The Making of the 20th Century

*This series of specially commissioned titles focuses atten-
tion on significant and often controversial events and
themes of world history in the present century. Each
book provides sufficient narrative and explanation for
the newcomer to the subject while offering, for more
advanced study, detailed source-references and biblio-
graphies, together with interpretation and reassessment
in the light of recent scholarship.*

*In the choice of subjects there is a balance between
breadth in some spheres and detail in others; between
the essentially political and matters economic or social.
The series cannot be a comprehensive account of everything that has happened in the twentieth century, but it
provides a guide to recent research and explains something of the times of extraordinary change and complexity in which we live. It is directed in the main to
students of contemporary history and international
relations, but includes titles which are of direct relevance
to courses in economics, sociology, politics and geography.*

The Making of the 20th Century

Series Editor: GEOFFREY WARNER

Already published:

David Armstrong, *The Rise of the International Organisation:
A Short History*
V. R. Berghahn, *Germany and the Approach of War in 1914*
Brian J. L. Berry, *Comparative Urbanisation: Divergent Paths
in the Twentieth Century*
Richard Bosworth, *Italy and the Approach of the First World War*
John Keiger, *France and the Origins of the First World War*
Dominic Lieven, *Russia and the Origins of the First World War*
Sally Marks, *The Illusion of Peace: International Relations in Europe
1918–1933*
A. J. Nicholls, *Weimar and the Rise of Hitler*
B. N. Pandey, *South and South-east Asia 1945–1979: Problems and Policies*
Esmonde M. Robertson, *Mussolini as Empire-Builder*
Zara Steiner, *Britain and the Origins of the First World War*
Richard Storry, *Japan and the Decline of the West in Asia 1894–1942*
Christopher Thorne, *The Approach of War 1938–1939*
Hugh Tinker, *Race, Conflict and the International Order*
Wang Gungwu, *China and the World since 1949*
Elizabeth Wiskemann, *Fascism in Italy: Its Development and Influence*
R. T. Thomas, *Britain and Vichy: The Dilemma of Anglo-French
Relations 1940–1942*
Fiona Venn, *Oil Diplomacy in the Twentieth Century*

Further titles are in preparation

Britain and Decolonisation

The retreat from empire in the post-war world

John Darwin

St. Martin's Press, New York

All rights reserved, For information, write:
Scholarly & Reference Division,
St. Martin's Press, Inc.,
175 Fifth Avenue, New York, NY10010

First published in the United States of America in 1988

Printed in China

ISBN 0–312–02464–9

Library of Congress Cataloging in Publication Data applied for.

Contents

To

Caroline, Claire, Charlotte and Helen

Preface

This book sets out to explain how and why the British gave up their empire after 1945 and accepted, with apparent equanimity, the radical diminution in their power and influence that followed in the wake of the Second World War. To do this, however, it was also necessary to try to explain something more far-reaching. The winding-up of the British imperial system cannot be studied as the sum of a hundred colonial retreats, amounting cumulatively to the dissolution of empire. The British viewed their colonial possessions as *components*, albeit special ones, of the wider structure of their world power, which was also based on naval and commercial primacy in particular regions and the effective domination of a number of technically independent states. Colonial policy, therefore, only makes sense in the framework of British external policy as a whole, and the history of one colony or region, viewed in isolation, will tell us little about the deeper causes and motives of decolonisation. Certainly, for the British, the problem of imperial decline appeared systemic: it was rarely possible to prevent the effects of change, weakness or defeat in one colonial area from spilling over into others, and the British themselves were always uneasily aware of the implications of change in one part of their imperial system for its other elements – even if they often misjudged the actual consequences.

Britain's response to the disappearance of the old colonial world order that had been a basic feature of global politics before 1939 and to the problem of her own growing imperial weakness in particular is therefore best studied by examining the whole range of Britain's post-war imperial relationships rather than by focusing in great detail on the bilateral connection between the mother-country and one of its dependencies. It is the approach which has dictated the organisation of this book. No attempt has been made to provide a continuous narrative for individual colonies. Instead, in the course of six chronological chapters (2–7) we trace, as far as possible comparatively, Britain's changing relations with the dominions, India, the colonial dependencies and the regions of informal predominance which together made up the imperial system. This will serve not only to emphasise the extreme diversity of Britain's imperial connections but also to highlight the dangers of generalising too boldly from the cases of India or Ghana about the thinking behind British policy or the fundamental causes of the fall of colonial rule. A comparative approach of this kind has two other advantages. It compensates to some extent for the shortage of archival sources. More important, perhaps, it may save us from the fallacy of believing that the decolonisation process was the intended consequence of the actions of British policy makers or colonial politicians.

Decolonisation remains academically a very underdeveloped subject. Vast archival sources have yet to be tapped: others may vanish or dissolve before they can yield their secrets. The interpretative framework through which we approach this sprawling wilderness of a topic is still for the most part rough and ready, heavily influenced by current political and international preoccupations and by the tendency to see decolonisation as a morality play in which Progress triumphed over Reaction. The purpose of this book is modest. It offers an unsentimental interpretation of Britain's retreat from empire and world power which may be useful as one of the reference points for more intricate archival investigation into the causes, course and impact of decolonisation. If nothing else, it may serve to mark out some of the main areas of controversy.

In a book of this kind, the writer is heavily indebted to the work of many authors in fields and on regions he can never hope to master for himself. The vast extent of my debts will be apparent from the notes and references that follow the text. But, in common with many others, I also owe a particular debt to the late Jack Gallagher, not only for interest and encouragement but because in the study of decolonisation, as over the whole history of imperialism in the nineteenth and twentieth centuries, his influence was seminal, liberating and profound. Few historians have left so great a mark on their subject, and with such wit and sympathy.

Maps

The British Empire 1920
Colonies and Bases 1967
Britain and the Middle East 1919–1967
Britain in Africa 1947–1968

The above maps are reproduced from *British History Atlas* by Martin Gilbert, by kind permission of George Weidenfeld & Nicolson Limited.

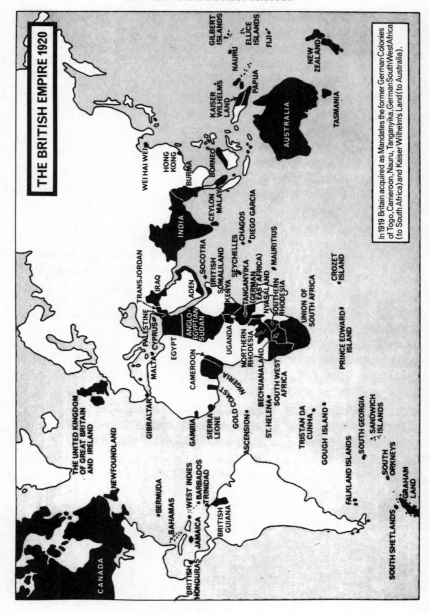

THE BRITISH EMPIRE 1920

In 1919 Britain acquired as Mandates the former German Colonies of Togo, Cameroon, Nauru, Tanganyika, German South West Africa (to South Africa) and Kaiser Wilhelm's Land (to Australia).

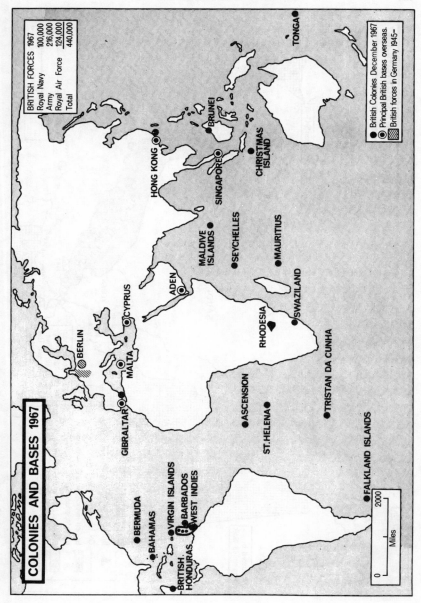

COLONIES AND BASES 1967

BRITISH FORCES 1967
Royal Navy 100,000
Army 216,000
Royal Air Force 124,000
Total 440,000

● British Colonies December 1967
◎ Principal British bases overseas.
▨ British forces in Germany 1945–

TONGA
BRUNEI
CHRISTMAS ISLAND
HONG KONG
SINGAPORE
MALDIVE ISLANDS
SEYCHELLES
MAURITIUS
ADEN
CYPRUS
SWAZILAND
BERLIN
MALTA
RHODESIA
GIBRALTAR
ASCENSION
TRISTAN DA CUNHA
ST.HELENA
FALKLAND ISLANDS
BERMUDA
VIRGIN ISLANDS
BAHAMAS
BARBADOS
WEST INDIES
BRITISH HONDURAS

Miles
0 2000

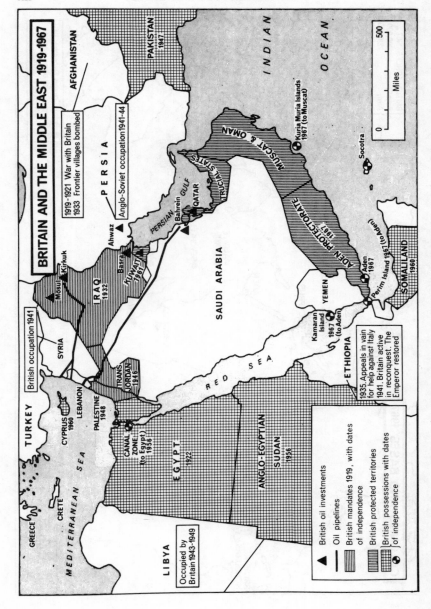

BRITAIN AND THE MIDDLE EAST 1919-1967

AFGHANISTAN

PAKISTAN
1947

1919-1921 War with Britain
1933 Frontier villages bombed

Anglo-Soviet occupation 1941-44

PERSIA

INDIAN

OCEAN

Kuria Muria Islands
1967 (to Muscat)

Socotra

MUSCAT & OMAN

Ahwaz

PERSIAN GULF

Bahrein

QATAR

TRUCIAL STATES

Kirkuk

Basra

KUWAIT
1961

Mosul

IRAQ
1932

ADEN PROTECTORATE
1967

British occupation 1941

SYRIA

SAUDI ARABIA

Perim Island 1967 (to Aden)

Aden
1967

SOMALILAND
1960

TRANS-
JORDAN
1946

YEMEN

Kamaran
Island
1967
(to Aden)

LEBANON

PALESTINE
1948

CYPRUS
1960

TURKEY

RED SEA

ETHIOPIA

1935. Appeals in vain
for help against Italy
1941. Britain active
in reconquest. The
Emperor restored

CANAL
ZONE
(to Egypt)
1956

EGYPT
1922

ANGLO-EGYPTIAN
SUDAN
1956

MEDITERRANEAN SEA

CRETE

GREECE

LIBYA

Occupied by
Britain 1943-1949

▲ British oil investments

── Oil pipelines

British mandates 1919, with dates
of independence

British protected territories

British possessions with dates
of independence

500

0   Miles

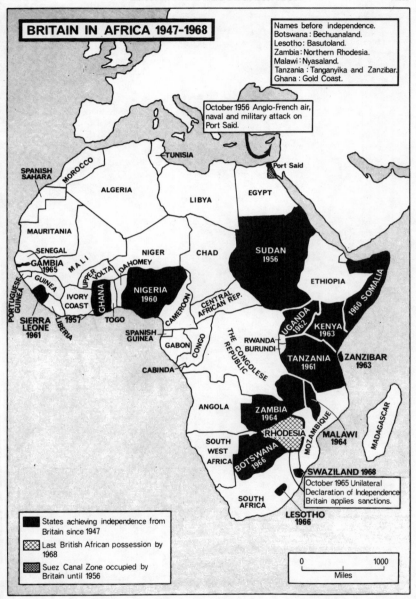

BRITAIN IN AFRICA 1947-1968

Names before independence.
Botswana : Bechuanaland.
Lesotho : Basutoland.
Zambia : Northern Rhodesia.
Malawi : Nyasaland.
Tanzania : Tanganyika and Zanzibar.
Ghana : Gold Coast.

October 1956 Anglo-French air,
naval and military attack on
Port Said.

October 1965 Unilateral
Declaration of Independence
Britain applies sanctions.

States achieving independence from
Britain since 1947

Last British African possession by
1968

Suez Canal Zone occupied by
Britain until 1956

0   1000
Miles

1 Decolonisation

The absence of large overseas colonial empires is one of the most striking features of the contemporary world. For the first time since the sixteenth century the regions under the direct colonial rule of Europeans form an insignificant portion of the world's surface – with the exception, that is, of the continental empire of Russia, last and most ruthless of imperial powers. From the sixteenth century to the twentieth the expansion of Europe proceeded with apparently glacier-like inevitability, defeating, absorbing or subjugating one civilisation after another. European settlement, trade and investment steadily thrust their way into the remoter corners of the world. Of course, this great expansion took a variety of forms: the creation of settlement colonies; the carving out of dependencies where an indigenous population was ruled by a thin stratum of European officials; and the development of semi-colonies or 'informal empire' where states that remained technically independent enjoyed so little economic and political freedom as to be almost in the position of a colony. The independence of most of North and South America from metropolitan control by 1830 modified this picture, but not significantly, since the new states merely served with varying degrees of efficiency as agencies of European economic and demographic expansion. Here were societies with an anti-colonial tradition but, for all that, with an underlying sympathy for the fundamental assumptions of European expansion.

By 1900, in fact, the United States had joined the exclusive fraternity of colonial powers which ruled so much of the world and presided over its international politics. At the same time, Japan, a much more emphatically non-European state, also became a somewhat uneasy associate of the colonial club. Periodically, between 1890 and 1939, the ranks of membership were thinned as colonial properties changed hands. Spain in 1898 and Germany in 1919 were stripped of their colonies – by envious rivals not by resentful subjects. But despite these adjustments and the inevitable jealousies of the main imperial powers the longstanding domination of Africa and Asia by a half-dozen imperial states (principally, after 1918, Britain, France, Russia and Japan, with the United States, Italy, the Netherlands, Belgium and Portugal as lesser colonial landlords) still seemed an inevitable feature of the international order before 1939. Moreover, the prime threat to their hegemony apparently lay much less in the resistance of their downtrodden clients and subjects than in the risk that the imperialists would fall out amongst themselves, or with the resentful miscreant expelled from the club in 1919 – Germany. In Asia, scarcely any country east of Iran, and very few to the west, enjoyed a real independence except Imperial Japan, a colonial power in her own right. In Africa, the only countries that had escaped the great partition of the late nineteenth century were Ethiopia and Liberia. Here were exceptions that proved the rule for Ethiopia became an Italian colony in 1935 while in Liberia a caste descended from American negro freedmen lorded it over the pagans of the interior.

Yet, quite rapidly after 1945 this old colonial order fell to pieces and much of the overt domination of particular regions, like China and the Middle East, by the colonial powers was swept away. The colonial world was replaced, nominally at least, by a 'world of nations'. With it vanished a whole catalogue of belief and dogma which had helped to prop up (as well as drawing credibility from) the colonial system: not least the rooted belief in the unequal intellectual and other capacities of whites and blacks. Enormous inequities of political, military and economic power remained; but the formal constitutional subordination of colonial peoples to European masters disappeared. Whatever qualifications we may make about the continuing dependence of new states upon developed nations, this alone marks a revolution in world history whose full effects may yet be barely visible. It has altered the pattern of international rivalries, modified the way in which non-European civilisations are viewed in the West and set in motion all over Africa and Asia a struggle to create durable new political and economic structures that will satisfy the aspirations of post-colonial rulers and ruled. Most important of all, perhaps, decolonisation has meant the entry into world politics of a large number of states imbued with ambitious theories of national sovereignty drawn from the European past but (usually) grossly out of keeping with their poverty and vulnerability. Not surprisingly, for many such states, radical discontent with the existing international order is axiomatic.

Nevertheless, the era in which colonial rule was abandoned and a multitude of successor states established in its place may eventually be seen as a crucial moment in the long evolution of the West's connection with the peoples and cultures of Africa, Asia and other ex-colonial lands.

In this book we approach this huge theme by way of the dissolution of Britain's imperial system. In the nineteenth and twentieth centuries Britain had by far the largest colonial empire – if we exclude the continental domain of Russia – and much the most valuable. Britain was also more active than other powers in exerting her will over extra-European regions by means other than direct colonial rule, for example through her virtual domination of the Middle East after 1918 or her financial and commercial pre-eminence in Argentina between 1880 and 1939. No other colonial power aspired to the same degree of global influence or had enjoyed it. No other country derived such extensive benefits from its empire or undertook such far-flung military burdens to protect it. Thus, though what holds true of Britain's experience of decolonisation will not necessarily hold true of that of France, Portugal, Belgium or the Netherlands, the sheer size and variety of Britain's imperial system, as well as Britain's involvement in other vital arenas of world politics, should allow us to see the most important elements of the decolonising process at work: the thought and action of the colonial rulers; political and social movements among the ruled; and the influence of wider changes in international politics – ideological, military, diplomatic and economic. At least, we may conclude, any grand theory of the causes of decolonisation that does not fit the British case will be like a history of Italy which ignores the Church.

THE MEANING OF DECOLONISATION

Britain's career as a world and colonial power since 1800 appears at first sight to fall comfortably into three distinct phases. In the century after Waterloo, the British embarked upon a prolonged expansionist movement, fuelled by commercial and industrial growth at home and aided by mercantile and naval supremacy on the oceans of the world. In this period the earlier colonial acquisitions, strategic footholds and spheres of influence built up since 1600 were dramatically enlarged and the scale of British activity in the world transformed. After 1914, by contrast, much of the steam seemed to go out of this drive for territorial possessions and economic influence, so that historians have tended to characterise the years between 1914 and 1945 as an age of gradual, grudging imperial retreat. The engines of empire – the great staple industries of cotton, coal and engineering – were running down. Britain's legendary financial resources were devastated by the costs of war and the ravages of depression. Her naval supremacy was abandoned. The subject peoples of the empire became more recalcitrant and in some places their resistance was more effective. At home the overseers of British world policy, the heirs of Palmerston and Salisbury, seemed to have lost the aggressive and expansionist instincts that had driven the Victorians forward and become resigned to the inevitable attenuation of British power, wealth and influence. In the third phase, the 30 years or so after 1945, all the trends apparently visible in the inter-war years were transformed into hard facts. The age of slow retreat turned into the era of dissolution. Britain's territorial empire passed out of her control; her economic influence declined precipitously; and the contraction of her military and naval resources ended her claim, sustained since the seventeenth century, to be a major power in Asia.

It is this third and final phase that has come to be regarded as the true age of decolonisation, even though historians in search of its roots have cast back to the beginning of the twentieth century and beyond. The hallmark of decolonisation became the surrender of political sovereignty over the peoples of Africa and Asia and the emergence of independent nation-states where once European administrators and settlers had ruled supreme. The 'third world' replaced the 'colonial world'.

But in the British case in particular this simple approach to decolonisation raises a number of difficulties. The facile notion of successive phases of expansion, stagnation and decline does not stand up to critical scrutiny.[1] If the concession of independence or internal self-government was symptomatic of decolonising then Britain was decolonising more rapidly between 1783 and 1914 than she was colonising. The Thirteen Colonies were granted independence and the British colonies in Canada, Australia, New Zealand and South Africa all received almost complete internal autonomy after 1850. Yet it was possible for a leading imperial enthusiast in Britain to declare in 1869 that 'for purposes of commerce and civilisation America is a truer colony of Britain than Canada'.[2] And in the British colonies the loosening of constitutional ties was accompanied by the reinforcement

of economic, social and cultural bonds through greater trade, investment and migration. Indeed, in their own eyes, as well as Britain's,
the dominions remained colonies in all but name up until the Second
World War.[3] The second difficulty lies in the fact that there were a
number of independent countries where, in terms of economic and
financial relations, the privileged position of Europeans and the
deference accorded to Britain's strategic and diplomatic requirements,
British dominance was as great as in any colonial possession proper.
Here were client states whose non-colonial status was purely technical.
The British regarded their position and influence in these client states
as of no less importance than their 'legitimate' authority in the
constitutionally subordinate colonial territories. Egypt or Shanghai
were scarcely to be counted less valuable than the Gambia, Nigeria or
Uganda. Lastly, it followed from this that the British had always been
prepared to secure their imperial ends – trade, security, influence – by
the widest variety of political means, using the inflexible and expensive
method of direct colonial rule only when necessary – and often
grudging the necessity. Wherever possible they preferred to influence,
persuade, inveigle (by economic benefits) or frighten local rulers into
cooperation with them. All this means that we cannot easily measure
the extent to which British dominance over client states and colonial
peoples contracted by the crude yardstick of a change in constitutional
forms. Just as in the mid-Victorian period the extent of Britain's
colonial possessions – her 'formal empire' – was an inadequate and
misleading measure of the scope of British power.[4] Decolonisation
was a subtle, intricate and deceptive process. External alterations
concealed inner continuities. The substance of the colonial relationship may have been unchanged by the concession of autonomy or
independence. If decolonisation is to mean more than a superficial
modification of constitutional status, it must refer to wider changes in
the relations between the developed and less developed states – even if
it is in the territorial possessions of the colonial powers that these
changes can usually be seen most distinctly.

Decolonisation is best understood, perhaps, as a partial retraction,
redeployment and redistribution of British and European influences
in the regions of the extra-European world whose economic, political
and cultural life had previously seemed destined to flow into Western
moulds. That is not to say that since 1945 the Afro-Asian world has
been liberated from external influences or economic dependence
upon the former colonial powers in the West. Far from it. But in

several crucial respects the relations between the colonial powers and the countries of the Third World have undergone a striking change since the Second World War. Before 1939 it was usual to suppose that even if the pattern of rule in the colonial world was modified, ultimate European control would continue indefinitely almost everywhere because Afro-Asian nationalism would remain too feeble to achieve the final demolition of the colonial apparatus. Even in India, where progress to self-government had gone further than in any other non-white colony, there was before 1939 no timetable for full self-government and a general expectation that in matters of defence and foreign affairs Indian deference to British commands would continue for the forseeable future. European influence in Africa and Asia would continue to be founded on the direct control of large tracts of both continents.

Secondly, it was not even clear before 1939 that European *expansion* had ceased and that colonial decay had set in generally. Italy began to carve out a new empire in East Africa. France commenced the vigorous exploitation of her newest North African acquisition in Morocco.[5] Portugal, the oldest European colonial power, reasserted her colonial mission in Africa.[6] And in much of Britain's domain in tropical Africa the years after 1918 saw the extension of effective colonial government as well as of white settlement into the paper empire acquired during the Scramble for Africa. To the young Jomo Kenyatta, writing in 1938, the most urgent task seemed to be not the throwing off of colonial rule but the organisation of resistance to the *expansion* of white settlement and control.[7] Away in India, Jawaharlal Nehru, Gandhi's lieutenant in the Indian National Congress who spent a good part of the 1930s in gaol, wrote despondently that it was impossible to prophesy when the British would leave India.[8]

These political assumptions were set in a frame of economic expectations. With few exceptions, the proper destiny of Africa and Asia was still seen as the fulfilment of a complementary but essentially subordinate role in relation to the economies of the imperial states. In particular, it was widely supposed that there would be a steady enlargement of the area of white settlement in parts of Africa and that such settlement would be compatible with the land needs, and beneficial to the economic well-being, of the indigenous peoples.[9] Elsewhere, in Asia, Europeans remained deeply entrenched in the economic life of India, Ceylon, Burma, Malaya, Singapore, French Indo-China, the Dutch East Indies and even in technically independent

China where Europeans still enjoyed privileged status in the treaty ports and concessions of the China coast.[10] And even where climatic, economic or political factors ruled out permanent settlement, the colonies and semi-independent states of the Afro-Asian world still seemed to hold out opportunities to the adventurous and enterprising. Whether as planters or businessmen or administrators, expatriate Europeans could hope to enjoy more satisfying careers, higher social status as boss, *baas*, *bwana*, *sahib*, *tuan*, and usually greater material reward than their own economies and rigid social structures could offer. Demographically, Europe still appeared in that phase of expansion that had populated vast areas in the nineteenth century, even if the Depression had brought a temporary check. The colonies were still, for all their limitations, Europe's open social frontier.

But at the root of the relationship between the colonial powers and their possessions before 1939 was the apparent power of the former to control *directly* the economic development of the latter. Where colonial rule prevailed, the effect was usually to forbid the erection of protective tariffs behind which local industries could develop. In China, Turkey and other formally independent states, the same effect had been achieved by 'unequal treaties'. Colonial governments were not expected to permit discrimination against the economic interests of those whose votes were needed by their political masters in London, or Paris or Brussels. Without tariffs, there seemed little likelihood that colonial economies could ever escape dependence upon European manufactures and the production of primary commodities to pay for them – or indeed diversify their economies significantly. In some parts of the British empire of course this strict prohibition on tariffs or a discriminatory commercial policy no longer applied. In the white dominions it had long been obsolete. India too enjoyed tariff autonomy after 1919 and, partly as a consequence, lost a good deal of her former value as a market for Lancashire cotton goods.[11] But the dominions remained dependent on Britain as the chief buyer of their minerals and commodities, as well as the supplier of capital and migrants to develop their economies. They remained to a greater or lesser degree economic and demographic satellites. India was different: she needed no migrants and her exports were sold to foreign countries. Like the dominions, however, she needed British capital. Moreover, while conceding tariff autonomy as part of India's partial self-government, the London government had retained strict control over the management of India's currency: a much more powerful economic lever.[12]

In general, whether in the self-governing dominions, the partially self-governing Indian Empire, the colonies where local autonomy had made little progress or in the technically independent client states whose trade policy was dictated to them, it seemed reasonable to suppose that these extra-European countries would remain economic satellites of the industrial world, and of Britain particularly. Consequently, it was easy to imagine that, insofar as the more backward colonial societies were 'modernised' at all, that modernisation would produce social and economic structures that would complement those of the industrial and capitalist societies. The social outlook and habits of the colonial peoples would come, in some cases with imperceptible slowness, to replicate, however crudely, the social order of their European masters – the touchstone, it was believed of their economic progress.

There was, therefore, a cultural or ideological dimension to the colonial or semi-colonial relationship that could be seen most clearly where Europeans ruled directly. For along with political tutelage and economic direction came the relegation of indigenous cultures and political systems to a position of permanent inferiority, while the superiority of European civilisation[13] (a word that acquired large overtones), intellect, institutions and morality was proclaimed in the apparatus and even the language of colonial life. This aspect of colonial expansion has often been attributed to racial arrogance or racism. But the hostility or contempt that Europeans often seemed to display towards their subjects' behaviour and beliefs actually derived from two different sources. The first and most obvious was fear. Wherever Europeans found themselves in a small, privileged but vulnerable minority, all but submerged in an alien, suspicious and unpredictable community, the tendency to seek reassurance in the assertion of superior virtue was very pronounced. For the same reason they tended to react with exaggerated alarm to the least symptom of recalcitrance. The price of their authority seemed to be an unbending insistence upon the outward display of subservience and comformity in the bearing and behaviour of subject peoples. Thus Gandhi's discarding of European dress and his notorious appearance before the Viceroy in the guise, as Churchill indignantly put it, of a 'half-naked fakir' was a dramatic gesture of disrespect to the Europeanising traditions of the Raj, and evoked the anger that Churchill expressed. But if some of the arrogance that Europeans showed was the product of anxiety or was deliberately cultivated to preserve the solidarity of a foreign ruling class, much of it was habitual and unselfconscious. For the second spring of European arrogance was the conviction which had taken root by the mid-nineteenth century that the achievement of intellectual, technological, moral – and therefore social and economic – progress was the birthright of those societies which enjoyed the peculiar social characteristics of north-west Europe.[14] All other societies, especially non-European ones, were seen as less successful variations of the European ideal, whose historic development had either been retarded or diverted altogether into a cul-de-sac. Their only salvation lay in the wholesale adoption not only of Western technology but of European morals, laws and manners as well. And despite the gradual erosion of this doctrine from the later nineteenth century onwards, there was little inclination to dispose of its fundamental premises while social theory was still compatible with political reality in the colonial world.

The meaning of decolonisation can best be grasped by contrasting the contemporary relations between the advanced industrial states (especially the former colonial powers among them) and the ex-colonies with the relationship that has just been described. The first but only the most obvious contrast with the pre-war years is the end of direct political control of the many dozens of former colonial possessions and the emergence of a large number of sovereign independent states in their place. This constitutional transformation turned out to have more far-reaching consequences than was originally expected – both internally and externally. In most cases, the withdrawal of colonial rule led to major changes in the political institutions of the former colony as the new rulers grappled with the characteristic problems of economic underdevelopment and political division. In some, the end of colonial rule precipitated internal conflict on a large scale – as in Nigeria. Externally, many ex-colonies shook off the guidance and direction of their foreign policies which the ex-colonial powers had expected to exercise even after independence. One result was the tendency, especially in the early post-independence years, for former colonies to show solidarity with each other in denouncing the policies of their ex-rulers, as well as any surviving relics of the old colonial order. A second was the increasing likelihood of colonial successor states coming into conflict with each other as a result of territorial claims or regional rivalry. In the colonial period, of course, such conflicts could hardly have been imagined. Thirdly, the concession of sovereignty to the former colonies made it much more difficult for the ex-colonial powers to use these territories for military purposes in the way that was second nature to pre-war strategic planners, for whom free access to the strategic facilities of their colonies was, especially in the British case, a vital part of the protection of imperial interests as a whole, including those in the technically independent semi-colonial states. For the British, India and Ceylon had once performed precisely this function in relation to China and the Far East. Without firm footholds in their 'own' possessions, it was bound to be much harder to maintain the control and supervision of independent non-European states which had been exercised previously by the colonial powers. And for their part, many former colonial states developed a range of interests and international friendships, sometimes arising directly from their internal difficulties or geopolitical situation, which pulled them sharply away from the old 'mother country' or made it politically undesirable for them to retain close military or diplomatic links with it.

The constitutional emancipation of the colonies brought, therefore, a wave of further changes helped on by the post-war shifts in the global distribution of power. The presence of so many new sovereign states changed the forms of dialogue, and to some extent the agenda, of international affairs, especially at the United Nations, the arena *par excellence* in which new international identities could be paraded and displayed. Above all, perhaps, and to a degree that would have horrified their pre-war masters, the ex-colonies have become the object of an open competition for influence among the greater powers and the superpowers – precisely the eventuality which the annexations of the colonial era had been intended to prevent. Colonial rule, after all, had very little to do, in most cases, with the energetic *internal* administration of a particular tract of Africa or Asia, and all to do with the exclusion of every other foreign influence but that of the annexing power. Now instead of the partition of much of the extra-European world into clearly designated spheres of influence and control, with only certain regions open to real competition, most of the extra-European world has moved into a much looser relationship with the old imperial states, and with the industrial world generally. Former colonial and semi-colonial states alike have been able to enlarge their freedom of manoeuvre and drive a better bargain with those who seek influence over them. And the old spheres of influence have been divided and re-divided among the new powers of the post-war world.

This was the constitutional and diplomatic face of decolonisation.

But decolonisation also meant a change in the demographic move-ment that had carried thousands of Europeans to the Afro-Asian colonies as expatriate planters, traders and administrators or as permanent settlers. The arrival of political independence usually became the signal for the reduction of the European community, the replacement of expatriates in administration and the retreat of Euro-pean settlers from the countryside in the face of local land hunger or violence. In some cases, as in Algeria, the Belgian Congo and Angola, the end of colonial rule led to the evacuation of almost the entire foreign population urban and rural alike. Even where a substantial body of Europeans remained behind, their *collective* social and eco-nomic influence was sharply modified. Without the guarantee of, or perhaps the desire for, permanency, their status declined from that of social leaders to that of tolerated aliens, highly vulnerable to the xenophobic pressures thrown up by local social and political discontent. Nor any longer did they enjoy the advantage that colonial rule had conferred of promoting their interests as a community with special political rights and privileged access to the government.[15]

By the end of the 1950s, therefore, and a decade and a half earlier in the Asian colonies, the notion that Europe and the West would continue to draw new regions into their economic and cultural orbit by the physical occupation of the land, through the activities of a permanently settled commercial class, or by the presence of privileged European communities with a rotating membership, had become almost wholly obsolete. In Africa and Asia, the old frontier of settlement and European communal expansion had been closed: only in the surviving bastion of white rule in southern Africa could Europeans hope for both the promise of permanency and the elevated social position that had once seemed their birthright in the colonial world. Migration continued from Europe, of course, but it was largely confined to the long-established areas of European settlement in the Americas and Australasia or to short-term contracts in Africa, Asia and the Middle East. But the contemporary patterns of migration would have surprised pre-war observers in another way. Thus an important proportion of British migrants today travel not to North America, South Africa or Australasia, but to Europe. And since the 1950s Britain, like other European countries, has been the destination for many thousands of migrants *from* Third World or ex-colonial countries.

The closing of Europe's settlement frontier in Afro-Asia was only part of the series of economic changes that have come to be associated with decolonisation. These changes represent the efforts of the newly independent states to restrict as far as possible the direct access of external influences (especially those emanating from former masters in the West) to their economies and societies. Thus the ex-colonial territories have generally striven to reduce their dependence upon the export of primary products to the industrial West – the dependence that had been the economic foundation of colonial rule. To do so, they have replaced the colonial 'open economy' with the post-colonial 'closed economy'.[16] Under the open economy, the colony was effectively prevented from limiting the entry of manufactures from the mother-country; the management of its currency was geared to the requirements of foreign trade and traders; there were no controls on investment from abroad, no direction of investment, nor any restraint on the full repatriation of profits; and, usually, every institutional encouragement to build up a close economic relationship with the ruling power. Under the open economy, the interests of the colony were thought to be best served by the fullest participation in the international economy whatever the immediate social or economic consequences (although in practice colonial governments often intervened to soften the impact of change).[17] By contrast, the closed economy set out to restrict the exposure of the ex-colony to outside economic forces by enforcing governmental control over foreign trade and foreign investment, in order to protect local manufacturing interests, retain a larger proportion of the profits earned by foreign investment and, normally, to prohibit the wholesale repatriation of foreign capital. The immediate objective was to use the political authority conferred at independence to improve the terms of economic cooperation between the West and the former colony. In the longer term the closed economy was intended to attain a degree of economic liberation consonant with the achievement of political independence.

The economic face of decolonisation, the closed economy, has produced as a result a number of practical modifications in the economic relations of the ex-colonies and semi-colonies with the industrial states. Except in the special circumstances of the oil states, decolonisation has done little to enrich the new countries at the expense of their former rulers. Indeed, by the late 1970s, many commentators had detected a *widening* gap between the wealth of the industrial world and that of the less developed countries. In many cases, too, the struggle to escape from commodity production for the

West into greater self-sufficiency, allied with the intense pressure for the redistribution of land in newly independent states, has weakened the commercial sector of agriculture and brought about a crippling shortage of both foreign exchange and foreign investment. The drive towards import substitution and the extension of economic controls has imposed on the operations of foreign companies a variety of often unpredictable political and bureaucratic constraints.[18] In some places decolonisation has drastically undermined the security of foreign enterprises either through the decline of public order or the threat of confiscation or compulsory purchase. At its extreme, it has led to the total exclusion of Western economic activity or its restriction to inter-governmental barter. In general, however, just as political independence did not so much expel all external political influences as change the setting in which they had to operate, so decolonisation in its economic sense has served mainly to expose the commercial activity of the industrial states to new social and political pressures whose force colonial rule had concealed or suppressed. The economic meaning of decolonisation, therefore, has not been the collapse of 'imperialist exploitation' but rather the rise of the branch plant and the multi-national company which could trade safely inside the defences of the closed economy, largely immune from the hostility displayed by post-colonial governments to foreign enterprise proper. The ex-colonial world may have freed itself from direct subjection to economic policies framed in the interests of the colonial powers, but often this has been exchanged for a looser dependence upon foreign economic aid with its strings and provisos.

Lastly, it is apparent that decolonisation has an ideological and cultural meaning as well. For the shock of political independence from European rule and the decline of the colonial economic nexus in its old form coincided with the passing of the confident belief, commonplace before 1939, that Afro-Asian societies would gradually adopt European values and habits and that their material progress was dependent upon the careful imitation of European models. Partly as a result of the end of colonial rule, the prestige of African and Asian cultures rose sharply so that today there may even be in the West a tendency to underestimate the influence of Western social and economic systems and to regard the social and political experiments of the Third World with exaggerated respect. While decolonisation has not produced the wholesale displacement of the values and mentality implanted in the colonial era, for which Frantz Fanon called in his famous manifesto *Les damnés de la terre*, the cultural and ideological relationship between the old colonial powers and their former subjects is marked by a certain public deference to the customs, ethos and aspirations of the latter which would have appeared astonishing to a generation reared at the height of Europe's colonial dominance. Moreover, to an extent that would have appeared remarkable even in the inter-war years, the notion that (almost) every former colony was entitled by right to a separate, independent national existence, and that self-government was invariably preferable to good government by others, became a dogma so deeply entrenched in the Western world that scarcely the hardiest controversialists dared, or troubled, to challenge it. In a response, perhaps, to the intellectual crisis of the Second World War, national self-determination had become by the later 1950s the supreme political value in the West itself.

Thus we might summarise the essential features of decolonisation as follows:

1. the dismantling of formal political and economic controls over non-European states, including in this the abolition of such institutions as the concessions and treaty ports in China, the restrictions on tariffs and the extra-territorial rights once enjoyed by Europeans in Turkey, Iran, Thailand, China and elsewhere.

2. the dismantling of the 'open economy' in colonial and semi-colonial states.

3. the changed character of Europe's demographic expansion into Afro-Asia and the partial check to its cultural and intellectual influence.

4. the open competition for international influence in areas once formally or informally reserved to a particular colonial or great power.

If these criteria are accurate they suggest that we should see decolonisation as something much more than the concession of political sovereignty to a large number of dependent territories; but as something much less than the collapse of the influence and power of the industrial states in the Third World. Indeed, it may be most useful to regard decolonisation as a sea-change in the relations between the two, symptomatic of one of those gradual shifts that occur periodically in the relationship between different continents, different cultures and different economic systems. In the eighteenth and nineteenth centuries global conditions – the rapid improvement in the technological and organisational efficiency of Europe and the decay of many

Afro-Asian political systems – allowed or encouraged the creation of the great colonial empires and their informal outriders. By the middle of the twentieth, these global conditions were changing sharply. Decolonisation signified in effect a new set of ground rules for the pursuit of national interests in the less developed world. In the age of empire and colonisation Britain had promoted her interests with outstanding success. Subsequently, fresh techniques and new resources were called for. In the era which opened up after 1945 the rulers of the British empire found, like the rulers of other empires before them, that a different and harsher climate had dried up the sources of their power.

THEORIES AND EXPLANATIONS

It is scarcely surprising that such a complex historical change affecting so many different parts of the world, and subject to wide variations of circumstances, should have proved difficult to define with precision. Still less, that it has attracted a multitude of explanations. Any general theory has to take account of the enormous variety of the colonial world, the very different forms of government to which colonies were subjected, the striking variations in their social and economic development, as well as the obvious differences in the circumstances, interests, political culture and power of the states that ruled over them. Even if we confine ourselves to the case of Britain, numerous alternative explanations for the termination of colonial rule and the subsequent general retraction of British influence have to be considered. There are those that emphasise the effects of political and social change within the colonial societies, culminating in the emergence of an irresistible mass nationalism; those which stress the accelerating decline of Britain's economic and military strength measured against the burdens of world power in a superpower age; those which see a growing *indifference* to empire in Britain and, to match it, an increasingly non-imperial orientation in the economy; and those which invoke chiefly the new conditions of global politics after 1945, in particular the obsolescence of colonial empires in the age of superpowers.

Of all these explanations the most widely favoured has usually been the part played by Afro-Asian nationalism, the emergence of which is commonly seen as the decisive moment in the defeat of colonial rule. Once nationalist leaders had begun to rally mass support for independence, the days of colonialism were numbered. It is easy to see the appeal of this argument. Nationalism in Europe had been a dynamic, if not lethal, force in the continent's modern history. As a political doctrine it seemed capable of mobilising enormous enthusiasm and the support of all classes. Moreover, the course of events in most colonies did appear to vindicate its significance: the end of colonial rule generally seemed to follow upon the rise of a mass movement demanding independence and threatening insurrection or civil disobedience if it were not granted in rapid stages. Nothing seemed more natural in retrospect than that the new educated elites in the colonies should have come to resent alien rule; that their resentment should have come to be shared by the mass of the population; and that with mass support behind them the nationalist leadership should have been able to dictate the timing of colonial withdrawal. Decolonisation, on this view, was mainly the achievement of mass nationalism. Both were the inevitable consequences of the gradual dissemination of European ideas about nationality, nationhood and political liberty, as well as of associated socio-economic changes that threw up the new educated class.

But although nationalist parties and movements appeared in most British colonies and although, in many cases, their leaders displaced the British colonial authorities in successive phases of constitutional change, the part they played in decolonisation and the transfer of power needs careful qualification. The creation of a mass nationalism strong enough to throw out colonial rulers was much more difficult than it appears with hindsight. Most colonies contained a great variety of communities with very little in common. It was usually very difficult to sustain mass support for very long. And there were major drawbacks to embarking upon an all-out confrontation with a determined colonial government, equipped with effective security forces. Open insurrection was politically risky and physically dangerous. Even the incitement of the masses to open civil disobedience or demonstrations was regarded by the educated and wealthy elite, as well as by the rural landowners and tribal chiefs whose support was needed for an effective mass movement, as a two-edged sword. The rural masses might refuse to pay taxes or recognise the authority of the colonial state. But supposing they went further and refused to pay rents and challenged the leadership of landlords and chiefs? Political action could easily topple over into social anarchy, more harmful to the leaders of colonial nationalism than to their imperial oppressors.

For all these reasons, mounting a political campaign for independence required careful timing and favourable circumstances. Indeed, it was most likely to be successful where the colonial rulers, for their own reasons, had already decided not to resist the demand for self-government. In some places after 1945 the British went further than that, positively searching out, grooming and coaching their successors. On occasion they even found it necessary to invent nationalism where it did not exist – as in northern Nigeria. By contrast, for local politicians to maintain an attitude of intransigent opposition and to refuse any cooperation with a colonial government might mean forgoing power, influence, office and patronage – perhaps for ever if a rival faction or party gained control with British assistance. On closer inspection, therefore, the simple picture of spontaneous resistance to colonial rule turning into an inexorable advance towards independence as nationalism won ever-increasing support looks less and less convincing. Even the most uncompromising nationalists had to make realistic political calculations. And it was usually the combination of nationalism with other forces that so enhanced its impact and cleared the path for decolonisation.

Not surprisingly, then, an alternative way of explaining Britain's imperial retreat has been to portray it as a deliberate, if not entirely willing, choice by post-war British governments. The relative decline of Britain's economic performance since 1918, the notorious sluggishness of her growth (relatively) since 1945 and the recurrent economic crises that punctuated the 1940s, 1950s and 1960s provided one obvious clue to the contraction of British world power. The loss of Britain's former pre-eminence as the greatest trading and investing power, the smallness of her industrial base by comparison with the United States or the Soviet Union, (starkly evident in the Second World War) together with the failure to modernise her industrial economy properly after 1945 reduced British influence in the world and made the military burden of defending a global empire intolerable. Reluctantly, on this argument, the British were forced to cut their coat according to their cloth. But economic change also worked, perhaps, in another way. Gradually Britain's commercial interests and principal trading partners ceased to be in the countries of the empire and became concentrated more and more in the industrial states of Europe and the North Atlantic. Empire and the imperial connection lost its old economic rationale; both ends of the imperial nexus were experiencing a long-term economic disengagement and reorientating their trade. At the same time, public opinion in Britain after 1945 demanded a much larger expenditure on welfare – rather than imperial defence. A consumer-orientated society became increasingly impatient with the old imperial patriotism. In this way, Britain simply drifted away from her old imperial role; the 'will to rule' slackened imperceptibly; indifference reinforced the effects of economic decline.[19]

In some versions, this account of changing British attitudes to empire lays greater emphasis upon the conversion of the policy makers to more liberal views of colonial advancement, or on the general recognition that failure to grant speedy independence would merely commit Britain to a series of bloody and unwinnable struggles. Harold Macmillan, the major political architect of Britain's African withdrawal, portrayed independence as the longstanding object of British policy, the triumphant culmination of Britain's mission to endow less fortunate peoples with her democratic heritage.[20] This was a picturesque invention worthy of Disraeli. There is, in fact, room for scepticism about any fundamental change of attitude towards empire after 1945. It is far from clear that the old assumptions about Britain's 'world role' died away after 1945 or even after 1960. Nor that the economic argument turned decisively against empire and global commitments in the 1940s and 1950s. Indeed, it seems likely that the economic repercussions of the Second World War encouraged a revival of British interest in parts of their colonial empire and in imperial economic integration generally. Moreover it is unsafe to argue from the fact that the British granted constitutional concessions and eventually independence that the one was *intended* to lead to the other or that the form which independence ultimately took had been expected or was desired. For much of the time, we may suspect, those who 'made' colonial policy were guessing, hoping, gambling – and *mis*calculating.

The same kinds of qualifications need to be made about the supposed effects of changes in the balance of world power or of other shifts in world politics. The relative decline of British world power in the age of the superpowers was evidently a new fact of profound significance. The rise of Soviet power in Europe forced Britain to commit herself to a peacetime alliance and a permanent military commitment on the European continent. Both the superpowers were avowedly anti-colonial in outlook whilst the ideological struggle against Hitler had made the assertion of pre-war colonial principles unfashionable. The creation of the United Nations Organisation and the stiffer terms for trusteeship (compared with the old League mandates) reflected a stronger bias in favour of the advancement of colonial territories to independence.[21] Above all, perhaps, the humiliating defeat of the European colonial rulers in Asia by the Japanese and the emergence of two extra-European powers as the arbiters of world affairs seemed to signify the passing of European primacy and of the colonial structures that formed part of it. After 1941, remarks one recent historian of the British Commonwealth, in the age of *Pax Americana* Britain declined 'almost to protectorate status'.[22] Amid such seismic changes in international relations, the contraction of British power and the liberation of so many countries from colonial rule (if not from Western influence) appears natural, inevitable, inexorable. Given the tough new requirements for being a global power, it was little wonder that the British soon found the going too hard and began the gradual winding down of their commitments and interests. Strategic dependence on the United States hammered home the lesson that, whatever her past glory, Britain could no longer be a world power and that, as a consequence, her colonial territories had to be disposed of. On this view, it only required a succession of diplomatic crises, especially the Suez crisis of 1956, to force British leaders and British opinion to accept the unpalatable truth.

The sharp decline of British power and influence after 1945 is unarguable. But it is much less clear that over the period 1945–70 British leaders consistently recognised the need to retreat from the old global commitments towards purely regional concerns in Europe; nor that the international climate was as consistently hostile as has sometimes been suggested. American attitudes towards Britain's great power pretensions turned out to be much more sympathetic than was feared, while the American guarantee against Soviet aggression in Europe (through NATO) offered Britain much greater security than she had enjoyed in the 1930s. Nor did the two new superpowers spread their influence immediately into every corner of the globe: a large sphere was still left in which Britain was for long the only major power. Moreover, although the British trailed far behind the Russians and Americans in military power, they remained for a decade or more after 1945 the world's third power, much stronger than any other middle-ranking country. These circumstances help to explain the curious reluctance of British leaders, so often noted, to read the 'message of the times' and abandon old habits of thinking in international affairs. They suggest that international pressures had a more subtle influence on British policy, offering more limited but important scope for the pursuit of British world interests. Arguably, not until the end of the 1950s did Britain's 'third power' status and the advantages it conferred begin to fall away sharply. Arguably, even then the abandonment of colonial empire was not an inevitable corollary of declining world status, as the case of Portugal indicates. The connection between international politics, British policy and the colonial setting has to be more carefully drawn.

Finally, an influential explanation put forward in recent years for the transfer of sovereignty and the transformation of the colonies into independent states has been to say that these constitutional processes were largely a charade, that the colonial powers made sure that power was transferred to politicians who could be trusted to look after the local interests of Western capitalism, and that decolonisation was in reality no more than a convenient change of technique whereby the industrial states sought to escape the political costs of directly controlling colonial territories while at the same time ensuring that their vital economic interests were defended, if not positively entrenched, by the terms on which decolonisation was carried through. The corollary of this argument is that the colonial powers timed their withdrawal to frustrate much more radical nationalist movements and to ensure that power was handed to 'safe', 'moderate' or 'conservative' nationalists.[23]

For those mainly preoccupied with the continuing economic inequities between the Third World and the industrial North this explanation may be persuasive. It also has an attractively conspiratorial flavour. But its plausibility is far from self-evident. It has certainly not been demonstrated in the British case that the acceleration of representative government in the colonies or the decisions on when and how to proceed to the full transfer of power were primarily determined by calculations as to how best to preserve Western business interests. The influence of multinational companies and other vested economic interests on colonial policy, may, in some cases, have been considerable, but its extent is unclear. Secondly, the approach to, and timing of, the transfer of power was inevitably affected by a much wider variety of considerations – among them the preservation of local order, strategic factors, international diplomacy and domestic politics – than merely the private advantage of certain commercial concerns. Thirdly, it is far from obvious that, if the protection of such interests had been their prime concern, British governments would have struck the bargains that they did with particular colonial leaders. Fourthly, this whole interpretation, with its strongly mechanistic overtones, overestimates the freedom of manoeuvre which the imperial policy makers thought they enjoyed, as well as the extent to which colonial nationalism itself represented a set of local vested interests that could be bought off and accommodated in this way.

There seems in fact little point in trying to isolate a single factor and attributing to it sufficient force to bring about the complex of changes we call decolonisation. Colonial rule and the whole pattern of international relationships that we may describe for convenience as the colonial 'order' depended upon the interlocking of a number of factors and circumstances, international, metropolitan (i.e. in the mother-country) and local. Thus at the international level the colonial system was sustained by a particular pattern of world trade, by the enthusiasm of the most powerful states for colonial rule, by their general reluctance to engage in colonial conflicts with each other, by the disparities in military technology which assisted European intervention in other continents and by an international culture which justified and esteemed European dominance over non-European societies. At the metropolitan level colonial activity similarly required a certain economic and military capacity, a favourable political climate and a sufficient economic compatibility with and orientation towards colonial regions. And in the colonial areas colonial rule or informal dominance was also conditional upon the absence of those defences by which some extra-European states (like Japan) kept Europeans at bay, on a social and economic structure which gave European intruders some purchase and a political environment which permitted the assertion of European control or influence, or even facilitated it. But if *any* of these necessary conditions were to disappear or change radically, then the stability of colonial rule and of the whole global pattern of colonial relationships would be jeopardised. Moreover, changes at any particular level – international, metropolitan or colonial – would be likely to have a 'knock-on' effect at the other levels, enforcing further consequential changes which would themselves set off a new round of movements and adjustments.

Thus, to give the simplest example, the involvement of the imperial mother-country in war was bound to entail political, social and economic consequences for its colonial territories with unpredictable effects on the colonial relationship. Theoretically, at least, the onset of a disruptive change at any level and among any of the necessary elements in the colonial system was capable of triggering off a long series of explosions which together might blow away the old colonial world.

But the rapidity and completeness with which decolonisation occurred in the two decades after 1945 encourages us to frame a slightly bolder hypothesis. There may indeed have been many local changes in colonial politics or economics, and even some modification of the external interests of the leading imperial powers in the inter-war years. But before 1945 there was no general change in the position of the colonial world remotely comparable with the revolution in its constitutional and international status that took place between 1945 and 1970. It is tempting, therefore, to suggest that, while decoloni-sation was the product of changes at the international, metropolitan and colonial levels, and can only be explained in terms of changes at all these levels, it may have been changes at the international level – in particular the Second World War and its aftereffects – that served as the *trigger* for an infinite series of transformations that cumulatively destroyed the old pre-war relationships of the imperial powers with the regions of colonial rule and semi-colonial domination.

In the British case, the sequence might be presented tentatively as follows. Prior to the Second World War, the evolution of the British imperial system – both in the colonies of direct rule as well as in regions such as the Middle East – appeared set on a path very different from that which it was ultimately to follow after 1945. But involvement in the war drove the British to make major changes in colonial policy and in their management of colonial resources. In doing so, they stimulated a new pattern of colonial activity and created novel political conditions in their colonies which generally made them harder to rule. Meanwhile the international and metro-politan side effects of the war (especially the emergence of such strong anti-colonial powers) encouraged colonial resistance to the old colonial powers, and, in Britain's case, made it harder to reassert authority without imposing unwelcome financial and political burdens on the home government, as well as jeopardising wider international interests outside the empire. In this way, a 'vicious circle' of imperial decline was set in motion, so that despite various strategies to sustain the main elements of the imperial system, it was progressively unravelled. The same kind of sequence, with local modifications, may be seen at work in the other European colonial powers: indeed the colonial empires ultimately depended on each other's support, and vicarious legitimation.

But of course this can only be the most general hypothesis with which to approach the enormous variety of colonial situations or seek to explain the widely differing outcome of decolonisation in different societies. We may find that it is of little help in understanding the course of events in Central Africa or South East Asia. In particular, we will want to guard against any presumption that in some mechanical way the actual pattern of decolonisation was the inevitable outcome of the Second World War. It was the *interlocking* of events, international, domestic, colonial, that determined that outcome. Only by picking our way carefully, noting how international, metropolitan and colonial politics ricocheted off each other and observing the (inevitably fallacious) assumptions of policy makers and politicians about the likely course of future events can we begin to understand why decolonisation followed the peculiar, unpredictable course that it did.

THE BRITISH IMPERIAL SYSTEM: AN OUTLINE

The British imperial system whose post-war dissolution is the subject of the following chapters was very far in reality from the political or constitutional unity that the expression 'British Empire' implies. Governments in London did not rule over an ordered phalanx of colonial governors: the empire did not march to the beat of Whitehall's drum. There was no logic and little system in its constitutional structure; no uniformity in its political development; and no unity in its economic life. Whatever the dreams of imperial enthusiasts, the British empire bore a closer resemblance to the ill-coordinated patrimony of Charles V than to the loyal imperial federation to which Joseph Chamberlain had looked forward before 1914. Above all was the fact that the British had never regarded their 'formal empire' of territorial possessions and protectorates as defining their most important economic or strategic interests.

This last was and remained a fundamental element in British thinking about their position in the world. For valuable though the countries of the formal empire were as markets and fields of investment, much British capital was invested outside the empire, in the United States, Latin America and elsewhere, and British trade depended as heavily upon foreign as upon empire markets. It was also an article of faith among British governments that London should remain the financial centre of the world (despite the competition from New York) and that sterling should continue to be the world's most widely used currency. The profits and advantages of being the world's banker were not to be given up. Thus any narrow policy of building a closed imperial economic bloc, insulated against the rest of world trade, rarely commanded much sympathy in London, and the experiment in an imperial economic policy based on tariffs and preferences, launched in the depths of the Depression in 1932, was considerably modified within a few years.[24] Commercial relations outside the empire held as high a priority as those inside and were regarded as essential to Britain's long-term economic health.

The same held true of political and strategic relationships. Before and after 1914 there was a passionate 'Blue Water' school in Britain which wanted to restrict British involvement in Europe to the barest minimum and to concentrate on building up an intimate partnership especially with the white dominions. But Britain's geographical position alone ensured that British governments could not remain aloof from European events since British security was bound up with the continental power balance.[25] Elsewhere in the world strategic and political interests had sucked British power into regions that lay outside the formal empire. By the 1930s both Egypt and Iraq were independent states and neither had ever been technically part of the empire. Yet both were regarded as of key importance to Britain's security interests as a great power in Asia and the Pacific, Egypt especially. The Suez Canal and the Persian Gulf were the gateways to the Indian Ocean. Hence Cairo was required to maintain a special relationship with Britain, to accept London's 'advice' in the conduct of foreign policy, and to make military bases available for British use. British influence was upheld through a treaty, but in practice by the presence of a British garrison and naval supremacy in the eastern Mediterranean. Much the same applied in Iraq. In both countries, the British enjoyed all the military benefits of colonial rule. But they were drawn, as a result, into the tangled politics of the Middle East and, by virtue of their mandate in Palestine (undertaken to exclude any other major power), into the deadly quarrel between the Arabs and the Jews.

There was thus no neat dividing line between Britain's imperial and non-imperial interests. Imperial security depended, or was thought to, upon Britain's position in non-empire countries. British prosperity required a liberal trading policy. Britain's diverse interests as a

European *and* world power obliged her to take account well before 1939 of the need to conciliate the feelings of other major powers including the United States. Imperial relations could not be conducted in a vacuum. They were bound to affect, and to be affected by, relations with other states. That is why the term 'imperial system' may be preferred to 'empire' which usually bears a narrower and more legalistic meaning. It was indeed once remarked in a brilliant image that the countries coloured red on the map – the formal possessions and protectorates of the Crown – bore the same relation to the overall shape of British world interests as the visible portion of an iceberg to its whole dimension.

For this reason the countries of the 'formal' empire could never demand, and certainly never received, any consistent priority in the eyes of policy makers in London. Indeed they themselves constituted a remarkably disparate collection of states and territories at different stages of political development and often with very little in common with each other save their connections with Britain. At the highest level in constitutional terms were the countries enjoying 'dominion status' – Canada, Australia, New Zealand, South Africa and the Irish Free State. By the 1930s they were fully autonomous in internal and external affairs.[26] They recognised the British Crown as their sovereign (after 1937 Eire's recognition was ambiguous and problematic) but their relations with the British government were, in theory, those of equals. In practice, of course, they were bound in varying degrees to Britain by economic self-interest, demographic links, sentiment and strategic dependence. But preserving good relations with the dominions to avoid potentially damaging political conflicts, required careful management on London's part. There was always an undertone of dominion resentment at British arrogance. In Canada, South Africa and the Irish Free State important sections of the community deeply resented the imperial connection and would have liked complete separation. Dominion economic interests had to be appeased and London found it expedient to emphasise not British leadership but fraternal solidarity and mutual interests. Nevertheless the object of British tact was to keep the dominions as closely aligned as possible to Britain so that in any major world crisis they would replay their part in the First World War: as a valuable reservoir of manpower; as sources of vital raw materials that could be bought without hard currency; and as safe and economically advanced bastions of British power and influence around the world.

The dominions enjoyed a special and intimate relationship with Britain and had to be treated as equals. But the Indian Empire was Britain's most important single colony. It was a valuable though declining market, an enormous bank of cheap manpower (extensively used in the First World War), the provider of a regular army available in emergency for British use, and, in geopolitical terms, a great zone of stability from which British influence could be exerted in East Asia and the Middle East. An India that was hostile or under the influence of a foreign power was simply inconceivable. Hence in London's eyes India's significance bulked larger than any other part of the imperial system and the defence of India was a vital strategic priority. By the later 1930s India was ruled by a complex system of partial self-government, although the Viceroy controlled defence and foreign policy absolutely. The Indian National Congress, dedicated to India's complete independence, commanded mass support, and, under the new constitution introduced in 1937, controlled the governments of the majority of Indian provinces in the last two years before the Second World War. An elaborate programme of constitutional development was planned to culminate at some unspecified stage in India's being granted dominion status and joining the other dominions as a partner rather than a subordinate in the imperial system. But for the time being this was pie in the Indian sky. The reality was still limited Indian participation in a structure of government in which British officials still occupied key positions, while their authority was backed up (if Indian politicians refused to cooperate) by an army and police force commanded and controlled by British officers.

From this point of view India was only the largest and most prestigious of British *dependencies* – those territories whose connection with Britain rested not on colonisation by British settlers but on rule by a thin stratum of British officials. These other territories formed a large and heterogeneous collection of crown colonies and protectorates, scattered across the globe like so many witnesses to a bygone century of carefree naval supremacy. In many cases population was small; in most the economy was commercially primitive. Moreover, most dependencies contained not a single culture, community, language or religion but several, perhaps dozens. Quite often, too, different parts of a dependency were governed under different constitutions (reflecting a multitude of local political and historical peculiarities) so that quite distinct forms of administrative and political organisation coexisted. In these circumstances it was the solidarity of the foreign ruling cadre of British officials that provided such unity as the dependency possessed.

The main clusters of dependencies reveal the extraordinary variety to be found in the colonial empire. In the British West Indies were some of Britain's oldest possessions dating back to before 1700. Once the jewel in the imperial crown, they were now poverty-stricken, overpopulated and, as the 1937 riots indicated, politically volatile. Poverty and the fierce local loyalties of the small island communities appeared to preclude any rapid progress towards self-government. In West Africa where there were four British dependencies there was great disparity between the social character of the coastal zones and that of the interior regions. This was particularly marked in Nigeria where North and South were like chalk and cheese. In general there was little sign of progress towards territorial self-government before 1939. In East Africa British rule was complicated by the presence of white settlers with aspirations to self-government and that of the Indian community whose status hovered uneasily between whites and blacks and who were regarded with mistrust by both. In central and southern Africa the British ruled over the protectorates of Northern Rhodesia and Nyasaland (now Zambia and Malawi), and over the High Commission Territories of Basutoland, Bechuanaland and Swaziland. Here too the continuation of British rule brought London up against white opinion in the self-governing settler colony of Southern Rhodesia (with which the 10,000 whites in Northern Rhodesia wanted to amalgamate) and in South Africa where the separate existence of the High Commission Territories was a source of grievance. Apart from Northern Rhodesia which yielded copper, the central and southern dependencies were desperately poor and politically comatose.

In Asia Britain's colonial dependencies stretched from Aden and the Hadhramaut to Fiji and the Pacific territories. The most important (outside India) were Ceylon (now Sri Lanka) and Malaya (now Malaysia), and the port-bases of Singapore and Hong Kong. Ceylon was affected by reverberations from Indian politics, but its deep ethnic and religious divisions – between Sinhalese and Tamils – seemed to rule out even the political concessions promised in India. In Malaya, too, Chinese and Indian immigrants were a potential source of communal friction: progress towards self-government would raise the thorny question of their status alongside the indigenous

Malays. But although politics in the Asian colonies were generally more lively than in the African, here too there was little to suggest on the eve of the Second World War that the rapid retraction of British colonial rule was on the cards.

The character of British rule in the Indian Empire and colonial dependencies is encrusted with popular myth and misconception. It is often depicted as a despotism exercised by pompous or bigoted *sahibs* in white shorts and pith helmets. Or (less fashionably) as a selfless struggle against the poverty, indolence and ignorance of the primitive masses. Both stereotypes miss the point that in general the cadre of British officials was so small[27] and the financial resources of most colonies so slim that colonial rule was obliged to rely upon locally recruited subordinates to man its bureaucracy and security forces and to win the cooperation of the indigenous social leaders – chiefs, landowners, sultans or sheikhs – who remained the main source of order and authority in the countryside. This cardinal fact of the colonial system imposed on the British great caution in its management. The poverty of the colonies and Parliamentary distaste for colonial expenditure made extreme economy of effort the guiding principle of policy. The colonies must be financially self-sufficient. Colonial governments must avoid actions which might incur heavy expenditure: above all, of course, they must not risk insurrection by offending too many powerful groups in indigenous society. Where possible local administration should be devolved on indigenous big-wigs and, in the interests of peace, quiet and economy, a blind eye turned to irregularities. This was the doctrine of 'indirect rule' which was in general favour between the wars.

Thus far from approaching their empire as a legacy to be ruthlessly exploited, the British in the two decades before 1939 seemed to treat it almost on a care and maintenance basis, perhaps in response to post 1918 financial stringency and economic depression.[28] As far as possible also the policy makers sought to keep colonial affairs out of politics at home, fearing the consequences of interference by ignorant parliamentarians playing to an even more ignorant gallery. Responsibility for the imperial system was in any case divided among four departments. The Foreign Office superintended British relations with the client states and semi-colonies including Egypt and the Sudan, technically co-administered with Egypt but in practice a British dependency. Relations with the dominions fell to the Dominions Office. The Indian Viceroy was supervised by the India Office. The rest was the province of the Colonial Office. Thus there was never a single departmental voice on imperial affairs which were also of concern to the armed services which had to maintain imperial security. In practice each department championed the interests of its own clients, dependents and allies.

The ramshackle appearance of the imperial system reflected the British instinct to keep their colonial authority flexible, to work with the grain of local societies, to rely upon indirect methods where possible and to avoid Napoleonic uniformity for its own sake. To that extent, the rickety exterior was deceptive. Nevertheless, even when run on a loose rein, the system was vulnerable to disruptive influences. In some colonies poverty, ecological disaster, economic depression or overpopulation threatened a social and political explosion. In others the light hand of colonial administration found it hard to restrain conflicts between rival communities. The struggle over land rights between immigrant groups and the indigenous population was a recurrent problem: common to Palestine, Burma, Kenya, Northern Rhodesia and Ceylon – among many. The social pressures behind the struggle were not easily relieved. Nor, for all their caution, were the British always able to avoid serious confrontation with their colonial subjects. The success of Gandhi and the Congress Party in fusing political discontents across the Indian sub-continent forced the British into reluctant coercive measures between 1930 and 1934, as well as constitutional concessions. Arab nationalism, fired by resentment at the influx of Jews, inspired an awkward and embarrassing insurrection in Palestine between 1936 and 1939. In 1931 there was a rising in Burma where Burmese nationalism throve on antipathy to the Indian minority. Defusing nationalist grievances by concession always risked whetting the appetite for more, as well as demoralising the government's own supporters and servants. Even the most artful schemes for dissolving a nationalist opposition into its various constituents by tactical concessions or constitutional change might be knocked sideways by external pressures: a veto from London or an international crisis. Finally, as different parts of the imperial system gradually acquired representative institutions or (in the case of the dominions) complete autonomy, it became harder and harder for London to prevent the affairs of one colony from provoking reaction in another: Indian resentment at the treatment of Indians in South and East Africa; Burmese or Ceylonese demands for parity of status with India; the demand by Kenya whites for the same privileges as their Southern Rhodesian counterparts.

There was one other respect in which the affairs of one colony jarred upon those of others. Ultimately, British rule in all their dependencies rested upon their ability to keep order and overcome rebellion. With the exception of the Indian army, the local military units in the colonies were of modest strength. Nor in the last analysis could they be relied upon to suppress a local insurrection if left unsupported by British troops. In India after the Mutiny of 1857 it was an iron rule (broken only in 1914–18) that there should be half as many British as Indian troops in the country at any time. The infantry battalions of the British army were the final sanction of colonial rule. The trouble was that there were relatively few of them – the army as a whole numbered under 200,000 men in peacetime – and they had to be posted around the world in penny packets, with a central reserve whose prime task was home defence. To reinforce a particular garrison adequately might take some time (hence the value of the Suez Canal). London had to hope that major internal security problems requiring a substantial military presence would not break out simultaneously, nor coincide with an *international* crisis. With so few men to play with, the margins were always fine.

By the later 1930s, however, these internal worries were over-shadowed by a much greater fear. It was not the machinations of wily nationalist politicians that London dreaded but the rapacity of Britain's three imperial rivals, Germany, Italy and Japan. Diplomatic capitulation or defeat at their hands would have far-reaching consequences. Key strong-points would be lost. In every colony the prestige and authority of British rule would be undermined, perhaps fatally. Local opposition movements would be patronised by the new victor powers. The morale of the colonial administrators and their local supporters would quickly collapse. The dominions would abandon their British connections looking elsewhere – perhaps to America – for trade and protection. So the fundamental imperial problem was defence, Britain's capacity to repel interference with her possessions, partners and spheres of influence. It was in this department that the weaknesses of imperial power in the 1930s were most obvious. It was in Britain's apparent inability to rearm more quickly and on a larger scale after 1935 that the consequences of her relative economic decline since 1914 could be seen most clearly.

To dwell only on the defects of the imperial system would be misleading. Every empire has weaknesses and it is unlikely that the British suffered more than most rulers from the characteristic imperial condition of political neurosis and strategic paranoia, mixed with nostalgia for a mythical golden age when internal opposition and external pressures had not existed. The British empire had survived the First World War and the great Depression. Despite the anxieties of the later 1930s, British leaders had yet to ask themselves whether the maintenance of a vast overseas empire was in Britain's interest any longer. Indeed, it did not occur to them to ask such a question. Had they been asked 'What is the empire for?' they might have found it difficult to frame a swift or convincing reply. But that would not be surprising. Large and complex institutions rarely lend themselves to easy rationalisation: their strength lies in complicated loyalties, multiple calculations, inertia and fear of the unknown. It is unlikely, however, that British leaders, or for that matter their colonial subjects, could have imagined a world in which Britain's connection with the empire countries and semi-colonies had been sundered completely. For all its imperfections, the British imperial system still appeared a necessary part of any stable world order. The alternative in much of the Afro-Asian world seemed mere anarchy.

THE PROBLEM

How far was Britain's long imperial career already played out by 1939? Was the writing already on the wall in India and elsewhere? Were changes in the more developed colonies steadily but irresistibly squeezing out colonial rule and British influence? Was the task of governing complex colonial societies that were undergoing further social change already too difficult and effortful and becoming rapidly more so? Were the British merely deluding themselves that by shrewd tactics, artful concession and ingenious constitutional rearrangements they could prolong their influence indefinitely and maintain a monopolistic 'special relationship' even after full self-government? Was the Second World War merely the last straw that broke the back of the imperial camel? As with all such hypothetical questions, it is hard to be sure, but right to be wary about deterministic explanations, unless all others fail. For all their disasters and humiliations, the British survived the Second World War as an imperial power. They suppressed a major Indian civil insurrection and reconquered lost colonies. Whatever pre-war tendencies may have existed, the pattern of post-war decolonisation was profoundly influenced by the course and impact of the war. To that we now turn.

2   War and Empire, 1939–45

Throughout the 1930s, British leaders had dreaded the outbreak of another great war not only because they feared its effects upon Britain and the British economy but because they suspected that a further round of global conflict so soon after the First World War and its nerve-wracking political aftermath might shake Britain's imperial system to pieces. Anxieties of this kind had periodically frightened British governments since the 1880s and 1890s. Conscious of imperial possessions and commitments for whose scattering across the globe the term 'far-flung' seems feebly inadequate; of the small scale of Britain's army; of the inevitable priority of home defence in any major war; of the financial and political constraints upon maintaining larger armed forces for imperial defence; and of the danger that defeat at the hands of an imperial rival would immediately threaten British control over India and the other dependencies where no bond of racial solidarity united mother-country and colonial population, governments in Britain, even before 1914, viewed the prospect of any war that might extend beyond Europe with doubt and gloom. In the hey-day of empire, British strategists anxiously debated whether, in the event of a Russian invasion of India through Afghanistan, Britain would be able to defend her grandest colony.[1]

Before 1914, however, the British were able to dissolve the nightmarish fear of a combined onslaught on their empire by the rival colonial powers of Germany, France and Russia. Alliance with Japan (1902), an entente with France (1904) and a further entente with Russia (1907) allowed the British to concentrate attention and resources largely upon Germany in the strategic rethinking that preceded the outbreak of the First World War.[2] In the decade that followed the armistice of 1918, the danger of any serious threat to British imperial interests appeared remoter than at any time since 1880, with the collapse of Germany, the weakness and internal preoccupation of Russia, the isolationism of the United States and the discretion with which Japan pursued her longstanding ambition of a larger influence in China. In 1928 Churchill denounced as absurd any notion of a naval conflict between Britain and either Italy or Japan.[3] But, notoriously, the difficulties of imperial strategy multiplied with appalling speed after 1930. The Japanese conquest of Manchuria in 1931 sounded the alarm about the defence of British possessions from India to Hong Kong, as well as of Australia and New Zealand, against a determined rival with a naval strength at least two thirds that of the Royal Navy, which had vastly larger commitments to meet. Then between 1933 and 1936 British strategists were confronted first by the spectre of a fiercely nationalistic Germany determined to rearm – and to acquire a new navy – and then by the gruesome prospect, with the formation of the Axis in 1936, of facing a simultaneous conflict in north-west Europe and in the Mediterranean and Middle East. On any calculation, the strategic and diplomatic revolution which occurred between 1931 and 1936 posed an appalling dilemma for the makers of British policy. Henceforth, in any crisis that involved Germany, Italy or Japan, they would have to take into account the danger of all three powers acting in concert against British interests – forcing the British to divide their already inadequate army, navy and air force between three widely separated theatres. And even if this 'worst-case' did not arise, there was an almost equal danger that a conflict with any one of these powers might result in such losses especially of warships that Britain's ability to defend her interests elsewhere would be decisively weakened. Thus it was precisely the fear of losing any of their precious capital ships – the mainstay of any defence against Japan – that dissuaded London from effective action to restrain Italian aggression in Ethiopia in 1935.[4] At no foreseeable date, the service chiefs told ministers, would Britain be able to contemplate with confidence a war against the three enemies that confronted her by 1936.[5]

Before 1914, faced by three formidable rivals, the British had made a useful regional alliance and struck a bargain with two of the three. There were powerful arguments for the same approach in the 1930s. But try as they might the British could not find a reasonable basis of compromise with any of the three revisionist powers – although Neville Chamberlain thought he had done so at Munich. Perhaps the internal dynamics of their opponents made any durable agreement impossible. Hence the anguish and uncertainty of British diplomacy in the later 1930s. Other factors as well told against Britain's general position – so much weaker by 1939 than it had been in 1914. Her only great power ally, France, was enfeebled and demoralised by internal divisions. Britain's own economy and industrial base seemed less well-equipped to provide the military strength required: rearmament was delayed by manpower shortages and anxieties over inflation and the balance of payments. The navy was considerably weaker in real striking power than in 1914, much of it being old or obsolete. The new technology of warfare – especially in the field of naval aviation – had been neglected, so that Britain's air power, barely adequate for the defence of Britain in 1940, was dismally deficient for the protection of the empire, particularly against Japan. Finally, to a greater extent than in 1914, the British had to take account of the political divergencies and unrest inside their imperial system: the hostility of many Afrikaners and most southern Irishmen to participation in a 'British' war; the insurrection in Palestine that complicated their political relationships in the Arab world; and the danger that Indian nationalism would mobilise popular feeling against the sub-continent's involuntary involvement in war. There were, in short, ample grounds for viewing Britain's entry into even a purely European conflict with a pessimism close to despair. If, that is, the object of fighting was to preserve Britain's place as an independent world power.

When war did break out in September 1939 the worst anxieties of British defence planners remained, temporarily, in abeyance. Neither Italy nor Japan joined the war, although Japanese pressure over the Tsientsin crisis in China forced the British to eat humble pie.[6] The British hoped that with France undefeated and the United States becoming more and more alarmed at Japanese expansion in China neither Italy nor Japan would dare exploit their preoccupation with Germany.[7] Hitler's lightning campaign in the early summer of 1940 wrecked that calculation. In June 1940 the fall of France ended all prospect of containing German power in Europe; permitted Mussolini to enter the war and commence the conquest of the Mediterranean and Middle East; and, by thus widening the war in Europe and threatening Britain with imminent invasion, provided powerful encouragement to Japan to seize an historic opportunity before it was too late. Thus it was the defeat of their continental ally which exposed the British to imperial ruin. Japanese intervention was deferred for a further eighteen months. But in the meantime Italian attacks upon Egypt and Suez, Axis propaganda aimed at Britain's discontented

Arab subjects and clients, the effective closure of the Mediterranean to British supplies, and, in 1941, the entry of German military power into the Mediterranean and North Africa, placed vast new burdens upon a British war machine scarcely capable of ensuring home defence. And were Mussolini to fulfil his boast and enter Cairo in glory, not only would a devastating blow have been struck at the authority of the London government over its dependencies, but, to all intents and purposes, the British imperial system would have been cut in half, leaving India, Malaya and the Pacific dominions to fend for themselves.

Worse was yet to come. As the British struggled to secure Egypt against an Axis attack reinforced by German troops and counted the losses of their abortive defence of Greece and Crete, the strategic nightmare of the 1930s at last became real. The greatest crisis of the war arrived with the defeat of the American navy at Pearl Harbor and the freedom this conferred upon the Japanese to commence the invasion of Malaya, the Philippines and the Dutch East Indies. Britain's accumulated military weaknesses now exacted their full toll. With utterly inadequate air power, especially at sea, the desperate effort to halt the invasion of Malaya resulted in forlorn tragedy, as two battleships, *Prince of Wales* and *Repulse*, that had been rushed to the Far East, were sunk by Japanese aircraft. Without air or naval protection, and with no prospect of relief, the fortress of Singapore – the iron gate that was to exclude any eastern invader from the Indian Ocean and be the launching pad for Britain's counterstroke – fell in February 1942 with a garrison of 130,000. The remaining units of the Royal Navy left Ceylon and fled westwards across the Indian Ocean. Burma was abandoned. In three months, the whole structure of British political and military power east and south of India had collapsed like a house of cards. The invasion of Australia, to whose defence British governments had repeatedly pledged themselves, appeared more than likely. In the North African battles to defend Egypt, the fall of Tobruk in June 1942 and the retreat of the British towards the Nile raised the spectre of fresh and worse disaster. Meanwhile in India, the Asian stronghold of British power, the failure of the Cripps Mission to find common ground with the Congress party leaders precipitated the great insurrection of 'Quit India' in August 1942. In Goebbels' phrase, England 'was on the toboggan'.

It was nevertheless in 1942 that the entry of the United States into the war at last brought some hope of ultimate victory, although in what form so far as British world power was concerned remained unknown and unpredictable. For though it brought enormous relief to British leaders, alliance with the United States, whose military and naval strength, like its industrial power, were potentially so much greater than Britain's, harnessed together two powers which, for all their common language, had very different approaches to world affairs; and in a relationship that was certain to be tilted sooner or later against Britain. Added to that was the fact that Roosevelt regarded the colonial empires of the European states with the same suspicion and dislike as had Woodrow Wilson. Antipathy to the British empire as an obstacle to American commerce and an affront to America's democratic anti-colonial tradition was also a key factor in American public attitudes to Britain, and not one which a president as cautious of public opinion as Roosevelt was likely to ignore.[8] For many Americans the notion of helping Britain to retain her colonial possessions was the unacceptable face of alliance; for them the corollary of Anglo-American partnership was British readiness to make sweeping changes in imperial policy: accepting the principle of trusteeship under international supervision in all their colonies; laying down a timetable (not necessarily a rapid one) for colonial independence. In particular, much American opinion, including Roosevelt himself, was very critical of the toughness the British had shown towards the Congress Party in India, and its claim to share the direction of India's war effort. Indeed, the Atlantic Charter of August 1941 which Roosevelt and Churchill had signed as a statement of common ideals could be read as an affirmation of the right of all peoples to choose the government under which they lived[9] – not a doctrine that was widely popular in the Colonial or India Office in London. 'The age of imperialism', remarked one of Roosevelt's most influential foreign policy advisers in 1942, 'is dead'.[10]

Ministers, officials and even academic opinion in Britain were all aware of the importance of reassuring or conciliating American feeling about the imperial system, and conscious of the need to present Britain's colonial policy in the most favourable light possible. Between 1942 and 1945 the question of how far Britain should accept any international supervision of her colonial territories in the post-war settlement, of what sort of declaration of colonial purpose London should agree to, was discussed continuously.[11] Enormous ingenuity was expended in framing ideas of regional cooperation and 'partnership' between colonial rulers and ruled as alternatives to internationally administered trusteeship: the object was to disarm the dangerous enthusiasm of American policy makers for the wholesale dismantling of the colonial order. As the sense of financial dependence upon the United States grew more oppressive, the fear increased that Washington would demand colonial changes as the price of continued economic assistance.[12] To make matters worse, Roosevelt made no secret of his desire to prevent the French from regaining control of Indo-China, his sympathy for China's great power aspirations in the Far East and his preference for Hong Kong to be handed back not to Britain but to Chiang Kai-shek. A settlement of this kind in the Far East, reasoned the British, would make their own case for resuming the government of Burma and their Malayan possessions almost untenable. Moreover, it seemed likely that America's overwhelming predominance in the Pacific war would enable Washington to impose its views by virtue of its unchallengeable military superiority in the region in the aftermath of Japan's defeat. By 1943–44, therefore, the defence of the British imperial system had become, in the eyes of British leaders, almost as much a diplomatic struggle against their ally as a military struggle with their enemies.

For whatever the ingenuity of the departmental experts in London, or the highmindedness of the outsiders they coopted to assist them, in the upper reaches of Churchill's wartime coalition government there was scarcely any serious division over the prime importance of Britain's retaining full control over her colonial possessions (particularly over their advancement to self-rule) and of regaining the colonies lost by foreign conquest. Imperial patriotism and the conviction that Britain must remain a great world power were cherished as much among such Labour members of the Coalition government as Bevin and Morrison as among the Conservatives. Even a Fabian colonial reformer like Creech-Jones resented the criticism of British colonial administration voiced in the United States. Among ministers directly responsible for Britain's overseas interests and possessions there was general determination to keep a firm grip on pre-war spheres of influence and control as far as possible. Amery, the Secretary of State for India, urged in 1943 the declaration of a British Monroe Doctrine over the Middle East.[13] 'The British Empire', declared the Colonial Secretary in the dark days of July 1942, 'is not dead, it is not dying, it is not even going into decline.'[14] In November 1944 Anthony Eden, the Foreign Secretary, reminded Mountbatten, the Allied Commander in South East Asia, of the importance of 'reconquering the British Empire with mainly British force of arms'.[15] But above all these lesser figures loomed the presence of Churchill.

In retrospect, Churchill has come to be identified with Britain's solitary island resistance to Hitler after the fall of France in 1940: the David who challenged the Nazi Goliath. But Churchill did not regard himself as the leader of a small people fighting to be free. More boisterously than any British premier of the century, he insisted upon unwavering adherence to Britain's manifest destiny as a world power and the greatest of imperial powers.[16] Even when the invasion fears of 1940 were at their height, Churchill remained concerned for Britain's strategic grip on Egypt and the Suez Canal – the hinge connecting Britain with her vast possessions in Asia – as well as with the defence of British power in India and the Far East. For Churchill, the cavalry subaltern in Victorian India, the veteran of Omdurman, the erstwhile director of British seapower (1911–15, 1939–40), the architect of Britain's special position in the Middle East after 1918, the thought of abandoning the Victorian legacy of world power was anathema. While his ideas on colonial government were not inflexible, he regarded the retention of some ultimate British control over the various elements of the imperial system as essential. Above all, Churchill insisted that Britain must preserve her authority over India which he saw with unchanging conviction as the second centre of British world power. In the 1930s he had fought a bitter political campaign against any vestige of Indian control over the central government of the Raj where questions of external policy and defence were decided. If Britain lost the Indian Empire, he once declared, she would sink in two generations to the rank of a minor power – like Portugal.[17] Churchill's wartime colleagues may have cringed sometimes at the bluntness of his imperial patriotism. But his fierce defence of British rights and status commanded their general support and checked any tendency towards offering, as a sop to American opinion, anything that smacked of international interference in the British empire. ' "Hands off the British Empire" is our maxim', minuted the prime minister in December 1944.

But even Churchill's exceptionally vigorous championship of Britain's imperial prerogatives (including the threat to resign the premiership if Roosevelt demanded concessions to Gandhi) might not have availed but for a series of fortunate circumstances. British world power had been in desperate straits in 1942 and might have been demolished before American military participation became effective. By 1944 Britain's manpower reserves had reached their limit;[18] her war economy was strained to the utmost.[19] By contrast, the American war effort was growing rapidly and in the middle of 1944, for the first time, the number of American troops in direct contact with the enemy exceeded that of British empire forces.[20] In 1944 also, the successes of the Russian armies at last made clear the likely scale of Stalin's share in the Allied victory, and, thenceforth, British leaders were to find a marked tendency for the emergent superpowers to negotiate over their head. In the war against Japan, American predominance on the Allied side was unchallengeable, and their likely influence over the Asian peace settlement correspondingly large. In all these respects, the difficulty of maintaining Britain's vast and over-extended terri-torial possessions let alone of recovering lost provinces and shattered influence might have been immense. But, for all their economic hardship and overstrain – perhaps because of it – the British were able to end the war with their imperial legacy astonishingly intact – at least to outward appearance.

Four circumstances in particular helped to bring this about. In the first place, American pressure for the internationalisation of the British colonial empire was moderated from an early stage by the fear that pressed too hard it might result in the disintegration of British power or the collapse of Churchill's government, before the war was won. Paradoxically, as Britain's status in the Grand Alliance declined with the rise of Russia, American attitudes were increasingly in-fluenced by wary calculations about Soviet power and the necessity of British friendship.[21] Secondly, American official enthusiasm for the repudiation of all forms of colonial rule was never wholehearted. In particular, the armed services engaged in the Pacific struggle were determined to retain the islands conquered from Japan under direct American control and looked askance at notions of international trusteeship. They thus made common cause with London to check the internationalist zeal of Roosevelt's other advisers.[22] The other circum-stances arose from the fortunes of war.

For the survival of the British imperial system, the second battle of Alamein in October 1942 was of the utmost importance. At the moment when Montgomery arrived to take command of the battered and demoralised Eighth Army the triumph of Rommel's German-Italian army seemed highly probable.[23] The British high command in Cairo contemplated the evacuation of Egypt and the withdrawal of the British and Commonwealth forces to Palestine and up the Nile to the Sudan, leaving the Suez Canal in German hands. Whether the British troops could have long escaped surrender deprived of the base facilities of Egypt and direct links with Britain seems doubtful. Had this disaster occurred, British power in the Mediterranean and Middle East would have been shattered. Britain's East African possessions would have been vulnerable. With Iraq and Iran under Axis influence, the security of India would have been threatened from two sides.[24] The South African government of General Smuts, deeply committed in North Africa and assailed by considerable Afrikaner discontent at home, might have collapsed. And even if, by dint of American assistance Axis domination of the Mediterranean and Middle East had eventually been overthrown, it is unlikely that British prestige and authority could have recovered, leaving the region to be divided between American and Soviet influence. It is little wonder that Churchill afterwards confessed that it was the outcome of this battle that caused him the most intense anxiety of the war. And it was *after* the battle of Alamein that Churchill threw down his famous gauntlet:

> Let me make this clear in case there should be any mistake about it in any quarter. We mean to hold our own. I have not become the King's First Minister in order to preside over the liquidation of the British Empire.[25]

Alamein and the subsequent victories in North Africa may have secured the British position in the Middle East; but South East Asia hung in the balance. Churchill was bent on recovering Singapore at all costs. This was, he said,

> The supreme British objective in the whole of the Indian and Far Eastern theatres . . . the only prize that will restore British prestige in this region.[26]

It was essential for Mountbatten's South East Asia Command to reconquer the lost colonies and, if possible, to restore the colonial order in the Netherlands East Indies and Indo-China. But much depended on how the struggle with Japan developed, and whether Britain's economic resources could sustain a major share in Japan's defeat if, as was expected, the Pacific war continued for a year or more after Germany's surrender, and if the Pacific victory turned out to be chiefly the handiwork of the United States and the Soviet Union. Here too the British were supremely fortunate. In the event it was American air and naval power in the central Pacific which played the major role in defeating Japanese power, while the atomic bomb brought the war to a much more rapid end than was expected. The main American military effort bypassed Indo-China and the Netherlands East Indies which were subsequently attached to Mountbatten's command. As a result, the British were able, however briefly, to restore colonial rule in the French and Dutch dependencies as well as in their own, and American influence in South East Asia in the immediate post-war years remained limited. Here, as in the Middle East, the British were able, to all appearances, to restore the *status quo ante bellum* to an extent which had seemed quite improbable in 1942.

Nevertheless, the outcome was not entirely satisfactory judged by Churchillian standards and, as we shall see, the restoration of the formal *status quo* masked the inner turbulences set off by the impact of the war in both Asia and the Middle East. Nor, when it came to the creation of the United Nations in 1945 were the British able to prevent the transformation of their old League of Nations mandates into the trusteeship territories of the new organisation. To make matters worse, Churchill agreed at Yalta, perhaps unwittingly, that the supervisory powers of the United Nations trusteeship council should be strengthened by allowing visits of inspection with all their disturbing effects. At the San Francisco conference in April 1945, it was also agreed that the trusteeship council could receive petitions from the population. Both these provisions, opening the prospect of external interference, were disliked by British ministers but reluctantly accepted to avoid British isolation and to conciliate the Americans.[27] The exact significance of these concessions in enhancing the status of anti-colonial opinions among the member states of the United Nations and encouraging the hopes of colonial nationalists is difficult to assess, not least because the crucial difference between the United Nations and the old League lay in the very different roles and importance of the United States and the Soviet Union – both ideologically opposed to colonial rule – in the latter.

Churchill, however, had made good his promise: what we have we hold. That he had done so, that no British colonies had been permanently lost as a *direct result* of foreign conquest was undoubtedly an important if immeasurable influence upon the outlook of successive governments anxious not to dissipate too obviously Churchill's legacy of world power and an intact empire. As a result, arguably until the middle 1960s, if not beyond, in external policy government after government felt the peculiar weight of that 'immense and brooding spirit' – the 'saviour of his country' and also the fiercest advocate of its imperial pretensions.

IMPERIAL SIDE-EFFECTS

At first sight, victory in 1945 seemed to be, as in 1918, a striking vindication of the resilience, loyalty and solidarity of the British empire-commonwealth. Despite the procession of disasters and humiliations in the first three years of the war the ramshackle structure of the imperial system had survived. Britain had drawn economic and military assistance from almost every part of the empire as well as from countries like Egypt whose involuntary association with the imperial war effort reflected the fact of Britain's undeclared domination. Even when the war became global, after December 1941, it had been possible, just, to preserve the political unity of the whole structure and to maintain relative harmony with self-governing empire countries over strategy and war aims. Nevertheless, the impact of the war upon the shape of British imperial power was profound. It raised new questions about British military power which affected opinion in Britain, the dominions, in India and the other British colonies, as well as in the semi-colonies where British influence was paramount. It created new international conditions, both politically and economically, and raised hopes of a new non-colonial world order. It generated new discontents as the British, in their struggle for survival as a world power, asserted control over their colonial economies more vigorously than ever before. For all the triumphs in Europe, the Mediterranean and the Pacific, it was certain that a return to pre-war 'normalcy' was impossible – not that anyone would have wished to return to the fear and insecurity of 1939. At the very least, a spasm of colonial unrest and uncertainty was likely to follow the end of hostilities; perhaps even a general crisis in the old bases of British world power. In the dominions, the dependencies and in Britain's semi-colonies, the old terms of cooperation and rule could no longer be taken for granted.

Before 1939 the five dominions, Canada, Australia, South Africa, New Zealand and the Irish Free State, already enjoyed constitutional equality with Britain. They shared a common sovereign but in every other respect were formally independent of any British control. In practice, they still felt bound to Britain by ties of sentiment and self-interest, or by fear of the consequences of seceding from the empire. In material terms Britain remained for all of them an irreplaceable market, an important source of capital and settlers (Eire was an exception) and, for South Africa and the Pacific dominions especially, their shield and guardian against external attack. They could not easily imagine a future cut loose from Britain, or if Britain were to be defeated and under foreign domination. Despite their remoteness, therefore, they felt bound up with Britain's European fate.[28] When Britain went to war against Germany in September 1939 the dominions followed. The single exception was Eire – the one dominion without a substantial population of British stock. Eire maintained her neutrality throughout the war.

The readiness to come to Britain's aid, as in 1914, showed that the dominions still regarded Britain as the key to all their external relationships. In Canada, Australia and New Zealand probably no government which refused to join Britain could have survived. But the course of the war, for all that it promoted a sense of common purpose, also emphasised the differences of interest between Britain and each of the dominions and the extent to which, for all the dominions, their links with the mother-country now had to be supplemented by other international relationships. The war set the seal upon Eire's withdrawal from all real participation in the imperial system and cleared the way for the eventual decision to enact a fully republican constitution outside the Commonwealth. In South Africa the economic and social changes brought on by the war, especially the great inflow of black labour into the towns, contributed to the revival of republican nationalism among Afrikaners and the triumph of the National Party in the 1948 election.[29]

The nub of the matter, however, was strategic and international. It was changes in this sphere rather than internal changes which altered the relationship of the dominions to Britain after 1945. Thus from an early stage of the war Canada had been anxious that her commitment to the Commonwealth war effort should not jeopardise relations with her vast southern neighbour. After the fall of France, the security of Canada's coast line and Atlantic sea links with Britain relied chiefly upon an overstretched Royal Navy confronted by a growing submarine threat. In these circumstances, American willingness to guarantee Canadian security under the Ogdensburg Agreement of August 1940, and to set up a joint defence board, was a great relief. But it was also an historic turning point in Canada's triangular relationship with Britain and the United States, signalling a strategic intimacy and mutual interest in the defence of the North American continent closer than the old bonds of empire. Canada's special relationship with Britain continued, but now it was counterbalanced more emphatically than ever before by her new defensive alliance – the first alliance contracted between a dominion and a foreign power.

Canada's need for more security and protection than Britain could offer was dramatically echoed in the case of Australia and New Zealand. Even before Japan's entry into the war, the Australian government had been uneasy about the effectiveness of British aid against Japanese attack, especially after the fall of France and the loss of French naval support. After Pearl Harbor, Canberra became understandably frantic. The lack of British air and sea power in the Far East was glaring. Much of Australia's army was in the Middle East fighting the desert war. In this situation of acute vulnerability, the Australian prime minister declared openly: 'Australia looks to America, free of any pangs as to our traditional links with the United Kingdom'.[30] With the fall of Singapore in February 1942, the loss of Burma, the threatened loss of Ceylon and the flight of the Royal Navy to the shelter of the East African coast, this sense of abandonment by Britain became extreme. Attlee, as Dominions Secretary, candidly told the Australian premier 'Your greatest support in this hour of peril must be drawn from the United States'[31] – a terse epitaph on 150 years of naval supremacy in eastern waters. For their part, Australian leaders were bitterly critical of Churchill's war direction[32] and of the general ignorance, indifference and bad management that they saw in Britain's Far Eastern policy.[33] American economic aid, the presence of American troops and a common Australian-American interest in clearing the islands north of Australia of Japanese invaders quickly replaced the old sense of strategic dependence on Britain so marked before 1939. After Singapore there could be no return to the old confidence in Britain's naval shield. A fundamental element in Britain's pre-war relationship with the Pacific dominions disappeared in February 1942. Ultimate victory did not restore it. The decisive role played by the Americans in defeating Japan and the persistence after 1945 of Australian fears about Far East aggression ensured that the lesson of Singapore was not forgotten.

Three of the dominions had seen at first hand the weakness of British power and the vulnerability of the imperial system, so much more evident than in 1914–18. Each had noted the indispensability of a new special relationship with the United States. A fourth, Eire, had been able to remain neutral even in 1940, partly because of American protection (Roosevelt had warned Churchill against trying to bully De Valera into the war).[34] The fifth, South Africa, had fought in the African campaigns, but at home anti-British republican feeling had grown rapidly among Afrikaners, especially through the *Ossewa Brandwag* movement.[35] To the British, close relations with South Africa seemed more and more dependent upon the authority of the ageing Smuts (b. 1870). 'After Smuts the political deluge', remarked one minister in March 1944.[36] And even Smuts, a longstanding South African expansionist, had grand ambitions to share control of Britain's African empire with the mother-country. Thus in different ways, each dominion had shrugged off a good deal of its pre-war subservience to Britain, discovered vital interests which its imperial connections could not provide for and developed new international ambitions and relationships hardly envisaged before 1939. The longer-term significance of these wartime changes we shall trace in later chapters.

Unlike the dominions, India and Britain's other colonies entered the war involuntarily without benefit of public consultation or approval. Moreover, here the job of mobilising resources and manpower for the imperial war effort, and of explaining the purpose for which the effort was being made, fell not upon local political leaders – as in the dominions – but upon British officials whose foreignness and apolitical training made them, at best, somewhat ill-adapted for the task, particularly in the crucial field of propaganda and persuasion. Consequently, the inevitable anxieties, discontents and uncertainties generated by a long and often daunting conflict became a direct challenge to the framework of British rule – because it was much harder than in Britain to redirect popular resentment towards the enemy – and the deficiencies of British administration were highlighted in a period of abnormal political excitement. In India as we shall see in a later chapter the political reaction against British rule was strongest and set off a major popular insurrection in 1942, judged by the British to have been (briefly) more dangerous than the Mutiny of 1857. The insurrection was suppressed but left its mark on Indian politics. In other colonies the political reaction was milder, although there were strikes, demonstrations and signs of popular unrest. For many of the sources of discontent in India were to be found also in other colonies.

Before 1939 in India and almost everywhere else, the golden rule of British colonial administration had been to let well alone, as far as was possible, at the local level in the economic and social life of their possessions.[37] In India, the policy was to turn over local affairs to Indian politicians; in other colonies to delegate it as much as possible to tribal chiefs or whatever set of local rulers could be found, under the doctrine of 'indirect rule'. The merit of this approach, it was thought, apart from its cheapness, was that it extracted British rule from direct confrontation with local feeling, denying nationalist politicians and agitators the kind of local issues which could galvanise the rural masses and rouse them against the colonial administration. In fact, of course, the onset of economic depression by 1930 created dangerous economic grievances among the rural masses anyway, grievances which colonial rule could do little or nothing to alleviate. But generally, even in India, the policy of masterly inactivity appeared the best way of reminding Britain's colonial subjects that, even though they might resent colonial rule, their differences with each other, on caste, class, religious or other social grounds, were too great to make an all-out struggle for independence worthwhile.

Mobilisation for war threw masterly inactivity into reverse, and forced colonial governments into actions they knew to be unpopular. Almost everywhere the intense pressure for the colonies to produce more goods to meet war needs led to more and more imperial direction over colonial economies. Their overseas trade was closely regulated. Schemes of bulk purchase, as in East and West Africa, turned colonial governments into monopoly purchasers of local cash crops – sometimes paying only half the price paid on the open world market.[38] In India, where the shortage of food became critical, government assumed full control over food-grain marketing and imposed rationing in many cities.[39] Production of cash crops was restricted in the interests of the Grow More Food campaign, and by the war's end even wider interference into the operations of the rural moneylenders and the price level of agricultural products was in view.[40] But intervention by governments could not prevent, and sometimes aggravated, the characteristic wartime problems of shortages and inflation. Rising prices meant, in many cases, falling living standards.[41] The lack of consumer goods, especially in India, led to the hoarding of grain, and then to famine.[42] In all these ways, despite itself, colonial rule bore the odium of inflicting unwelcome interference on farmers, traders and businessmen, and harsh sacrifices on the urban and rural masses.

There were other ways, too, in which wartime administration meant overturning previous conventions about governmental inter-ference. In some colonies, for instance, the colonial authorities resorted to the arbitrary impressment of labour to meet production targets in agriculture enjoined by London.[43] Substantial numbers of Indians, Nigerians, Kenyans, Tanganyikans, Gold Coasters and other colonial peoples were recruited for military service.[44] The methods employed by local dignitaries may have been anything but fair and equitable. In the Gold Coast, the colonial governor, at London's insistence, reluct-antly introduced the unpopular novelty of an income tax.[45] Indeed, the war saw the general introduction of this tax in the colonial empire.[46] Rates of taxation and import duties also rose substantially.[47] In Nigeria, Kenya, Northern Rhodesia, Ceylon and the Gold Coast (now Ghana) public revenue more than doubled over the period 1939-46.[48] In East Africa, the priority given to war production and the new importance, in this role, of the white settler community, pushed the colonial government towards constitutional concessions to them and raised African fears of large-scale white immigration at the end of the war.[49] All or most of these innovations were bound to have a disturbing effect on the relations between the alien rulers and their colonial subjects, to whom the actions of the government often appeared arbitrary, unpredictable and inexplicable except in terms of some deep-laid plot to impoverish the indigenous peoples to the benefit of outsiders.

The danger of a widening gulf between resentful colonial popu-lations subjected to new burdens and restrictions and a colonial administration preoccupied with London's demands for a greater colonial contribution to the war effort was accentuated by the effects of the war on the 'steel frame' – the cadre of British officials on whom imperial control ultimately depended. In every colony, the new tasks of wartime – food control, propaganda, censorship, security, war production – absorbed much of the time and energy of the admini-strators, whose ranks were already depleted by departures for military service. The result of this extra work and deteriorating conditions of service was sagging morale.[50] It also meant that desk-bound admini-strators in many colonies gave up the practice of touring – the essential means whereby colonial officials kept in touch with opinion in the countryside[51] as well as sustaining the prestige and authority of their rule. Not for nothing did the Governor of the Gold Coast urge his officials to travel by horse or even bicycle rather than the too-rapid car.[52] At the war's end, when vast new problems of adjustment to peacetime conditions in a novel political climate came in sight, the administrative machine in many colonies, especially in India, was badly run down, exhausted and demoralised.[53]

Not surprisingly, the British officials in the colonial governments were deeply anxious about the effect of these enforced changes on the stability of their rule, dependent in almost every case very largely upon the acquiescence of the local population and its social leaders. The 'thin white line', even in pre-war times, was usually very thin indeed.[54] They looked back to the unrest which had followed the First World War and expected the same upsurge of political excitement at the end of the Second. They were eager if possible to anticipate the growth of new political movements and to conciliate local interests irritated or outraged by wartime exactions and restrictions. Thus the Governor of the Gold Coast wanted to sweeten the bitter pill of income tax by promising a majority of 'unofficials' (i.e. local representatives) on the Legislative Council a concession designed to appease local bigwigs.[55] In India, the Viceroy was convinced that a speedy return to representative government at the war's end was essential, and would mean cooperation with the Congress Party and a further move towards full self-government. In the Sudan, where the side effects of the growth of Egyptian nationalism were felt as well, the colonial administration made preparations for larger local participation in government at the war's end.[56] The same pressure to conciliate local interests whose help in the colonial war effort was necessary led colonial governments in Kenya and Northern Rhodesia in a different direction. There fear of antagonising white settler communities led to promises of greater *settler* participation in government and the Colonial Office in London even briefly considered full internal self-government for the Europeans in the White Highlands of Kenya[57] – a decision that would have created a second 'Rhodesia' in East Africa.

The anxiety of the men on the spot chimed in with the sharp wartime change of outlook at the centre of imperial affairs in London. Even before the war, the defects of a colonial policy based on extreme parsimony and *laissez-faire* had been demonstrated by the disturbances in the West Indies. The beginnings of a new attitude towards colonial economic and social development could be seen in the Colonial Development and Welfare Act of 1940.[58] But the war carried matters much further. 1942 brought defeat and humiliation in Asia as Hong Kong, Malaya and Burma fell. The Quit India insurrection followed in August. At the same time, Britain now found herself in a Grand Alliance alongside the two great anti-colonial powers, the United States and the Soviet Union. Democracy, on the one hand, and socialist planning, on the other, suddenly came into fashion.[59] A chorus of criticism arose at the management of imperial affairs, set off by the fall of Singapore. 'The British imperial game is up', remarked the influential writer R. H. Tawney. More to the point, it now seemed essential, as we have noticed already, to portray British colonial policy in ways that would appease anti-colonial sentiment in the United States: new and attractive justifications had to be found for the exercise of colonial rule; new promises made about its objectives.

This ideological revolt against the old approach to imperial power thus produced a major shift in the assumptions about what was possible and desirable in colonial administration. It was strongly reinforced by pragmatic arguments. The fall of Malaya had raised obvious questions about the efficiency and effectiveness of the colonial government. The pressure on colonial administrations elsewhere to contribute to the war effort and undertake a vast range of new tasks revealed that they too were chronically under-engined for the functions of a modern government, above all in the field of economic management and social development. It was also perceived that necessary changes in the character of colonial governments would have local repercussions as well. As it happened, even before the full extent of London's dissatisfaction with its colonial authorities had been reached, the Colonial Office had despatched Lord Hailey to survey the political changes that might become necessary in British Colonial Africa. His report was to have a major influence on the thinking behind post-war colonial policy.

Hailey was perhaps the most eminent British colonial official of the day. After a career in India, culminating in a key provincial governorship, he had turned on his retirement to the compilation of *An African Survey* (1938), a massively authoritative work of reference on almost every aspect of colonial administration on the continent. Hailey became particularly expert in the varieties of local administration employed in different colonies, especially differences in the participation of Africans. His conclusions were unlikely to be radical; but being grounded in the practicalities of colonial government, their force would be all the greater.

Hailey's report flatly ruled out going on as before. The number of educated and politically-minded Africans was bound to increase as social and economic changes made themselves felt. Political movements would become more frequent,[60] and some means would have to be found of canalising them safely. But Hailey was much less concerned with preparing for a rising tide of nationalism – which he claimed was scarcely visible in Africa – than with the problems and consequences of expanding the social and economic functions of government, hitherto almost negligible.[61] Colonial governments would have to plunge into new fields in their role as the agents of development. Opinion at home now required this. But the more they regulated the social and economic life of African societies the more they would be caught up in local grievances and controversy.[62] Indeed, the promotion of any social and economic change at all would force colonial governments to make difficult and unpopular choices. The result might be to shake the foundations of imperial authority: 'Can we be sure,' Hailey asked, 'of the continuance of that degree of acquiescence in our rule which is a necessary condition of administrative progress?'[63] – especially since the current world conflict was likely to have unknown but far-reaching effects on colonial societies.[64]

Hailey's prime concern was with the stability and effectiveness of the British colonial governments in Africa, but he was also anxious that British policy should be seen, especially by American opinion, as contributing positively to the attainment of self-government in some indefinite future. Significantly, he rejected the idea that the tribal and traditional local authorities of the countryside could be the basis for more self-government.[65] What was needed was African participation through regional councils, and the recruitment of Africans into the administrative machine (as in India). For in its new tasks, a colonial government now needed the assistance of educated Africans rather than their tribal or traditional fellows, and had to make room for them in its political and bureaucratic structure. Hailey opposed 'premature constitution-mongering' and suggested no precise programme of constitutional change. Nevertheless, his insistence that a new style of colonial rule required new local allies and institutions marks a watershed in London's approach to colonial policy. Not all his ideas were accepted. But the broad implication of his report that development was now at the head of the agenda in colonial administration, and that development, in order to work, required political change in the direction of more self-government, was clearly in tune with the wartime need to find an 'acceptable face' of imperialism and to modernise the colonial economies in the wider imperial interest.[66]

The old basis of Britain's relations with the dominions and the colonial territories had been deeply disturbed by the reverberations of the world war. But this was not the full measure of the war's imperial side effects. There were also regions where Britain had little or no *direct* colonial authority at stake, but whose stability and responsiveness to British influence was of the greatest concern to London. Here, too, the war had unleashed new forces to threaten British interests and test the strength and determination of an already over-extended imperial system. The two regions where these dangers seemed most apparent and Britain's interests least dispensable were the Middle East and East and South East Asia.

Between the wars Britain was the dominant foreign power in the Middle East. Palestine and Trans-Jordan were administered as mandates. Egypt and Iraq – strategically the most important countries of the Middle East from the British point of view – were reluctant allies on whose soil the British maintained substantial bases. Both were expected to conform their foreign policy with Britain's. Saudi Arabia, infinitely weaker and poorer then than now, was dependent on British subsidy. In the petty Arab states of the Persian Gulf, British authority was paramount. But impressive as Britain's position appeared, its stability depended upon the careful management of Anglo-Arab relations. British military power and the readiness to use it on occasion had to be convincingly displayed. Interference with local society and religion had to be kept to a minimum to avoid conflict with what the British thought of as the inflammable masses. Above all, the British had to be extremely careful to do nothing which would allow or encourage Arab nationalism to be mobilised against them, or which might force the usually conservative rulers of the independent Arab states to disavow their British connections. By the mid to later 1930s, this meant applying in Palestine a policy broadly acceptable to the leaders of Iraq, Egypt and Saudi Arabia; in other words, the limitation of Jewish immigration and the promise of Palestine's eventual independence *as an Arab state*.[67]

Between 1940 and 1942 British control of the Middle East was tested almost to destruction. But by early 1943, the battles of Alamein and Stalingrad had together removed the danger of a German-Italian conquest of the Middle East from the north and west. Henceforth, the strategic importance of the Middle East lay in its role as a supply and transit zone for theatres of war elsewhere in Europe and Asia. British control appeared stronger than ever: compliant regimes now ruled in Cairo and Baghdad; Vichy French rule had been overthrown in Syria and Lebanon. The whole region swarmed with British administrators, experts, advisers, technicians and soldiers. Ambitious plans began to be hatched for the post-war development of the Arab world. But the British soon found that by exacerbating the social and political tensions within Arab societies, by introducing new and unpredictable external influences into the region and by forcing them to abandon their cautious pre-war stance, the war had weakened not strengthened their position.

The first source of difficulty for the British was the necessity, at the worst crisis of the Middle East war, to coerce their reluctant Arab partners into full cooperation. In 1941–42 the British overthrew the pro-German ruler of Iraq and imposed on the king of Egypt a prime minister of their choice – by the simple expedient of surrounding his palace with tanks. They also brought Syria and Lebanon under British control. To conciliate and reassure Arab opinion, after these abrupt moves, London promised Syria independence and declared British sympathy for Arab unity.[68] Arab nationalism, it was hoped, would still find British imperialism an acceptable partner. In fact, these gestures triggered off new rivalries among the Arab states (including Egypt), the effect of which was to multiply their suspicions of Britain's real policy. Meanwhile the strain of participation in the war effort showed itself in inflation and shortage, doubling prices in Egypt and Palestine and increasing them sixfold in Iraq.[69] An elaborate bureaucratic machine – the Middle East Supply Centre – staffed by Anglo-Americans, was clamped onto the economy of the region, regulating trade, dictating grain and food prices, monopolising transport.[70] Everywhere the military and administrative presence of the British became more and more intrusive: and Arab and Egyptian fears that economic and political controls riveted on in wartime would continue indefinitely grew correspondingly more intense.[71] Above all, discussion of Arab unity, the part played by Zionists in the war effort, the entry of the United States into the war, highlighted the problem that the British had struggled to play down: the future of Palestine. Already before the end of the war, a chorus of British officials in the

Middle East was warning that any change in pre-war policy – to accommodate American opinion or humanitarian concern for Jewish refugees in Europe – was incompatible with Anglo-Arab cooperation.[72]

All this was bad enough. But from 1942 onwards the British had also to reckon with the erosion of their inter-war primacy in the region. The joint occupation of Iran with the Soviet Union in 1941 brought Russian influence back into the Middle East. By the end of the war, Russian demands were being heard for a louder voice in Turkey, for effective control of the Bosphorus and Dardanelles and even, in September 1945, for the trusteeship of western Libya.[73] In Saudi Arabia, American influence grew rapidly in the war, and London resigned itself to the necessity of an enlarged American stake in the Middle East, not least in the oil industry, as a counter to the more sinister power of Russia.[74] But although the British took a generally complacent view of America's new presence in the region, they were soon to find that it complicated their own dealings with Arabs and Jews.

Altogether, the political, economic and diplomatic consequences of the war aroused the latent internal tensions of the Middle East, intensified local suspicion and resentment of foreign interference and control, stimulated new hopes of independence and unity and added a dangerous new twist to the one question on which local feeling might unite in hostility to Britain: Palestine. At the same time, London's freedom of manoeuvre – to settle the Palestine problem in accordance with imperial interests and to buy off Arab nationalism by relaxing diplomatic and military control over Egypt and the Arab states – was being reduced sharply by the rise of Russian and American influence. In a region still deemed of vital importance to Britain's global interests, and of growing economic importance, there was every reason to expect that the end of the war would bring not tranquillity and security but turbulence and danger.

Prior to the Japanese onslaught on China in 1937, Britain's position as the leading Western power in the Far East had not been *directly* challenged since its beginnings in the 1840s. Even in the 1920s, Britain and her Hong Kong colony together controlled more than a third of China's foreign trade.[75] With naval bases at Hong Kong and Singapore, their colonial territories in Malaya and Borneo, a dominant position in Far Eastern banking and finance, and privileged use of the Chinese treaty ports – especially of the great city of Shanghai, regarded by London as practically a British possession – the British enjoyed an enormous influence in the region, with the prospect of benefiting from the long-awaited 'opening-up' of China to real economic development.[77] Political influence and naval power had gone hand in hand with financial and commercial profit. But the expansionism of Japan after 1930 had rapidly revealed the flimsy foundations of that power and influence, and, by the late 1930s, the British had ruefully recognised their inability to protect their Chinese interests against determined Japanese incursion.[78]

The outbreak of the Pacific war in 1941, as we have seen, exposed the weakness of Britain's position not just in China but everywhere east of India. Hong Kong, Singapore, Malaya, Borneo and Burma were all overrun and their colonial administrations ejected. Even after the eventual defeat of Japan had become inevitable, the British knew that the reimposition of their control would be a delicate, perhaps dangerous, operation. For, in the hiatus, while Japan's 'new order' had prevailed in the Far East, new forces had emerged to challenge the old colonial regime. In Burma the Japanese had granted independence and encouraged the creation of a Burma National Army. In Malaya, opposition to Japanese occupation had led to the growth of a communist guerrilla movement among the large Chinese community. Everywhere the ignominious collapse of British power in 1941–42 had undermined the prestige on which colonial rule depended so heavily.

In fact, of course, the Pacific war had brought wider changes of fundamental importance all over East and South East Asia, so that the context of British policy had altered dramatically since the 1930s. Before the war almost all South East Asia, with the exception of Thailand, had been partitioned between the colonial empires of the British, French, Dutch, Portuguese and, in the Philippines, the Americans. China was weak, divided and vulnerable to Imperial Japan, a colonial power herself. But Japan's violent onslaught in South East Asia had led to the downfall of all the colonial empires there. In Indo-China, the nationalist Viet Minh had emerged as the only resistance to Japanese rule: when Japan was defeated, it was they who were best placed to control the colony. In Indonesia the Japanese occupying force had encouraged anti-Dutch sentiment and the formation of nationalist political groups – chiefly as a means of mobilising the population for their war effort. Here, too, at the moment of Japan's surrender, a new regime of Indonesian nationalists stepped forward to take power before the Dutch could return: Sukarno declared Indonesian independence on 17 August 1945, three days after Tokyo's capitulation.[79]

To make matters worse, the regions under Japanese occupation had suffered great wartime privations since their trade patterns had been broken and the Japanese had requisitioned supplies and labour with the ruthlessness, after 1942, of desperation. Shattered economies, starvation, impoverishment, the bitterness which the occupations brought into internal social relations, these were the conditions in which the post-war future of Indo-China and Indonesia had to be settled. For the British, the fear was that, left to themselves, both these colonies would relapse into anarchy (with serious economic consequences) or xenophobic nationalism, whose effects would be felt across the whole of South East Asia, affecting Singapore, Malaya, Burma and even India.[80] The Dutch and French, however, were determined to reimpose colonial rule with the help of the mainly British occupying forces sent to 'liberate' Indo-China and Indonesia in 1945. Reluctantly the British complied, nervous of American resentment on the one hand, but equally of the colonial and European repercussions if they refused. But although British and Indian troops occupied Indo-China until January 1946, and Indonesia until the end of that year, as matters turned out, neither the Dutch nor the French were able to re-establish a stable colonial regime, nor even to find an acceptable settlement with local nationalism. British policy in South East Asia had, therefore, to take account of the fracturing of the colonial order throughout the region, and to reckon with the effects that the independence struggle against the French and Dutch would have upon their own colonial subjects.

There was, of course, a further dimension to the political consequences of the war in Asia. The defeat of Japan meant the liberation of China. Under American auspices and with American aid, it looked in 1945 as if a new nationalist China would emerge under Chiang Kai-shek as the strongest local power in the region. With large Chinese communities in Malaya, a frontier in Burma, a long history of friction over Tibet, an old Chinese grievance in the British possession of Hong Kong, as well as substantial commercial interests in China, London had grounds for some anxiety about Britain's relations with this new power, especially since it enjoyed open American patronage and support, and had been accorded the dignity of a great power in the embryonic organisation of the United Nations.[81] The British gloomily accepted that their influence in post-war China would run a bad second to that of the United States. Over the future of occupied Japan, too, it rapidly became clear that MacArthur would resist any British interference, and that post-war Japan would be a vehicle of American influence.[82]

With so many disruptive forces in this vast region, with the old colonial powers struggling to reimpose their authority, with the likely development of a Sino-American partnership implicitly hostile to the colonial powers, and with the Pacific dominions anxious for American strategic partnership, the British had cause to ponder whether they could ever re-establish their pre-war interests. In the aftermath of the war, particularly, faced with so many calls on their resources, and nervous of employing the Indian army for long in Indo-China and Indonesia, the British recognised the limits of their influence and even abandoned in October 1946 their token occupation of Japan. But London's recognition of a new age in Asia should not be overdone. For all the difficulties they foresaw, the policy makers were determined to restore British control in Burma, Malaya, Borneo and, most exposed of all, Hong Kong; and to determine wherever they could the pace of political change.

Wherever they chose to look in 1945, the British could hardly doubt that they faced new challenges to their authority and influence in the dominions, in the colonies and semi-colonies and in their spheres of influence. Tumult, upheaval, conquest and reconquest were a poor prescription for empire-on-the-cheap. Of course, British interests were not equally threatened everywhere. In colonial Africa anti-British nationalism had yet to come out into the open – except among some white settlers. But in the Middle East and much of Asia east of India, local turbulence and new external pressures seemed certain to make the defence of British interests a good deal harder than in the halcyon days before the later 1930s. In India itself, the question by 1945 was not whether independence would come but merely how soon and on what terms. In nearby Burma and Ceylon, the demand for self-government was building up. And even in those parts of their empire least affected by the world struggle of 1939–45 the British had come to recognise the necessity of energising their colonial rule and winning for it more vigorous local support.

But none of this meant that the British had given up their imperial ideas and settled for a modest role as an offshore island. As we shall see, British leaders were preoccupied not with a timetable for colonial dissolution but with ways and means of adapting their imperial policies to post-war circumstances. Even in the dark days of 1943, a cabinet committee had declared roundly that for many parts of the Colonial Empire 'it must be a matter of many generations before they are ready for anything like full self-government'; and that for those (many) colonies inhabited by peoples of two or more different races, 'it is impossible to say how long it will take to weld together these so-called plural communities into an entity capable of exercising self-government'.[83] In short, it remained in 1945 quite uncertain how rapid the constitutional evolution of all the various dependencies would be, and under what conditions independence would be conceded. It was also unclear what pressure would come to bear on Britain's imperial interests from the post-war pattern of international relations or from opinion at home. Hailey had talked of growing public interest in colonial policy. But was post-war Britain, exhausted, impoverished and preoccupied with internal recovery, prepared any longer to shoulder the burden of empire?

BRITAIN AND THE BURDEN OF EMPIRE

In August 1945 Britain emerged for the second time in 30 years a victor power in world war – an achievement unique among the European states. Her empire was intact and the defeats and humiliations of 1939–42 had been avenged. As in 1918, Britain was to be one of the arbiters of the post-war settlement. Her prestige as the champion of freedom against Hitler in 1940–41 was, if anything, higher than it had been at the end of the First World War. But from an *imperial* point of view, Britain's situation was, in almost every respect, much less favourable.

In the aftermath of German defeat in 1918, the British had enjoyed remarkable freedom of manoeuvre to promote their world interests and shore up their empire. Both the United States and Russia largely withdrew, for different reasons, from international diplomacy: certainly they played a self-effacing role. Germany's defeat and the destruction of her navy removed the more serious threats to British sea power. No country was strong enough to dominate continental Europe, or threaten Britain's home security, so that rapid demobilisation of the army was possible. In the Far East, Britain and the United States combined to force, by diplomatic pressure, the renunciation of Japanese claims on China and her withdrawal from Siberia and Manchuria – checking Japanese imperial expansion for a decade.

Meanwhile Britain herself was able to strengthen the defences of her own imperial system by the extension of British influence and control in the Middle East and by gaining for herself and the dominions the lion's share (under mandate) of Germany's lost colonies in Africa and the Pacific.

There was, moreover, no serious question in 1919–22 of the fundamentals of the colonial order being swept away despite the turbulence that afflicted almost all the regions of the colonial and semi-colonial world in the aftermath of the war. With the retreat of the United States and Russia into different forms of isolation, it was the two greatest colonial powers, Britain and France, who stood forth as the leaders of the post-war 'New World'. Despite the chronic economic difficulties that set in after 1920 there was no question of Britain's being incapable of sustaining her imperial commitments on economic grounds. Nor were her debts to the United States seen as limiting her national independence. Once the war was over, no new economic assistance was sought from the American government. Instead, parity of naval power with the United States was successfully negotiated in 1922. All these circumstances permitted British leaders to view with a certain calmness the wave of unrest that swept over their imperial possessions in 1919–22, especially in Ireland, India and Egypt, although their post-war drive for added imperial security encountered significant checks in Turkey and Persia in 1921–22. Britain's position was secure enough to contemplate without any fear of an imminent imperial collapse a substantial devolution of power in India, Egypt and Southern Ireland. Opposition was to be appeased, colonial nationalism tamed and British influence streamlined, even strengthened, by a timely policy of decentralisation. But the continuation of British imperial power was axiomatic.[84]

In 1945 Britain's situation and prospects were radically different. Her survival as a great power depended, as we shall see, upon American economic assistance. American military and naval power was enormously greater than in 1918. Washington now had the capacity to influence events in the Middle East and South East Asia which it had lacked in 1918. American resources and prestige also gave them a new influence in other British preserves – among the dominions and in India. Meanwhile in Europe, the demolition of Nazi power revealed, gradually, a new menace to the continental balance of power. If, as was widely expected, the United States withdrew its forces promptly from Europe, only a weakened and impoverished France could serve as Britain's ally against the military power of Soviet Russia. Yet a great continental military commitment was scarcely compatible with the continuation of the far-flung defensive obligations of the imperial system; and in 1945 those *imperial* obligations were greater still than in 1918. For now, as well as the Middle East, there was recaptured South East Asia to be garrisoned. With conscription already in force for six years at home, the politics of post-war defence were likely to be contentious, while the use of Indian troops, that old imperial stand-by, was certain to be affected by the negotiations over Indian self-government at the war's end. And, as we have seen, in the Middle East, India and elsewhere, the post-war turmoil of 1919–22 seemed certain to repeat itself on a more extensive scale. Finally, in their efforts to preserve the main elements of their pre-war world power, the British could no longer take comfort in the axiomatic nature of the colonial order. In vivid contrast to the inter-war years, it was now the anti-colonial powers who dominated world politics and whose political outlook influenced the aspirations of colonial peoples, not least through the new United Nations Charter. With France in eclipse, only Britain remained, for the time being at least, as an effective champion of the old colonial system. No longer could recalcitrant colonials be so easily threatened that independence would only mean absorption into another less liberal empire. The old 'closed system' of the high imperial age was visibly breaking down.

There could be no doubt, therefore, that to remain a power on a scale remotely comparable with the United States or the Soviet Union would be an extremely difficult task, even if the new international organisation served, as the Foreign Office hoped, to inflate British influence artificially.[85] Ultimately, of course, the readiness of British leaders to contemplate a renewed peacetime effort to maintain their world power and preserve both colonial rule and the special relationships with the dominions and other semi-colonial countries was a question of political attitudes at home. Historically, the makers of British foreign and imperial policy had depended upon the acquiescence of home opinion in their defence of imperial interests, rather than on any positive imperial enthusiasm. They had taken pains to reduce the visible burden of empire as much as possible, to clothe imperial purposes in a suitably moralistic rhetoric and to represent the empire as a vital national interest from which *all* sections gained. Certainly, before 1939 a number of convictions, deeply entrenched, so it appeared, in public opinion, had made the relinquishment of the empire politically unthinkable and imposed quite close limits on the flexibility of official policy. There was the instinctive reluctance to give up any of Britain's colonial possessions, whether to those previously familiar only as agitators or troublemakers, or to foreign powers. There is little doubt that public opinion at large accepted the official view that British colonial stewardship was wise, enlightened and humane, and regarded any alternative set of rulers as inferior in efficiency, in benevolence or in both. Secondly, it was extremely difficult in such a vast territorial empire to persuade opinion at home that to give up British control over any particular territorial unit was not symptomatic of declining strength and power, and indicative of ineptitude or betrayal at the top. Any change of constitutional regime, as British ministers found in the great battle over India in 1930–35, had to be presented with the greatest care. Thirdly, there was before 1939 only a very limited decline in that confidence in cultural and technical superiority by which British expansion and colonial rule had so often been justified. More to the point, perhaps, although the depression of the 1930s had exposed the vulnerability of British overseas trade and although Britain by 1939 was relatively a weaker industrial power than in 1914, there was little sign of any serious public debate over whether Britain had the resources to be a great world and colonial power indefinitely. Indeed, it was scarcely a matter of argument that Britain *was* a great power with global interests and *had* to remain one if those interests were to survive. Because of Britain's peculiar evolution as a food importer, and her longstanding tendency to seek export markets in the less developed world, it was easy to conclude that the economic basis of British independence required the energetic defence of far-flung colonial and semi-colonial commitments.

These widely-held assumptions were encouraged and exploited by the vested interests which empire itself had generated. Former members of the armed services and of the colonial bureaucracies were a well-connected and vociferous check on any backsliding in imperial matters – especially through the Conservative Party organisation. The influence of commercial interests is harder to assess. For many concerns operating in less developed countries, the disappearance of all British political influence would have appeared disastrous, especially where, like the Anglo-Persian Oil Company, they relied on diplomatic pressure to help defend unpopular concessions.[86] Elsewhere, however, in China and India for example, some British businessmen seemed ready to come to terms with local politicians and commercial interests without relying on official protection or gunboat diplomacy, preferring instead to draw local interests into partnership.[87] But even here, it is likely that they assumed that a British presence would continue in the background as the ultimate guarantee of their commercial survival. Similarly, for British banking and financial interests so widely scattered around the globe, Britain's world power status was an important if unspoken element in their dealings with local governments. The promotion of financial stability and free multilateral trade – key British objectives in the depressed world of the 1930s – could hardly have made much headway without the deployment of Britain's great power influence and prestige. The recovery of prosperity through the liberalisation of international trade seemed to depend more than ever on the close alliance of government and business and the readiness of government to defend embattled overseas commercial interests.

Of course, the imperial *status quo* did not go unchallenged in Britain. To some writers on the Left like John Strachey, it was the empire which alone propped up a bankrupt capitalist system in Britain and barred the way to socialism.[88] To the veteran J. A. Hobson, whose classic tract *Imperialism: a Study* was reissued in the 1930s, tropical dependencies encouraged investment overseas better used at home as well as helping to undermine parliamentary government and the liberal political tradition. As war approached, yet others like Leonard Barnes asserted that until 'old-style imperialism' was abandoned in favour of independence for some colonies and internationalisation for the rest, no lasting peace was possible since '. . . Hitlerism is unlikely to disappear so long as the British and French empires survive in their present economic and social structure'.[89] The Labour Party was deeply attracted by the idea of internationalising colonial possessions and sympathetic to Indian self-government.[90] But there was also a powerful strand of enlightened paternalism in its approach to colonial issues, while the T.U.C. for its part bluntly favoured maintaining the old division of labour between an industrial Britain and the agrarian countries of the empire.[91] There was in fact little if any sustained interest in the Labour Party as a whole in imperial questions: the party's advisory committee on colonial affairs was very rarely attended by senior party figures.[92] Party activists recognised well enough that the electorate had little interest in schemes for colonial reform.[93]

The effect of the war was to encourage a leftward shift in British opinion across the whole range of political and social issues.[94] But how did this affect prevailing attitudes towards the desirability of maintaining a world empire? Two countervailing tendencies may be seen at work. On the one hand, the experience of the war brought the most compelling evidence of British weakness and vulnerability. The desperate isolation of 1940–41; the sufferings of the Blitz; the sense of impotence against German power in Europe; the humiliating defeats by Japan; the evident superiority of American military power and resources; the dependence on American aid for economic survival: even the most complacent confidence in British world power could hardly remain undented by these. Against this background, Cripps' offer to India of prompt self-government at the war's end created scarcely a ripple in British politics. Imperial supremacy and the assertion of racial superiority were no longer an appropriate rhetoric. But on the other hand, a number of wartime influences helped to moderate the reappraisal of British imperial commitments when peace came. Britain was, despite all, a victor power and the lost colonies were successfully reconquered. To abandon territories recovered with such sacrifice was likely to draw protest. Then, too, the curious two-stage ending of the war may have helped to mute the demand for rapid demobilisation which had overwhelmed the Lloyd George government in 1919. More important, perhaps, the war had seen the emergence of a rough consensus on colonial policy. When the Labour Party's pamphlet on the colonies was published in March 1943, it contained nothing objectionable to either the Colonial Office or the Conservative Party.[95] Both party leaders agreed, publicly at least, on a progressive colonial policy that would encourage the dependencies along the road to self-government[96] – a much blander formulation than anything the Labour Party had agreed to since 1918.[97] Under the pressure of American criticism a new and plausible doctrine of 'partnership' was devised that proved acceptable across the political spectrum in Britain, especially now that Labour had taken on some of the attributes of a 'patriotic' party. Nor in the circumstances of 1945 was there much force left in the old anti-imperialist war-cries. Hitler had been defeated without the renunciation of empire; the new rhetoric of partnership and self-government denied the incompatibility of democracy at home and empire abroad; and the abandonment of empire no longer appeared necessary to Britain's own economic and social well-being. On the contrary, the manifesto of the new economic and social consensus, Beveridge's *Full Employment in a Free Society*, (1944) insisted on Britain's need to maintain a substantial overseas trade and on the importance of Britain's playing a forceful role in the framing of a new international economic order.[98] The desirability of Britain's recovering her old role as an industrial, trading and financial power was explicitly affirmed, just as the obligation Beveridge saw of promoting economic development in backward regions assumed that some of the main elements of the old colonial system would remain in place.

Taken together, these various wartime developments indicated that British opinion was likely to be docile and accommodating on imperial issues and ready to fall in with the need to modify the imperial system which had struck the policy makers (though not Churchill) so forcibly after 1941. Significantly, when India returned to the political agenda after 1945 there was no repetition of the fierce public controversy which had delayed constitutional reform between 1930 and 1935. Of course, the triumph of the Labour Party in an election in which colonial issues played no part coincidentally destroyed the power of the Conservative Party rank and file and their diehard allies in the House of Commons to check the flexibility or pragmatism of the policy makers. Even so, as we shall see, the leaders of the Labour Party, far from relishing the opportunity to make radical changes in imperial policy, regarded with nervous apprehension the reaction of the electorate to anything that might be branded as a 'scuttle' or as the 'liquidation of the British Empire'.

The real question that hung over British imperial policy – indeed over all British external policy – at the end of the war related not so much to public opinion as to the capacity of the economy to sustain the burdens of world power. To remain an independent great power on pre-war lines, Britain would have to meet the costs of a worldwide defence system, to repay the accumulated debts of the war, to finance the economic development of the empire countries and undertake, at least in the short term, the military occupations which victory in Europe and Asia required. All these burdens, old and new, would be thrown on to a British economy that had been severely weakened between 1939 and 1945. The diversion of other resources to war needs and the physical destruction of houses, factories and shipping cost Britain perhaps 25 per cent of her national wealth.[99] A substantial part of Britain's foreign assets, especially dollar investments, had been sold to pay for essential imports, reducing the income from abroad that had previously contributed very considerably to British economic stability and strength. Instead, Britain had run up enormous foreign debts amounting to £3,000 million. The merchant fleet, another important source of overseas income, was 30 per cent smaller in 1945 than before the war. In addition, the huge scale on which the economy had been mobilised for war after 1940 (with 45 per cent of the labour force in the Services or producing war goods) meant that the civilian economy, and especially exports, had been run down very greatly. Exports had fallen to 29 per cent of their pre-war value in 1943, and generally through the war years stood at only 40 per cent of pre-war levels. In practice, this meant the loss of valuable markets, perhaps for ever; an arduous and costly task of reconversion; and a huge increase in foreign debts – to obtain on credit what could not be bought from income. Because Britain concentrated on getting on with the war as quickly and efficiently as possible, commented Keynes bitterly in May 1945, 'we and we only end up owing vast sums, not to neutrals and bystanders, but to our own Allies, Dominions and Associates . . . '.[100]

The implications of Britain's economic sacrifice were drastic. Although Lend-Lease had allowed the British to obtain large supplies of munitions from the United States without charge, the end of the war was expected to bring enormous difficulties for her balance of payments. With the civilian economy in disarray and huge debts to repay, how could Britain hope to meet the cost of importing food and raw materials, let alone other vital products? Worse still, much of the goods the British would have to import to get their manufacturing economy on its feet, as well as food and other supplies, would have to come from the United States, the only major industrial economy left intact. Once Lend-Lease ended, imports from America would have to be paid for in dollars or hard currency that Britain simply did not have. The British were confronted, wrote Keynes just before the defeat of Japan, by the threat of a 'financial Dunkirk'.[101] This would mean a precipitate withdrawal from all overseas responsibilities and accepting a position comparable to that of liberated France. It would mean the loss of London's ancient prestige and 'hegemony' as a financier which Keynes treasured as much if not more than most other British leaders and policy makers. It would mean the surrender of all economic power outside the Soviet Union to the United States – with unfathomable consequences for Britain's economic future. Such a prospect was to Keynes and, no doubt, to all British official opinion, utterly unthinkable.[102]

Yet to avoid this catastrophe, so Keynes argued, would also mean taking some unpleasant medicine. There would have to be an intense concentration on the production of exports and the home population, starved of consumer goods for five years, would have to endure further austerity. 'Drastic and immediate' economies would be necessary in overseas expenditure, especially in the military and political out-goings associated with the war in the Mediterranean, and the Middle and Far East. Finally, Britain would have to seek a substantial dollar loan from the United States on terms acceptable to both sides.[103] Without the loan and American financial cooperation, Britain's career as a post-war world power was likely to be brief and inglorious, with serious political and social unrest at home into the bargain.[104] But on what terms would American aid be forthcoming, especially since much American commercial opinion regarded Britain as an industrial rival set on stealing America's new markets? And how far would dependence on American loans be compatible with an inde-pendent great power existence, given American distrust of British imperialism? Was London's recovery of its old financial hegemony, American loan or no, a realistic prospect?

These questions are a stark reminder of how much more vulnerable Britain appeared at the end of the Second World War than at the end of the First – above all in economic terms. In 1918, as we have seen, no financial Dunkirk threatened British independence. But in 1945, even if the kind of economic catastrophe pictured by Keynes was avoided, and even if American aid was forthcoming, a prolonged phase of economic weakness held all sorts of dangers. The United States might insist on the opening up of Britain's remaining economic preserves in the empire countries to American commercial penetration. The decline of British trade from pre-war levels was likely to bring a proportionate decline in British influence in many regions. Any major reduction of domestic living standards might set off a political explosion at home. Without a buoyant manufacturing and trading economy, Britain could not afford to remain a serious military power – certainly not on the scale required to defend such large and scattered interests. Lastly, if her economy contracted too severely, the whole economic basis of empire would crumble. If Britain was too poor to buy what the colonies and dominions produced, to invest in their economic development or to provide the exports they wanted, one of the most powerful agents promoting cooperation between the mother-country and the empire countries, self-governing and dependent alike, would vanish. The alternatives then would be coercion (beyond Britain's means) or dissolution.

Even in the last weeks of the war, however, the severity of Britain's economic situation was not fully recognised. In the Treasury there was optimism that Britain would secure from the United States a 'just' financial settlement, including a refund on Britain's war purchases before Lend-Lease and a large loan without strings attached and at nominal interest.[105] Right up to the time of the Anglo-American loan negotiations, Keynes himself continued to believe that the United States would make a large free gift of dollars to help Britain over the transition from war economy to peace. But, as it turned out, American attitudes were less generous. Lend-Lease was ended abruptly when Japan surrendered and a loan was only forthcoming on terms that were to plunge sterling into crisis in 1947. As a result, the British were to find that although a great power role was possible their external policy in the critical aftermath of the war was dominated, far more than in 1918–22, by the fear of economic collapse.

3 The Crisis of Empire, 1945–48

It was inevitable that the British should have found the aftermath of the war a period of intense strain in the organisation and defence of their worldwide interests. With their economic resources stretched beyond their limit, new commitments at home and abroad and a lowering international landscape, it required strong nerves to be the landlord of so much far-flung, ill-defended and turbulent real estate. But the years beteen 1945 and 1948 were not simply a phase of anxiety and overload in the management of the imperial system. They formed a critical turning point in Britain's post-war career as an international power. In these years the rough outline of Britain's last phase as an imperial power took shape; the commitments which dictated her foreign policy until the late 1960s were established; and their validity recognised by the main body of political opinion at home. By 1948 most, though not all, of the huge uncertainties of 1945 had begun to clear away.

But in the meantime it seemed that the whole future of the imperial system, defended and recovered so laboriously from 1939 to 1945, hung in the balance, and with it Britain's entire place in world politics. Some of the most vital issues lay far beyond the control or influence of British policy makers. There was the critical question of what part the United States would play in world affairs. If the Americans were to withdraw once more into isolation, as Attlee feared, almost the whole burden of organising resistance to Russia in Europe would fall upon Britain, with profound consequences for her defence commitments outside Europe. If the Americans declined to play any role in the Mediterranean, the support of Greece and Turkey against Russian influence would again fall largely upon Britain. And, as Keynes insisted, if Washington refused a loan or other economic assistance, Britain herself would have to undergo a savage regime of austerity and international withdrawal like Russia between the wars. In all these cases, American decisions seemed likely to determine whether Britain would have the resources to exercise anything more than a minimal influence in her old spheres of activity in the Middle East and South and South East Asia, let alone among the dominions.

With American aid, it was thought in 1945, Britain could recover much of her old position as an industrial and trading power before 1939. But even if such aid were forthcoming, it was in fact far from clear that Britain could ever 'return to go' and resume her old premier place in the international economy. If she could not, how could her old commercial and financial influence be sustained? How could she afford the greatly increased costs of defending her interests around the world? What would be the justification of the expense of running an imperial system if Britain was too poor or weak to reap the economic benefits? As if these questions were not enough, new ones were piling up in 1945. For in the July general election the electorate voted heavily for social reform and returned a majority Labour government for the first time on a programme which envisaged sweeping and expensive social improvements. After an exhausting war, how easy would it be now to win popular support for overseas commitments or heavy expenditure on defence in money and manpower especially if the going got rough? How ready would a Labour government be to try, given the longstanding aversion of the party to 'imperialism' and 'militarism'? Would not politicians of the Left find it easier to cut loose from Britain's imperial traditions and seek a new international alignment?

Between 1945 and 1948 British intentions about their imperial system were tested most severely in South Asia and the Middle East. In these two regions they were faced with hard decisions and un-welcome compromises. The outcome – since both regions were of central importance to the structure of their pre-war imperial system – was to exercise a profound influence over the last twenty years in which British world power remained a reality (if on a constantly diminishing scale). At the time the turbulence of the two regions threatened to wreck British influence over them altogether and do much damage beside. By the end of 1946, it was an open question whether Britain could escape entanglement in a bloody conflict in India. Granted that an independent India was London's policy, the kind of post-colonial relationship that would emerge was no less uncertain. Would India remain united and in the Commonwealth, or neither? In the Middle East the questions were no less drastic. Whether Britain should remain in the region at all was debated in London. If Britain did, how were her strategic interests to be reconciled with the new aspirations of Arab nationalism, particularly in Egypt? What was London to do about the appalling problem of Palestine? And how could the British prevent their involvement there from destroying the basis of Anglo-Arab cooperation?

It is easy to see in retrospect that had Britain abandoned or been driven out of the Middle East, or been dragged willy nilly into an Indian civil war, much of her post-war history might have been different. There might have been internal political side effects in the way that colonial catastrophe helped to destabilise French politics. The whole shape of Britain's post-war colonial commitments would have been affected and perhaps the whole approach towards the point and purpose of retaining them. The attitude of British policy makers to colonial nationalism could scarcely have been the same. And the whole complex interplay of world politics, especially the role of the United States in world affairs, would have followed a different pattern with very different consequences.

THE HOME BASE

Whatever their opponents may have feared or expected, the Labour government elected in 1945 turned out to be remarkably unradical in its approach to foreign, defence and imperial policy, especially if it is borne in mind that no government confronted by the post-war conditions could have maintained pre-war policies and commitments unchanged. Significantly for their outlook, the Labour ministers had come to power in Churchill's wake. The senior figures in the new government had served under him for five years in the wartime coalition. Inevitably they still breathed the atmosphere of the great patriotic war for Britain's survival and shared the exaltation of victory.

The most powerful figures in the new government were Attlee, Ernest Bevin, the new Foreign Secretary, Herbert Morrison, overlord on the economic front, and Cripps who had acquired a wartime reputation as a dynamic and brilliant leader. None of these now subscribed to any radical conception of Britain's place in world affairs. None of them regarded with *distaste* the continuation of Britain's colonial empire or objected to Britain's pursuit of an independent great power position based on her pre-war spheres of influence outside Europe. Bevin in particular exemplified a bluff patriotism reminiscent of Lord Palmerston. The contraction of British power was anathema to him and unlike many of his colleagues he was fundamentally unsympathetic to the idea of Indian independence.[1] Attlee, for all his pragmatism and unsentimentality, had a similar outlook (although not on India). His alliance with Bevin in foreign and defence policy was the most powerful rivet holding the cabinet together. Attlee had no doubt that Britain was and should remain a great power. Morrison and Cripps, as economic ministers, both criticised the burdens that Attlee and Bevin were prepared to accept. But neither did so because he objected on principle to the exertion of great power influence abroad. Morrison shared Bevin's no-nonsense patriotism. Cripps, a much more complex figure who had passionately denounced imperialism before 1939, had apparently undergone an ideological sea-change during the war which had brought a strain of nationalism to the surface. As Chancellor of the Exchequer after 1947 he was to preside over the economic integration of the empire-commonwealth (in the form of the sterling bloc) with all the enthusiasm of a pre-1914 Chamberlainite Tory.

These attitudes were not uncharacteristic of the Labour Party in the House of Commons, or, probably, in the country at large. Before the war the party had criticised aspects of imperial policy. There had been a concern for labour conditions in the colonies. The seductive influence of Gandhi and Nehru had encouraged the illusion that the Indian National Congress was really an oriental labour party. But there had been no question of dismantling as opposed to reforming the apparatus of colonial rule elsewhere, and the 'paternalist tradition' as well as a 'sub-conscious streak of racial typology'[2] remained entrenched in party policy. Belief in the desirability of a strong British voice in world affairs was held just as firmly on the Left as on the Right of British politics. The colonies were seen not as useless encumbrances, nor as a shameful legacy best disposed of, but as an opportunity for planned redevelopment. Thus although there was considerable dissidence in the party over external policy this was largely concentrated on the emotive issues of Anglo-Russian relations and the future of Palestine. There was also, as we shall see, considerable discontent over the manpower and financial costs of defence. But the retention of a colonial empire and the panoply of a great power role evoked little real controversy.

A number of influences, some discussed in Chapter 2, help to account for this. There was also the pervasive belief, to be found in a wide cross-section of contemporary opinion, that Britain derived her uniqueness, as well as cultural, economic and political benefits, from her maritime and imperial contacts around the world; and that her independence and even survival were bound up with their preservation. These ideas owed much to Seeley's famous account of how Britain acquired an empire[3] which inspired a generation of writers and historians and became the common currency of schoolroom and popular literature. Even in 1945 their status as proverbial wisdom was scarcely tarnished. Then, too, neither the party nor its leaders could ignore the emotive power of Churchill's legacy to his post-war successors: an empire saved and Britain, by virtue of that empire, a member by right of the 'Big Three'. As they showed on several occasions, the Labour leaders were extremely anxious not to give Churchill the opportunity of accusing them of a 'scuttle' or of the 'liquidation' of the British empire. Policies that could be represented in that light were thought to be electorally disastrous. It is likely too that Labour members in the Commons were no more immune than their leaders from the gratified sense of Britain's share in victory in 1945 and from the feeling that victory and the sacrifices made *entitled* Britain to be a great power. Finally, these feelings were probably strengthened by the growing rivalry of the two new superpowers, and the suspicion felt equally by many in the Labour Party for Soviet communism and American capitalism. More perhaps than at any other time in the post-war years, British leaders saw Britain as offering a distinctive ideology to the world, a practical, democratic middle way. Independent world power had an acceptable ideological matrix.[4]

There was thus no disposition to seek a new post-imperial future, although the necessity of modifying the imperial system – especially by making India a dominion – was recognised. But the real question that faced Labour leaders and their followers was not so easy to answer. In Britain's acutely difficult economic circumstances what resources were they prepared to allocate to the defence of interests overseas? At what price was world power to be maintained? And which interests should enjoy the highest priority?

All these decisions had to be taken against a background of looming economic disaster: indeed it is likely that economic fears were at the forefront of most ministers' minds through the whole period from 1945–48, and beyond. The task of repaying Britain's debts, meeting her import bill and restoring her lost position in world trade, ministers decided, required British industry to sell abroad half as much again as before the war. But three major dangers obsessed them. The possibility that Britain would simply run out of hard currency and be unable to import vital supplies of food, fuel and raw materials – with total economic collapse ensuing. The risk that lack of sufficient manpower – especially in export industries – would bring such a catastrophe closer. And the threat that the very high level of government spending that followed on from the war would jeopardise financial stability and bring on a major inflation, the effect of which would be to undermine cooperation with the trade unions as well as damaging Britain's recovery as a trading and financial power. The successful, though protracted, negotiation of an American loan temporarily relieved the first of these anxieties. Nevertheless, it was clear from the beginning that the burden of Britain's defence commitments overseas was a vital element in the economic struggle. Maintaining large forces abroad was a heavy drain on external finance as well as upon the groaning taxpayer at home. But, above all, the armed forces soaked up manpower vital to recovery in the export economy while the burden of supplying their needs absorbed the energies of a large proportion of the working population. In agreeing that the services must be reduced to 1.2 million men and women by the end of 1946, the cabinet accepted that even this burden could not be borne for long and heard Dalton, the Chancellor of the Exchequer, warn that the balance of payments could not stand the strain.[5] This was only the first salvo in a long exchange.

Dalton kept up the pressure during 1946. In June he told the cabinet that the occupation of Germany was costing Britain £100 million a year and that 'we could not continue to bear this heavy expenditure'.[6] In July, partly to help feed the British occupation zone there, bread rationing, unknown during the war, was introduced at home. In October, the Treasury began to sound the alarm about Britain's ability to pay for dollar purchases the following year, especially in view of the promise given in the American loan agreement to allow free exchange between sterling and the dollar by July 1947.[7] In November, Dalton opposed British aid to Greece, Turkey and Afghanistan. 'I sent a minute to the P.M. saying that we have not got the money for this sort of thing and that, even if we had, we should not spend it on these people'.[8] Nevertheless, despite Dalton's complaints, 1946, for all its anxieties, turned out to be the lull before the storm, a year in which the export drive appeared to be going well and the government retained its impetus and cohesion. But this 'annus mirabilis' (Dalton's phrase) was to be succeeded by 'annus horrendus'.

Troubles began promptly with the new year. Morrison as economic overlord circulated a warning that Britain's dollar resources were being rapidly depleted as American prices rose, and questioned whether the burden of 1.4 million in the armed forces, serviced by some 12 per cent of the whole working population, could be sustained.[8] This was the cue for a furious cabinet row over the manpower requirements of the services. 'We cannot afford either the money or the men for which the Minister of Defence asks', declared Dalton.[10] But the economic ministers, Morrison, Dalton and Cripps, made little headway in cabinet against Attlee, Bevin and A. V. Alexander, the defence minister.[11] Dalton's implied threat of resignation eventually brought a 5 per cent reduction in defence estimates, but, as Britain's economic position deteriorated, the disagreement remained. In February and March 1947 the fuel crisis imposed a further strain, damaging Britain's export performance. In March, Cripps, the personification of asceticism, told the Commons that years of austerity lay ahead in the struggle for economic revival. By the early summer, as the hour approached for Britain to abandon exchange controls and permit sterling to be sold freely for dollars, the Treasury grew more and more nervous about the dollar reserves and Dalton's forebodings steadily grimmer.[12] By June, the Treasury was warning that without substantial American aid, the world shortage of dollars would drive the British economy to the wall with a complete breakdown in international trade. In July, a senior Treasury official told the Chancellor that unless American help came 'we should require a desperate export drive . . . it is difficult to see how this could be done without direction of labour and indeed a complete and total national mobilisation as far-reaching as that of 1940'.[13]

Inevitably, in these conditions, the free convertibility of sterling into dollars to which London was committed lasted scarcely a month before the threat of the pound's complete loss of value against the dollar led to the reimposition of exchange controls. At the same time, the demand for defence cuts, resisted in the spring, was revived with new force. Early in August, Dalton reminded Attlee of his resignation threat in January and asked for cuts in the armed services.[14] Attlee and the Defence Committee refused to reduce manpower below 1,007,000 in 1948. In August and September dissatisfaction with Attlee among his colleagues threatened to break up the government. Morrison, Cripps and Dalton were all involved in plots to overthrow the prime minister and in September both Cripps and Dalton discussed resignation over the government's economic strategy.[15] With the cabinet in disarray, and new measures of austerity in prospect – including the rationing of potatoes and a general reduction of food rations – Attlee, Bevin and Alexander gave ground over service manpower. Now the 1948 figure was to be 937,000, with the promise of a sharp reduction to some 700,000 in 1949.[16] Even so, despite further import reductions, and a full apparatus of exchange controls, Britain's economic situation on the eve of Marshall Aid still seemed almost desperate, with the collapse of the sterling area system and a 'downward spiral of employment' at home if American aid was not prompt and substantial.[17]

In the crisis year of 1947 economics and strategy interlocked painfully. In economic circumstances infinitely less favourable than before the war, the British were struggling to keep more than four times as many men in the services and spending between two and three times as much on the task as they had done before 1939. Attlee, Bevin and Alexander had stubbornly refused any wholesale redefinition of Britain's overseas commitments, standing equally firm against their economic critics in cabinet and the professionals who argued that defence resources were too thinly stretched. Attlee had not always taken this attitude. Soon after becoming prime minister he had startled the service chiefs by arguing that because of the atomic bomb and air warfare 'the British Commonwealth and Empire is not a unit that can be defended by itself [and] . . . can only be defended by its membership of the United Nations Organisation'. 'If the new organisation is a reality', he went on, 'it does not matter who . . . controls the Suez Canal'.[18] Attlee continued to talk along these radical lines. In February 1946, he told Dalton that with Indian independence on the way, the value of the Suez Canal to Britain was much less obvious. 'We should be prepared to work round the Cape to Australia and New Zealand'.[19] In March, Dalton recorded Attlee's view that Britain should withdraw from the Middle East altogether, including Egypt and Greece, to a defensive line across Africa from Lagos to Kenya, thus placing 'a wide glacis of desert and Arabs between ourselves and the Russians'.[20] Attlee's ideas represented a sharp break with long-standing notions of strategy and foreign policy, but they were not based on a repudiation of world power. They reflected instead acute alarm at the prospect of American withdrawal into isolation and Britain's being drawn into confrontation with Russia not only in

Europe where it was inescapable but in the Middle East as well. Attlee posed an alternative strategy of world power to take account of this and the loss of India, part of which required that 'we should put a large part of Commonwealth Defence, including many industries, into Australia'.[21] By the spring of 1947, however, he had abandoned such ideas for a much more conservative position.

The pressure to do so came partly from Bevin and partly from the Service Chiefs. Bevin and his Foreign Office advisers had never accepted that it was necessary or desirable for Britain to withdraw from the Middle East, and, as we shall see, they were determined to entrench British influence in the region by a flexible and sympathetic policy. The Service Chiefs regarded Attlee's proposal to write off Britain's longstanding and bitterly-defended strategic positions in Egypt, Palestine, Iraq and elsewhere with horror and incredulity. When Montgomery became Chief of the Imperial General Staff in June 1946 he immediately prepared a paper insisting on the vital importance of the Middle East. When Attlee persisted in his view, he was, in Montgomery's account, told privately that the three Service Chiefs would resign rather than change theirs.[22] In March the three Chiefs of Staff triumphantly prepared a lengthy paper setting out the strategic value of the Middle East to Britain and recording the endorsement of the prime minister.[23] Thereafter Attlee defended Britain's Middle East commitment as stubbornly as Bevin, encouraged perhaps by signs of American interest as well as by Russian withdrawal from her threatening forward positions in northern Iran. Indeed by April 1948 Attlee had so completely reversed his earlier views on the danger of any new commitments that he could be found arguing for effective British control of eastern Libya, Italy's lost colony.[24]

But economic pressures could not be resisted altogether: in some spheres they told with considerable effect. Manpower shortage and financial strain led to the abandonment of British military aid to Greece and Turkey in February 1947 – a decision which paved the way for the Truman doctrine of containment and American aid in the defence of the eastern Mediterranean. The British also gave up all thought of reviving a real naval presence in the Pacific or along the China coast. Economic crisis at home enforced a slow but steady contraction of military manpower despite the complaints of the Service Chiefs. The difficulty of reorganising the army after the war meant that despite its nominally enormous manpower there were fewer infantry battalions – the backbone of military power in much of the world – available for service than before the war. In 1948 the Service Chiefs were driven to urgent and dramatic warnings about the state of British defences.[25] Nevertheless, given the continuous atmosphere of impending economic catastrophe, what is remarkable is that the strategic commitments which Attlee and his colleagues accepted were so extensive, especially since it was apparent by the end of 1947 that the large British garrison in Germany was likely to remain there indefinitely.[26] For although in 1947–48 the British withdrew from India and Palestine (decisions which, while not taken for military reasons, considerably reduced the pressure on military manpower) in neither case did they redefine their strategic interest in the surrounding region. Most strikingly, Attlee's decision to accept a public time limit for the end of British rule in India coincided with his recognition of a continuing strategic role in the Middle East, while the security of the Indian Ocean was considered as important a British interest as ever.

Nor was the strategic conservatism of the Attlee government merely a matter of hanging on to existing obligations with such resources as came to hand. Two major decisions taken in 1947 in the worst year of economic crisis cast a revealing light upon the view taken by Attlee and his most senior colleagues of Britain's future as a world power. The first was the acknowledgement – in stark contrast to post-war attitudes a generation before – that conscription would have to be retained in peacetime to meet military requirements, despite its unpopularity on the Left and its novelty. The second was the secret decision taken by Attlee and not revealed to the cabinet as a whole to build an independent nuclear deterrent, a decision based principally on the belief that as a great power Britain *must* have the most advanced weapons available.[27] This was, to put it mildly, a far cry from that reliance on the United Nations which Attlee had recommended only fifteen months before.

Why was it that the oppressive sense of economic weakness and vulnerability made so little impression upon the strategic thinking of the Labour government? Part of the answer lies in the tough discipline which Attlee and Bevin imposed on their cabinet colleagues who were not permitted to debate the fundamentals of strategy at all. But the explanation runs deeper. Bevin and Attlee were convinced that American assistance in the containment of Russia was vital. To obtain it, they argued implicitly, Britain would have to display resolution herself whatever the short-term cost, and prevent Russian influence spilling over into new spheres. Their gamble was successful. But they were helped also by the paradox that Britain's very economic weakness made out the case for securing vital sources of dollar-free oil and raw materials. In January 1947 a joint paper by the Foreign Secretary and the Minister of Fuel pointed to the critical importance of Middle East oil which supplied 60 per cent of Britain's oil needs.[28] In Britain's parlous post-war condition, dollars were even scarcer than military manpower. In economic, political and strategic terms, so it appeared, the alternative to the further exertions demanded by Attlee and Bevin was even more unattractive: there was no 'safe' region to which Britain could withdraw in comfortable isolation. Nor, perhaps surprisingly, was there any significant public pressure for a major rethink of world policy. For all the flurry on the Labour Left, continued conscription was widely accepted. The Conservative opposition was in broad agreement with the approach of Bevin and Attlee. The public emphasis upon *shortages* rather than the need for strictly *financial* economy made imperial commitments easier to justify. Everyone drank cocoa. But ultimately what made Bevin and Attlee's strategy viable was that at two crucial moments, in 1945 and 1948, American economic assistance in the form of a loan and then of Marshall Aid saved London from the nightmare austerity which the Treasury forecast, with its unpredictable but painful consequences across the whole range of overseas commitments. Agonising re-appraisal was postponed.

THE CRISIS OF BRITISH POWER IN ASIA

India

In 1945 the future of India was one of the most difficult and important questions with which British leaders had to deal. India's sheer size, the value attached to her strategic relationship with Britain (magnified by the experience of the war), the appalling scale of the commitment should British rule there be engulfed in chaos and disorder, American interest in Indian affairs and the implications for colonial rule elsewhere if India's progress towards self-government were mishandled, elevated Indian policy almost to a par with economic policy in the preoccupations of the London government. The actual outcome of the struggle to decide *how* India would become independent was bound to have important implications for Britain's position as a world power, as well as revealing her post-war strengths and weakness. But overwhelming as was India's significance among Britain's possessions in Asia, the course of British policy in the sub-continent needs to be set alongside developments in Burma, Ceylon and Malaya. Firstly, because events in India exercised a powerful influence upon their politics. Secondly, because British policies in these other Asian colonies give some indication of how they saw their future in Asia, and thus of the thinking behind their Indian policy. And thirdly because British difficulties elsewhere in Asia are a reminder of the great tide of unrest that washed over the agrarian societies of the continent in the aftermath of the war. Fear that this wider turbulence would wreck an orderly transfer of power had become a powerful influence on British policy by 1947.

The end of British rule in India between 1945 and 1947 was neither sudden nor unexpected. The British had long accepted that there must be political change in India. Even before 1900 they had recognised that the greater participation of Indians in the machinery of government was essential if government itself was to be effective, and if India was to remain a useful and valuable part of their imperial system. Indians had to be persuaded to tax themselves more heavily. They had to be cajoled into accepting an ever-increasing degree of intervention by the state to improve the rural economy, to eradicate social abuses and to encourage the most efficient use of resources of all kinds. This was no mere altruism: as we have seen, the British expected India to provide an army of comparable size to their own to help defend the empire at large, and India's ability to do so depended ultimately upon the development of her economy and the modernisation of her institutions. But the price of this steady extension of state activity was the modification of alien and arbitrary rule by British officials, and the formation of representative bodies – such as municipalities – so that as far as possible Indians should be seen to tax and regulate themselves. The alternative was to risk arousing widespread popular unrest and a confrontation with the united opposition of Indian opinion; and, conceivably, a second Mutiny.[29]

These schemes of reform were originated at a time when it seemed unlikely that Indians would ever aspire to control the commanding heights of British rule in New Delhi or that Indian politicians in the diverse and distant provinces of British India (let alone in the States) would be able to combine in a common struggle against British rule.

But after 1918 this is exactly what had happened. The Indian National Congress under the inspiration of Gandhi claimed to represent the interests of Indians all over the sub-continent, and threatened British rule with a general withdrawal of the political and social cooperation on which the stability and effectiveness of the Raj depended. For five years after 1918 and again in the early 1930s Congress waged campaigns of civil disobedience designed to force the British into conceding control of British India to elected Indian politicans – in effect, as it was thought, into the hands of Congress. No longer would Indians be content with the lower levels of power in town or district or even province. Now British control of the army, the police and the financial system was to be swept away. The special powers of the Viceroy to govern, if need be in defiance of Indian opinion, should be obliterated; and India's status as a dependency of the British Crown should give way either to independence outside the empire, as Nehru demanded, or, at best, to dominion status – on a par with Canada or Australia – within the British Commonwealth.

The British response to this new pattern of Indian politics after 1918 was variable. They had recourse frequently to the arrest and detention of Indian political leaders. Nehru spent nine years in gaol between 1921 and 1947. The prestige of the Raj and the morale of its servants required the repression of those who challenged too openly the authority of government. But the British also embarked upon policies designed to attract positive Indian cooperation and to weaken support for the more extreme forms of nationalism that called for the complete independence of India. The reform act of 1919 promised Indians a share in the government of the provinces and set up a Legislative Assembly at the centre in New Delhi. Then in a further extension of the same approach the British carried through after 1930 a second round of constitutional change: complete control of provincial government was now given to elected Indians and India's future progress to dominion status as a federation of the provinces and the princely states clearly implied. In the meantime, British control of the central government, of currency and, above all, of defence and foreign relations was preserved. But the goal of eventual self-government at all levels had now become clearly visible even if the timing remained vague and undecided.[30]

But it would be a mistake to conclude from these constitutional changes that the eventual pattern of independence and partition had become inevitable before the Second World War. By the later 1930s the British knew that they could not destroy Indian nationalism and that the attempt to do so would be counterproductive in India and politically embarrassing at home and abroad. They had recognised that sooner or later Indian self-government must come. But acknowledging these two facts of life left an enormous stake still to play for. Whatever else they were prepared to give up, the British had not resigned themselves to India's becoming an independent country without special links and ties with Britain. They were determined that when India eventually reached independence it should be as a dominion and that her leaders should be ready to cooperate freely with Britain in trade and commerce and especially in the defence of the British imperial system (under its new soubriquet 'British Commonwealth') to which the Indian army had always made an important contribution. India was to remain within the ambit of British influence, and to contribute voluntarily to the defence of a world system under British leadership – a vital concern in the later 1930s.[31]

But how were the British to persuade the leaders of Indian nationalism to compromise their struggle for independence in this way, and how could they hope for Indian cooperation once they had handed over the last instalment of self-government and made India a dominion? How could they stop India going her own way internationally? Chiefly, London thought, by so moulding Indian politics that *before* self-government was attained those they thought of as the extreme wings of the Congress and Indian nationalism – the Left under Nehru with its admiration for the Soviet Union, and the supporters of a self-sufficient Gandhian utopia on the Right – should have been defeated by a moderate centre, eager for continuity both internally and in India's foreign relations. The methods by which the British expected to influence Indian politics in this direction both before and after independence are a measure of the political resources which the imperial power still seemed to enjoy even as its formal authority began to melt away. Indeed, as we shall see elsewhere, the extent to which Britain was able to go on drawing on these informal political resources was a vital factor in shaping the decolonising process and the kind of relationship that emerged out of the constitutional transfer of power.

Thus after 1935 Indian politics remained a mixture of self-rule at provincial level and below (with a narrow franchise) and modified autocracy at the all-India level where the Viceroy retained the last word over finance, security, defence and foreign affairs. To make this clumsy system work from day to day and to enlist Indian cooperation over the longer term, the British exercised considerable political ingenuity. In the first place they observed a fundamental rule of conduct: to avoid actions or policies that appeared to be against the interests of Indians of different classes, castes and regions and which could be used to whip up anti-British feeling. Taxation had to be kept as low as possible; religious practices carefully deferred to; and, so far as government could prevent them, rapid and unsettling social changes avoided. This timid policy reflected the belief that the Congress was a vast unnatural coalition of divergent caste, class, religious, regional, social and economic interests only held together by the artificial stimulation of anti-British grievances. If those grievances could be mitigated, and fresh ones avoided, then, the British hoped, Congress would begin to shed the character of a mass national movement and might even transform itself into a number of parliamentary parties concerned more with social and economic than with 'national' issues.[32] At the very least, encouragement would be given to cooperative and moderate elements.[33]

Secondly, the British tried to propitiate ambitious and influential elements in Indian society by adjusting the regime to meet their aspirations. Well before any question arose of India's becoming a dominion, London conceded 'fiscal autonomy' to New Delhi. This allowed the Viceroy to place tariffs on imports – including those from Britain – in order to protect infant industries in India from foreign competition. Powerful commercial and industrial interests were to be persuaded that there was nothing inimical in the connection with Britain. The same motive led to the gradual introduction of Indians into the hitherto predominantly European cadres of the senior civil service and the officer corps of the Indian army. 'Indianization', like fiscal autonomy, was intended to demonstrate that Indian ambitions and interests could find satisfaction within a British-Indian framework. As self-government approached, (at the speed in pre-war India of a country bullock-cart) loyal Indian army officers and civil servants were expected to ensure continuity and preserve a strong core of pro-British feeling at the heart of the state.

Thirdly, the British were careful to build into the new pattern of Indian political life a set of institutional checks and constitutional devices intended to shape the way in which provincial and ultimately national self-government functioned. One of the most important of these was the arrangement whereby the appointment of civil servants was vested not in Indian ministers but in public service commissions nominated by the governors.[34] Ostensibly this was to avoid corruption and favouritism, but it could as easily be used to preserve some influence over the civil servants upon whom the ministers would have to rely. In a more general way, the governors, limited monarchs as they were in the provinces after 1937, could use their position to interpret the constitution. But much more important was the British insistence that India could only reach full self-government as a federation: amalgamating a decentralised British India and the locally autonomous Princely States. This would force the nationalist politicians of the Congress to come to terms with the conservative-minded rulers of the States: for any parliament of the future Dominion of India would contain a large bloc of members from the States to check the more radical elements of Congress. All together, with the Muslim minority in north India, the Princes, the divergent interests of the provinces, the commercial and industrial interests and the Indian element in the civil service and army all acting as a collective brake on Congress, the British had some reason to hope that even the most ardent nationalists in the Congress would recognise the impossibility of turning their back on Britain long before India became a self-governing dominion.

Lastly, even after India became a dominion, a trinity of long-term factors was expected to preserve the substance of the Anglo-Indian relationship. Of these the British laid, and long continued to lay, the heaviest emphasis upon India's supposed inability to defend herself against external attack, whether from Japan or from Russia.[35] The assistance of British military power would go on being an indispensable element in Indian security, and provide the most powerful argument against the repudiation of the British connection. That India might become neutral or 'non-aligned' in a world of voracious imperialist powers was inconceivable to the policy makers in London. Secondly, before 1939 Britain was India's most important creditor. Powerful pragmatic arguments expressed by Indian financial and commercial interests were expected to countervail nationalist rhetoric and maintain close ties – as with Australia, New Zealand or South Africa. Lastly, the advent of dominion status was not expected to signal the abrupt withdrawal of all British personnel in the country. In the army and civil service, as well as in the specialised and technical services such as agriculture or forestry, contingents of British would remain to help, advise and influence.

It might be suggested that such British calculations were merely fanciful and self-deluding. The constitutional reform of 1935 which had conceded full internal self-government to the provinces of British India, while laying down the federal principle as the basis for All-Indian self-government, may have been intended to weaken and divide the Congress with whom the British had been locked in struggle since 1930. But in the elections of 1937 Congress scored a great victory and formed the largest party in seven provinces out of eleven. Congress ministries took office and set about strengthening the foundations of local power and patronage: the vital base for a further confrontation with the Raj and the drive for full independence. The extent of Congress's triumph should not be underestimated, but it was very far from complete. In the two great Muslim majority provinces of Bengal and Punjab anti-Congress ministries were in power. In the States, with their vast area and large population, Congress had yet to make much headway. Meanwhile, within the Congress itself there was good reason to expect that the attainment of provincial power would accentuate the fissiparous tendencies against which the movement had always had to struggle; and, by forcing the Congress to act like a government rather than a popular movement, expose the fault-lines of socio-economic division that nationalism had papered over. The outbreak of war cut short this fascinating experiment in constitutional politics, on which the British had staked so much, before the outcome of this new phase of manoeuvre and counter-manoeuvre became apparent.

It was with such short and long-term assumptions that the British contemplated the gradual approach of self-rule. The importance of what can be seen in retrospect as highly optimistic suppositions was not only that they mitigated the consequences of ending direct rule but indeed that they made direct rule unnecessary and even self-defeating. At all events, what is clear is that before the Second World War the British expected and accepted that the Indians would rule themselves, probably sooner rather than later. What they did not expect, and emphatically did not intend, was that the approach to full national self-government would take place in an atmosphere riven by anti-British agitation, communal violence and widespread disorder; that British authority would ultimately fail to preserve a united India (the greatest memorial, the British thought, to their rule); least of all that a self-governing India would prove unable or unwilling to contribute to a Commonwealth system of security in Asia and the Middle East. The significance of the independence of India and

Pakistan in 1947 was that the *way it was reached* constituted a devastating reversal for British plans and the almost complete defeat of pre-war policy.

Why did this happen? Why did the British lose control over the pace and direction of political change in India so that at one point in 1947 they almost contemplated abandoning it to civil war? Before succumbing to the determinist view that such an outcome was inevitable from the 1930s it is worth noticing the effects that Britain and India's involvement in the Second World War had upon the political calculations we have been tracing. For the war damaged or demolished most of the instruments whereby the British hoped to control India's political development; and it transformed the setting in which the British had intended to carry through India's rebirth as a federal dominion.

In the first place the war forced the British to break their own golden rule of avoiding government action which might unsettle the Indian masses and make them susceptible to agitation. As we have seen, in India as elsewhere in the imperial system mobilising resources for the war effort produced shortages, inflation, the dislocation of markets and transport together with a sharp increase in the scope of government regulation and interference. Hence discontent was likely to become more widespread just as the Raj became a more visible target for resentment. For this reason political cooperation between the British and the Congress was all the more important. But here, too, the side effects of war made it infinitely harder to move towards the kind of partnership pre-war policy makers had envisaged. When Britain went to war in September 1939, India followed automatically as a dependency of the Crown. There was no consultation with Indian opinion, no vote, as in the white dominions, in an Indian parliament. This threw into sharp relief precisely those elements of British domination which pre-war reforms had sought to play down. At the very moment when Congress politicans had begun to play the parliamentary and constitutional role designed for them, a great fillip was given to those who wished Congress to remain a movement of confrontation, not a constitutional party. For his part, the Viceroy refused to make concessions to Congress that might have sweetened the pill, fearing that to do so would risk the efficiency of India's imperial contribution. To the Congress leaders, however, full partici- pation in what might turn out an unpopular, even disastrous, im- perial war looked certain to crack the fragile unity of their movement and might even destroy its hold on the Indian masses.

Both sides, therefore, moved towards a reluctant confrontation, and the flexibility of British policy was further reduced by the advent of Churchill as prime minister in May 1940, for Churchill was an old enemy of Congress. In 1940 Congress began an ineffective campaign of civil disobedience. In the spring of 1942 it rejected the proposals of the Cripps Mission for a larger Indian share in the day-to-day administration of the central government and held out for concessions that would have weakened British control over India's war effort.[36] In August, Gandhi launched a violent insurrection against British rule, the 'Quit India' movement, which was ruthlessly suppressed. The Congress leadership was interned and all prospect of partnership while the war lasted vanished completely. Instead there grew up a barrier of mistrust and even hatred between Congress leaders and British officials, who had taken over the administration in those provinces where Congress ministries had resigned in protest in 1939. Far from seeking to mould Congress views and influence Indian opinion by indirect and subtle means, the British now seemed intent on the eradication of Congress altogether. Thus between 1939 and 1942 the strains of a war which, from the standpoint of Britain's world interests, was going from bad to worse, utterly transformed the setting in which pre-war policy had been expected to function.

Other consequences too flowed from this revolution in Indian politics. In their desperate attempt in early 1942 (as the Japanese swept over Malaya and into Burma) to lure the Congress leaders into agreement, the British promised unequivocally to facilitate complete Indian self-government as soon as the war ended. They thus surrendered control over the timing of constitutional change in what was certain to be an extremely turbulent post-war period. Secondly, as they plunged into conflict with the Congress the British searched anxiously for Indians who *would* cooperate with them and lessen the authoritarian appearance of their rule.[37] They found such allies among the enemies of Congress, for whom its disappearance as an open political force after 1942 presented a golden (and perhaps unrepeatable) opportunity. Chief among the enemies of Congress was Jinnah's Muslim League, dedicated from 1940 onwards to the creation of a separate Muslim state and the defeat of Congress' ambition for a united India with a strong central government. After 1939, the British increasingly recognised the League's claim to represent all Indian Muslims in return for Muslim loyalty to the war effort:[38] the supreme importance of promoting Indian unity receded temporarily into the background. Thirdly, the violent lurch from cooperation into confrontation after 1939 placed massive strains, further accentuated by the needs of the war, on the administrative machine which held India together. Fewer and fewer British officials were available to preserve the balance of British and Indians in provincial administrations, while open war with Congress eroded the loyalty of Indian officials of Congress sympathies. When the war ended, it was little wonder that the once-vaunted 'steel-frame' of Indian administration was badly run-down and only doubtfully reliable in a full-scale crisis.[39]

Thus the war drove the largest Indian party into open resistance, strengthened the forces of division and weakened the framework of government. But it also had a corrosive effect upon that trio of long-term factors which had underlain pre-war British calculations about their relationship with a self-governing India. Before 1939 it had been reasonable to expect that when India became a dominion, much of the rest of Asia would still be under colonial rule (or semi-colonial domination), that China would be weak and divided, that Japanese power would be a potent threat, while the Soviet Union loomed darkly to the north in central Asia. British power on land, sea and in the air would be recognised by Indians as indispensable to their security. Even after 1945, the British clung to this belief, but the transformation of Asia between 1941 and 1945, the defeat of Japan, the rise of American power in the Pacific, the enhanced prestige of Russia, the emergence of China as an 'honorary' great power (under American auspices) and the terrible blows dealt to British prestige in the Anglo-Japanese conflict undermined the credibility and, perhaps in Indian eyes, the necessity for such a close strategic relationship. Secondly, the war brought about a fundamental change in the financial relationship. Far from being a debtor, dependent on British goodwill, India ended the war as a creditor of Britain to the tune of £1,000 million: the financial boot was on the other foot. Thirdly, with the colossal drain on British manpower that the war had brought, and the exhaustion of many British officials in India, the availability of British administrators, experts and army personnel to service a new Indian dominion was far less certain. Moreover, the war had brought about a sharp and involuntary acceleration in the Indianisation of the army[40] and civil service which could not easily be reversed.

So, when the British came at the end of the war to consider with some urgency how India was to be given the self-government that had been promised and in a way that was compatible with Britain's own global interests, they found that the basic elements of India's political life had changed and that the instruments of authority and influence upon which they had chosen to rely were cracking in their hands. The struggle for India's future was beginning in earnest.

The war against Japan ended with unexpected suddenness in August 1945, but the new Labour government was determined to move as quickly as possible towards granting India full self-government.[41] Speed was thought desirable partly because it would impress international opinion with the sincerity of British intentions but even more so that London and the Viceroy could keep the initiative in India.[42] The cabinet were very anxious to lay down a clear programme of constitutional progress before Indian politicians could begin to mobilise popular agitation against British rule, and while a calm atmosphere prevailed. Both the Viceroy (Lord Wavell) and London were very eager to restore the pre-1939 pattern of Indian participation in provincial government, and to create an interim central government which would enjoy *de facto* most of the rights of a dominion government.[43]

But this did not mean that the Labour cabinet had in mind a radical new scheme for Indian independence. What Attlee and his colleagues wanted to implement was the offer made by Cripps in 1942: the election of a constitution-making assembly as soon as the war was over; the creation of a federal India (individual provinces and states could opt for separate independence); and an Anglo-Indian treaty to regulate mutual interests. Moreover, they hoped and expected that a swift constitutional settlement would ensure that India's relationship with Britain would be very similar to that envisaged before 1939. India, they thought, would continue to look to Britain for assistance in her defence and this would be the dominating factor in her external relations.[44] In return India would help Britain with the defence of South East Asia and provide facilities for British operations in the region.[45] Indeed, the planners hoped to profit from India's growing industrial power and what were seen as her aspirations to play a much larger part in the affairs of post-war East Asia.[46] A more powerful and assertive India, closely allied to Britain, would lift some of the old burdens of imperial power from weary British shoulders – an attractive prospect at such a moment. Cooperation of this kind reasoned the Labour cabinet, would be their reward for constitutional generosity. By the same token, the essential objects of post-war British policy in India were geared to these long-term strategic and political aims. Three requirements were fundamental: 'a stable and contented India';[47] India's willing membership of the British Commonwealth; above all else, the preservation of Indian unity and the avoidance of partition or balkanisation in the sub-continent.

But it was hardly to be hoped that an outcome so agreeable to British interests would be easily attained in the circumstances prevailing at the end of the war. Far from eagerly embracing the British proposals and pledging friendship and cooperation the leaders of the Congress scorned British promises and talked instead of another mass movement to eject the British from India neck and crop.[48] The cause of this intransigence was the Congress' belief that the British were deliberately encouraging the claims of the Muslim League to represent all Indian Muslims, and its fear that the League would exploit the 'opting out' clause to achieve partition.[49] Worse still, the Congress leadership feared that the British proposals would allow Muslim electoral majorities in Punjab and Bengal to take the whole of these provinces with their millions of Hindus and their enormous economic and political importance, out of the Indian federation altogether. Moreover, if the rulers of the princely states, whose accession to a federal India had been a fundamental part of the pre-war British plan, took their cue from the Muslim League and demanded separate independence, all prospect of creating a united India would vanish and the sub-continent would dissolve into political fragments.

The British stuck to their insistence that neither provinces nor states could be forced into a federation whose central government was certain to be dominated by the Hindu majority. This was not because they harboured any secret desire to weaken India by partition or postpone the hour of independence by playing upon Indian divisions. The reverse was true: as we have seen, if India was to play the role in Asia which the British hoped for; if indeed her relations with Britain were not to be poisoned by bitterness and mistrust, the preservation of Indian unity was essential. British refusal to let Congress *impose* Indian unity and a Congress 'raj' was grounded in several powerful objections. It would have represented a complete change from existing policy and come under fierce attack, especially from Conservatives in Britain, as a capitulation to those very political forces who had shown disloyalty during the war and as a gross betrayal of Muslim loyalty. It might even damage considerably British relations with the Muslim states of the Middle East. These were reasons external to India. Internal Indian reasons seemed even more compelling. The British were deeply impressed by the growth of support for the Muslim League and by the gathering strength of communal feeling – a growing force in Indian politics for the past 40 years. They feared that to *coerce* Muslims into unity would be a recipe for rebellion and civil war. And because Muslims formed an element in the Indian army out of all proportion to their share of the population, they had a particular and immediate reason for dreading Muslim unrest. If the army mutinied all would be lost. By some means, therefore, Muslims must be convinced that their interests would be safeguarded and that partition was unnecessary and undesirable.

At the end of 1945 it was apparent that a swift constitutional settlement acceptable to the League and Congress, and a smooth transfer of power were not in prospect. Relations between the Congress and the League were getting steadily worse. Jinnah, the leader of the League, was determined not to agree to any constitutional formula that would prejudice the attainment of a separate state – Pakistan. The League had made great strides in winning Muslim support away from Congress and other Muslim parties during the years when Congress had been under ban. But with Congress back in the field competing for Muslim votes (and not without success) Jinnah and the League had to assert their claim to be the true voice of Indian Muslims with even greater vehemence and to insist that nothing short of Pakistan would meet Muslim aspirations. Post-war uncertainties and fear of what a strong Congress central government might do helped their cause;[50] but they also made it harder for Jinnah to draw back at all from the full extent of his demands. For its part, the Congress leadership utterly rejected the claim that the League spoke for the Muslim community. Nehru contemptuously attributed its growth to British favour[51] and believed that if it were withdrawn the League would start to wither away.[52] The object of the Congress therefore became to resist any binding promise that would permit the secession of the Muslim majority provinces; and to postpone the settlement of India's internal affairs until after British withdrawal and the attainment of self-government. With Congress in command of the Indian centre and the apparatus of government, the 'fantasy'[53] of Pakistan could be exploded, the League deflated and the princes called to order. Congress would rule and Indian unity would be assured. Hence the more intransigent the League became over partition the more determined grew Nehru and the Congress leadership not to cooperate in a constitutional plan which would allow it; and the more eager they became instead to drive out the remaining power and influence of the British: the crucial obstacle, they thought, to the defeat of the League and the coercion of the recalcitrant princes.

So far from presiding benignly over the emergence of a friendly new dominion the British found themselves confronting two unpalatable alternatives: civil war in northern India leading to partition; or a successful Congress insurrection that would expel British influence from India by force, and impose a Congress solution. London and the Viceroy toyed briefly with the idea of repressing Congress if only to provide a breathing space in which to wait for calmer times. It would, said the Viceroy in November 1945, be 'relatively easy'.[54] But ministers decided then that such a course could not easily be justified.[55] British, American and international opinion would not understand. There was a further, graver objection. If Congress as the undisputed representative of the mass of Hindu opinion (and of the great majority of Indians) was driven out of politics, what were the British to put in its place?[56] Repression would postpone the solution of India's constitutional problems, but at the price of intensifying the difficulties and costs of British rule: a larger garrison and the recruitment of new British officials 'on a scale never before attempted'.[57] The burden of a further period of emergency rule was intolerable alike to ministers in London and British officials in New Delhi. By the spring of 1946 it was clear enough that even this grim option was closed. The demands on Britain's contracting army were reducing available military power even while the 'general sense of insecurity and lawlessness' in India grew.[58] The crunch had come. 'On the whole', wrote the Viceroy's principal adviser on internal security in April 1946, 'I doubt whether a Congress rebellion could be suppressed'.[59] In June 1946 the cabinet accepted this as a governing fact of their policy.[60] Coercion, as the ultimate weapon of British policy in India against recalcitrant nationalism, as the bedrock of British rule for 190 years, was defunct.

How then could Indian unity be preserved? Dissatisfied with their Viceroy and naively convinced that Muslim support for a separate Pakistan would collapse under the weight of reasoned argument,[61] the cabinet despatched a delegation of senior ministers with Cripps (next to Attlee's the most powerful voice on Indian affairs) at their head to negotiate with Jinnah and the Congress. Cripps was determined throughout that partition must be avoided.[62] His solution was

ingenious. India should have not a two-tier but a three-tier federation.[63] The provinces should be sorted into three groups or sub-
federations, one for Hindu-majority provinces, one for Muslim majority provinces and one for Bengal and Assam as special cases. The
sub-federal governments should enjoy whatever powers the provinces
conceded to them but foreign relations and defence would be reserved
to the top tier, the federal centre.[64] The object was to buy off the
Muslim League with the promise of a Muslim sub-federation instead
of a sovereign Pakistan, to find a middle road between Congress and
League and to meet what London saw as the vital strategic requirement. At first both sides seemed ready to accept this elaborate
compromise. But soon the objections piled up. Nehru and the Congress feared that making grouping compulsory would actually encourage Muslim separatism, strengthen the League's power to veto
the formation of a real federal centre and pave the way for partition.
Jinnah feared that to concede the principle of federal unity and enter
the quicksands of negotiation would enable Congress to discredit him
and sap his bargaining power. Above all, both sides were consumed
with the fear that compromise and concession would undercut the
loyalty and obedience of their supporters as the growing violence and
disorder inflamed communal feeling. With the future of northern
India – of the whole sub-continent – at stake, neither movement dared
risk the erosion of its popular support at the very outset of the
constitutional struggle.

Instead the object became to control the machinery of the existing
central government, perhaps in the belief that if no constitutional
agreement could be made the party which commanded the resources
and military power of the dying Raj would prevail. The British were
eager to see Congress and League politicians working together in an
interim central government in the hope that shared responsibility
would promote constitutional compromise. First Congress and then
the League did indeed join the government sharing the major departments between them. Preparations for a constituent assembly to draw
up the constitution went ahead. But the interim government was in
practice scarcely a government at all. Far from working together the
two parties turned the cabinet into a debating chamber with the
Viceroy as referee. Central government was paralysed. Both sides
redoubled their efforts to ensure that the procedure of the forthcoming
assembly should favour their cause. The assembly met but was
repeatedly adjourned. As 1946 drew to a close, the open struggle for

power in the provinces as at the centre, mixed with intensifying communal antagonism and social and economic unrest, seemed to be driving northern India faster and faster towards an explosion of anarchy and the outbreak of civil war.[65] The last shreds of British rule were vanishing.

These events converged to force London to revise its plan for India. Wavell as Viceroy was determined to get the cabinet to decide what it would do if there were no progress towards a peaceful transfer of power and an accelerating decline in public order. Wavell insisted repeatedly that British power merely to keep order was melting away as British civil servants and police retired or resigned and their Indian subordinates responded to communal loyalties. A year or eighteen months would see its final collapse.[66] What the Viceroy wanted was a 'breakdown plan' that would declare openly a date for British withdrawal and allow him in the meantime to withdraw British troops, police and officials from those parts of India where no communal differences stood in the way of the transfer of power.[67] This blunt warning and the danger that thousands of British lives would be lost in an Indian anarchy undoubtedly frightened ministers. They toyed with ways of planning a withdrawal if only as a means of jolting Congress and the League into cooperation. A statement was drafted declaring Britain's intention to withdraw by 31 March 1948.[68] Then at the very end of December, encouraged by a short-lived compromise patched up between the Indian parties, the cabinet at Attlee's prompting decided to defer this announcement and to recast its form radically.[69]

Their reasons are revealing. The more ministers thought about a declaration of withdrawal the less they liked it. What damned Wavell's plan for a gradual withdrawal, quite apart from its disintegrating effect on Indian unity, was that it would mean repealing the 1935 Government of India Act and subjecting the government's whole Indian policy to prolonged parliamentary scrutiny.[70] Even the declaration of intent to withdraw by a stated time alarmed a section of the cabinet because it 'might be regarded as the beginning of the liquidation of the British Empire'.[71] Instead the deferred statement was to be redrafted so that British withdrawal should be presented not as 'the first step in the dissolution of the Empire' but 'as a voluntary transfer of power to a democratic government'.[72] Indeed, the more ministers argued about India the further its political realities receded from their minds; and the more anxious they became about public reaction at home to a policy of 'scuttle'. 'I am convinced', Bevin told Attlee, 'that if you do that our Party in this country . . . will lose and lose irrevocably when the public become aware of the policy of the Cabinet at this moment.'[73] Bevin urged instead that Britain stand firm in India, at least for the time being. Even at this late stage, and in a Labour cabinet, the imperial urge was still strong. But it was borne down by two influences which swept ministers towards the cataract they dreaded. By February 1947 the last hopes of compromise were vanishing as the Congress renewed its demand for the removal of the League ministers and the League refused to work the constituent assembly. Secondly, Mountbatten, whom Attlee had chosen to replace Wavell (perhaps originally as a substitute for a real change of policy) insisted upon a public time limit as the price of his acceptance. On 18 February 1947, the cabinet bowed to the inevitable and authorised the statement. British rule was to end, come what may, by June 1948.[74]

Thus Mountbatten arrived in India in March 1947 as the last Viceroy, but determined to present himself as the honest broker of Indian politics, wholly committed to Indian independence and devoid of any desire to prolong British authority. The statement of 20 February 1947 declared Britain's intention to hand over power to a representative Indian government or, failing that, to *governments* London considered representative: a clear indication that partition might have to be accepted. But Mountbatten's instructions from Attlee made clear that the achievement of a united India was still the 'definite object' and that 'the defence requirements of India' as well as her part in the defence of the Indian Ocean should be given 'full regard'.[75] Mountbatten himself was eager to preserve Indian unity by any means possible; and equally convinced that only by announcing a plan for the transfer of power within weeks of his arrival could civil war be averted.[76] The result was the clumsy and abortive 'May Plan' by which power was to be transferred first to the provinces, which were then to choose between an Indian Union, Pakistan and separate independence. Perhaps Mountbatten hoped, by offering independence to Bengal and the Punjab, where there were strong Muslim reservations about partition,[77] to frighten Jinnah and his supporters into at last accepting federation in some form.[78] If so he failed. Instead the plan was vehemently denounced by Nehru, now the real leader of Congress, as a blueprint for the balkanisation of India.[79]

With dazzling rapidity, and to the astonishment of the cabinet,

Mountbatten, claiming that the London government's gloss on his plan had made it unacceptable in India, dropped it completely and devised instead a second, the so-called June Plan. In this plan all thought of securing unity was put aside, and the 'independence option' scrapped. Mountbatten proposed, in effect, that power should be transferred to two separate dominions, India and Pakistan. The provinces and states could choose between them, but Bengal and the Punjab would be partitioned unless both communities could agree upon their choice. London made no objection and agreed to Mountbatten's demand that the transfer of power take place far earlier than expected, in August 1947. Congress and the League reluctantly accepted the new plan, while in Bengal and the Punjab the assemblies voted for partition. Thereafter, at hectic pace, the preparations for independence were driven forward. The army was divided; the new partition boundaries drawn out (though not published) and an independence bill rushed through Parliament. Mountbatten himself cajoled and threatened the Princely States into joining the new dominions and giving up their treaty rights to British protection. On 15 August 1947, before even the new boundaries in the Punjab and Bengal had been made known,[80] India and Pakistan received their independence as dominions in the British Commonwealth.

The speed and efficiency with which Mountbatten had ended British responsibility in India was a remarkable prize for a government which, at the time of his appointment, had been devoid of any idea save how to avoid political embarrassment at home. When Mountbatten had arrived in India there was every expectation of a total collapse in the framework of government and widespread civil conflict. Without the humiliating 'scuttle' the cabinet dreaded, Britain could scarcely have avoided being sucked into the maelstrom of communal struggle, a commitment whose political and military consequences threatened to unbalance her entire foreign policy and endanger her relations especially with the Muslim world and the United States. There was, into the bargain, every sign that both Indian parties, and certainly the Congress, would reject membership of the Commonwealth and demand a republican constitution. In short, as Wavell left India, British policy makers faced a disaster of major proportions that would have reverberated throughout the rest of their imperial system as well as in domestic politics.

In these circumstances, to have persuaded Congress and the League to accept Pakistan and partition, as well as dominion status, seemed almost miraculous. The real reasons were inevitably more prosaic. For Mountbatten's arrival in India coincided with a fundamental shift in the attitude of Congress towards partition. Having so long resisted any constitutional solution that might permit Pakistan, Nehru and the Congress leadership had come by the early part of 1947 to fear that without a swift settlement of some kind their own authority, like that of the British, would collapse in a storm of provincial disorder.[81] Partition, if only temporarily,[82] was the price that had to be paid if any form of central government was to survive, if the balkanisation of India was to be avoided, and if Hindu minorities in Bengal and the Punjab were not to be abandoned to Muslim domination. The way was opened for Mountbatten's June Plan. The same pragmatic outlook brought Congress to accept Commonwealth membership, at least for the time being. For the supreme convenience of dominion status (independence within the Commonwealth) was that it allowed power to be transferred *before* new constitutions for India and Pakistan were drawn up, by a simple amendment of the existing 1935 constitution.

Thus the transfer of power in India was effected in a way that neither British officials nor Congress politicians could have dreamt of before 1939, even perhaps in their worst nightmares. For both British policy makers and the Congress the terms of Indian independence were a shattering defeat measured against their pre-war aspirations. The political and social upheavals that the war had brought simultaneously destroyed the foundations of British influence in India and the political supremacy of Congress. Beset by European, Middle Eastern and other Asian difficulties,[83] harassed by economic and manpower crises at home, the British lacked the resources or the will to reassert their authority and impose the constitutional solution they really wanted. Congress, in its turn, bobbed like a cork on the waves of social and communal unrest in India, as much the victim as the beneficiary of political change. But although the worst catastrophe was averted, the British now had to face the imperial consequences of India's partition: the division of the Indian army; the strategic weakening of the subcontinent; the loss of the contribution that a united Indian dominion had been expected to make to the stability and strength of their world system.

Burma

In India the most strenuous efforts of British policy failed to create a federal dominion or preserve the unity of the sub-continent. But at least both India and Pakistan had been retained for the time being within the British Commonwealth and their special links with Britain temporarily safeguarded. Burma refused to remain in the Commonwealth and insisted upon an independence untrammelled by any surviving links with Britain. Moreover all British attempts to check the headlong pace of Burma's constitutional progress after 1945, or to moderate the demands for a complete break with London, came to nothing. In no part of British Asia was the rejection of British influence so complete. The comparison with India is interesting: the contrast with Ceylon and Malaya striking.

Burma had been acquired in the nineteenth century as a strategic outwork of the Indian Empire, and became a province of British India. It was developed rapidly by British capital and Indian immigrants as the great 'rice bowl' of Asia, producing large quantities of rice for export.[84] In 1937, as part of the general reconstruction of the Indian states and provinces, it was separated from India proper and granted responsible government. Five years later it was overrun by the Japanese and the apparatus of British rule destroyed. In 1943, as part of Japan's new order, it was declared independent and a government of Burmese nationalists installed. Then in the summer of 1945 Burma was reconquered and British rule restored. After two violent political convulsions, with its export economy in ruins,[85] its towns devastated, Burma was once more part of Britain's Asian empire.

The instinct of the British government in London was to cling to the pre-war policy of allowing gradual progress towards the ultimate goal of full self-government within the British Commonwealth: like India, Burma was eventually to be a dominion accepting the rights and obligations of dominion status. In 1943 the Burmese had been promised complete self-government 'as soon as circumstances permit'[86] – a somewhat ironic promise under the circumstances of the time. In May 1945, with Burma reconquered, but with the Pacific war expected to last a further year or more, the promise of dominion status was reiterated. But, ostensibly to allow time for the revival of the economy, communications and the administrative apparatus necessary for elections, Burma was to be given over to the direct rule of British officials until December 1948: the responsible government constitution of 1937–42 was suspended. Moreover, the so-called 'Scheduled Areas' – the ethnically distinct hill states which fringed Burma proper – were to remain under British control until their people showed the desire to be amalgamated with the rest of Burma.[87] In June 1945 this policy was enshrined in legislation.

Burma's need for economic reconstruction was incontrovertible. But clearly three and a half years of direct British rule was intended to promote more than just a physical recovery. British influence had to be restored and the memory of 'independence' erased if Burma's pre-war constitutional programme was to be revived. It required, however, more than the raising of the Union Jack over Rangoon to rebuild British power and prestige. The British would have to regain real control over the administration and police and reassert their authority in the towns and villages of Burma. They would have to displace the native Burmese for whom the beheading of the British presence in 1942 had been the opportunity of a lifetime. Above all, they would have to suppress the private armies and other clandestine organisations which had grown up in the countryside in the years of chaos; in particular the Burmese 'national army' which had been formed under Japanese rule and of which Aung San, the nationalist, was the leader.[88] These tasks were beyond Britain's capacity at a time when so many other urgent calls were being made on her military resources in Asia. In September 1946, following a strike of police and public servants, Aung San was appointed a member of the executive council: the cooperation of his party, the Anti-Fascist People's Freedom League (AFPFL) had become indispensable to British control.

Aung San and his followers were not content with the temporary constitution of 1945 and the prolongation of direct rule. Nor would they accept the revival of the pre-war constitution for an interim period. 'The Burmese and AFPFL . . . are determined to have their freedom and have it quickly', reported the governor.[89] The AFPFL leaders were anxious to exercise control over defence, external relations, finance and the administration of the 'Scheduled Areas' before the elections which the British had promised in April 1947,[90] and before the new constitution was drawn up. Their motives were obvious. With Burma's administration in disarray, with growing support for local communism, and with the threat that the British might permit the hill states to go their own way,[91] it seemed vital to establish full authority as quickly as possible before delay and discontent undermined the AFPFL's prestige and popular support, and to ensure that the forthcoming elections produced a satisfactory result.

The Attlee government was reluctant to make such concessions. As over India, it dreaded making its imperial policy a party issue and feared an adverse parliamentary reaction if it conceded the AFPFL's demands. Secondly, it was afraid that the appearance of weakness in Burma would weaken British authority in Ceylon, where progress to full self-government was expected to be slower, and in Malaya where it had not yet begun.[92] But a stream of telegrams from the governor made it clear that the means to resist were lacking: the police force was unreliable and would strike if the AFPFL left the government; and if the AFPFL joined forces with the communists to drive out British rule, there was little military strength with which to oppose them, a view endorsed by the Chiefs of Staff.[93] Overwhelmed by these arguments and encouraged by the hope that Aung San could be won over by concessions and might prove a staunch enemy of communism, ministers approved the concessions to the AFPFL delegation that had come to London: immediate *de facto* dominion status was to be offered.[94]

Thus the logic of British weakness on the ground in Burma had been to transfer effective power to that party which seemed best able to hold Burma together and which looked likely to deal firmly with communist insurgents in the countryside. To strengthen their new allies, the British were prepared to abandon their original consti-tutional programme and propel the hill states towards amalgamation in a Burma Union.[95] In return they hoped and expected that Aung San would elect to remain within the British Commonwealth and would enter into a close partnership with Britain especially in defence, but perhaps also in economic development. These hopes had soon to be abandoned. In the spring of 1947 it became clear that Aung San would insist on Burma's becoming a republic, erasing from its constitution any reference to the British Crown. London cajoled (the benefits of membership) and threatened (no financial assistance) in vain. Neither Aung San nor the new Constituent Assembly would modify the demand for a republic; and in 1947 (though not after 1949) a republican constitution was incompatible with membership of the Commonwealth.

At stake was more than just a form of words. As in India, the object of British policy was to transfer power on terms that would preserve a special link with the British imperial system, minimise the *inter-national* and *strategic* significance of self-rule and encourage com-mercial cooperation. Commonwealth membership would be a visible symbol of Burma's loyalty to the British connection and a vital channel of British influence. Her secession, so it seemed to British officials in Rangoon and Singapore – the great bastion of British power in South East Asia – would be a damaging blow to British prestige in Asia and an encouragement to anti-British nationalism everywhere.[96] Burmese intransigence was attributed to 'immaturity' and excessive 'self-confidence', but its roots were more complex. Partly it reflected the old obsession about parity of status with India: for the Burmese leaders expected that Nehru would insist on an Indian republic.[97] Of far greater significance, it may be suggested, was the profound mistrust felt by the Burmese, especially the rural cultivators, for any vestigial connection that might allow the return of British commercial interests, the Indian moneylender and Indian migrant labour. Before 1939 these three groups had dominated Burma's agricultural economy. During the Depression resentment against them, above all against the large Indian minority, had become increasingly bitter, as cultivators were driven deeper into debt and dispossessed.[98] The collapse of British rule in 1942 had destroyed an economic as well as a political system. The prospect of its revival in any form, chaining the Burmese peasant once more to the world market and restoring his liability for pre-war debts to Indian bankers and usurers, was anathema. Rural crisis before 1939 had bred a lasting xenophobia.[99] The leaders of the AFPFL dared not resist this feeling, convinced that if they did so agrarian communism 'advocating no rents or taxes and forcible seizure of the land'[100] would win over the rural masses. Foreign conquest had shattered British *rule*. But British *influence* had been destroyed by racial antipathy, deeply-felt social and economic grievances and the side effects of internal disorder and division. In January 1948, Burma passed into independence and out of the British Commonwealth.

Ceylon

In both Burma and India the British had begun by believing that the promise of constitutional change would secure local cooperation and make possible the construction of two new Asian dominions looking to Britain. But these plans broke down because London had failed to realise how far the war had destroyed the old pattern of politics in both India and (even more dramatically) in Burma. After the war neither the determination of Congress to restore its position and break the Muslim League, nor the after-effects of the total collapse of British authority in Burma could be simply wished away. Yet the alternative course, to reassert British power by the insertion of large garrisons and a strong corps of administrators, was rendered impossible by Britain's own shortage of manpower, the urgent need to reduce her towering overseas expenditure and the concatenation of crises in Europe, the Mediterranean and the Middle East that beat upon her between 1945 and 1948. In these circumstances there was neither the will nor the means to seek to *impose* an imperial design: on the contrary there seemed every reason to avoid a confrontation with Asian nationalisms at so delicate a moment.

But it would be wrong to deduce from British policy in India and Burma that British interests, still less British ambitions, in Asia had disintegrated. Even while they struggled to preserve the unity of India or find any workable formula for a transfer of power, and while Burma turned her back on the Commonwealth, the British carried through the transfer of power in Ceylon with flamboyant ease and persuaded Ceylonese leaders to accept not only Commonwealth membership but, as the price of independence, two agreements that guaranteed Anglo-Ceylonese cooperation in defence and external affairs. With its Westminster-like constitution and its eagerness for British friendship, Ceylon indeed seemed the very model for the successful creation of new Asian dominions.

The greater cooperativeness of Ceylon politicians did not mean of course that they would have been content to languish in the colonial status to which they were restricted before 1939. Ceylon's constitutional development had been slower than India's or Burma's. Between the wars the Colonial Office had rejected the idea of granting full internal self-government with a ministerial cabinet responsible to an elected assembly on the grounds that local politics were too strongly influenced by racial or communal animosities.[101] (Large minorities of Tamils and Indian immigrants as well as other small communities made up some 30 per cent of the population.) To encourage racial cooperation, a constitution modelled on the English system of local government had been laid down: instead of being collectively responsible to the assembly, the ministers were to be the chairmen of, and individually responsible to, the several executive committees into which the assembly or 'State Council' was divided. By this means, and by abolishing communal electorates, it was hoped to discourage the growth of communally-based political parties. Meanwhile the governor, and thus London, retained control of Ceylon's defence and foreign relations as well as a veto on the financial policy of the local ministers.

Even before the outbreak of war the rise of racial tensions and the inability of ministers responsible to different committees to cooperate with each other and with the governor had made constitutional reform necessary.[102] The impact of the Asian war multiplied the pressures for change. From being an insignificant outpost of empire Ceylon became, after the fall of Singapore, of vital strategic importance for the defence of Britain's sea communications with India.[103] With the advent of Mountbatten's South East Asia Command, it became the headquarters of the whole British war effort to defeat Japan. It acquired a vastly greater importance as a supplier of rubber, after the loss of Malaya almost the only remaining source to the Allies in the East.[104] In these circumstances the value of local political cooperation was distinctly enhanced.[105] In 1942 the State Council, aware of the promises being made in India, demanded the guarantee of dominion status at the end of the war. In May 1943 London responded with an assurance that Ceylon would be granted full responsible government in internal affairs with only external relations, defence and currency questions reserved to British control. Meanwhile the Ceylonese ministers were invited to draw up constitutional proposals for London's consideration.[106]

The demand for rapid progress towards cabinet government and dominion status arose chiefly from the leaders of the majority Sinhalese community. It reflected their desire to end a political system which, apart from its clumsiness, had been designed to prevent them from monopolising the executive through control of a parliamentary majority. In the later 1930s and during the early years of the war this motive had been joined by another. The depression had strengthened Sinhalese dislike for the entry of immigrant labour from India and had made the question of their voting rights a fierce controversy.[107] Sinhalese politicians were keenly aware that while the franchise and control of immigration remained under the jurisdiction of British officials pressure from the government of India on behalf of its immigrant workers, and British concern for minority interests, might combine to impose a constitution in which minority rights were entrenched at the expense of the Sinhalese majority. Cabinet government and dominion status were the vital means of ensuring that this could not happen. Sinhalese pressure was successful. Well before the Asian war ended, and long before it was expected to end, a commission under Lord Soulbury reported in favour of granting responsible government and acknowledged the desire of the Ceylon population for dominion status. Dominion status was, however, deferred on the grounds that the defence and external affairs of the country remained of vital imperial importance.[108] But this denial was softened by three crucial concessions: the franchise of Indian immigrants was still to be restricted by residence and domicile regulations;[109] and both the control of immigration and the administration of the franchise were to be treated as internal matters over which the British governor-general would have no authority.[110] In October 1945 the Labour government added the promise that Ceylon should proceed to full dominion status 'in a comparatively short space of time'.[111]

The 'Soulbury Constitution' reflected London's desire to preserve full control over Ceylon as a military and naval base in the chaotic aftermath of Japanese defeat in South East Asia as well as unwillingness to permit headlong constitutional change before normal times had been restored. Reluctantly the Sinhalese ministers accepted the delay. Drawn as they were very largely from a class of landowners, the alternative course of rousing popular agitation against the British had little appeal. Instead, Senanayake, the leading Sinhalese politician, attempted to strengthen his hand and to ease British fears about minority interests by creating a political party that would appeal to the Tamil and Muslim communities.[112] In the event, the standstill in Ceylon's constitutional progress was short-lived.

In the elections of September 1946 Senanayake and his United National Party emerged as the strongest grouping in the Ceylon parliament, but failed to win an outright majority. Both the Tamil and Indian communities had held aloof. Far more serious, however, both for Senanayake and for London, was the success of the Communists among the Sinhalese especially in the towns swollen by Ceylon's war economy.[113] The Communists and their allies formed an opposition controlling over 40 of the 100 or so seats in the lower house. They demanded not dominion status but complete independence outside the British Commonwealth and without close ties in defence and external relations which London thought vital. Still more alarming was the surge of social unrest that followed the elections as the artificial prosperity of wartime fell away. Between October 1946 and June 1947 there were strikes among transport workers, government and municipal employees and among workers in the tea and rubber trades. The use of the Defence Force to preserve order raised the dangerous possibility that this social unrest would become an anti-British campaign. For Senanayake, the need to secure dominion status without delay, thus to demonstrate his nationalist credentials, became overwhelming. Pressure from within his own party, and the fear that Ceylon might languish indefinitely as a colony while India gained independence, drove him back to London to ask for an immediate promise of independence within the Commonwealth. Unnerved by the spectre of extreme nationalism, fearful of yet another colonial crisis in Asia and anxious to bolster the forces of moderate nationalism, the cabinet gave way: Ceylon was to become a dominion provided that satisfactory agreements could be negotiated for cooperation in defence and foreign affairs.[114] These pacts were concluded in November 1947, and Ceylon became a dominion in February 1948.[115]

The pattern of decolonisation in Ceylon was thus very different from that in India and Burma and, from a British point of view, infinitely more satisfactory. Power had been successfully transferred to local politicians who, as a junior minister reported in March 1948, 'are extremely friendly and want to maintain and deepen the British connexion',[116] and who had pledged themselves to strategic cooperation. In Ceylon constitutional generosity seemed to have reaped the reward which had eluded the British in India and still more in Burma. The reasons for this success should be sought in the far more favourable circumstances which British policy enjoyed in Ceylon during the Second World War. There was no repetition in Ceylon of the catastrophe that overwhelmed British rule in Burma, nor even of the political revolution which in India had destroyed the fragile pre-war cooperation of the British and Congress. Friendship between the British and the Sinhalese politicians comfortably survived the stresses of war. No less important was the conservative nature of the Sinhalese politicians, almost all of them 'extremely rich landowners with local power and influence comparable to a whig landlord's in George III's time'.[117] There was no parallel in Ceylon to the political dominance of a xenophobic agrarian radicalism such as had confronted the British in Burma; and the landowning class was undoubtedly anxious to preserve Ceylon's preferential export market in Britain. Finally, to a much greater extent than in Burma, the leaders of the Sinhalese majority in Ceylon were fearful of Indian domination and saw in close ties with Britain the best guarantee against it.[118] All the makings of a partnership existed so long as Britain was careful to respect the forms of independence. Gordon-Walker's memorandum aptly described the spirit of British policy:

'It is hardly too much to say that if we treat them strictly as a dominion they will behave very like a loyal colony: whereas if we treat them as a Colony we may end in driving them out of the Commonwealth'.[119]

Malaya

In India, Burma and Ceylon the British displayed after 1945 a striking readiness to come to terms with local nationalism, and a keen anxiety to avoid open political conflict. As we have seen, their policies were founded on the calculation that only by the concession of independence could a special connection with Britain be preserved. But the speed with which Britain abandoned colonial rule in these three territories at the end of the war has sometimes suggested that now London had written off completely the old supremacy in South and South East Asia and accepted a severe contraction in Britain's global role. But in Malaya British policy showed no hint of any desire to cut and run. The plans drawn up in London during and immediately after the war revealed instead a determination to extend and strengthen British control of the peninsula. Notoriously, after June 1948 Britain was drawn into a prolonged and expensive struggle to prevent the emergence of a communist regime hostile to British influence. Why did the British adopt towards Malaya an attitude so much at variance with their approach elsewhere in British Asia? And why should they have supposed that the restoration of their colonial rule there would escape the fate that had overcome it in Burma or Ceylon?

Before 1939 the name 'Malaya' described not a single territory but rather three separate groups of territories under varying degrees of British influence or control. Under direct British administration were the Straits Settlements, four pockets of land – including the island of Singapore – acquired as trading stations in the eighteenth and early nineteenth centuries. The Straits Settlements were a crown colony. Then there were the Federated Malay States (FMS), four states ruled over by Malay sultans who had accepted British protection in the later nineteenth century. Here the sultans were pledged to accept the advice of British Residents and a staff of British civil servants under the nominal authority of the sultans conducted much of the work of administration. In 1895, partly because of the growth of European enterprise in the mines and plantations, these four states were formed into a federation with a central government at Kuala Lumpur and with a common budget. Lastly there were the five Unfederated Malay States (UMS) which had come under British protection somewhat later. Here too the Malay rulers were bound to follow British advice and were 'assisted' by British administrators. Economically they were less developed than the FMS and the five rulers had resisted federation and the loss of control over their own revenues. They enjoyed separate treaties of protection with Britain. The governor of the Straits Settlements based at Singapore was high commissioner for the FMS and UMS and was also responsible for the outlying British possessions on the island of Borneo (Labuan, the Brunei protectorate, North Borneo and Sarawak).

Thus before the war British Malaya was a patchwork quilt of dependencies with different political and administrative traditions. Nowhere had there been any significant development of representative institutions such as could be found in India, Burma or Ceylon. On the mainland peninsula of Malaya the British relied upon the cooperation of the traditional rulers, and in return helped to bolster their authority. But the political life of the Malayan territories was further complicated by the results of four decades of rapid economic development. The expansion of tin mining on a large scale and the growth of rubber plantations had brought an inflow of European capital but also a huge influx of migrant labour from China and India. By 1941 the population of British Malaya including Singapore was 43 per cent Chinese, 41 per cent Malay and 14 per cent Indian.[120] Even outside the overwhelmingly Chinese city of Singapore the indigenous Malays were equalled in numbers by Chinese and Indian migrants (49 per cent each). There was little intermarriage between these communities and no sign of their fusing into a common Malayan nation. Nevertheless, neither the Chinese nor the Indians had been granted political representation, partly on the grounds that they were foreign-born and transient.[121] Thus the traditional Malayan sultans of the FMS and UMS enjoyed an influence over government which was less and less in accord with the actual balance of the communities, and a power which was increasingly threatened by social, economic and demographic change.

This old Malayan system was swept away by Japanese conquest in 1941–42, and until August 1945 Malaya passed under Japanese control. The policy makers in London drew up their plans for the future of post-war Malaya: there, as in the rest of the colonial empire, the ultimate goal was to be self-government within the British

Commonwealth. But that was less than half the story. For the planners were determined to turn the disaster of 1942 to imperial advantage. The ramshackle pattern of pre-war Malaya was not to be revived when liberation came. Instead, the whole block of territories in Malaya and Borneo was to be unified with Singapore as their capital.[122] Later this was modified to exclude Singapore and Borneo; but the purpose remained the same. Malaya was to be transformed into a proper colonial state: an effective central administration, long resisted by the sultans, would accelerate Malaya's economic development and provide far more effectively for its defence.[123] A new Malayan Union was to be erected on the wreckage of the old Malaya.

These sweeping changes reflected London's belief that the weakness of the old system had contributed to the catastrophe of 1942;[124] and the expectation that the gradual military reconquest of the colony would inevitably create a highly centralised administration in its wake.[125] But they also revealed two vital assumptions about Malaya's future importance to the British imperial system. Before the war, Malaya had produced one third of the world's tin and a very substantial share of its rubber. The bulk of both products had been sold in the United States, for dollars. Malaya's trade was more valuable than that of New Zealand and more than half that of India. Economically, Malaya was a young and dynamic colony whose value to Britain was certain to increase: indeed its ability to earn dollars was likely to be critical after the war. Secondly, as we have seen, the British did not intend to abandon their old commercial role in East Asia and China when the war ended. To guard their eastern sea routes they were determined to re-establish themselves firmly in Singapore with a stronger Malaya under British rule to protect its hinterland. India, Burma and Ceylon might advance to dominion status, but the Indian Ocean and the Bay of Bengal would remain a British lake. Malaya was the vital strategic bulwark on the eastern flank of British Asia, as well as its weakest and most fragmented unit. Now it was to be soldered together the better to serve the purpose of imperial policy.

As soon as the war ended, therefore, a senior British ex-proconsul was dispatched to Malaya and extracted from the nervous sultans an agreement to surrender their old treaties with Britain. In January 1946 the new Union constitution was announced. It reduced the sultans to figureheads and their states to little more than English counties. Administrative and financial control was to be centralised in a new government presided over not by a high commissioner but (ominously) by a governor.[126] No less objectionable in Malay eyes, citizenship in the Union was to be extended to the bulk of the Indian and Chinese population, a measure which was designed not simply to remedy an injustice but to check the growing appeal of communism among Malayan Chinese and to align Chinese interests with the British drive to bundle the Malays and their sultans down the road to economic development and political centralisation.[127] The result, though not predicted, was predictable. The sultans, having caught their breath, protested bitterly. In March 1946 a new nationalist movement, the United Malays National Organisation (UMNO) sprang into life to protest against 'annexation'. By May, the local British authorities, alarmed by Malay reaction and already grappling with extensive political and social unrest among the Chinese, had effectively abandoned the Union and reopened negotiations with the sultans. The outcome was a revealing compromise. The sovereignty of the sultans was restored; the governor reverted to a high commissioner; the States regained some of their financial powers. But a real federal government nevertheless emerged uniting the old FMS and UMS and controlling the bulk of Malayan revenues. In return the British scrapped the citizenship proposals of 1946: now only a small minority of Chinese and Indians were to enjoy the benefits of federal citizenship.[128] Malay predominance was assured.

Grudgingly London agreed to this embarrassing U-turn in June 1947, significantly at the moment when the partition crisis in India was reaching its height, when Britain's future relations with Burma and Ceylon still hung in the balance, and, above all, at a time when the cabinet was seriously alarmed that Dutch resistance to Malay nationalism in Indonesia might intensify Malay opposition to British rule on the peninsula.[129] But though they had been forced to modify the drastic boldness of their original scheme, the British had achieved their prime object of pulling their Malayan dependencies together into a stronger political unit. Nor had they conceded any promise of early self-government, let alone of independence. The contrast with Burma, where British rule had also vanished in 1942, is striking. In Malaya the British enjoyed two vital advantages denied them elsewhere in Asia. Firstly, Malay nationalism was very largely under the control of socially conservative rulers who were reluctant to attempt all-out conflict with the British and keenly apprehensive that it might lead to the kind of democratic and republican nationalism that had grown up across the straits in Indonesia. Secondly, the Malays as a community were fearful of Chinese domination in political, as already in economic life. To resist it, and to suppress the wartime Chinese guerrilla units still at large in the peninsula required British assistance. Thus the federation scheme concealed a classic colonial trade-off, a mutual dependence. But within four months of its inauguration a new and far more testing emergency was to begin.

THE CRISIS IN THE MIDDLE EAST

Even as they struggled with increasing desperation to bring Mohammed to the mountain in India, the British suffered setback after setback in their search for a new political settlement in the Middle East which would combine stability with the protection of their all-important security interests in the region. Some of the same forces which helped to shatter British political authority in the Indian sub-continent – inflation, ideological turbulence and the hideous twist that the politics of the war period gave to communal conflicts – were at hand in the Middle East as well. The problem that confronted the British was, as in India, how they should define or redefine their interests, and how far they should go in defending them if, in doing so, they risked a major armed confrontation with local opinion, Arab or Jewish. At a moment when they were extremely nervous of intervention from outside in the form of Russian expansion and under intense economic pressure at home the premium on caution was unusually high.

When the war ended the British dominated the Middle East militarily and politically. In their two mandates, Palestine and Trans-Jordan, they were the ruling power. Iraq and Egypt, the leading independent states of the region, were bound to them by treaties of alliance which conferred extensive military rights on the British. In both countries the British had enforced cooperation during the war years. Syria and Lebanon – defunct French mandates – were under effective British control. The only exceptions to this predominance were in Saudi Arabia where American influence was growing, and in Iran which had been jointly occupied with Soviet Russia in 1941 and where the British waited anxiously to see if Stalin would withdraw. But for all the convenience of this wartime supremacy, the British well knew that they had to find ways of pursuing their interests that did not depend on massive military power with its colossal costs. Once the war was over, cooperation with Middle Eastern politicians would have to replace the coercive methods on which they had relied since 1940.

Throughout the whole period from the end of the war to their baffled withdrawal from Palestine in May 1948, the overwhelming preoccupation of British policy was fear of Soviet expansion into the Mediterranean and Middle East as Russian influence poured back into regions it had abandoned in the collapse of 1918 and the era of isolation that followed it. Greece, Turkey, Iraq and Iran – the 'northern tier' of Near and Middle Eastern states – all seemed vulnerable to Soviet pressure, subversion or conquest. Stalin's refusal to leave Iran at the agreed time in 1946, and the struggle for communist rule in Greece seemed hard evidence of the dangers that the strategists foresaw. As we have seen, Attlee's reaction was to question the value to Britain of attempting to defend such a vast and unstable region and to urge a great strategic withdrawal that would place a 'wide glacis of desert and Arabs' between British possessions and Russia. But the government's professional advisers in the Foreign Office and among the Chiefs of Staff, as well as the new Foreign Secretary, Bevin, regarded the exclusion of Soviet influence and the maintenance of Britain's pre-war ties with the Arab states as of overriding importance. If Britain withdrew, to be replaced by Soviet Russia, a fundamental shift would have occurred in the strategic balance of the world. Russian power, not British, would dominate the eastern Mediterranean, the north-eastern approaches to Africa up the Nile, the Red Sea and the Persian Gulf with its access to the Indian Ocean. With the future of Anglo-Indian relations in the balance, one of the most powerful arguments for continuing friendship and co-operation – shared strategic interests – would have vanished. Britain's dollar-free oil would be at risk. And the great power prestige which lubricated British diplomacy around the world would have drained away. All these arguments could be deployed against any suggestion that Britain could afford to evacuate the Middle East. And as the fear of a general conflict with Russia developed in 1946–47, the Chiefs of Staff reinforced them with a new and dramatic claim that the strategic value of the Middle East to Britain, quite apart from its growing oil production, had been decisively enhanced by the outcome of the war.

Their reasoning was based upon the crucial importance of air power to the defence of Britain. If Britain was to find herself at war with the Russians without her strategic positions in the Middle East, they argued, 'we lose the air bases vital for the action which alone can decrease the weight of attack on the United Kingdom . . . .'[130] Britain would begin the war in the 'outer ring' of the North American continent, South Africa, Australia and New Zealand with no effective air bases except those at home from which to strike at Russia. The United Kingdom, they concluded in a grim reminder of 1940, 'would begin the war by fighting in the last ditch, and it is open to serious doubt whether she could survive so long'.[131] By contrast, retention of the Middle East, especially of its air bases, would allow Britain to strike at Russia's industrial heartland in the Ukraine and at her oil supply in the Caucasus, less than 500 miles from Britain's Arab ally Iraq. Standing firm in the Middle East, according to this strategic view, was no longer a matter of guarding the routes to empire. Now the Middle East was a vital defensive outwork of Britain herself.

Nevertheless, Bevin and the Foreign Office intended that Britain's post-war presence in the region should be remodelled in ways that would reconcile Arab feeling and avert anti-British nationalism. They were sensitive to the growing signs of resentment and unrest and anxious that Britain's influence in the region should not be damaged by disorder and upheaval in the Arab states. There were three aspects to this new approach. The first was the successful operation to lever the French out of the Middle East by securing the independence of Syria and Lebanon.[132] This would be popular and would simplify Anglo-Arab relationships. The second was Bevin's brainchild. British influence should be thrown behind projects for the economic and social development of the Middle East, and Britain should make friends among the radicals and reformers in Arab societies, whose power was visibly growing, and win their acceptance for a 'partnership' with Britain. Thirdly, as part of the New Look of the British presence, the pre-war treaties with Egypt and Iraq would be renegotiated in a spirit of mutual goodwill and cooperation, to take account of Arab susceptibilities. The signs of British domination, distressingly visible in the war years, would be replaced by tactful self-effacement. After all, the reduction of the military presence to the minimum required by the strategic purposes described above appeared as much in Britain's interest as that of the Egyptians or Iraqis.

This was the healing ointment with which Bevin and his advisers proposed to soothe the inflamed condition of Arab and Egyptian opinion at the end of the war. Unfortunately, two large and troublesome flies prevented any cure it might have effected. The first of these was the impossibility of reaching any agreement with the Egyptians on a new treaty.

After 1945, as before 1939, Egypt lay at the heart of British strategic thinking about the Middle East. The Second World War like the First had brought home what an incalculable asset it was in a world war to control Egypt with its air fields, its large labour force, its agriculture, its front door on the Mediterranean and its back door into the Red Sea and the Indian Ocean, and, above all, the Canal. The bases built up in the Canal Zone were, by 1945, a huge military investment with ten air fields and nearly 40 camps, together capable of servicing and maintaining an army of half a million or more. During the Second World War, in fact, the British treated the whole of Egypt as one huge base, and British troops were stationed in Cairo and Alexandria.[133]

But as soon as the war ended the Egyptian government asked for negotiations to end Britain's military presence in the country altogether. A wave of strikes, demonstrations and bombings in which a number of British were killed emphasised the need for speed and flexibility in London. At the outset Bevin told the cabinet that the aim was to draw Egypt into a regional defence system while retaining peacetime facilities in the country for the army and the R.A.F.[134] But as violence persisted in Egypt, Attlee and Bevin became more and more nervous about a serious clash between British troops and Egyptian demonstrators.[135] They pressed the Defence Committee and then the cabinet to agree that the British negotiating terms should offer to withdraw British troops from Cairo and Alexandria immediately and from the whole of Egypt in five years – an offer which, it was hoped, would create a friendly atmosphere in which defence cooperation could then be discussed.[136] On 6 May 1946, not without opposition, the cabinet agreed that this historic offer should be made.[137] But as so often happened in Middle East or colonial affairs, the British were disappointed at the response to their magnanimity. The Egyptian negotiators refused to agree to Britain's automatic right to reoccupy the Canal Zone bases in the event of an emergency.[138] Lord Stansgate, the Air Minister who had led the British team, now argued that sufficient concessions must be made to win the Egyptians over. 'The Cabinet must realise', he delared, 'that the alternative to a treaty on the lines now proposed would be an Egypt united in hostility to us and supported by the Arab world'.[139] Britain should accept a Joint Defence Board but without the *right* to re-enter the bases. In a crisis there should be consultation on mutual assistance. This argument was denounced by Alanbrooke, the professional head of the army as 'the slippery slope of concession' and there was other opposition. But the next day Bevin and Attlee pushed through the concession, arguing that without Egyptian goodwill no treaty was any use and claiming that the alternative was to maintain Britain's military rights by main force – a course, they suggested, that Parliament would reject.[141]

As it turned out, this discussion was academic. The Egyptian negotiators were apprehensive of agreeing to a treaty which bound Egypt to give any form of military assistance to Britain: popular feeling (however manipulated) and the threat of assassination made the risks of 'political suicide' peculiarly real in Cairo. Party rivalries worked against compromise, partly because no group wished to see its competitors win the political jackpot by making a successful and popular settlement of the pre-eminent national question – anyway a difficult enough task. Negotiations actually broke down over the future of the Sudan – once Egypt's colony, theoretically co-administered with Britain since 1899, but in practice controlled by the British. Egyptian leaders demanded a much larger say in Sudanese affairs and the promise that one day the Sudan would be re-united with Egypt. Perhaps such a concession might have won over enough politicians in Cairo to make a treaty work, but the British refused. Discussions were broken off in January 1947. The British insisted on their right to stay in the Canal Zone until the 1936 treaty expired in 1956, and the Egyptians tried eventually to persuade the United Nations Security Council to declare that treaty void and to order the British troops out.

In the light of subsequent events the readiness of Bevin and Attlee to agree to withdraw all British troops from Egypt and the Suez base in exchange only for a Joint Defence Board and a treaty requiring consultation on mutual assistance if the Middle East was threatened by external attack, but with no *right* to reoccupy the vital base facilities, appears very striking, confirmation seemingly of their implicit recognition of Britain's decaying power. Here, perhaps, was a first step towards giving up domination in the Middle East altogether. Closer inspection suggests that (however matters turned out in the longer run) this was not their *intention* and makes the reaction of Egyptian politicians more understandable. For the British were not of course talking of pulling out of the Middle East altogether. Far from it. When Montgomery succeeded Alanbrooke as Chief of the Imperial

General Staff in June 1946, he accepted the political case for leaving Egypt, but his list of conditions is revealing. As well as the right to return to the bases, Montgomery gave as minimum requirements: full military rights in Libya with air bases; land and air forces in Cyprus; air bases in Trans-Jordan; a strong position in the Sudan and full military rights in Palestine.[142] Although they discarded the right of return, Bevin and Attlee accepted the rest of Montgomery's conditions. Bevin himself told the Defence Committee in January 1947 that Palestine was strategically necessary to retention of Britain's Middle East position.[143] Ringed by British bases, with the Royal Navy at Malta, Egypt was unlikely to refuse British 'requests' for assistance and the use of the Suez base in time of war – any more than King Farouk in 1942 dared refuse to change his premier when his palace was surrounded by British tanks.

The most important of the conditions laid down by Montgomery was the use of Palestine, conveniently situated and ruled by Britain, as a mandate. Palestine was also vital to British efforts to improve Anglo-Arab relations and win Arab cooperation in the defence and development of the region since it was *the* great issue that could create a common Arab front against Britain. The British intended to find a solution to Arab-Jewish conflict in Palestine which would satisfy the Arab states, but at the same time permit them to use the country as their main Middle East base in peacetime – so as to withdraw from Suez and clear the way for better Anglo-Egyptian relations. But this ambitious plan went disastrously wrong. At the very moment when the British began to regard Palestine as of greater strategic value than ever before, their control of the country collapsed.

In 1945 British policy in Palestine was still based upon the famous White Paper of 1939, the terms of which had been designed to allay Arab fears that they would be swamped by the Jewish immigration set in motion by Hitler's policies in Europe. No more than 75,000 Jews, it said, were to be admitted over the following 5 years. Further Jewish immigration would require the (unlikely) consent of the Arabs. And an independent Palestine was to be established within ten years. The implications were obvious. The Jews would remain a minority and Palestine would become independent as a predominantly Arab state. The Zionist dream of a separate Jewish state was definitely ruled out.[144]

Before the war, the main consideration in London had been the necessity of damping down the Arab hostility to Jewish immigration which had led to the insurrection of 1936–39; and, at a time when Britain's diplomatic and military resources were already strained past their limit, of preserving good relations with all the Arab states. After 1945, these objectives seemed just as vital, but now there were countervailing pressures. Among the refugees and displaced persons left in the ruins of Hitler's Europe were many thousands of Jews desperate to go to Palestine. Knowledge of the Holocaust made their wishes much more difficult to resist and intensified the feverish determination of the would-be immigrants. Their plight and the cause of Jewish immigration generally aroused intense concern in the United States where the Jewish community was wealthy, influential and, in certain places, of key electoral importance. It would be acutely difficult for debt-ridden Britain, dependent on American aid, to ignore the wishes of the American government whose cooperation was necessary over such a wide range of issues. Thirdly, as a result of the war in the Middle East and the reaction of many Jews to the 1939 White Paper, Anglo-Jewish relations had changed decisively. The Jewish leadership had swung away from cooperation with Britain and increasingly regarded the Mandate government as an enemy to be defeated. The Jewish underground army, the Haganah, was now well-armed and organised, while the later years of the war had already seen the emergence of Jewish terrorist organisations like the Stern Gang and the Irgun. The narrow path along which the policy makers had trod before 1939 had become razor thin.

The initial problem confronting the British was how far to give way to the pressure, emanating from Washington, to allow in perhaps 100,000 Jewish immigrants immediately. The trouble was that the immigration question would raise all kinds of other issues. Any concession was bound to antagonise the Arabs. Moreover, allowing in a substantial number of Jews would mean either partitioning Palestine – an extremely difficult operation, anathema to the Arabs and ruled out in 1939 – or prolonging British administration indefinitely to keep peace between the two communities and to prevent an independent Arab-run Palestine closing the door. In either case the promises made to the Arabs in 1939 would be broken with unpredictable political consequences. But clearly the great effort that Bevin wanted to build a new Anglo-Arab partnership was likely to be an early victim.

Bevin and the Foreign Office were determined to avoid partition if possible. Instead the British set out to draw the Americans into the Palestine problem, partly as a way of dampening ill-informed enthusiasms in the White House, partly in the hope that as American policy makers recognised the complexities of the issue, and the strategic significance of the Arab world, they would exert moderating pressure upon the Zionists. But even though the American officials in the State Department understood and sympathised with London's fears, this approach made little headway. Truman and his White House advisers dared not ignore the electoral weight of Jewish votes nor the influence inside and outside the Democratic Party of Jewish organisations and pressure groups. In October 1946, to British rage and dismay, Truman publicly supported the swift entry of 100,000 Jews and the partition of Palestine. All efforts to agree a common Anglo-American policy acceptable to Arabs and Jews came to nothing.[145]

Meanwhile the urgency of some agreement on Palestine's future was increasing all the time. This was not an old-style colonial problem which could be relied upon to die away in due course as a wave of discontent spent its force and receded. The construction of an Anglo-Arab partnership against Soviet influence, the creation of a regional defence system, the negotiations with Egypt were all affected by Arab perceptions of British policy in Palestine – or were thought to be. In Palestine itself the British were obliged to maintain some 100,000 troops by 1946 to help keep order as the Haganah and the Jewish terrorist groups began a campaign of bombing and assassination, the most dramatic instance of which was the explosion at the King David's Hotel in Jerusalem in July 1946 when some 92 people were killed.[146] The pressure of terrorist violence, the pressure of Arab relations, the pressures of the Anglo-American relationship, the pressure for economy and demobilisation, all drove the British remorselessly.

The solution most favoured in the British government had arisen out of an abortive Anglo-American plan in the middle of 1946. It proposed not partition but a system of provincial autonomy in which Palestine would be divided into Arab and Jewish provinces under a central administration over which a British high commissioner would preside. With direct control of Jerusalem and the Negev Desert, and over defence and foreign affairs, the British would be able to use Palestine for whatever military purposes they wanted.[147] But by early 1947 it was clear that neither this plan nor any variant of it could attract enough backing among Jews or Arabs to have any chance of success. In February 1947 Bevin put to the cabinet his last throw:

Britain would refer the issue to the United Nations with the implied threat of British resignation of the mandate if some agreed solution failed to emerge. In the short term, the British probably hoped that the prospect of international discussion and a decision by the United Nations (discussion could not take place before the session in September 1947) would push the two sides into moderation and compromise. There was no question as yet of actually giving up British control.[148]

In India, as we have seen, the declared intent to end British rule had helped to push both sides into reluctant agreement on the terms of partition. In Palestine a similar prospect had no such effect. There were several reasons. On the Arab side almost everything conspired against the acceptability of a compromise. The Palestinian Arabs themselves were divided and without an effective leadership. The pre-war leaders, exiled for their part in the revolt of 1936–39, had gambled on an Axis victory and lost. The organisation of the Palestine Arabs into a new political movement whose leaders would have sufficient authority to negotiate had hardly begun. Instead the initiative was taken by the leaders of the Arab states as self-appointed trustees of the Palestinians. But they too were divided by rivalry and mutual suspicion: the king of Saudi Arabia against the Hashemite kings of Trans-Jordan and Iraq; Trans-Jordan and Iraq against Syria for pre-eminence in Palestine. Both Trans-Jordan and Iraq dreamt of the absorption of Syria. The king of Trans-Jordan was eager to annex the Arab areas of Palestine to his own desert state. Egypt wanted to maintain and enhance her status as the leading Arab state. To all, except perhaps Trans-Jordan, to settle along the lines of a compromise, let alone of partition, risked not only loss of prestige in the Arab world but also a furious agitation at home where popular opinion had been encouraged to view Palestine, rather than domestic social and economic questions, as the acid test of their leaders' political virtue.[149]

On the Jewish side conditions were no more propitious. The old Zionist tradition of friendship with Britain had been smashed by the shock of the 1939 White Paper. During the war, the emergence of the terrorist groups and the Holocaust changed the climate of opinion in the Yishuv – the Jewish community in Palestine. The Zionist political leadership was fearful of a compromise which would allow the dissident leaders of the Stern Gang or the Irgun to discredit them and erode their political authority. They dared not settle for anything short of a Jewish state, and one large enough to absorb many more immigrants. Moreover, they were buoyed up in 1946–47 by encouragement from the United States and hopes of American aid. Above all, perhaps, the Zionist leaders were aware that the aftermath of the war presented them with an historic opportunity which was unlikely to recur. Palestine was still a mandate. The Arabs were disorganised. Much vocal international opinion was deeply sympathetic. The convulsion in Europe, the hundreds of thousands of Jewish refugees it had created, and the magical appeal that Palestine held for them, offered the hope that the great diaspora of so many centuries before could be reversed – if only the tide of Jewish migration was allowed to flow in. It was now or never. If the Zionist movement failed to secure a Jewish state, if the flood of refugees was turned elsewhere, if Arab opinion was allowed to organise a more effective resistance, then Zionism in Palestine would become a lost cause. The momentum towards expansion and the attainment of a Jewish state had to be maintained.

It was thus not simply the conflict of Arab and Jewish interests that frustrated the British and led them to throw in their hand. It was the degree to which Palestine had become an *international* problem, and the peculiar international difficulties the British faced at that moment which made it insoluble. On the one hand there was the extent to which the Arab states had come to be involved in Palestine's affairs, their jealousies and rivalries, and Britain's apparent need, no less than in 1939, to retain their goodwill in the face of a great power enemy, on the other, the extent of American sympathy for the Zionists and Britain's dependence on American friendship and cooperation. Not least there was the additional complication that a local settlement would require the sanction of the United Nations – since Palestine was a Mandate not a colony.

It was hardly surprising therefore that Bevin's gesture failed to achieve a breakthrough. Instead it proved to be the prelude to the cabinet decision in September 1947 to resign the Mandate and withdraw both troops and the civil administration by the middle of 1948 in an act of abdication for which there was no imperial precedent. Two factors lay behind that decision. The first was the increasing ungovernability of the Mandate and the growing embarrassment this was causing the government in London. Ever since the middle of 1946 ministers had drawn back from the prospect of repressive measures against the Jewish community sufficiently draconian to root out the terrorist organisations or intimidate Jewish opinion into disowning them. Undoubtedly this hesitation was based on concern about

American reaction,[150] though the longstanding Zionist associations of the Labour Party itself were a further restraint. It was also open to doubt whether the British garrison in Palestine had the resources to undertake a full-scale operation of the kind required – given the extent to which the Jewish community was politically mobilised.[151] Ministers preferred to pin their hopes upon winning the cooperation of moderate Jewish leaders. But whatever the reason, the result by mid 1947 was a situation in which Jewish terrorists attacked the government and army with impunity, destroying their ability to operate effectively.[152] Frustration and resentment at home reached a climax over the affair of the two British sergeants kidnapped as a reprisal and then hanged by their Irgun captors.[153] The second factor was the report drawn up by the United Nations special committee on Palestine (UNSCOP) which recommended partition. As the mandatory power, it would fall to Britain to carry this through if it were approved by the United Nations General Assembly.

This was the actual trigger for the British decision to withdraw. Whatever else, Bevin was determined that Britain should neither carry out such a policy nor be implicated in it. Partition, he told his cabinet colleagues, would lead to an Arab rising. If Britain tried to implement it 'we should . . . be engaged in suppressing Arab resistance in Palestine, and thus antagonising the Arab states, at a time when our whole political and strategic system in the Middle East must be founded on cooperation with those States'. The existence of a Jewish state was bound to damage British interests. Yet Britain could not easily impose a solution contrary to the wishes of the United Nations (if it adopted the UNSCOP report). The only answer was to resign the Mandate and leave:[154] a conclusion endorsed by the cabinet on 29 September 1947. The date of departure was eventually fixed for the end of May 1948.

It was not to be hoped that this drastic if unheroic solution would leave Britain's general Middle East position intact. The British could no longer directly influence the outcome of the Palestine conflict. They were sure to lose their old military rights in the Mandate. Their prestige was bound to suffer.[155] Nevertheless, as Bevin had made clear, giving up the Mandate was not part of a staged withdrawal from the Middle East, but a deliberate and calculated step to relieve British influence in the Arab states of a dangerous incubus. Mean-while, other efforts were being made to recoup the loss of strategic facilities, especially since the future of British bases in Egypt remained somewhat uncertain. Attlee and Bevin agreed that Britain must have ample military rights in eastern Libya. Indeed, no sooner had they washed their hands of Palestine than they were intriguing for a new mandate from the United Nations preferably for Libya as a whole.[156] The uncertainty over Anglo-Egyptian relations, insisted Bevin, made it essential to strengthen Britain's grip in the Sudan,[157] whose strategic value would be much enhanced if the Suez base was abandoned. And when it came to the partition of Palestine, the British hoped that the Arab share would be peacefully annexed to the kingdom of Trans-Jordan, their closest ally in the Arab world with whom they already had a treaty of alliance.[158] Moreover, once it was clear that the Egyptians were not going to accept the terms offered in June 1946, the cabinet, on Bevin's advice, decided to stand firm and insist on British military rights under the 1936 treaty.[159] When the Egyptians appealed to the UN Security Council to declare the treaty void, the British delegation resisted vigorously. In September 1947 the issue was shelved indefinitely in the absence of any agreement. As so often before in Anglo-Egyptian relations, the British had decided to sit out the storm, to wait for popular excitement to subside and a more compliant government to emerge. Certainly, in 1948 political conditions were unpromising, as the British found again when they tried to renegotiate their alliance treaty with Iraq. There too they were forced to stand pat on their existing rights.

By 1948, indeed, the optimism and confidence of Bevin's plans for a constructive, reforming British role in the Middle East had completely disappeared. Far from holding the initiative in building a new Anglo-Arab partnership, the British found themselves embattled in their old treaty rights, the butt of popular resentment and the whipping boy of local politicians – especially in Egypt. By resigning the Palestine mandate they gave up all control over the Zionists whose subsequent (and unexpected) military successes in the Arab-Jewish war further destabilised the politics of the Arab world. Britain had escaped a general Arab campaign against her interests in the region – the Foreign Office's nightmare. And Egyptian nationalism was still far too feeble to *enforce* British withdrawal from the Canal Zone. But now Britain was forced to defend her military rights and bases by a large and costly garrison, in contrast to pre-war practice, while the policy makers remained uncomfortably aware that with the bases question unresolved the turbulence of post-war Egyptian politics was always liable to focus on Britain's military presence as a target for unrest and disorder. With Russian and American interest and influence growing, the strains and stresses of remaining *the* great power in the Middle East could only increase, whatever the arguments about grand strategy and oil. Even so, despite their post-war difficulties, the British had yet to conclude that their general position in the region had become untenable.

CONCLUSION

Withdrawal from India, Burma and Ceylon, the abandonment of the Palestine Mandate, the readiness to contemplate military withdrawal from Egypt, expectations of economic catastrophe. All these might be thought unmistakable signs of imperial decay and impending collapse – the imperial system very near the end of its tether. And in a sense they were. British experience in India and Palestine seemed to show that the old empire-builders no longer had the strength or the will to impose their rule on volatile alien populations stirred into large-scale turbulence by forces beyond Britain's control. But should the post-war crisis, for all the weaknesses it revealed in British world power, be seen as a clear demonstration that the retention of a world empire was now beyond Britain's strength? Was this the conclusion the policy makers drew? Was it so in fact?

There can be little doubt that, while the retreat from colonial rule in South Asia and Palestine was not *simply* a consequence of economic weakness and an overstrained military machine, it was a response to the general pressure which the multiple crises and commitments of the aftermath of war brought to bear upon the nerve centre of the imperial system in London. Although they resisted a drastic run-down of Britain's armed services on the model of 1919-21, Bevin and Attlee could not have contemplated courses of action which actually *increased* the demands on British manpower and finance. That rule out confrontation and repression except in the very short term, in the most vital places or in the most favourable circumstances. This was not a radical conclusion to draw. Since the early nineteenth century at least British foreign and imperial policy had made a virtue of flexibility and of an acute appreciation of the limits of British strength. Britain's long career as a world power could be attributed, as much as to anything else, to the wary caution of her policy makers in a century in which Spain, Russia, Turkey, France, Italy, Germany and Japan had all come to terrible grief through catastrophic misjudgements in foreign policy. Faced in 1945–48 with a very real danger of being heavily embroiled simultaneously in Europe, the Middle East and in India, it is hardly surprising that London's instinct was to reckon discretion the better part of valour. After all, there had never been a time when British power had been equal to a triple burden of that kind.

It is therefore highly misleading to view the events of this crowded period simply in terms of a clash between a decaying imperialism and the new and vigorous Afro-Asian nationalisms (including Zionism) that opposed it. Equally, it would be unwise to regard British policy as infused with a new post-war liberalism in colonial matters, or even with a pragmatic recognition that Britain's great power days were over. In 1945–46, the British had clear ideas about the reshaping of the Middle East and South Asia in ways that would preserve these regions within the ambit of British influence. They would have liked to have swept Jinnah off the board, to have bullied the Congress leaders, to have imposed a settlement in Palestine and to have destroyed the Stern Gang and the Irgun by the kind of repression used in the past (and subsequently in Malaya and East Africa). Without the concatenation effect of 1945–48 it is conceivable that London might have intimidated the Jews into accepting provincial autonomy, or the Arabs into agreeing a partition. The Arab states might have been bribed or threatened into compliance. But everything was against these kinds of tactics. In the Middle East American pressure inflated Zionist hopes and expectations. Russian expansionism magnified the importance of Arab goodwill. In India and Burma, external influences were less immediate, but the British dared not ignore the tide of chaos engulfing Indo-China, Indonesia and China itself and hold out for federation and unity. Everywhere multiple commitments weakened British nerve and muscle and forced the policy makers into hasty bargains that ran counter to British interests as they had once been conceived. For the true significance of the withdrawal of British rule in Palestine, India and Burma (though not Ceylon) was not that it took place, but that the British were unable to prevent the transfer of power occurring in ways that ultimately conflicted with their vital interests in the region. In both cases the *force majeure* of circumstances obliged the British to tolerate outcomes they thoroughly disliked and might, in better times, have struggled much harder to avert.

Unsatisfactory though they were, there is little sign that their experiences in the Middle East and South Asia convinced British leaders that Britain's great power position was untenable or that the imperial system was a white elephant. Palestine's independence had been officially projected before the war; India's widely discussed since the mid 1930s and effectively promised in 1942. Of course, the circumstances in which their independence was achieved were radically different from anything previously envisaged. But the superficial continuity of policy, combined with the survival of British links with the Arab states, India and Ceylon made it difficult to predict how British interests would fare and tempting to assume that with tactful management a great deal might be saved from the wreck. As we shall see in the next chapter, the more favourable turn (from a British point of view) in international politics after 1948 gave considerable encouragement to the notion that Britain's position as the world's third power was safe for an indefinite period.

Even so, as contemporaries were uneasily aware, the events of 1945–48 had weakened British power. The end of the Raj and the partition of India meant the loss of the Indian army whose value as a supplement to British military resources in Asia had always been considerable – not least in two world wars. Henceforth, a divided India would not be the source of strength the planners dreamt of in 1945–46. Never again would the Indian army be available for imperial purposes in the Middle East or South East Asia. Inevitably the burden was transferred to the British army, strengthening the case for national service but inconveniently highlighting the military burden of empire in domestic British politics. Arguably, without their Indian empire the British lacked both the resources and the motive to remain dug in in the Middle East – although this argument was discounted at the time. Arguably, too, by abandoning Palestine so precipitately the British merely accelerated the collapse of the Anglo-Arab relationship rather than, as they hoped, averting it. For the Palestine question after 1948 was to be a powerful destabilising force in the external and domestic politics of the Arab states and hence in Anglo-Arab relations. British inability to settle the question was symptomatic of the new pressures threatening Britain's influence in the region: pressures that grew rapidly in the early 1950s. Finally, there was the 'demonstration effect' which the British as old hands at managing an empire with the minimum of costly coercion took very seriously. If British power could be levered out of *India*, why should it not be blown out of the Gold Coast, or Kenya or Malaya?

But if it was easy to deduce from the immediate post-war years that British power was in decline, it was much less easy to calculate just how fast that decline would be or how far it would go – questions that every colonial nationalist had to ask himself. If the multiple pressures of 1947–48 could be maintained at full intensity, perhaps decline would turn quickly into fall. If not, if the British struck up an alliance with a superpower, if their economy and their nerve recovered, their decline might be of Byzantine slowness. For their part, the British deduced from their travails in India and the Middle East, and from developments to be surveyed in the next chapter, that they both could and should exercise great power influence in large spheres of the world. Post-war changes, far from teaching them the inevitability of a retreat into Europe, stimulated a pattern of great power activity which lasted until the early 1960s.

4   World Power or Imperial Decline?

Whatever their ultimate causes, the events of 1945–48 in India and the Middle East had torn a gaping hole in the fabric of the old pre-war imperial system. British interests in the Middle East were now exposed to new forms of instability. Indian military power was no longer available to meet imperial needs east of Suez. The passage of India, Pakistan, Ceylon and Burma to independence was likely to stir up dormant nationalisms elsewhere. Overall, the implications for the rest of the dependent empire were bound to be substantial. For all its decentralised character, the British empire was a system of sorts. The East African possessions had been acquired to help defend India. Britain's rule in South East Asia and her influence further east had originally been based to a considerable extent on the power, wealth and economic connections conferred by the control of India. How were these subsidiary activities to be maintained once the main base in Asia was lost? More to the point, perhaps, was it not clear by 1948 that the days of colonial empire were numbered? If the British could not summon the power or the will to hold India what would they be able to hold? What indeed would be worth holding? And were not the difficulties of the other main colonial powers in Indo-China and Indonesia a sombre warning that the old colonial order was disintegrating rapidly?

A consideration of these issues might have been expected to overcome any lingering conservatism in London and propel the Labour government, however reluctantly, towards a general reappraisal of colonial policy and imperial strategy – especially since Attlee himself had shown a fitful tendency to take up radical attitudes (in private) on strategic and imperial questions. In fact, of course, although they displayed a remarkable pragmatism over a whole range of issues in colonial and foreign policy, there is no sign that British leaders or their advisers gave up their overriding belief that, by hook or by crook, Britain should remain a great world power.

One commonplace explanation for this apparent determination to

cling to the wreckage maintains that the failure to think radically was
the result of an unthinking adherence to old mental habits and the
persistence of delusions of grandeur. Nor should bureaucratic inertia
be dismissed too readily as a prime factor in the making of policy since
it is reasonable to suppose that in the absence of strong inducements
elaborate administrative systems are slow to abandon the unspoken
assumptions which often justify their very existence. But in the post-
war years this familiar argument is less plausible than usual. The
necessity of change and the severity of the external pressures on
Britain were extraordinarily obvious and generally acknowledged.
The governments of the day responded with a variety of radical
expedients: the construction of a welfare state; nationalisation; the
imposition of peacetime conscription; devaluation. In external policy
particularly, Attlee and Bevin showed a capacity to think out new
policies, and to Bevin belongs the main credit for one of the most
radical innovations of all, the making of the Atlantic Pact. However
fixed in their ways, the policy makers could hardly respond to the
cascading international changes of 1947–52 with a weary 'plus ça
change . . . '. The Berlin crisis, the advent of Russian nuclear weapons,
Britain's entry into NATO, the emergency in Malaya, the triumph of
communism in China, the outbreak of the Korean war, Britain's
setback in Iran and the surge of colonial unrest in West Africa:
collectively, if not singly, their implications for British world power
were far-reaching. Even if their conclusions were conservative, the
policy makers were obliged to ponder the effects of these dramatic
events.

It is conceivable that in some circumstances British leaders, confronted by the evidence of their economic weakness and dwarfing by
the new great powers, and obliged already by the end of 1947 to
authorise retreat from India, Ceylon, Burma and Palestine (except in
Ceylon, without explicit provision for imperial interests) might have
accepted the need for a drastic revision of Britain's international
liabilities or, at the very least, for a sharp turn towards indirect and
informal means of sustaining imperial interests and an acceleration
of constitutional devolution. There had, after all, been some such
response in much less unfavourable circumstances once the dust had
settled at the end of the First World War. There are, indeed, ample
signs that the importance of flexibility and informality was recognised.
But in the five years after 1947 a variety of factors militated against
the tendency to question the fundamentals of British policy and even,

in several important cases, against the adoption of less formal devices for the defence of British interests in the colonial and semi-colonial world.

There was, in the first place, no inclination to assume that the granting of independence in India, Ceylon and Burma carried any direct implications for the treatment of colonial territories elsewhere, especially in Africa whose political evolution was expected to be very different from that of Asia. Indeed, when they looked at their colonial possessions, the British were struck not by the similarities of their constitutional subordination (as were outsiders) but by the extreme variety of their internal social, economic and political conditions. Thus colonies where there were white settlers were approached in quite a different way from those where they were absent. The British were slow to recognise that not everyone would approach colonial issues with their fine sense of distinctions. But, undoubtedly a more powerful consideration in the later 1940s was the seeming impossibility in most British colonies of finding any plausible successor regime on which the running of the colonial state could be devolved – so that 'Indian' solutions to Britain's over-extended commitments appeared quite out of the question. The corollary of this was that in very few places indeed did they face the kind of internal pressures that had driven them out of India. A precipitate colonial withdrawal to match that from India was thus never on the agenda. Moreover, if it had been, it would have had to contend with the sharpened sense in the 1940s of Britain's dependence on colonial sources of supply for her industry and population as well as a strong conviction that the restoration of British trade and finance – a top priority in domestic and external policy – required stability in the extra-European world and a loud British voice in all post-war economic arrangements.[1] Thus a second factor in British thinking was the calculation that, as well as the direct protection of particular economic interests in the Middle East, Malaya or China, the preservation of Britain's wider interests as a trading and investing nation in the emerging international economic order required all the resources of global influence that could be mustered.

The third factor was the belief that the confrontation with the Soviet Union ruled out in many cases the kinds of political solution that might otherwise have been appropriate to British interests and circumstances. Military withdrawal and constitutional progress could not be embarked on where they threatened to create a vacuum for

Soviet influence to enter. This was most obviously true of Malaya and the Middle East states and seemed to be vindicated by the Berlin crisis of 1948 (as evidence of Soviet aggressiveness), the uprising in Malaya, the creation of the People's Republic of China and the launching of the Korean war. Generally, it might be argued, the containment of communism became a new and pressing imperial commitment that showed few signs of diminishing.

The last major influence that argued for caution and conservatism in external policy after 1947 was the absence of any obvious alternative to Britain's striving to remain an independent world power, a power, that is, with interests in every region and the means to defend them. It was considered axiomatic that as an offshore island without wider connections Britain could not retain her independence let alone her standard of living. The character of world politics required her participation in some larger unit or partnership. Subsequently, British failure to recognise the potential of European unity, to take up the leadership of the European movement or to seize the opportunity to construct a united Europe along the lines of British political tradition has been counted as an epic misreading of the writing on the wall: clinging to the imperial coach and four the British missed the European bus. But even at the end of the 1940s, the European option was regarded as a dangerous distraction from Britain's real interests. The European states, their politics and economies devastated by the war, seemed weak and unstable, a source of embarrassment not of strength. 'On merits', concluded a meeting of senior officials from the Treasury, Foreign Office, Board of Trade and Commonwealth Relations Office in January 1949, 'there is no attraction for us in long term economic cooperation with Europe. At best it will be a drain on our resources. At worst it can seriously damage our economy.' Britain had an interest in European recovery. But 'in no circumstances must we assist them beyond the point at which assistance leaves us too weak to be a worthwhile ally for U.S.A. if Europe collapses – i.e. beyond the point at which our own viability is impaired.'[2] Deep distrust of Europe's post-war prospects, combined with memories of Dunkirk and the wartime imperative of Anglo-American strategic partnership to create what might be termed a 'Dunkirk-D-Day syndrome' in British thinking.

The price of accepting the logic of world power was a great and perhaps growing burden of defence and imperial commitments. But acceptance of these was eased politically by the persistence of certain attitudes that were widely shared among professional advisers and the circle of ministers and politicians. If Britain was not a great power on the scale of the United States or the Soviet Union, and if it was doubtful whether she could 'afford to take on any other power whatever in single combat',[3] she was still recognisably a great power, partly by virtue of the wide gulf separating her from the next most powerful state and partly because Britain was still accepted as one of the managers of international society by opinion at home and abroad.[4] Economic weakness could be dismissed as a passing phase. 'Let us wait until our strength is restored', Bevin urged Attlee, 'and let us meanwhile with U.S. help as necessary, hold on to our essential positions'.[5] Amid all the multiple uncertainties of world politics after 1947 it would have needed great desperation to give up Britain's claim to great power status and to accept the degree of vulnerability and dependence then characteristic of the mainland European states. Moreover, British official thinking, as Bevin indicated, was remarkably confident that American help would continue to be forthcoming to prop up British world power and that the Americans would gratefully accept British guidance in the joint management of Anglo-American interests.[6] The development of Anglo-American relations from 1947 to 1950 seemed to provide corroboration for such optimism. World power was a good thing in itself, British leaders might have reasoned at the end of the decade. It was necessary to guarantee British independence and prosperity and with American assistance its burden could be borne.

The apparent viability of great power status had extensive implications for British imperial policy. If it was *desirable* to remain a great power the precipitate abandonment of the empire without provision for British interests was clearly objectionable. If great power status was *viable* for the indefinite future, then colonial self-government could in some cases be deferred and in others made the instrument for defending or promoting British interests and influence. If Britain had a future as a great power, it was worth treating the Commonwealth relationship in a flexible and pragmatic spirit. Indeed, as will be suggested later, assumptions about Britain's place in the world were of key importance in London's approach to colonial self-government, the shaping of the Commonwealth and the timing of the transfers of power. Ironically, those assumptions turned out to be uniformly ill-founded.

It is, therefore, not difficult to explain why, even after transfers of power in India, Burma and Ceylon and the debacle in Palestine, the British showed so little inclination to draw too many gloomy conclusions about their world-position. Nevertheless, it would be wrong to assume that after 1947 London was not confronted by major difficulties. The strain of meeting the defence burdens was immense. In 1947, 1949 and 1951 financial and economic disaster seemed near and in 1951 at least the crisis was directly associated with the costs of rearmament. Britain's economic capacity to remain a world power even with American aid was challenged by the fragility of her trading and financial position. Secondly, the outbreak of the Cold War and its extension round the globe raised the central question of whether an inescapable British commitment to the defence of Western Europe was compatible with global defence arrangements except at an unacceptably high cost. Thirdly, it was far from clear after 1947 that the special relationship with the self-governing states of the Commonwealth which constituted one essential support of Britain's great power influence and status could stand the strains of constitutional diversity and strategic realignment. Commonwealth relationships underwent a fundamental transformation between 1947 and 1952 the full effects of which only gradually became visible. Fourthly, while British authority in colonial and semi-colonial regions escaped the severity of the challenges posed in India and Burma at the war's end, it was subjected in West Africa and Egypt to pressures that tested the resource of the policy makers. In Malaya and Iran where their interests were of great strategic and economic importance, the British were forced into open conflicts, one military the other diplomatic, whose course by the end of 1951 marked out some of the limits of British world power in the post-war era.

THE ECONOMICS OF POST-WAR EMPIRE

The secret of British imperial expansion before 1914 and of her resilience between 1914 and 1945 lay not so much in her military power as in the economic strength which sustained a world-wide influence. Commercial energy and industrial primacy had between them carried British connections into almost every corner of the globe by 1914. In the early inter-war years they continued to be an immensely important foundation for the formal constitutional bonds and less formal ties of sympathy which held the imperial system together. At the economic level, what bound the dominions, the dependencies and the semi-colonial regions where she was dominant to Britain was, in varying degrees, their reliance on British markets for their principal exports, their eagerness to use the banking facilities of London for their international trade, their hunger for British manufactures, capital and, in some cases, immigrants and, not least, their use of sea routes guarded by the Royal Navy for trade and ordinary communications. While Britain remained the world's greatest source of development capital, the principal centre of international finance and the largest market for primary products, the possibility of the colonies achieving real, as opposed to merely constitutional, independence from the mother-country was somewhat limited.

The classic pattern of the imperial economy was, however, considerably modified in the depression years of 1929–39. The drastic fall-off in world trade and the slump in the prices of primary products encouraged self-sufficiency and local industrialisation and undermined the old complementary relationship between metropolis and colonies. The overproduction of primary goods brought the export of British capital virtually to a halt and ended the flow of British migrants to the dominions and settler colonies. Britain herself seemed to turn away from her old preoccupation with export markets. The proportion of her workforce engaged in the production of exports fell from about one in four in 1914 to one in eight at the end of the 1930s.[7] Investment at home in new industries and housing became far more attractive than investment in depression-hit railways in agricultural countries overseas. It looked as if under the terrible battering of the world slump the basic elements of the imperial economy – the financial and commercial connections that underpinned Anglo-dominion relations and held the colonies in thrall – were breaking up.

Of course, the crisis in the world economy which stretched the cohesion of many societies to the limit and which transformed the politics of two of the world's largest industrial nations was bound to affect the trading links of a far-flung empire. But it would be wrong to suppose that those links were snapped. The demand for the primary products which the empire countries exported might have fallen away, but Britain remained by far the best and largest market for them.[8] Moreover, by offering Imperial Preference in 1932 she allowed empire countries to increase their share of that market at a critical time. The relative *stability* of the British market stood out in contrast to the wild fluctuations of demand elsewhere.[9] And because she was still their most important trading partner, Britain continued to act as the banker of the empire not just for the colonies who had no choice but for the dominions as well. Even after London ended the link between sterling and gold in 1931, the dominions (but not Canada) continued to bank their foreign reserves there and to maintain a fixed link between their currencies and sterling. This voluntary association, the 'sterling bloc' was testimony to the strength of long-established trade patterns and the value which even self-governing empire countries attached to their special privileges in the London capital market.

It was the war and not the depression that really transformed Britain's economic relationship with her imperial system. During the war, Britain purchased great quantities of goods and services from the dominions, India and the colonies and paid for them not with exports which had been drastically cut but by crediting their value to the sterling reserves held by empire countries in London. Thus Britain became a great debtor (to the tune of some £3,700 million by 1945) where once she had been the great creditor of the empire. Her wartime inability to supply exports hastened the industrialisation of her dominion partners and India while the mobilisation of the home economy for war, coupled with the demands of reconstruction at its end, transformed the old abundance of manpower and capital – traditionally exported when the economies of the imperial system were expanding – into grave shortages of both. On a broader front, the liquidation of overseas assets in the Americas and elsewhere, and the loss of important markets outside the empire greatly weakened Britain's power as a trading nation and undermined her importance as a marketplace and banker; while the United States emerged unmistakably as the most powerful industrial and trading state for whose goods and currency there was an insatiable demand. The general effect of this transformation on British influence in regions where it had rested on commercial and financial predominance rather than on any constitutional bond was bound to be adverse.[10] But her relations with her own imperial system could not help but be affected also. For her capacity to fulfil her old function as the metropolis of a world empire was now in question. Could she supply manufactured exports in the quantities that the post-war economies of the empire would require? Could she promise the development capital for which most of them were once more eager? Could she even honour promptly the sterling debts incurred during the war? Could she afford to buy the primary products of the empire countries in any volume? Could she recover that old position as a great trader and investor that made her the natural and not just the formal head of a mainly non-industrial empire? If not, then it could be only a matter of time before the empire countries who were free to do so looked elsewhere for economic partners and financial patrons, while the unfree dependencies rebelled against a colonial system that offered no economic benefits. Nor, indeed, without her old financial strength would Britain long have the power to enforce her control of the dependencies.

While the war lasted, these vital issues were left unresolved. The empire countries had accepted the pooling of their export earnings to provide a common fund of dollars and foreign currencies which Britain managed on behalf of the empire-commonwealth war effort. Strict controls were imposed on the exchange of sterling and shortages tolerated as the price of victory. But it could hardly be expected that this willingness to let Britain buy on tick *and* to control the use of hard-earned dollars and gold would continue for very long into the peace, especially if she failed to provide goods on which the wartime accumulations of credit could be spent. As we have seen, in 1945, as part of the terms of the American loan, (that 'economic Munich' as one angry M.P. described it) the British agreed to allow sterling to be freely converted into dollars by mid 1947, restoring at a stroke the old voluntary character of the sterling bloc and ending the elaborate regulations by which the dominions had agreed (and the dependencies been obliged) to forgo the right to exchange their exports for non-sterling goods. But in the crisis year of 1947 the result of this commitment was predictably catastrophic. When sterling became convertible in July, its foreign holders hastened to exchange it for dollars, threatening to wipe out Britain's dollar reserve and destroy the value of sterling as a trading currency. In August the British government abruptly changed course and reimposed strict controls on foreign exchange.

This repudiation of a key condition in the Loan Agreement might have been expected to incur the wrath of the United States and produce a rebellion among the overseas members of the Sterling Area. (Indeed, fear that the empire countries would resent restrictions on the exchange of sterling had been used as an argument for convertibility back in 1945.) But no such storm occurred. American reactions were greatly softened by the new perspective of cold war and of Britain as a battered comrade-in-arms in this new fight. The sterling countries accepted with apparent docility the need to revive regulation of non-sterling transactions and to pool all the dollar earnings of the Area once more in a central fund managed in London. They also accepted by agreement or informally[11] that the large reserves they had built up in London could only be drawn upon at a rate that would not impose too great a strain on the British economy – since the credit concerned would have to be redeemed by British exports. Altogether, the various measures agreed to in 1947 tied the independent members of the Sterling Area far more closely than before 1939 to a common trade policy, limited their rights over the credit they had accumulated and obliged them to purchase a considerably larger proportion of their imports from Britain than they had done in 1938.[12] The much closer economic integration carried through as an emergency measure after 1939 was to be prolonged indefinitely into the peace. It was a paradoxical companion-piece to the independence of India and Pakistan, and the new conception of a more truly equal Commonwealth of Nations.

Why did the dominions accept these constraints on their economic freedom at a moment when Britain's declining strength as a world power had been starkly revealed by the debacle in Palestine, the failure to preserve the unity of India and near economic collapse at home? Partly, because of the sense of loyalty that the war had reinforced. But also because there remained extremely powerful elements of mutual economic dependence. Because Britain was their banker and the bulk of their assets were expressed in sterling, the dominions had an overwhelming interest in keeping her solvent: her financial collapse would ruin them too. Britain was still for most oversea members of the Sterling Area their most important market – in some cases by a huge margin. They were tied to her by longstanding arrangements in their commercial life, by imperial preference, by their links with London's great commodity markets, by the schemes of bulk purchase set up in the war and by their regard for the past stability and reliability of Britain as a customer.[13] The prospect of finding alternative buyers for their great output of primary products was poor: neither food-rich America nor war-torn Europe were so attractive as the British market. The dominions were also anxious to continue their tradition of borrowing for development in London and had reason to fear that unless they cooperated with Britain in the defence of the sterling zone, such capital would not be forthcoming. The British quelled a recalcitrant South Africa by threatening to stop capital exports there if she refused to provide gold for the sterling pool.[14] At this stage, the United States showed little interest in supplying the kind of foreign investment which Britain had long provided.[15] Last and by no means least was the vital fact that the dominions were themselves unable to meet their purchases of dollar goods by their own exports: they too had a vested interest in pooling the reserves of the whole Sterling Area. Indeed it was the dollars which Britain and the Irish Republic received under the Marshall Plan, together with the dollar earnings of the dependent territories (especially Malaya and British West Africa) which provided the hard currency the dominions lacked: a powerful quid pro quo for blocked sterling balances and strict exchange control.[16]

Thus in the looking-glass world of post-war economics, the dominions, including the new dominions in Asia, found that despite British economic weakness and their huge new credits in London, they were less free than ever to break the old imperial economic connection. When the British resorted to devaluation in 1949, without consulting their Sterling Area partners, the latter meekly followed suit.[17] Solidarity and cooperation were strengthened by fears of economic catastrophe, by the belief that the dollar shortage would be a permanent factor in post-war trade, by Britain's near monopoly in the supply of industrial goods, except those paid for in dollars, and by the great increase in exports which Britain actually achieved between 1945 and 1950, at the price of continued domestic austerity.[18] At a time when their survival as a trading state had seemed in doubt, the British had drawn upon the stores of financial and economic influence built up in the great age of expansion before 1929 and had successfully reoriented their trade to escape the disaster that had loomed in 1947. But this new economic pattern with its much heavier dependence on Commonwealth and empire markets than before the war was tied to circumstances of doubtful permanence. By the early 1950s, the dollar shortage had begun to ease; the industrial economies of Europe and Japan revived; the pressure to relax austerity in Britain intensified; the need of Commonwealth countries for investment grew too great for Britain alone to satisfy; and new pressures arose in many Sterling Area countries to diversify their economic relationships and review trading priorities. As the world moved out of the economics of siege and into a freer economic order, Britain's claim to the economic and 'natural' leadership of the Commonwealth-Sterling Area would once again come to depend upon her own industrial strength, commercial enterprise and capital resources. Just as it had done in the century before 1939.

Before the Second World War the idea that the British government should initiate and finance the economic development of her colonial empire had made little headway in London. The orthodox doctrine laid down that colonies should be financially self-sufficient and should raise their own development funds on the London money market. Financial aid from Britain was reserved for emergencies or special circumstances and was usually accompanied by irksome Treasury controls on local spending. In 1929 the first Colonial Development and Welfare Act had relaxed this attitude very slightly by making one million pounds a year available for grants and loans. But the prime object of this measure had been to encourage colonies to buy the products of Britain's older industries, hard-hit by depression and unemployment and it in no sense represented a comprehensive colonial development plan.[19] At the end of the 1930s there was a more significant shift in official attitudes as the depression which struck agricultural countries with particular severity not only destroyed the prospects of economic progress in most tropical colonies but seemed to be actively impoverishing them still further. The report of the Royal Commission which investigated disturbances in the British West Indies indicated a new official awareness that without funds from Britain to encourage new industries and improve health and education, the vicious circle of economic decline would create a spiral of social and political unrest and erode the stability of colonial rule. The relevance of these conclusions to many other tropical colonies smoothed the path for the second colonial development act in 1940 which offered some five million pounds a year to be spent on economic and social improvements.

During the war the propaganda need to present colonial rule in a favourable light as a form of partnership in economic development, and the war-time tendency towards state direction of the economy strengthened this new official orthodoxy, and paved the way for a third act in 1945 providing a total of £120 million over 10 years.[20] But more compelling than economic fashion or public relations was the wartime drive to increase the productiveness of the tropical colonies and to encourage them towards greater self-sufficiency in manufactured goods which Britain could not supply. It was the urgencies of war production which dictated that colonial governments should no longer act as nightwatchmen and become instead a dynamic force promoting economic and social change. Even so, it is likely that the end of the war would have brought about a sharp decline in London's enthusiasm for colonial economic development (as after 1918) but for three connected circumstances.

The first of these was the necessity to find and exploit sources of food and raw materials which did not require payment in dollars, a necessity that grew more urgent once the convertibility crisis of 1947 had revealed the weakness of sterling against the dollar and the danger of a sharp decline in living standards in post-war Britain. The justification for the notorious and ill-fated project to grow groundnuts in East Africa was that without a great new supply of vegetable oils either a reduction in the margarine ration or heavier dollar expenditure would be necessary.[21] The same urgent need to find sterling substitutes for imports from dollar countries lent the white tobacco producers of Southern Rhodesia a new importance and transformed the prospects of what had been a struggling settlement colony. Secondly, London was anxious to encourage the production of colonial commodities that could be sold for dollars and help pay for the essential imports of the Sterling Area as a whole.[22] 'It would gravely worsen the whole dollar balance of the Sterling Area if there were serious interference with Malaya exports' the Colonial Secretary warned the cabinet at the beginning of the Emergency there.[23] As we have seen, the dollar deficit of the Sterling Area was largely redeemed by West African and Malayan exports.[24] The third circumstance was that political subordination of the tropical colonies made them especially vulnerable to restrictions on their economic freedom, in particular the freedom to spend their export earnings where and how they wished. Unlike the self-governing countries of the Sterling Area the colonies had no choice at all but to bank their foreign earnings in London and to obey London's command to pare their dollar purchases to the bone. Moreover, British officials who ruled the tropical colonies had little option but to agree to the bulk purchase schemes by which Britain bought entire crops at what turned out to be considerably below world market prices.[25] And because they controlled the marketing of export crops such as West African cocoa, these same officials were able to channel a large part of the sale proceeds back not to the producer but into reserve funds to be used for capital development. In this way the producers' demand for consumer goods which Britain could not supply was artificially suppressed by a system of forced saving.

Thus the wartime acquisition of extensive regulating powers and the inflated value that the dollar shortage had given to tropical products go a long way towards explaining London's post-war enthusiasm for colonial development. Broadly, economic development was in two forms. The production of crops directly needed to sustain Britain's living standard was to be undertaken by the Overseas Food Corporation. The general encouragement of development schemes designed to improve the productivity of the colonies was to be the province of the Colonial Development Corporation set up with a capital of £100 million in 1948.

But the very suddenness of London's conversion to the gospel of development brought difficulties. The obstacles to rapid economic change, especially in colonial agriculture, were little understood; often basic research had yet to be undertaken.[26] In many colonies even the population statistics were a matter of bold guesswork. The scale of the capital resources required to initiate a real economic revolution was far beyond what Britain could provide in the straitened post-war years. Consequently, colonial governments turned for funds to the reserves which the marketing boards had accumulated by holding back from producers the full proceeds of crop exports. They also levied export taxes on cash crops, thus laying further burdens on rural producers. Whatever the merits of this policy, and they have been vigorously debated,[27] it was unlikely to be popular in the colonial countryside. Nor was the new zeal of colonial officials for the efficiency of native agriculture. Administrative interference and compulsion, the insistence upon new and more onerous methods of cultivation – like terracing – the destruction of diseased plants and livestock, more stringent controls on the rearing of animals, however necessary from a developmental point of view, were easily represented as oppressive or confiscatory acts aimed at subduing the colonial population. Continued pressure on living standards in a number of colonies in the later 1940s made such resentments still harder to dispel. To make matters worse, as the programmes for development got under way, indigenous colonial populations, already suspicious of the widening ambit of governmental intervention, encountered a growing influx of European administrators, experts, instructors, technicians and, in some colonies, settlers, as well as other camp-followers of this new model imperialism. It was scarcely to be expected that this 'second colonial occupation' would pass unnoticed by local society, or that its social and political implications would be welcome.

It is at first sight a curious paradox that as Britain's power declined her economic grip on her imperial system seemed to tighten; that as her economic strength waned the old distaste for turning the empire into a trading bloc made way for the doctrine of Sterling Area cooperation and discriminatory controls. Likewise it seems strange that at a period of maximum economic strain at home policy makers in London should have contemplated with greater enthusiasm than ever before the economic uplift of the tropical colonies. But of course the paradox is more apparent than real. The post-war years did see a great reorientation of British trade and investment towards the countries of the empire-commonwealth, and the importance of the colonies as consumers of British exports was markedly greater after 1945 than before 1939. But these changes were principally a reflection of the special circumstances of the early post-war years and were, at bottom, symptoms of economic weakness and insecurity. The five years after 1947 did not provide a clear indication of Britain's postwar economic prospects although a number of warning signs appeared. British economic recovery had occurred at a time when austerity at home and devastation in Europe and Japan made the exporters' task unusually easy. Even so, devaluation in 1949 and the very severe balance of payments crisis in 1951 showed how acutely vulnerable Britain now was (without the old cushion of a considerable investment income from abroad) to the vagaries of the world economy and how sensitive to the economic policies and performance of the United States. The crisis of 1951 was also a terrifying reminder of the dangers of over-extended defence commitments and of the need to return as much manpower as possible to the civilian sector, if more, worse, sterling crises were not to come. The electorate, too, had signalled (or so it seemed) its impatience with austerity and control. Thus the years 1951–52 marked the end not only of the Labour government which had presided over the post-war defence of empire but also of an 'emergency period' when the ordinary laws of British and international economic behaviour were suspended. The defence of empire and its political management would soon have to be conducted in a cooler and more competitive economic climate.

COLD WAR AND IMPERIAL DEFENCE

Before 1939 it had been a standing object of British foreign policy to avoid entanglements in Europe and membership of any permanent military alliance that would impose peacetime obligations on Britain. At the end of the Napoleonic Wars in 1815 and after the First World War of 1914–18 British leaders had hoped to shake the dust of Europe from their feet and to escape the necessity of ever again intervening on the continent by promoting post-war settlements that eradicated apparent sources of conflict and established a more effective balance of power against aggressor states. By a mixture of luck and judgement, the 1815 settlement performed this function with remarkable success from a British point of view. The settlement of 1919–23 proved less durable and satisfactory and sucked Britain back into the vortex of European politics in less than twenty years. After 1945 the attempt to construct a settlement along these lines was rapidly condemned to complete failure.

Britain's motive for avoiding fixed commitments in Europe was simple. In the first place, membership of a continental military alliance was thought to entail the maintenance of a much larger army than Britain could afford and the use of conscription, odious on economic and libertarian grounds. After the First World War, conscription, so reluctantly introduced in 1916, was abandoned precipitately in 1919. Secondly, and more fundamentally, firm commitments in Europe were widely held to be incompatible with the promotion and defence of Britain's own *global* interests, which required her army, navy and air force to be deployed around the world to garrison her colonies and protect her sea lanes. Generations of policy makers had insisted that for Britain to bind herself rigidly to the maintenance of a particular *status quo* in Europe would destroy the freedom' of action that was vital if her very limited military power *on land* was to be used effectively. At most times, indeed, the defence of India and the settlement colonies had appeared a far more important British commitment than the independence and integrity of 'far-off' European countries such as Poland or Czechoslovakia. The only exceptions to this general rule were the vulnerable Low Countries with their Channel ports and, periodically since 1904, the declining power of France.

Towards the end of the Second World War there were some voices in Britain which called for a revival of the old policy as soon as hostilities ceased, so that Britain could concentrate all her energies on imperial consolidation. But the most influential school of thought was that which looked forward to a consortium of great powers – the United States, the Soviet Union, Britain, France and China – to regulate international affairs, each enjoying a special sphere of interest but cooperating in the maintenance of world peace. Working through the United Nations Organisation, and with a lower rung of regional organisations, this consortium held out the promise of a new international order tough enough to withstand the pressures that had eroded world peace in the 1930s. For the British it held the particular attraction that it would spread the burden of safeguarding Europe against a recurrence of war while allowing them to pursue their own global interests through a more flexible but still closely-articulated empire-commonwealth. Such a scheme seemed to offer the best of all worlds to a declining power. In actuality, of course, this attractive prospect scarcely survived the early months of peace.

What destroyed it was the combination of Russian pressure in eastern, central and south-eastern Europe and the fear that opinion in the United States would reject any formal European commitments after the war. Fear of an internal communist takeover with Soviet encouragement, and of a Soviet military presence in the Mediterranean, forced the British to lend economic and military aid to Greece and Turkey. Eagerness to encourage anti-communist regimes in France and Belgium contributed to the making of the Treaty of Dunkirk in 1947 by which Britain bound herself to come to the aid of France if she were threatened by German resurgence. Between the spring of 1947 and the summer of 1948 East-West tensions in Europe hardened into cold war as Russia confirmed her grip on Eastern Europe and the anti-communist parties, with American economic aid, struggled to restore stability in Western Europe. In these circumstances, all British hope of slowly reducing their European obligations gradually vanished. In January 1948 Ernest Bevin as Foreign Secretary made his famous plea for a union of Western Europe. In March, following the communist coup in Prague, Britain joined France and the Benelux states in the Brussels Pact, a defensive alliance clearly aimed at the threat of Soviet expansion. The prolonged crisis over Berlin in 1948 brought home the dangers of a further European war and accelerated the involvement of the United States in the defence of Western Europe. But the price of American participation in an Atlantic defence organisation was Britain's own military commitment to a permanent European alliance system: the North Atlantic Treaty Organisation established in April 1949. Moreover, on the outbreak of the Korean war in 1950, British leaders plainly felt it expedient to lend military support to a predominantly American war effort and framed their foreign and defence policies more and more on the assumption that Britain's role was to be America's junior partner in a worldwide struggle against communism. The transition from 'splendid isolation' and even from the era of 'limited liability' before 1939 seemed complete.

What significance did this new orientation in British foreign policy hold for the old imperial concerns? Was it a prime cause of Britain's willingness to transfer power in her colonies as the need to concentrate strength in European defence became pressing? Did it mark the real beginnings of a grand turn away from empire and towards Europe? Were the new burdens of the cold war only tolerable if the old burdens of imperial defence were sloughed off? The answers in the short term are broadly negative. Bevin might talk of Western Union, but Attlee was quick to point out that Britain was a power with interests in every continent.[28] Bevin himself was an ardent champion of Britain's extra-European interests. All sides agreed that Britain could not make European commitments incompatible with her empire-common-wealth role, and of which the dominions did not approve. The Commonwealth prime ministers' approval of the Brussels Pact was explicitly sought and given.[29] Nor were Britain's military commitments in Europe seen as marking a new departure with definite implications for the overall structure of imperial defence. The new obligations of the Brussels Pact and NATO were to be discharged not by stationing the bulk of the army on the Rhine but by an air-maritime strategy (after 1949 with an American nuclear component) which assumed that in any future European war Anglo-American forces would repeat the invasion strategy of 1944–45, backed up by a great bomber force.[30] Only with great reluctance did Attlee and the other chiefs of staff accept Montgomery's demand that the need to fight on the ground in Western Europe should be recognised at least in principle.[31] The great virtue of the Atlantic Treaty lay precisely in the fact that it helped to cover Britain's obligations in Europe by the formal extension of the American nuclear umbrella; and relieved Britain of a part of the escalating burden of what was essentially a problem of *home* defence.[32]

Not until the 1950s with the advent of Soviet nuclear weapons did the balance of European and imperial commitments change significantly.[33] In the meantime, there was little sign of any serious revision of pre-war strategic thinking about the need for a British military presence in the Middle and Far East. The division and uncertainty of the service chiefs about the need to stand and fight in Western Europe contrasted vividly with their vehement and united insistence on just such a plan in the Middle East. Thus the loss of Palestine as a base in 1948 hardened British attitudes against military withdrawal from Egypt and reinforced their determination to demand the trusteeship of first Cyrenaica and then the whole of Libya.

In fact, of course, the growing confrontation between the West and the Soviet Union which had begun in Europe served rather to confirm than to undermine the old basis of British imperial strategy. As we have seen, it was fear of Russian expansionism in Greece and Turkey (as well as Iran) after 1945 that made the British so determined to maintain a military presence in the Middle East. The intensification of the cold war after 1947 simply underlined the value of advanced air bases in the region to strike at Russia's southern flank. Similarly, the extension of the cold war to Asia, fear of communist subversion in Malaya and the outbreak of the Korean war checked the kind of debate on strategic objectives which withdrawal from India might otherwise have stimulated.[34] In another more indirect way the growth of antagonism in Europe helped to underpin far-flung imperial commitments. After the First World War, popular resentment had swept away conscription within weeks of the armistice, and wrecked all plans for maintaining a large army. But after the Second, public attitudes were strikingly different. An opinion poll early in 1947 found two-thirds of those polled to be in favour of retaining national service.[35] Limited at first to twelve months in deference to Labour backbench criticism, conscription was extended in 1948 under pressure from the service chiefs to eighteen since 'the progressive liquidation of our overseas commitments which we expected . . . has not been realised as fully or as rapidly as any of us hoped'.[36] Justified implicitly by the prolonged crisis over Berlin, the real aim of the extended term was to offset the extra travelling and training period required for troops serving not only in Germany but in imperial outposts in the Middle and Far East.[37] In the short term at least, a large conscript army,[38] sanctioned by home opinion, filled the manpower gap created by the loss of the Indian army – Britain's great auxiliary source of military power east of Suez before 1939.

But it would be wrong to see the cold war as merely confirming long-held doctrines about the defence of empire while providing a convenient political justification for heavy military spending. There were other less desirable side effects. The instinct of British policy makers had always been to evade, for sound logistical reasons, any sort of worldwide confrontation and to search for ways of separating and localising the threats to their imperial interests. They had good reason to know how easily strategic and political difficulties in one region could enforce unwelcome changes of policy in another. Secondly, they had always feared an encounter with any foreign power that could subvert the loyalty of their colonial subjects and clients. On these grounds, the British had from the first regarded with great apprehension the transformation of their old imperial rival in Asia into the patron of a virulent and extreme anti-colonialism. After 1945, these apprehensions were reinforced by the great growth in the power and prestige of the Soviet Union, and the signs that communism might have great appeal in colonial societies wracked by post-war economic and social turbulence. The Colonial Office was quick to suspect the influence of communism behind the Gold Coast riots of 1948. The policy makers were bound to be uneasy about the impact of such a pervasive and adaptable political creed which invited colonial nationalists everywhere to see themselves as part of a worldwide struggle against an obsolete capitalist imperialism. Although in retrospect a more realistic view may be taken of communist success in penetrating colonial societies, in the 1940s and 1950s the political implications of a global struggle to contain communism introduced an unwelcome external complication into the management of colonial politics and the tempo of constitutional advance.

Secondly, fear of Soviet expansion and engagement in a worldwide cold war forced the policy makers in some places into much less flexible postures than they would have liked and enhanced the influence of the military. Nowhere, perhaps, was this so true as in the Middle East where the logic of compromise with the militant national-ism of Egypt was blunted by vehemently asserted strategic imperatives. Here, and in the Middle East as a whole, the pressures of the cold war encouraged what turned out to be a fatally exaggerated notion of imperial interests. Lastly, there was a more insidious consequence of the new Anglo-American strategic partnership so eagerly desired by British leaders and largely constructed between 1947 and 1952. It was true that American attitudes towards the imperial system had mellowed, that, as the Colonial Secretary reported in 1948, 'the United States have largely come round to our point of view . . . [and] are at present too much preoccupied with communism to spare much time for "British imperialism" '.[39] But it was not to be expected that this patience would endure indefinitely. Driven, as they had been, by fear of the Soviet Union into strategic partnership with the United States as the price, in part, of remaining a great power at all, the British were poorly placed to resist if Washington altered the unofficial conventions by which Britain was allotted predominance among the Western Powers in certain regions; or if their attempts to cling to imperial power met with American disapproval. For the time being, however, it was the *benefits* of strategic partnership that appeared uppermost, as the British enjoyed greater security for their worldwide interests than at any time since the early 1930s. It was only later that the full consequences of global competition, unequal partnership and declining imperial resources made themselves felt.

COMMONWEALTH RELATIONS

British interest in the economic potential of the tropical colonies was a striking post-war novelty. But it did not alter the fact that of the various states and territories that made up the empire-commonwealth it was the five autonomous and self-governing dominions together, after 1947, with India and Pakistan that were regarded in London as by far the most important and valuable. Between them they contained almost all the industrial strength of the overseas empire. In both world wars it was they who had provided the vast additions of fighting manpower to enable the British to carry on the struggle in theatres of conflict thousands of miles from home as well as in Europe. Above all, the 'white dominions' – Canada, Australia, New Zealand and South Africa – were thought of as Britain's most reliable friends and allies, tied to Britain not merely by common interests and political traditions but by the deeper emotional bonds of kith and kin – the legacy of the great and continuing flow of migration from the British Isles.

Before 1939, despite the changes brought by the First World War, it had been possible to assume that the five dominions would continue to maintain a special relationship with Britain, would follow, if sometimes grudgingly, her lead in international affairs, and, when it came to the crunch, would come to her aid in a great war. Strategic and economic interdependence, racial and cultural sympathy, were the bedrock of Anglo-dominion relations and, in British eyes, far out-weighed the formal independence conceded in 1931.[40] But by the latter part of the 1940s, it was clear that the old nexus between Britain and the dominions (now called 'members of the Commonwealth' or 'Commonwealth countries') had changed its character. Economic ties had been modified and strategic relations profoundly altered by the war. The rise of American power in the Atlantic and the decline of British power in the Pacific inevitably affected Britain's relations with Canada, Australia and New Zealand. The Irish Free State had repudiated the fundamental obligation of dominion status by remaining neutral in the war. In South Africa the election of 1948 brought to power a government of strongly republican sympathies fiercely hostile to the British connection. At the same time after 1947 the wisdom of relying on kith, kin and common culture as the invisible cement of Anglo-dominion relations was put in doubt by the extension to India, Pakistan and Ceylon of the same constitutional status as autonomous members of the British Commonwealth. Then in 1948 India and Eire precipitated the issue of whether a republican constitution was compatible with Commonwealth membership. For the British, however, with their economy *in extremis* with vast commitments hanging over from the war, with the challenge to their influence posed by the emerging superpowers, the importance of dominion cooperation and loyalty was greater than ever. Only with their help, reasoned many British policy makers, could Britain remain a world power at all.

Three great issues dominated Britain's relations with the self-governing Commonwealth states in the post-war years. The first was how far the Commonwealth could be fashioned into a much closer grouping with a common foreign policy and an integrated defence, transforming the largely informal partnership of the pre-war era into a close-knit bloc of associated states. The second was whether it would be possible, or desirable, to reconcile the republican aspirations of the Irish and the Indians (and possibly others) with the strongly monarchist traditions of Britain, Australia and New Zealand, and with the entrenched principle of common allegiance to the British Crown. The third was whether the new dominions in Asia could be absorbed into the Commonwealth 'club' of dominions without undermining its habit of informal cooperation and consultation in international affairs. The resolution of these issues was likely to affect Britain's ability to sustain her great power position but also to shape decisively the Commonwealth relationship on which so much store came to be laid.

Well before the war ended the idea that Britain could only match the power of her two mighty partners in the Grand Alliance by welding the Commonwealth into a 'third force' had exercised a considerable attraction for British leaders.[41] The success of wartime military cooperation between Britain and the dominions, the legacy of the years alone between 1939 and 1941 and a sense of shared dependence on American power encouraged a somewhat fanciful conception of future Commonwealth solidarity which glossed over the likely changes that peace would bring. Thus in the autumn of 1945, Attlee, despite his own reservations about the viability of a Commonwealth system of defence,[42] raised the question of defence cooperation with a reluctant Mackenzie King, the Canadian premier.[43] In readiness for the dominion prime ministers' meeting in May 1946, the British Chiefs of Staff prepared an elaborate plan which invited the dominions to see themselves as 'main support areas' in the defence of the Commonwealth, with responsibility for guarding the surrounding strategic zone, and jointly responsible with other Commonwealth members for the defence of sea and air communications between them.[44] Behind all this lay the conviction that without the promise of dominion help the burdens of defence would be too much for an exhausted British economy. But the course of the prime ministers' meeting left little doubt about the fate of such plans. Mackenzie King reiterated his objections to any form of centralisation in the making of defence and foreign policy. When Attlee and Bevin stressed Britain's difficulties and fished for promises of aid and cooperation, he refused to make any commitment. The South Africans and Australians promised consideration.[45] But six months later they had still made no proposals.[46]

London took the hint. The 1946 white paper on defence organisation carefully rejected the idea of any centralised machinery and merely proposed the exchange of liaison officers between Britain and the Commonwealth countries. Instead emphasis was laid on the value of 'regional associations' as a 'starting point for future progress in Commonwealth defence'.[47] There was nothing new in the aversion of the dominions, especially of Canada and South Africa, to a common foreign policy in which London's views would predominate. What was new was the extent to which the dominions after 1945 looked outside the Commonwealth for their security. The Ogdensburg Agreement of 1940 had recognised the strategic interdependence of Canada and the United States; and in 1946 it was not Commonwealth defence but the terms of Canadian-American cooperation that preoccupied Ottawa. Australia and New Zealand, with their eyes on the revival of Japanese power, sought a defence agreement with Britain in 1946 but their real objective was to obtain an American guarantee of their security.[48] For Canada, entry into NATO in 1949 alongside the United States and Britain conveniently reconciled an old conflict of loyalties and interests and emphasised her status as an equal partner with Britain in a larger regional alliance. But Australia and New Zealand, alarmed by American commitments in Europe and the rearming of Japan in the wake of China's fall to communism and the outbreak of the Korean war, gratefully seized the opportunity of alliance with the United States and dared not insist on British participation to which Washington was opposed.[49]

By 1952, with the making of the ANZUS treaty, a new pattern of Commonwealth defence relationships was developing that was quite different from that obtaining before 1939. Before the war, none of the dominions had been in alliance with a foreign power, and while their loyalty to Britain could not be taken for granted, it was not limited by any other formal commitments. Thirteen years later, one old dominion was neutral (Eire) while three of the remaining four, anxious as they may have been to preserve their British links as a counterbalance to American influence, had formally recognised their strategic dependence on the United States. Henceforth, diplomatic or strategic cooperation with Britain was likely to be subject, to some extent, to American approval or acquiescence. By the same token, for the British themselves, strategic cooperation with the United States had become the centrepiece of their defence thinking, even if in the early 1950s the latent conflict between this and the pursuit of imperial strategic objectives elsewhere had not been exposed. Moreover, the value of Anglo-dominion defence partnership was still acknowledged, as the later readiness of Australia and New Zealand to participate in the defence of Malaya indicated. But paradoxically, by the early 1950s it was South Africa, one of the most troublesome dominions between the wars, who became, in strategic terms, Britain's closest Commonwealth partner,[50] because in southern Africa the old basis of pre-war imperial power – territorial possessions and naval supremacy – remained largely intact, and was reinforced by a new local awareness of weakness and isolation.

It was clear then from an early stage after 1945 that the old decentralised tradition of Anglo-dominion relations was to continue in an accentuated form and that the dominions, whether they wished to or not, would find themselves taking a more independent line towards London than had generally been true before 1939. Indeed, in their own interests, it was necessary for the dominions to assert their separate identity lest at the United Nations or elsewhere they be treated by the superpowers as mere appendages of the British empire, colonies in disguise, without an independent stake in the post-war settlements. In general, the British were anxious to fall in with the new mood, recognising that their Commonwealth partners were more valuable as friends if their independent status were fully recognised in Moscow and Washington. To emphasise this, the Dominions Office was tactfully renamed in 1947 and became the Commonwealth Relations Office. In 1948 a cabinet committee recommended that the term 'dominion' be dropped altogether.[51] The same deference to dominion sensitivities about their international status led to the phasing out of the old Imperial Conferences and their replacement by the informal meetings of the Commonwealth premiers. None of these changes, of course, was intended by London to erode the special relationship between Britain and the Commonwealth states: preserving the broad alignment of the Commonwealth countries with Britain in international affairs was a vital part of defending British interests around the world with straitened resources. The real question was how that special relationship could be maintained, and what formal constitutional connection, if any, was needed to uphold it.

Before 1939 the dominions, as members of the Commonwealth, were required to recognise the British Crown as their own head of state. The British insisted that a republican constitution was incompatible with membership of the empire-commonwealth and in the 1930s waged a successful campaign of economic pressure to prevent De Valera from declaring an Irish Republic (although after 1937 Eire only recognised the King by virtue of her 'external association' with the Commonwealth). This insistence was partly aimed at countering criticism at home of the extension of full self-government to the Irish and the oversea dominions. But it was also regarded as an ultimate guarantee that Britain's former dependencies would not act in ways hostile to her or damaging to her interests – since to do so would be *ipso facto* against the wishes of their sovereign, coincidentally the British Crown. Of course, the Crown, in its capacity as head of state in South Africa or New Zealand, could not command a dominion to go to war by Britain's side. But the existence of such a powerful constitutional link was one of the most important of the influences on which the British relied in the inter-war years to preserve the unity of their decentralised imperial system.[52]

In 1949, however, this constitutional principle, hitherto so vigorously defended was relaxed at the request of the Indian government which was permitted to remain in the Commonwealth with an explicitly republican constitution subject only to recognising the British Crown as 'head of the Commonwealth'. The wholly voluntary character of Commonwealth membership was reaffirmed. This change has sometimes been represented as merely a natural and inevitable stage in the evolution of the Commonwealth,[53] a counterpart to the recognition of the aspirations of nationalism in the dependencies. But the British attitude on this issue was nothing like as simple or uncalculating as this would make it seem. In 1947 London had refused to bend the rules to allow Burma to become a republic and stay in the Commonwealth. In 1948 no effort was made to persuade Eire to remain within the Commonwealth once the Dublin government had announced its intention of removing the last vestiges of the Crown's role and proclaiming an Irish Republic. But the Indian request produced a flurry of cabinet activity to find ways and means of reconciling a republican India with the entrenched tradition of common allegiance.[54] Moreover, without strong British support for the eventual compromise formula, it is doubtful whether the reservations of the other dominions (though not South Africa) and the objections of the lawyers would have been overcome.

British support did not reflect any enthusiasm for constitutional variety in the Commonwealth. In March 1948 Attlee had urged Nehru to accept common allegiance to the Crown and dismissed a republican constitution as something alien to India.[55] Mountbatten pressed him to abandon the term republic in favour of 'commonwealth' or 'state'.[56] Attlee and some of the dominion premiers were anxious that any new formula should stress the role of the Crown.[57] The virtues of a Commonwealth Privy Council and of a formula by which the Crown would delegate certain powers to the President of India were urged on Nehru,[58] to no avail. And when the final settlement was hammered out in April 1949, it carefully referred to India in particular and avoided sanctioning a new general principle. Far from revealing a positive new concept of the Commonwealth, British policy was shaped by the deliberate calculation of the value of a special Anglo-Indian relationship and of the minimum concession required to preserve it. Burma had not been important enough to justify the trouble and difficulty of revising the constitutional apparatus of the Commonwealth. In Eire the determination of the government to leave the Commonwealth and the lack of any articulate support for continued membership[59] were balanced by the fact that unchanged strategic, economic and demographic realities forced even an avowedly republican government to recognise that the real substance of Anglo-Irish relations would not be affected. But the case of India was very different. It could not be written off like Burma. Nor could there be any confidence that Anglo-Indian relations could take the strain of India's departure or expulsion from the Commonwealth.

The British feared indeed that India without Commonwealth links might turn sharply away from Britain and attempt instead to build up a bloc of Asian states united by their antipathy towards Western colonialism.[60] In 1948–49, with the emergency in Malaya, the continuing independence struggle in the Dutch East Indies, a growing colonial war in Indo-China, the approach of communist victory in China and considerable Anglo-Indian friction over the future of Hyderabad and Kashmir, such fears were far from fanciful. Nehru himself was under pressure from Hindu communalists on the right and communists on the left: neither favoured the Commonwealth connection. Mindful of India's value as a trading partner but above all of its value as a zone of political stability in a continent where communism and Soviet influence seemed to be advancing rapidly, the British were anxious to find ways of preserving the special status of India's links with Britain, and to avoid pushing Nehru into an anti-Western stance. They wanted also to keep open the possibility (not then as remote as it later became) that once the troubled aftermath of independence had settled, India would return to closer economic, diplomatic and perhaps even military cooperation.[61] As it turned out, Nehru too preferred to keep India in the Commonwealth (though his view of its uses was very different from London's) to help counter Soviet pressure and animosity, to balance India's growing dependence on American economic aid and to deny Pakistan the diplomatic advantage of Indian withdrawal.[62]

Thus the London declaration had its roots in the mutual interest of Britain and India in maintaining the tradition of close and informal consultation in international affairs and the avoidance of antagonistic policies: the central elements of the Commonwealth relationship. Faced with turbulence and unrest, especially in South East Asia, the British were eager to foster the impression that Asian nationalists could cooperate with Britain and forestall a wave of anti-Western xenophobia. Plainly, too, close relations between London and Delhi were vital if the British intended to remain the leading foreign power in western Asia and the Indian Ocean[63] – a role highlighted by their retention of Malaya and Singapore and the defence agreement with Ceylon. At its most ambitious this kind of thinking envisaged a new Anglo-Indian partnership which would underwrite the stability of South and South East Asia: a substitute for the vanished Raj. But it was already uncertain by 1949 how far the Indians could be persuaded to contemplate again so old-fashioned a role.

As a solution to the immediate issue of whether Britain and India would drift into mutual indifference and perhaps antagonism this new and more liberal definition of Commonwealth membership was a striking success. It removed what had seemed a formidable barrier to preserving British links with those former dependencies where a different culture and a different tradition of colonial nationalism made the position of the Crown a symbol not of shared equality but of continued subjection. But the extension of Commonwealth membership to the three new Asian states could not by sleight of hand ensure that the pre-war pattern of Anglo-dominion relations would be perpetuated. The new Asian members could not be expected to share the enthusiasm of the white dominions for the great power pretensions of Britain; still less their tolerance or support for British colonial rule. There was in addition a bitter bone of contention between India and South Africa over the treatment of Indians there. Moreover, the far more serious antagonism between India and Pakistan over the outcome of the Partition inevitably reduced the general intimacy of Commonwealth relations and greatly complicated Britain's relations with both. If the purpose of the post-war Commonwealth was the building of a group of like-minded states sharing historical links with Britain, its choice of members was eccentric. But that of course was not the object. For the Commonwealth was not a club in the real sense of the word nor even really an association. It enjoyed no 'natural unity'. Its members had little in common with each other apart from the strength of their *bilateral* ties with Britain. New members were admitted not by the choice of existing members but, in effect, at the discretion of the British government. The post-war Commonwealth was a British creation, constructed for British purposes.

It became a commonplace in the 1950s and 1960s that the Commonwealth was a natural successor to the empire and was held together by devotion to common ideals, especially of democracy and racial partnership. A frothy and grandiose rhetoric sprang up to trumpet its virtues. Colonial rule became in the authorised version of the recent past merely a stage en route for full independence within the Commonwealth. But it is unlikely that policy makers in the later 1940s viewed their pragmatic actions in such a light. Their objects were essentially defensive: to protect old spheres of interest from the inrush of new and potentially hostile influences (not excluding, in the case of India, that of the United States); to buoy up sympathetic elements in the successor states by the offer of international status and prestige, and a certain favouritism in trade and military assistance; and to prevent the dominance within the successor states of parties and movements committed either to Marxism or to the cultivation of xenophobic or utopian self-sufficiency. Acceptance of republican India was symptomatic not of the growth of a new equality, unity and intimacy among members,[64] but of the Commonwealth's transformation into a far more deliberate and self-conscious instrument for the preservation of British influence in the Afro-Asian world. Thus the celebration of racial partnership as a central purpose was of little relevance and still less appeal in the older dominions. At the end of the 1940s these tendencies were still little developed. With Europe's recovery at an early stage, with the future political landscape of East and South East Asia scarcely defined, before Suez or the onset of real transfers of power in Africa, it was perhaps easy to believe that the post-war Commonwealth would serve as an enlarged and effective vehicle of British influence, that the new dominions would become like the old. And difficult to appreciate how acutely the whole structure of Commonwealth relationships really depended on Britain's own capacity to fill the economic and strategic role that had been taken for granted before 1939.

COMMITMENTS AND CONFRONTATIONS

It was clear by 1947 that the war had brought about radical changes in the geography of great power influence and domination across the globe. The Soviet Union's control of Eastern Europe was soon to be completed by the events of 1948, and the revival of Russian influence was already apparent along the northern tier of the Middle Eastern states. The United States, long predominant in the western hemisphere, had assumed by 1947 new responsibilities in the Mediterranean and, most strikingly, seemed to have won an unchallenged primacy in East Asia as the patron of China and the occupier of Japan. In Europe it was the rivalry of the two emerging superpowers which dominated the continent's politics. But extensive though the power and influence of Russia and America had become, it was not yet universal. There was still in the later 1940s a vast region where the British enjoyed a fair field and, at worst, limited competition. What had once been christened the 'Southern British World' stretched from the Middle East and South and East Africa across the Indian Ocean to Malaya and Australasia. It was guarded to the north at Suez and by the British air bases in Iraq; to the east by Singapore; and on the west by the British naval base near Cape Town. For all the upheavals in Asia since 1939, the Indian Ocean was still, much as it had been since 1815, a 'British lake'. As we have seen, London hoped by its independence arrangements with Ceylon and its constitutional flexibility over India, to preserve the strategic partnership which had underpinned British control of the region in the era of colonial rule. For here, in a world region relatively remote from the centres of their great power rivals, the British could still hope to enjoy most of the benefits of empire: secure fields for settlement and investment and complementary trading partners offering privileged (in currency terms) access to foodstuffs, raw materials and minerals – especially gold, rubber and tin. For as long as Britain remained pre-eminent in this huge maritime realm, she would remain a great power of some kind. But the basis of British power in the region was more fragile than before 1939. The realignment of India and the Pacific dominions away from their British connections could not be ruled out. In the meantime, in Africa, South East Asia and the Middle East the British found themselves after 1947 grappling with the political turbulence that continued, long after the immediate post-war disturbances had died down, to threaten British interests and authority. Of the various challenges that confronted them in the five years after 1947 the most dramatic were the Malayan Emergency that began in 1948 and the Iranian oil crisis of 1951.

The British response to the Malayan Emergency throws an interesting light on their post-war imperial outlook and reveals both the new limitations on their power and the conditions that permitted still the survival of British influence. Certainly, the struggle against the Chinese communist guerrillas became a considerable military commitment requiring eventually the services of 20 battalions of the British army as well as of nearly 50,000 local police and special constabulary. It jeopardised the production of Malayan rubber and tin, two essential dollar-earning commodities that sustained the Sterling Area's effort to meet its dollar purchases and, indirectly, British hopes of eventual freedom from economic dependence on the United States. And, it threatened, if British countermeasures were not successful, to pave the way for Chinese domination (leading, perhaps, to a further struggle with the Malay majority population) and the ideological reorientation of Malayan politics at the very moment when Mao Tse-Tung and the mainland Chinese communists were setting up the People's Republic of China. Had the guerrillas made the Malayan interior ungovernable and forced the British into compromise, the implications for the British economy, for British control of Singapore, for British relations with the Malay majority and for Western interests as a whole in South East Asia would have been extensive and damaging.

The communist guerrilla movement had taken root among the Malayan Chinese during the Japanese occupation and exploited the difficulties the returning British encountered in restoring full administrative control over a colony abandoned in headlong flight four years before. Among the Chinese population of Malaya proper (excluding Singapore) post-war conditions encouraged support for the communists: alienation from a government which granted only limited citizenship to non-Malays; the economic strains of adjusting from war to peace which provoked widespread labour unrest including a general strike in Singapore in 1946; and the large-scale squatting by rural Chinese which created extensive settlements beyond government purview, whose populations were outside the law and antagonistic to all authority.[65] Indeed, with the abolition of the 'Chinese Protectorate' – the pre-war agency supervising Malayan Chinese – as part of the reorganisation of Malayan government, the British had lost their old sources of guidance and information.

The main symptom of administrative breakdown was labour unrest in the countryside. By August 1947 planters in Malacca were complaining that their labour force was out of control.[66] Despite a growing sense of insecurity, it was not until the murder of three planters in June 1948 that an emergency was declared and the struggle with the guerrilla bands began in earnest. For the British, the difficulty lay in choosing which tactics to adopt. They had far too few troops and police to protect the 3,000 rubber estates whose production was so important. Wholesale arrests and repression had little effect beyond alienating the Chinese population of the towns still further.

And the wide sweeps through the jungle prescribed by the standard military guides to guerrilla war proved ineffective against fighters able to take refuge among a sympathetic rural population. Despite the adoption in 1950 of the Briggs Plan which aimed to resettle the squatters in controlled villages, to grant them security of tenure and to end their alienation from government by more generous citizenship regulations – to drain the pool in which the guerrilla fish were swimming – even in late 1951 the Emergency was far from over. Contacts with guerrillas and security forces' losses both reached their peak.[67] And in October, the High Commissioner, Sir Henry Gurney, was ambushed and killed. Not until 1953 did the British achieve a real breakthrough and begin to eliminate large numbers of guerrilla bands.

The British government begrudged the military burden of the Emergency. But there was no question of contemplating withdrawal while it lasted. Attlee refused to announce a constitutional review after the disturbances began in 1948 and insisted in 1949–50 that there would be no 'premature withdrawal'.[68] Plainly, quite apart from the obvious objection to making concessions to the Malayan Communist Party, any package of constitutional concessions acceptable to the communists was unlikely to appeal to the sultans who still occupied a commanding position in Malayan society or to the Malay nationalist party UMNO. Moreover, for the British, the military costs of the Emergency had to be set against Malaya's extraordinary importance as a dollar earner. Whereas most colonial commitments appeared more and more burdensome in periods of financial crisis at home, in the case of Malaya the reverse was true. Between 1945 and 1949, the London government spent some £85 million in grants and loans to Malaya chiefly to stimulate rubber and tin production.[69] In the great devaluation crisis of 1949 it was enhanced Malayan dollar earnings, helped by a relaxation of American import restrictions, that were primarily responsible for the Sterling Area's return to dollar solvency in the first quarter of 1950.[70] There was no sign by 1952 that London could afford to let Malaya go its own way or take its dollars where it would.

But although the British remained firmly committed to defeating the insurrection and ruled out early self-government for Malaya, the Emergency modified the basis of their rule considerably. In 1948 it was assumed that progress to self-government would take at least 25 years.[71] Two years later, Malcolm MacDonald, who supervised as Commissioner-General British policy all over South East Asia, was talking of ten to fifteen years and perhaps less. Attlee, while discounting early withdrawal, repeated the British promise of eventual self-government. The British had several reasons for wanting to accelerate the constitutional pace. They were anxious to win maximum cooperation from the Malays who formed the vast bulk of the local security forces, and to reassure Malay leaders that the centralisation of power for security purposes would not work to their political disadvantage. Secondly, they wanted as far as possible to draw 'moderate' leaders in the Chinese community into full political cooperation as part of the struggle for 'hearts and minds'. Thirdly, they were aware of the fragility of Western influence in Asia at a moment when India, Pakistan, Burma and Ceylon had so recently gained independence; when China had been won for communism; and when the fate of both Indo-China and Indonesia was hanging in the balance. 'If we were to resist the pace of change', Malcolm MacDonald told British ministers in 1950, 'we should lose the present support of Asian leaders . . . we must be in harmony with Asian leaders so that there is no discernible difference in views on which world opinion can take sides against us.'[72] Bevin put it more bluntly. 'Our support of nationalism in South and South East Asia provides the best possible counter to communist subversion and penetration'.[73] Lyttelton, the new Conservative Colonial Secretary in 1951, briskly announced at the end of his Malayan tour that only communism held up progress to self-rule.[74]

Even so, in 1952, the end of colonial administration was, apparently, far from imminent. London still believed that much more had to be done to create a multi-racial society before self-government could work.[75] What the British experience in Malaya in the post-war years illustrates vividly is the complexity of the factors influencing constitutional change and the timing of any transfer of power. The communal problem, the security problem and concern for the stability of a vital dollar-earner argued strongly for continued British supervision. But the reassurance of both Malay and Chinese leaders, and the need for a real incentive to political cooperation among the communities (not forgetting the Indians) made constitutional concessions essential. Chiefly, the British had to consider how their interests in this valuable but vulnerable colony, with its major communal divisions and exposure to internal and external disruption, could be safeguarded at a time of extreme uncertainty in the politics of eastern Asia. In 1952, France was still committed to the battle for Indo-China. In Korea the war went on. The future course of Chinese foreign policy was unpredictable but alarming. The Japanese peace treaty had only just (April 1952) been ratified. It seems likely that it was the subsequent shifts and changes in the international politics of Asia, as much as the internal situation in Malaya itself, let alone any significant change in British attitudes to empire, which led with unexpected speed to Malayan independence only five years later.

What emerges clearly from the Malayan case is that the preservation of British authority in the face of insurrection depended heavily on the acquiescence if not loyalty of the Malay majority and perhaps especially on the distaste of the Malay ruling class for radical opposition to colonial rule. The British were also fortunate in the sea-girt geography of the Malay peninsula which made the containment and isolation of the guerrillas far easier. Even so, despite these advantages, international considerations and local politics required constitutional progress. The key questions still unresolved in 1953 were when, and in what form, independence would come.

In Iran in 1951 the British faced a very different sort of challenge, but one which has often been seen in retrospect as yet another symptom of a precipitous decline in British power. In defiance of British threats and warnings, the Iranian government of Mossadeq nationalised the British owned and operated Anglo-Iranian Oil Company in May 1951. After much debate, the London government reluctantly ruled out military intervention and decided instead that all British staff should be withdrawn and legal action taken to prevent the foreign sale of Iranian oil. When Mossadeq's government was eventually overthrown in 1953, with the covert assistance of the British and Americans, nationalisation was partially reversed, but the AIOC was now to be only part of an international consortium with a 40 per cent share in the reorganised company. For all this consolation prize, the rebuff in 1951 had been humiliating. Harold Macmillan had told the Commons with Churchillian melancholy: 'The day when the last British employee leaves Abadan will mark the end of the association of Britain with the development of Persian oil. It means, still more, the collapse of British power and prestige in the East'.[76]

In fact, Iran had always been a difficult field for the operation of British influence, lying as it did on the old frontier between the Russian and British spheres in Asia. In 1919–21 the British had tried and failed to formalise Iran's reduction to the status of an unofficial protectorate.[77] But between the wars there had been little reason to fear Iran's becoming an ally of Bolshevik Russia, and the British generally approved of the centralising and independent policy of Reza Shah. After 1939, however, Iran's precarious stability disappeared. In 1941 the British and Russians jointly intervened to enforce the abdication of Reza Shah who seemed inclined to favour Germany against his overmighty neighbours. The removal of the shah, foreign occupation and the familiar economic and social consequences of involuntary participation in total war, set off a wave of turbulence in Iranian politics and saw the rise of the communist Tudeh [Masses] Party to prominence. Even after the Soviet Union's delayed withdrawal in 1946, the Tudeh Party remained a formidable force, and the strength of the Iranian regime, under Reza's youthful son and heir, uncertain.

The British concern was to preserve the Western orientation of the Iranian government and resist the expansion of Soviet influence. As elsewhere in the Middle East, London saw itself acting as the custodian of Western interests as well as defending Britain's own longstanding position in the Persian Gulf and Indian Ocean. In this task, the question of Iranian oil was a vital complication, since, under an agreement that went back before 1914, the production and marketing of Iranian oil was in the hands of the AIOC which paid the Iranians a royalty on oil sold abroad and a percentage of net profits.[78] Inevitably, the relationship between the powerful foreign-run monopoly, backed and partly owned by a great power government, and the host country was uneasy and often ill-tempered. Iranian governments long before 1939 believed that the payment they received was inadequate and unfair and that only control over the company's worldwide activities would ensure equitable treatment. The fluctuation of royalty payments was a constant irritant. For their part, the company had resisted Iranian control and what it regarded as unreasonable financial demands. Predictably, in the disturbed internal and international conditions of the later 1940s, the royalty question, last settled in 1933, revived as an issue in Anglo-Iranian relations.

After 1947, in fact, circumstances combined in a way less and less favourable to British interests. The reaction of most Iranian politicians to the foreign occupation of 1941–46 was vehement dislike for any new agreement that smacked of dependency. At the same time, the intensification of the cold war and Iran's key position as part of the 'Northern Tier' of Middle East states, heightened American interest in the country[79] and made its treatment by Britain a matter of much greater delicacy than in earlier times. Thirdly, the politics of oil underwent a very considerable change after 1945. The international competition for concessions in the Middle East became much sharper. The oil-producing states demanding better terms from the companies. First Venezuela, then Kuwait and, in 1950, Saudi Arabia extracted 50–50 profit sharing agreements – radically better terms than the British were prepared to offer the Iranians. Last and worst for the British was the growing instability in Iran in 1950 which thrust their oil interests into the cockpit of local politics and brought into power the enigmatic nationalist Mossadeq.

Mossadeq believed that Iran must follow a policy of strict non-alignment in international affairs and refuse to grant major concessions to foreign enterprise.[80] His objection to the AIOC was not simply to the level of royalty but to its entire role as a Trojan horse of foreign influence, provoking great power rivalry and intrigue and threatening Iran's fragile independence. As disorder worsened in the early months of 1951, the attractions of a direct assault on the oil company grew. 'The only way to save Iran', declared one member of the Majlis [parliament] 'is to unite all classes against the foreign enemy'.[81] Mossadeq became prime minister in an atmosphere of fear, desperation and near anarchy. Almost immediately he abandoned the negotiation over royalties and nationalised the company. The confrontation began.

The British refused to accept nationalisation and were deeply concerned that, if unpunished, it would encourage the seizure of British assets elsewhere. But the difficulty was how to persuade or compel Mossadeq to withdraw nationalisation or at least agree to a form which left the actual operation and management of the company in British hands. In mid-July 1951 the cabinet rejected military action in the oil fields as impracticable, unlawful and certain to alienate American as well as other international opinion.[82] In August there was an abortive mission to Teheran to persuade Mossadeq to agree to a reorganisation that would have preserved British operational control, but Mossadeq would have none of it. In September, the British, having toyed for three months with the idea of seizing Abadan where the principal oil installations were sited, finally abandoned all idea of a military solution recognising Washington's implacable hostility and that 'we could not afford to break with the United States on an issue of this kind'.[83] The cabinet declined to deal further with Mossadeq or to accept his takeover. Instead ministers decided to wage a war of attrition against him by withdrawing the company's staff and taking measures to prevent Iranian oil reaching the world market.

But, nevertheless, the whole episode appeared an embarrassing exposure of British impotence and was felt to be so at the time. The interesting question, however, is why the British were unable in 1951 to protect the company in the way they had done in the past. For it had never been very easy – and often impossible – for London to exert direct leverage on the Iranian politicians in remote Teheran. In earlier times, the standard tactic of British policy, faced with Iranian recalcitrance, was to threaten military intervention in south Persia and encourage the local appetite there for autonomy if not independence. Given the slender hold Teheran had on its far-flung provinces, and the accessibility of south Persia to British sea power, this had often been enough to ensure British interests a second hearing: indeed it was always an implied threat in Anglo-Iranian relations. But by 1950 this vital diplomatic instrument had been struck from British hands. The American government made it very clear that it regarded intervention in the south as likely to prompt Russian action in the north of the country.[84] Deprived of this tactic, the British could choose either to accept Mossadeq's coup or to sit tight and play for time. There was little chance that they would merely cave in. The AIOC was far too important an asset to abandon easily. It yielded a substantial tax revenue to a hard-pressed government at home, but above all it was a great source of dollar-free oil – since Iran was paid in sterling – and an important earner of foreign currency. As in the case of Malaya, as Britain's economic difficulties grew in 1950–51, her Iranian assets took on an enhanced significance. So London fell back on the hope that Mossadeq would soon be replaced by a more pliable figure and that chaos in the oilfields, together with the loss of oil revenues, would accelerate his disappearance. This was the hope and the intention behind evacuation.

Mossadeq's removal in 1953, albeit with the assistance of the Central Intelligence Agency, vindicated to some extent British views of the apparently brittle nature of Iranian nationalism. Nevertheless, despite the partial recovery of the AIOC's position, it is clear that the Iranian oil crisis held a darker significance for British power and influence in the Middle East. What had happened in Iran was symptomatic of the growing difficulties the British were encountering all over a turbulent frontier region that had never been fully under their control and in which, after 1945, they had to take account of two new great power presences both strong enough to cause them serious trouble. Mossadeq, like Nasser after him, was able to exploit a delicate strategic position poised between East and West, as well as disunity and disagreement among the Anglo-Americans. Where Mossadeq was vulnerable, unlike Nasser, was in his failure to remove the monarchy and control the army, the vital allies, as it turned out, in the revival of Anglo-American influence. But attractive as it is to see the Iranian crisis as a milestone in British imperial decline, two important reservations have to be made. Firstly, 1951 marked the end of an extraordinary period in which the British had enjoyed (since 1918) far greater influence in Iranian affairs than at almost all times between 1800 and 1918, when they had had to compete actively with Russia. Secondly, it was by no means clear that the circumstances that had proved so awkward in Iran would apply elsewhere in the Arab Middle East: Iran had always represented the extreme limit of British influence in the region. Even so, within a week of British withdrawal from Abadan in October 1951, Cairo had unilaterally abrogated the Anglo-Egyptian treaty of 1936, the key diplomatic warrant for Britain's Middle East presence.

CONCLUSION

After the travails of the immediate post-war years, British leaders had expected that the end of the decade would find them in calmer waters, with their economy recovered, Europe settled and the empire tranquil. In these conditions, they might have hoped to maintain a very deliberate pace in the recasting of imperial commitments which the war and its aftermath had shown to be desirable – since no-one disagreed that progressive colonial self-government and a less obtrusive British presence everywhere, especially in the Middle East, were much the best ways of maintaining British influence. Hopes such as these were doomed to disappointment. The beginning of the new decade brought not relief and revival but a further round of crises. To a senior American diplomatic observer Britain seemed almost at the end of her tether. 'Having gone thru another economic crisis this year', he reported to Washington,

British leaders now feel that they are fighting a last-stand battle for survival as a world power. They see themselves confronted by a host of life or death problems. They are trying simultaneously to balance their trade, modernise their industry, balance their budget, fight off inflation and prevent a fall in their standard of living.

Since there are no margins, even trivial things, such as a battalion despatched to Eritrea; a million pounds expenditure on this or that item; a million gained or lost in overseas trade; a penny rise in the price of bread or a dime in the price of coal become critical problems of major dimensions that require Cabinet attention.[85]

In this exhausting administrative maelstrom, ministers found the burdens of world power taking on a peculiarly physical reality.

Between 1950 and 1952, indeed, British overseas policy was jolted by one shock after another. The outbreak of the Korean war in June 1950 and the recognition that some British troops would have to be committed there, if only in the interests of American goodwill, confronted British strategists with the prospect of a conflict with the communist powers on two fronts separated by 11,000 miles of sea. Then, after early successes, came the Chinese counterattack in November and the possibility of a full-scale conflict between the Untied States and China including the use of nuclear weapons. In a wave of panic the cabinet envisaged that China, if blockaded or bombed by the Americans, would retaliate by seizing Hong Kong and 'moving south through Indo-China to Malaya'.[86] In December 1950 Attlee apparently dissuaded President Truman from authorising a direct attack on China but only at the price of offering a massively enlarged British programme of rearmament. A series of hasty revisions jerked British defence spending up from some £830 million in 1950–51 to a proposed £4,700 million over the following 3 years: a staggering increase that would have devoted some 10 per cent of total output to arms production.[87] Not surprisingly, this evoked protest among ministers: Bevan, Wilson and Freeman all resigned in April 1951. But what made matters much worse was that the vast expansion of the defence programme coincided with a sharp rise in the price of raw materials and the onset of serious new difficulties in Britain's balance of payments.

It was in this gloomy context that the cabinet faced the Iranian oil crisis, the apparent deterioration of the security position in Malaya and the prospect of a violent confrontation with Egypt following Cairo's abrogation of the Anglo-Egyptian treaty in October 1951. After the general election and the Conservative return to power,

Churchill was warned by the Treasury that the payments crisis was worse than it had been in 1947 and might lead to a crash more severe even than that of 1931.[88] Sterling seemed weaker than at the moment of devaluation in 1949. These worst fears were not realised and, as we have seen, British difficulties in Malaya and Iran did not inflict as much damage as might have been feared on British oil, rubber and tin interests. Nevertheless, the multiple shocks of 1950–51 provided a reminder, if one were needed, of the fragility of Britain's post-war economic recovery and of the danger that the simultaneous outbreak of international or colonial conflicts in Europe, the Middle East and East Asia would impose a breaking strain not only on Britain's military resources but perhaps also on her vital diplomatic relationship with the United States.

But as in 1945–47, the crisis passed without, to all appearances, enforcing any drastic change of external course upon British leaders. As they looked back from 1952 the policy makers might well have remarked on the strain imposed by Britain's share in the containment of communism and the new strategic liabilities of the cold war. Within the empire-commonwealth they had had to face local colonial emergencies and a major adjustment of Britain's relations with the self-governing dominions, now including India, Pakistan and Ceylon. But on the other hand Britain's international position by 1952 appeared from many points of view infinitely better than it had been between 1931 and 1939. The vast bulk of the empire had been retained, so it appeared, within the ambit of British influence or under British rule. No immediate great power challenge threatened Britain's established imperial positions. And in Europe, the most demanding commitment of all, an American guarantee had been secured which permitted the continuation of Britain's old extra-European activities. In the unfamiliar new setting of international relations, in which the seven great powers of before 1939 had been reduced to three, the implications of the complex changes in global politics since 1945 were by no means yet so obviously unfavourable to British pretensions to remain a great power. The disposition of British policy makers, as the American State Department had irritably noted in 1950, was to hang on and hold on; to preserve their separateness from Europe; to consolidate their Commonwealth connections as far as possible; and to maintain the 'fraternal association of the English-speaking world'.[89] It is against this ambitious background that the post-war tinkering with colonial constitutions in Africa must properly be seen.

Britain had achieved a precarious stability as a world power by 1952. But as her whole post-war experience had shown, especially in 1950–51, the viability of world power and the empire that went with it, depended upon several pre-conditions. To uphold their spheres of influence and rule, the British needed American cooperation, colonial quiescence and a sound economy at home. Their delicate position, poised between the superpowers, was vulnerable to the extension of superpower rivalry, to the revival of the European states which would erode their own special claim on American goodwill and to an upsurge of colonial discontent. In the first decade after 1945 the British escaped the interlocking of all these factors to their disadvantage. Thereafter they were not to be so lucky.

5 Nationalism and Empire in the 1950s

It is not difficult to see the 1950s as a period in which the gradual disintegration of British imperial power accelerated sharply in the face of the challenge of Afro-Asian nationalism. In West Africa, the British conceded full independence to the Gold Coast (as Ghana) in 1957 and set in motion a timetable for Nigerian independence three years later. The Sudan became independent in 1956. Elsewhere in Africa the British steadily enlarged the participation of Africans in colonial government. In South East Asia, Malaya too became independent in 1957. In Cyprus the British grappled with EOKA terrorism until the tripartite agreement (Britain, Greece and Turkey) that provided for Cypriot independence in 1960. Most dramatically of all, the Suez crisis marked the final collapse of Britain's dominance in the Middle East and seemed to confirm that her pretensions to independent world power were at an end. By the end of the 1950s, it might be argued, it merely remained for the British to acknowledge formally their reduced international circumstances, to complete the technical operations required to transfer sovereignty to the colonial peoples and wind up their empire.

As the next chapter will argue, too much can be made of the impact of Suez on British aspirations to world power influence. Equally, the British approach to colonial nationalism can easily be misread with hindsight. For what is really striking about the pattern of British relations with Afro-Asian nationalism is not the uniform tendency towards the collapse of British power but the wide variation in British attitudes and policy between one region and another, and the very different kinds of accommodation which they reached, or sought, with different nationalist movements. Indeed, it is in these variations, and in the success or failure of British tactics towards nationalism, that we can best see both the thinking behind British policy in the age of imperial retreat and the factors which most influenced the outcome of their efforts.

Ever since the 1840s, the British had recognised that the stability of their imperial system depended upon establishing a working relationship with colonial leaders and politicians, since to govern against the grain of local politics was to risk either serious damage to imperial interests or unacceptable costs for their defence. As colonial politics were modified by the rise of new movements and parties, the requirements of this working relationship altered. Thus, long before the Second World War, British policy makers had generally accepted that colonial nationalism could not be crushed; it had to be accommodated: it might even prove benign. But none of this meant that they felt obliged to comply with every demand that nationalist leaders might advance or that they believed in the necessary incompatibility of colonial nationalism and their imperial interests. Instead, they deliberately sought to mould local politics in ways that would encourage the emergence of 'moderate' or 'responsible' nationalists with whom it would be possible to do business, and who would recognise the continuing interdependence of colony and metropolis. On occasions, in their pursuit of this ideal, the British showed a ruthlessness towards those they characterised as 'extremists' which belied any notion that they had lost by the 1950s the 'will to power' or abandoned their old conception of British world interests.

But of course their success depended upon circumstances: the pressure they could bring to bear upon particular colonial societies; the leverage that nationalists could find to enlarge their freedom of manoeuvre or drive out British influence altogether. The balance of forces in the colonial or semi-colonial relationship was determined by the interplay of domestic, international and local politics, yielding, as the regional studies of this chapter show, different outcomes in different places. What seems unlikely, however, is that the general tendency of British policy after 1950 towards a refashioning of colonial relationships and the gradual implementation of self-rule owed very much to a major shift of mood or opinion at home, before or after 1956. The rise of a more strident anti-colonialism in the Labour Party may have modified the political climate in which colonial policy was made to a modest extent.[1] But with a Conservative government in power and a Labour Party still committed to the Commonwealth and a British 'world role', this new radicalism should not be exaggerated. National Service in Malaya or Cyprus may not have been popular, but public clamour against the draft and the burden of imperial defence was not a feature of British politics. British leaders were undoubtedly constrained in colonial matters – as they always had been – by the desire not to be seen to take on new financial or military burdens of indefinite duration. After the trauma of 1951, there was every incentive to reduce the manpower demands of British defence. But no British colonial commitment in the 1950s became a major political issue at home – with the exception of Suez. And there was no significant popular pressure to carry through an accelerated transfer of power except from minority groups whose views were unlikely to carry much weight with a Conservative cabinet. If there was little evidence of public enthusiasm for empire – something which Salisbury, Cromer and Milner had lamented in the 'high noon' of empire – this was unlikely of itself to disturb policy makers for whom popular indifference was both familiar and convenient.

But if domestic pressures were not a major inducement to rethink the basis of colonial empire in the 1950s, international considerations were a different matter altogether. Between 1952 and 1959 world politics underwent a further transformation whose implications for colonial rule and Britain's spheres of influence could hardly be overlooked. Already by 1952 the emergence of communist China and the Korean war had signalled the extension of the cold war to Asia. After the *de facto* partition of Vietnam under the Geneva Accords of 1954, the direct challenge of communist guerrilla activity was replaced by the subtler Sino-Soviet appeal to the new post-colonial states of Asia to resist involvement in Anglo-American treaty systems and preserve their neutrality or non-alignment.[2] The success of this appeal seemed to be vindicated at the Bandung conference in 1955. For the British, who were eager to retain their special relationship with India, Pakistan and Ceylon, the urgency of countering this Eastern siren-song was plain. The general effect was to make Anglo-American diplomacy in Asia more anxious than ever to cast off the embarrassing legacy of colonial rule wherever possible in the new struggle for friends and influence in the uncommitted world, and to reinforce Washington's impatience with the old-fashioned imperialism of its French[3] and British allies. Then in 1955 came Kruschev's new forward policy: an eagerness not shown by Stalin to carry Soviet influence into the extra-European world. At the end of 1955, Kruschev toured India, Burma and Afghanistan. In the same year, the Soviet Union deliberately entered the labyrinth of Middle East politics and, by selling arms to Egypt, openly challenged British influence in the region.

In the new era of competitive coexistence, the British found the international pressures on their system of rule and influence intensified sharply. On the one hand it was necessary to pre-empt the seductive appeal of Sino-Soviet rhetoric among the new states of Asia and the Middle East by demonstrating more convincingly than before that British commitment to colonial self-government was genuine. On the other, London now had to contend with American anxiety that failure to forge friendships with Afro-Asian nationalists in time might jeopardise the global balance outside Europe; as well as Washington's impatience with what was seen as British complacency and self-interest. For their part, the British were determined to preserve their own influence where they could and were mistrustful of American motives. Certainly, where the international pressures were weak – as in most of Africa before 1959 – they showed little sign of abandoning their claim to a special position founded variously upon influence or rule.

With the fall of their Indian empire and their setbacks in the Middle East, the British had good reason after 1947 to reflect on the destructive effect of Afro-Asian nationalism on their imperial position. After all, the pre-war optimism that nationalism could be steered and channelled and made to harmonise with British interests had been discredited by the failure to preserve Indian unity and the political maelstrom in Palestine. Curiously, however, the British did not draw the pessimistic conclusion which these failures seemed to warrant – partly because they did not give up all hope of a close Anglo-Indian partnership until the mid-1950s and partly because they were convinced that political conditions in their Asian colonies bore no real comparison with those in the African. Consequently, they continued to act in their dealings with Arab leaders and African politicians on the assumption that, if only the clouds of bogus sentiment could be swept away by the humouring of local amour-propre, then strategic, economic and administrative realities would persuade nationalist leaders that their best interests lay in a lasting accommodation with the imperial power. Even the most strenuous nationalism, so they reasoned, would surely recognise that strategic (as in Egypt) or economic cooperation with Britain was perfectly compatible with the fullest independence. Where their expectations were disappointed, and nationalism remained 'unreasonable', the British, as we shall see, were sometimes prepared to strike hard in the effort to rearrange the local political balance.

Of course, nationalism as a political force (and the imperial response it evoked) varied enormously across the vast regions that formed part of the colonial empire or were of vital interest to British imperial power. Nationalism was a political label of bewildering vagueness and ambiguity: nationalists of one time and place appeared to have little or nothing in common with those of another. What was called nationalism in one colonial society might be no more than a diffused sense of resentment by the governed against the governors: to be a nationalist might signify little more than an attitude consistently critical of an assertive centralised administration – itself an unwelcome novelty in many colonial territories. Nationalism of this sort embodied specific local or sectional grievances and could be met by piecemeal concession or administrative adjustment. At the other end of the scale nationalism might represent an assertion of national identity and a coherent programme for the attainment of full national independence, backed up by a highly organised popular movement imbued with a powerful and emotive rhetoric. Plainly, this form of nationalism was far harder to tame by the prescribed methods of British policy, though not impossible. Commonly, the colonial nationalisms the British encountered in the post-war era combined elements of very different kinds of politics.

Yet the transition from a nationalism that was localised, timid and inarticulate to one that was united around a central leadership and a single programme and capable of mobilising mass support was nothing like so smooth in practice as has sometimes appeared in retrospect. Too much stress on the inevitability of colonial independence obscures the difficulty that local politicians encountered in trying to challenge colonial administrations more effectively. As we shall see, the emergence of a full-blown nationalism even in black Africa was very uneven, with some colonies lagging far behind; colonial politicians in Africa as a whole were far slower to organise and mobilise than their Asian counterparts. Part of the reason at least was that before nationalism could become more than the vaguest of slogans, and before it could attract a mass following, certain preconditions had to be met.

The most basic of these was the appearance of some measure of common interests binding together different regions and communities. As long as different parts of a colony were separately administered or remained ethnically, culturally or economically quite distinct, there was little prospect of organising more than the most localised opposition to colonial rule. Indeed, even where a successful unified movement could be launched, regional differences were a constant threat to its survival, just as they were to hamper the cohesion of so many post-colonial states.

However, the growth of common interests and identity was likely to be a very, perhaps infinitely, long, drawn out process. In the colonial era what chiefly mattered was the political and administrative unification of the territory rather than the attainment of real social or economic cohesion. For until there existed effective institutions for the exertion of central authority over the whole territory of the colony, the notion of national sovereignty and independence was bound to be no more than the emptiest of pipe dreams. In many colonies before 1939, especially in Africa, it was not the solidity of the administrative apparatus which enabled the central government to govern its remoter districts after a fashion but the *solidarity* of the expatriate colonial officials who were largely immune from the tug of regional or local loyalties. The emergence of such an administrative apparatus – which could be operated by other hands and inherited by a post-colonial regime – was an indispensable precondition for an effective national movement and, appropriately, control over it became the main object of political activity.

Thirdly, there was the question of personnel. While the number of those with a degree of Western education remained miniscule, it was difficult for colonial nationalism to move beyond its localised stage. This was not because Western education was necessary to learn political skills, nor even – as has sometimes been suggested – because the idea of self-rule was a foreign importation acquired by reading Rousseau. It was because dealing effectively with a colonial government and its agencies required both a considerable level of literacy as well as some insight into its inner workings – and preferably some knowledge of its metropolitan overlords as well. It was mastery of the baffling processes of a foreign government that conferred on a new educated elite of lawyers, teachers, clerks or businessmen the prestige needed to weld together the coalitions of local notables into the parties and movements that challenged colonial rule.

Fourthly, the mobilisation of a large-scale movement required some deeper motivation than the occasional spasm of xenophobia or religious fanaticism. The necessity of political organisation on a colony-wide basis had to be recognised by a multiplicity of local interests usually distracted by parochial rivalries. Opposition to colonial rule might prosper in the towns where racial feeling, a sense of displacement, economic insecurity and the influence of Western political ideas were all likely to be powerful. But nationalism in the colonial world could only triumph if it penetrated the rural interior and won over its local leaders. The more that central government interfered in the social and economic life of the countryside, and the more obvious it was that the exertion of central authority could only be contained by something more than localised opposition, the easier it became to fuse chiefs and tribes, communities and castes, traders and peasants into a unified movement capable of bringing diffuse local grievances to bear upon the distant and previously inaccessible commanding heights of the colonial administration.

Lastly, the escape from parochialism and the political appeal of independence and nationhood depended to some extent upon the image of the world outside, just as the structure of international politics helped to determine how much leverage colonial leaders could apply against their rulers. So long as the world was dominated by colonial powers, and escape from one colonial empire seemed merely the prelude to absorption within another, the achievement of real independence was bound to appear unlikely and even pointless. For nationalism to have more than a purely internal meaning, for independence to be 'real', a new international order was needed in which self-government would actually confer a genuine choice of external relationships.

What is striking about these preconditions is that, although their fulfilment required considerable initiative on the part of colonial societies and local politicians it was usually the impetus of colonial rule or imperial influence that brought them about. European diplomacy demarcated the territorial units which colonial politicians aspired to rule. Colonial rulers created, for their own purposes, the apparatus which gradually bonded these units together and eventually made possible their independent survival. Colonial governments, for their own reasons, pushed forward the political and economic changes without which nationalism might have remained an affair of the urban educated few. And it was the climactic outcome of the far-flung rivalries of the colonial powers, most dramatically in Asia, which brought about the freer international order without which true independence would have remained a chimaera.

If, then, we wish to explain why colonial nationalism flourished earlier in some places than in others part of the answer at least may lie in the gradual emergence of these preconditions. In pre-war India they were plainly far more visible than in colonial Africa. Indeed, even after 1945 their impact varied greatly across the colonial and semi-colonial world. In the Middle East, where direct British rule had disappeared in the 1920s (except in Palestine) it was perhaps only the fragile fiction of military and diplomatic supremacy which underpinned Britain's influence by the 1950s. Elsewhere, as in East and Central Africa, the preconditions for independence only began to emerge in the later 1950s and the final erasure of the imperial presence was delayed until after 1960.

One last qualification is necessary. It would be a mistake to suppose that the relations between colonial rulers and local politicians were always in the nature of a tug of war, that colonial governments always sought to obstruct the growth of nationalist politics. In a number of important cases the British, far from being bent on repression, played fairy godmother to nationalisms whose chances of survival against the strength of ethnic divisions or local particularism would otherwise have been slim. For colonial governments partnership with nationalist movements dedicated to the unity of the colonial state was often a far more attractive alternative to being harnessed to fissiparous tribal coalitions or regional movements jealous of central authority, even if the latter enjoyed well-organised grass roots support. So the key decisions on when, how and to whom power should be devolved or sovereignty transferred usually reflected not so much a nervous collapse in the face of overwhelming nationalist sentiment as a more elaborate calculation about the qualifications of any other set of local rulers for holding the flimsy colonial state together in the light of what was, after 1950, a rapidly changing international system.

WEST AFRICA

British West Africa provides a striking case study in the history of post-war decolonisation. The two leading colonies, the Gold Coast and Nigeria, were among Britain's most valuable colonial possessions by the later 1940s. As late as 1947 neither was expected to attain self-government let alone independence in much less than a generation. In both the loyalty and general contentment of local opinion contrasted strongly with the rebelliousness of Britain's Asian subjects. Yet, as it turned out, both colonies underwent such rapid political and constitutional change that independence was plainly in view by the early 1950s. And in neither case did the British offer any serious resistance to the demolition of colonial rule stage by stage; so that progress towards independence in both countries was almost completely free from the kinds of confrontation or violent protest common elsewhere. The end of colonial rule in West Africa, therefore, raises a number of interesting general questions. Why was political advance so unpredictably rapid? What part did the growth of nationalism play in the acceleration of self-government? And why were the relations between nationalism and imperialism so strangely amicable?

In 1946 the Gold Coast seemed the very model of a well-run tropical colony: a tactful government, no troublesome settlers, a local elite composed of traditional chiefs and a small class of Western-educated notables remarkable for its loyalty and cooperativeness, and an economy buoyed up by the rising price of cocoa. In the gratifying absence of nationalist opposition, the British introduced in 1946 a constitution designed to bind the coastal and inland regions more closely together and to provide a larger representation of local opinion. This was to be the first step in the slow, carefully timed march towards the distant horizon of self-rule, perhaps a generation or more away. Less than five years later, this vision of the Gold Coast's development seemed pitifully myopic. The formation of the United Gold Coast Convention (UGCC) in 1947 to campaign against the new constitution, the outbreak of rioting that rocked the colony in 1948, the emergence of Nkrumah's Convention People's Party (CPP) in 1949 with its appeal to popular nationalism and its doctrine of 'positive action', the concession of a large measure of self-government under the new constitution of 1950 and the installation of Nkrumah as, in effect, chief minister after the CPP landslide of 1951, destroyed the deliberate constitutional timetable drawn up at the end of the war. In 1954 Nkrumah obtained full internal self-government: three years later the Gold Coast had become independent Ghana.

The transformation had taken place with electrifying speed: the crucial period of change in local politics had been between 1947 and 1951 when the pressure of a mass movement in the form of the CPP was first brought to bear on the colonial government. The origins of this political revolution lay, however, largely in the actions and plans of the colonial administration whose efforts to extract more revenue and impose closer control forced chiefs and westernised notables alike to look to the defence of their interests and gave them a keener motive than before to seek to influence the policies of Government House in Accra. In 1943 the British imposed an income tax for the first time. In 1944, through the Native Authorities Ordinance, they greatly enhanced central control over rural local government and its finances and enforced the amalgamation of many of the small 'states' or chieftaincies.[4] Then in 1946 the Burns Constitution, by bringing the inland region of Ashanti and the coastal 'colony' under a single legislature hammered home (though not intentionally) the lesson that if local and other vested interests were to be protected against the interference of government, political influence at the capital, not personal influence with the district commissioner, was the key. But perhaps the decisive spur to political mobilisation was the belief among the small class of businessmen and lawyers in the coastal towns that the new constitution would give too much power to the chiefs and traditional notables who disliked the permeation of western-ised or democratic ideas, and promote a new alliance between these conservative interests and the colonial government. It was this fear that led to the formation of the UGCC in 1947 by the wealthy lawyer J. B. Danquah.[5] Danquah and his friends were not social radicals. But their open challenge to the government was a vital stimulus to wider popular unrest.

This unrest fed on several major grievances. In the countryside, the spread of commercial farming (of cocoa) and the social and mental changes that came with it created growing dissatisfaction with the privileged position of the chiefs especially among wealthier 'com-moners'.[6] In the towns which had grown extremely rapidly since 1930[7] there was an increasing class of 'verandah boys', young people who had received an elementary education of a Western type but who were either unemployed or unable to gain the prestigious non-manual jobs to which they aspired.[8] Both these groups were impatient with chiefly dominance and potentially volatile. Then in the aftermath of war, the colonial government became identified with two sources of bitter resentment in town and country. The first was the combination of food shortages and inflation, particularly serious in the towns,[9] blame for which was fastened on government and the European traders. The second was the drastic measures employed by govern-ment to control the virulent disease attacking the cocoa trees on which the colony's economy depended. The compulsory destruction of diseased trees enraged farmers unconvinced by official explanations and fearful for their livelihood. Nothing could have dramatised more effectively the farmers' need for protection against the unpredictable actions of government. Thus when riots and disorder broke out after a demonstration by unemployed ex-servicemen in early 1948, there was already widespread popular discontent in the coastal towns and in the Ashanti region, the rural heartland of the cocoa industry.

The British suppressed the disturbances but they had been startled by the success with which Danquah had apparently mobilised popular support. In response they set up a committee of some 40 notables, all local, to recommend constitutional change.[10] The object was probably to capitalise on the unease of Danquah and his allies at the prospect of further unrest, and to encourage the traditional and more westernised notables to come to terms. After hesitation, Danquah joined the committee which produced a new constitutional formula calling for a much larger elected assembly, universal suffrage (voting was to be indirect in most places) and devolution of much of the Gold Coast's internal affairs to local politicians. The British accepted this recommendation, calculating (like, no doubt, its designers) that the beneficiaries would be a moderate, socially conservative coalition of chiefs and urban notables that would happily return to the old tradition of cooperation. British control would become less overt, but British influence would remain deep and powerful. On all sides this was a profound miscalculation.

The actual beneficiaries were Kwame Nkrumah and his Convention People's Party. Ironically, Nkrumah had been brought back from London, where he had been studying, to organise the UGCC campaign in 1947 and build a popular base for it by drawing in the trade unions and the local societies and associations into which farmers, traders and other interests were organised. Nkrumah was too successful; the leaders of the UGCC began to have cold feet about the consequences of mobilising the 'verandah boys'. But when they attempted to destroy his position, Nkrumah retaliated by forming the popular organisation he had created into a new party, the CPP, claiming to be the true voice of Gold Coast nationalism, and demanding 'self-government now'. A campaign of 'positive action' – strikes, boycotts and demonstrations – dramatised the conflict with the British and led to Nkrumah's gaoling in 1950. But Nkrumah's imprisonment could not stop the electoral triumph of his party: with as much grace as they could muster the British released him from gaol in February 1951 to become chief minister in the new assembly.

Superficially, the victory of the CPP seemed to reflect the rapid growth of nationalism on the Gold Coast, attributable partly to external influences, partly to the effects of Western education and partly to the charismatic appeal of Nkrumah himself[11] – 'Iron Boy',

'Great Leader of Streetboys'. In fact, for all Nkrumah's rhetoric, there was little to choose ideologically between him and his opponents. But if Nkrumah's ideology was old-hat, his organising talents were supreme. The success of the CPP revealed not the appeal of its particular brand of nationalism so much as its enormous superiority as an organisation and as a machine for the representation of local interests in the new institutions the British had created. It was this which appealed to the hard-headed farmers and traders of the interior whose support was vital if the CPP was not just to be an urban and coastal party.[12] Almost by accident, Nkrumah had seized the opportunities opened up by the two central facts of Gold Coast politics in the post-war years. The first was the determination of the British to weld the colony together, to bring the localities more into touch with the centre, and to do this by creating larger representative institutions with a wide suffrage. The effect was to place a huge premium on electoral organisation and the fusing of local interests into a single movement. The second prime fact was the eruption of social and economic grievances felt equally in the towns and the rural interior and breeding a resentment against the colonial government that was intense enough to dissolve for a brief but crucial interval the regional, tribal and local animosities in a broad anti-government coalition. Inflation, shortage and cocoa control carried the CPP to power.

But, as it turned out, the machine-like character of the CPP and the pragmatic outlook of its leadership were highly acceptable to the British once they looked beyond the extravagance of Nkrumah's speeches. Nkrumah accepted office and avoided any open confrontation with London. He sought self-government *within* the Commonwealth. He loyally accepted the rules of the Sterling Area and the dollar pool.[13] London wanted the Gold Coast to press ahead with economic and administrative improvement. The CPP readily taxed the farmer to provide the finance,[14] and threw the weight of party propaganda behind the exaction of local rates by the new district councils.[15] Despite Africanisation, the number of British officials actually increased after 1951.[16] The price of this amiable partnership was a blind eye to CPP misuse of official funds[17] and willingness to concede full internal self-government and then independence. This price London was ready to pay, insisting only that before independence there should be a further general election and that insubstantial concessions to regional feeling (which had revived strongly after 1954) should be written into the independence constitution.[18]

London's flexibility reflected two calculations. One was that independence with the CPP in power would make little fundamental difference to Britain's material interests which were primarily economic (the Gold Coast held little strategic significance) and might even ease the political difficulties of economic development. The second was that whatever its faults the strength and cohesion of the CPP made it infinitely preferable to the factions and regionalist groupings that opposed it, and whose success might have fractured the fragile unity of the new state in which both the British and the CPP had a deep common interest. To have refused Nkrumah independence would only have driven him into a sterile confrontation and encouraged tribal and regional separatism. As so often elsewhere, the real nightmare of British policy was not the transfer of power but the disintegration of the administrative unity they had laboriously constructed. In that sense, the Ghanaian nationalism of the CPP was the favoured stepchild of British imperialism.

The smoothness of Anglo-Ghanaian cooperation after 1951 owed a great deal to Nkrumah's success in fastening the grip of the CPP all over the country and checking the rise of regional or tribal movements. The wide extent of commercial agriculture, binding the cocoa producers of the interior to the coast and the lack of a fundamental cultural divide between the Ashanti states and the coastal populations were also vital elements in Ghanaian unity. But in Nigeria the state-building ambitions of the British and the evolution of Nigerian nationalism suffered alike from the marked absence of such cultural or economic bonds. In religion, politics and social organisation, the Muslim north, with its Fulani aristocracy and its landed estates was a different world from the provinces south of the Niger-Benue line where Western, Christian and commercial influences were far stronger and social forms quite distinct. To make matters even more complicated, the southern provinces were divided between the Yoruba people of the west and the Ibos of the east, not to mention the large number of minority tribes scattered across the middle and south. Nigeria, remarked an aspiring local politician in 1947, 'is not a nation. It is a mere geographical expression'.[19]

The standing object of British policy after 1945 was to transform this vast and loosely-articulated collection of provinces into a modern state, to improve its administration and develop its economy. They wanted to cultivate self-government as a means of drawing the communities together and to promote ideas of modernisation and 'uplift'.

But, as in the Gold Coast, they found that these administrative schemes produced unforeseen political consequences, with the result that the leisurely progress towards self-government contemplated in 1945 had become by 1955 an unseemly rush, culminating in independence in 1960.

What part in this sudden acceleration was played by the emergence of a Nigerian nationalism? The short answer is that its effects were significant but limited: curiously the popular notion that colonial rule was expelled from Africa by the rise of African nationalism can only be applied to the largest country in black Africa with the heaviest qualifications. But that is not to say that there was no opposition to colonial rule. Between 1945 and 1950 the southern region was disturbed by a succession of upheavals: the 1945 general strike of public workers protesting against inflation; the abortive campaign against the 1946 constitution; the more violent campaign of nationalist extremists between 1947 and 1950; and the Enugu mine riots of 1949. Local traders resented the power and influence of the large European firms, especially in post-war conditions of shortage.[20] The growing number of literate Nigerians resented their exclusion from the upper echelons of government and limited job opportunities in the bureaucracy. Inflation and government regulation aroused discontent in the countryside. But there was little sign before 1950 that these various discontents would be fused into a political movement uniting town and country, farmer and trader, tribe and tribe even in southern Nigeria let alone in the north. Enthusiasm for the creation of a Nigerian nation was largely confined to small circles in the coastal towns, and even there had been divided after 1941 by Ibo-Yoruba antagonism.[21] The concept of a single Nigerian nation was vigorously attacked in 1947 by Obafemi Awolowo, the most prominent Yoruba politician.[22] The main political association, the National Council for Nigeria and the Cameroons (NCNC) was dominated by Ibos, completely failed to extract constitutional concessions from the Colonial Office and abandoned in 1947 its boycott of the new Legislative Council.[23]

Nevertheless 1948 saw a significant change of course in British policy here as in the Gold Coast. Higher administration was to be opened up to Nigerians; the provision of higher education was enlarged; local government in the east was reformed at the expense of traditional authorities and to the advantage of the educated 'new' men. Above all, the constitution was to be revised by an elaborate system of consultation culminating in a general conference. This move forward was prompted by a number of calculations. It was thought unwise to refuse concessions granted to the Gold Coast and British officials in Nigeria were anxious to anticipate any hardening of the educated class against them[24] – apparently the main cause of trouble in the Gold Coast. At the same time, London was pressing for the further improvement of local government – in effect the replacement of tradition-ridden 'native authorities' by district councils on the British model so that the work of development would be carried on more effectively.[25] Democracy and efficiency, Whitehall decreed, were natural companions. But the logic of reforming local government required changes in the regional councils as well, because they were largely selected by the native authorities and in their old form were of little use as legislating and improving bodies. So Lagos and London smiled sweetly when the consultative conference brought forward proposals for giving the regional legislatures wider powers and a more representative character in a system of limited ministerial government. Now the articulate and educated in the south could be drawn into the constructive business of state-building.

The British expected that this carefully balanced devolution of political power would make government more popular and effective, but without removing their ultimate control.[26] Instead, their main concern was the unity of north and south and the danger that the traditional rulers, whose sway in the north was unchallenged, would refuse to participate in a constitution increasingly geared to the aspirations of Western-educated politicians in the south.[27] Separatism and disintegration, not nationalism, frightened the policy makers most: the growth of Nigerian nationhood was their most ardent desire. Probably, their original intention was to stage the further instalments of self-government at a pace which would preserve overall British control until political differences between north and south were less marked and a strong federal government could be established with the consent of all three regions – the Yoruba west, the Ibo east and the Muslim north. In the event, it was precisely the supreme difficulty of persuading the three regions – especially the north – to cooperate in a federal government and to agree upon its powers that led them to accelerate self-government and promise in 1957 that full independence would be the reward for agreeing to work a proper federal system. In British policy independence was the horse and unity the cart: the one was meant to pull the other.

The root of the problem was the unexpected rapidity with which party government developed in the two southern regions. As in the Gold Coast, this was less a consequence of spontaneous popular nationalism and more a result of the pragmatic judgement of local interests that regional governments whose regulatory powers and financial resources were expanding rapidly could best be controlled through a disciplined phalanx of representatives in the legislature. Nor were the local leaders of the Action Group in the Yoruba west or of the NCNC in the Ibo east men of long nationalist pedigree. Generally, they were traders, teachers or businessmen whose prominence reflected their local value as intermediaries between the illiterate and inarticulate and the baffling demands of modern government.[28] Once in power, however, these new politicians had little choice but to press for wider self-government and even independence: to hold their gimcrack parties together, the leaders had to reduce the influence of British officials and enlarge their own command of patronage and public finance. Thus within two years the demands of party politics had made the 1951 constitution unworkable.[29] Even worse from the British point of view, the party governments in the regions wanted greater freedom from central government and greater control over the revenues raised in their region: demands that London 'regretfully'[30] conceded in the new constitution introduced in 1954.

At first sight, one possible strategy for the British was to let each region develop at its own pace, to concede self-government to the Eastern and Western Regions but delay it in the conservative north; and to allow almost complete regional autonomy. But a whole series of objections stood in the way. Both the main southern parties believed that they could win support in the Northern Region given the chance and they wanted the three regions broken up into a much larger number of states. Both feared the economic consequences of dismembering Nigeria completely. London was afraid that, with too much autonomy, the outlook of the regions would diverge so much that federation would become unworkable; and that virtual independence in the regions would build up irresistible pressure for complete command over revenue – in which case the centre would collapse. The British dared not create a situation in which the centre was visibly less 'democratic' or 'representative' than the two southern regions. Hence the 1954 constitution was a desperate attempt to balance regional autonomy against greater involvement by the regional politicians in the affairs of the centre. And to achieve this, the

British had to promise self-government and the prospect of independence for the centre as well as chivvying reluctant conservative politicians in the north to become as 'nationalist' as their counterparts in the south.[31]

Thus, by the time that the 1954 constitution was reviewed in 1957, the British were ready to offer independence as the reward for the establishment of a working federal government commanding the support of a federal parliament.[32] The prospects of federal power proved sufficient inducement for the leaders of the Northern and Eastern Regions to form a coalition inspired chiefly by fear and dislike of the Action Group.[33] And it was this coalition that took Nigeria into independence in 1960.

The outcome is a telling commentary on the realities of the political struggle between nationalism and colonial rule. For what drove the British out of Nigeria was not nationalism in full cry but the danger of nationalism going off at half-cock and fragmenting the country along tribal, regional and religious lines. Certainly there existed in post-war Nigeria some vague conception of Nigerian nationhood among a narrow educated circle. Certainly, but again only in the south, there was resentment against the exclusiveness of colonial rule. But the crucial process whereby the ideas of the few and the resentments of a minority were transformed into a demand for self-government was set in motion by the British, originally for their own purposes. It was the unexpected growth of party rule in the south and the rooted conservatism of the northern potentates which enforced a series of constitutional adaptations whose prime purpose in British eyes was to hold Nigeria together. On one view, then, the post-war innovations in colonial rule revealed an extraordinary miscalculation – if the defence of British *rule* was the centrepiece of policy. In fact, it is more likely that after 1950 the British regarded even independence (as in Ghana) as a highly acceptable price for a unified state and the cooperation of local politicians. Especially since they expected – how wrongly we shall shortly see – that the predominant influence that Britain had enjoyed in West Africa since c.1840 would be enhanced by skilful statecraft and the timely transition to an informal presence.

EAST AFRICA

The British response to the political aspirations of West Africans had been flexible and accommodating: their relations with West African politicians were for the most part amicable and relaxed. But this was not the resigned good nature of a weary titan anxious to slough off intolerable burdens. Elsewhere in Africa, the British sustained throughout much of the 1950s a far tougher and more unyielding attitude towards the claims of African politicians: in East and Central Africa they dismissed African nationalism as an agitator's ramp, a retrograde racialism, and a rejection of the requirements of economic and social progress. For most of the period between 1952 and 1959, either directly or through settler proxies, they harassed the exponents of African majority rule relentlessly – except, as we shall see, in Uganda where special conditions applied. The British did not regard their policies in the Gold Coast and Nigeria as a blueprint for the political development of their other African colonies: far from it. Their approach in East Africa was dominated by considerations which had little or no force in West Africa: the existence of a self-confident white settler population enjoying significant local power and capable of mobilising political support at home; the presence of an Asian community which was deeply entrenched in retail trade and on whose behalf the governments of India and Pakistan were periodically active;[34] the much greater strategic importance of East Africa for the protection of British interests in the Middle East and the Indian Ocean; and the belief that the economic development of the region depended heavily on the role of the immigrant, rather than the indigenous, population. All these factors, combined with the far shallower penetration of European cultural and commercial influences in East African societies, predisposed London towards schemes for constitutional and economic development that had little in common with the comparatively simple and generous formula applied in British West Africa.

Kenya was by far the most valuable and important of Britain's East African possessions. It enjoyed a better climate than Tanganyika (from a European point of view) and far superior agricultural potential. Unlike Uganda which had remained a 'black man's country' closed to white settlers, Kenya had been open to white settlement since the 1890s. In the development of commercial agriculture, industry and trade, Kenya had far outstripped the neighbouring territories and was certain to predominate in any East African federation or union. With a substantial port at Mombasa, good internal communications and the most advanced economy of the region, Kenya was also a very useful alternative base for the exercise of

British military and naval power, overlooking the Indian Ocean and within striking distance of the Middle East and Persian Gulf. Several times after 1945 London toyed with the project of making Kenya the prime centre of its military power east and south of Suez.[35]

But the key fact about Kenya was the size and strength of its white settler population,[36] and the very large political influence which the white community exercised locally. Kenya indeed could be regarded as the northernmost limit of the tide of white settler expansion which had colonised the Rhodesias before moving into the highlands of East Africa.[37] Although the Kenya settlers had so far failed to turn Kenya into a self-governing settler state on the model of Southern Rhodesia or South Africa, by the later 1940s they were deeply entrenched in the political and economic life of the colony. A great block of some 16,700 square miles in the heart of the country was reserved exclusively for their use: these were the 'White Highlands', a colony within the colony, the tribal homeland of the whites and the guarantee of their political and economic survival. Of the three communities in Kenya, African, Asian and European, the whites alone possessed an effective political organisation. Through the ministerial system, their representatives shared executive power with British officials answerable to the Colonial Office in London, while African political representation was limited to a handful of nominated members. With the new emphasis on economic development carried over from the war years, their cooperation and goodwill as farmers and producers seemed more important than ever to governors anxious for solid achievements to report. With agriculture prospering as never before, with London encouraging new settlers to enter the country[38] and with a colonial administration that seemed closely attuned to their outlook, the Kenya whites had some justification for their aggressive confidence that, even if self-government and dominion status were denied them, Kenya was and would remain a 'white man's country'.

Inevitably, the growth of a settled European population and the creation of a great white 'reserve' (carried through in the later 1930s) aroused alarm among the African population – especially among the Kikuyu whose tribal 'land unit' bordered the White Highlands. The Kikuyu were the largest tribe in Kenya, making up some 20 per cent of its population, as well as the most energetic and enterprising. Many of them had taken enthusiastically to Christianity and Western education; and such political organisation as existed among Kenya Africans before 1939 was largely a Kikuyu affair. The prime grievance of the Kikuyu was land hunger: the shortage of new land available for a growing tribal population in search of new homesteads. Kikuyu leaders insisted that the White Highlands were 'stolen lands', the lost patrimony of their tribe, a charge fiercely rebutted by the Kenya government. During the Second World War, Kikuyu political activity was suppressed on security grounds. But after 1945 their resentment was intensified by the sharpening social pressures of land shortage, by the apparently growing power of the settlers and by the local inter-ference of the Kenya government through more and more elaborate agrarian regulation. For the government was convinced that the real cause of the land hunger and overcrowding in the Kikuyu reserve was the deterioration of the land through overstocking and bad agri-culture. The real solution lay therefore in compulsory destocking and the strict enforcement of soil conservation – especially through the arduous task of terracing eroded hillsides – often accomplished by compulsory labour. To buy off Kikuyu resentment by opening the White Highlands to peasant farmers at the expense of European commercial agriculture 'would destroy the whole basis of the Colony's economy and put an end to development'.[39]

Right up to and after the outbreak of the Mau Mau emergency in 1952 the demands of leading Kikuyu for a revision of the land settlement and for a larger representation in the Kenya legislature received short shrift in London. That Kenya might one day become an African state was about as likely, remarked the governor in 1948, as the creation of a Red Indian republic in the United States.[40] Official policy was committed to the development of the economy (and the raising of all living standards) primarily through the ex-pansion of *European* agriculture, and to the creation in slow and cautious stages of a multiracial constitution under which no racial group would be allowed to dominate the others – a conception which conferred in the short term hugely disproportionate influence on the white population and, in the long term, a promise of protection against the aspirations of other communities. Perhaps it was this unsympathetic attitude towards African, and especially Kikuyu, grievances which encouraged the growth of the violent opposition that became Mau Mau.[41] But Mau Mau was not simply a terroristic expression of extreme frustration and bitterness at the injustices of colonial rule, even if its following was swelled by the landless and by squatters evicted from European farms. It was also a symptom of social crisis within a tribal society exposed to the full force of external influences that challenged deep-rooted customs, habits, hierarchies and supernatural beliefs. For all the prominence accorded to atrocities against Europeans, what occurred between 1952 and 1956 amounted to a civil war within Kikuyu society in which those who had adopted European ideas (including Christianity) or who had profited from cooperation with colonial rule, land shortage and inflation were violently assaulted by those who believed that collaboration with the colonial government and its policies was the source of all their grievances. In the four years from 1952 to the end of 1956, by which time Mau Mau resistance had been broken, 95 whites were killed but over 14,000 Kikuyu – 1,000 of them by execution.[42]

Mau Mau was suppressed by the extensive deployment of British troops and local security forces, by the device of new guarded villages and security fences to pen the Mau Mau fighters in the forests, and an elaborate programme of screening Mau Mau suspects and 'rehabilitating' them in special camps. But the result seemed to be not only the repression of a savage rural uprising (there had also been Mau Mau activity in Nairobi) but also a shattering setback to African nationalism in Kenya and the dream of African majority rule on the model of Ghana or Nigeria. In official eyes, and even more in the minds of the settlers, Mau Mau was not the articulation of grievance and fear but a barbaric throwback, deliberately engineered by Jomo Kenyatta and other radical Kikuyu politicians and held together by the use of oaths of 'unspeakable debauchery',[43] playing upon the lowest and most primeval instincts. Kenyatta himself was sentenced to seven years hard labour, and his Kenya African Union, the only real vehicle of African nationalism in Kenya, was banned. Indeed, from 1955 until 1960 no form of political organisation for Africans above district level was permitted. To policy makers and settlers alike it appeared obvious that without the strictest control political activity among the Kikuyu would rapidly degenerate once more to the horrors of Mau Mau.

At first sight, therefore, the effect of Mau Mau was to confirm European primacy in Kenya and to give it new conviction: the contrast between civilisation and barbarism was now more sharply drawn than ever in black and white. In fact, the struggle against Mau Mau set in motion political and economic changes which were to undermine steadily the power of the white settler community and their hold over British policy. In 1954, partly to allay settler criticism of the government's handling of Mau Mau, a Council of Ministers with three elected European members was created. But London and Baring, the governor, were also very anxious that the settlers should accept a greater sharing of power with Asians and Africans,[44] and that both loyal Kikuyu and other tribes as yet untouched by Mau Mau should be given a greater sense of participation in the government.[45] So two Asians and one African were added to the Council of Ministers. In 1956 further seats were created for Africans in the legislature and for the first time Africans were enrolled as voters on a qualified franchise. In 1957 a general election was held as a result of which a new group of elected African members emerged to demand a larger representation. Further constitutional changes in 1958 increased the number of African members from eight to fourteen, two of whom were to be members of the ministerial council.[46]

Alongside these political innovations, the British embarked after 1954 upon a fundamental reform of African agriculture. Partly this was a revival of the pre-Mau Mau schemes for soil conservation and improvement, but its real aims were far more ambitious. Henceforth Africans were to be encouraged to grow cash crops and to adopt a thoroughly commercial approach to farming. They were to receive a large measure of help and guidance from a new corps of advisers and instructors. Above all, the old and destructive pattern of fragmented holdings and collective ownership was to be replaced by the consolidation of holdings and the conferment of individual title. This programme, the so-called 'Swynnerton Plan', was put through at breakneck speed especially in Kikuyuland where, by 1959, consolidation had been largely achieved. Its purpose was twofold: to break the vicious circle of rural impoverishment and soil deterioration and to create a new class of conservative rural proprietor who would be immune from the siren call of Mau Mau xenophobia and extremist nationalism.[47] The political price for all this was the cautious extension of African political representation as a means of gaining 'moderate' African support, rewarding cooperation and thwarting troublesome rural agitators.

But neither constitutional nor economic innovation signified British willingness to install African majority rule in Kenya. The real purpose of the series of constitutional reforms adopted after 1952 was to create a system of government in which Europeans, Asians and Africans would have to share power and which would exclude 'extremist' politicians of all races – in particular African politicians who demanded universal suffrage and majority rule. Hence the device of a 'Council of State' which could veto legislation discriminating against any racial group and the effort to move away from the tradition of communal electorates towards a system in which only individuals who were acceptable to voters of all races (i.e. 'moderates') would be successful. Hence, too, the continuing ban on African political associations above district level: 'national' organisations, it was thought, were the breeding grounds of extremism and irresponsible nationalism. As late as the summer of 1959, the policy makers were still confident that this programme of 'multi-racialism' could be sustained and would form the basis for Kenya's eventual progress towards self-government; and that full-blooded nationalism could be checked and outmanoeuvred. Their determination was reinforced by the belief that any other course would bring anarchy in Kenya and discredit a far more delicate experiment in racial partnership in Central Africa, and also by the new emphasis after 1957 on Kenya's strategic importance for the defence of British interests in the Middle East and Indian Ocean.[48] 'I cannot now foresee a date' proclaimed the Colonial Secretary in the House of Commons in April 1959[49] 'when it will be possible for any British Government to surrender their ultimate responsibilities for the destiny and well-being of Kenya'. These ringing tones in London were soon to be followed by the wringing of (white) hands in Kenya.

In what turned out to be the last decade of their rule, the British pursued in Kenya a variety of policies designed to achieve what appears in retrospect as an extremely ambitious scheme for a multiracial constitution that would preserve European leadership for the foreseeable future. In Tanganyika and Uganda they adopted political strategies which were almost equally ambitious and which were intended to realise two principal objects. The first was the emergence in both territories of an African political leadership which would cooperate in economic and administrative improvement. The second, much more discreetly veiled, was to adapt Tanganyika and Uganda for membership of an East African federation in which a multiracial, European-led Kenya would play a dominant role.

Tanganyika had a special significance in these plans for building a federal East Africa. In the later 1940s and early 1950s, settler influence in Kenya predominated and Kenya was still a 'white man's country'. Uganda, on the other hand, had only a handful of European permanent residents, and although there was a considerable Asian population (some 70,000 by the late 1950s) it was plainly a 'black man's country'. Tanganyika, formally a United Nations trusteeship territory, stood halfway between the two. The white settlers, while they were a forceful and articulate group and were represented in the legislature,[50] were far less numerous and less well-entrenched than their fellows in Kenya and the case for regarding Tanganyika as a future 'black man's country' correspondingly stronger. But in any federal scheme, Tanganyika would hold the balance between Kenya and Uganda.[51] Hence the importance of ensuring that its political development kept both settler interests and black nationalism firmly in check, and demonstrated the practicality of racial cooperation in politics.

This external consideration had a far-reaching influence on the policies of the Tanganyikan government and the growth of African nationalism. As in other colonial territories, the post-war period saw a determined bid by government to impose much stricter measures for the conservation and rehabilitation of the soil both to raise productivity and to meet the demands of population growth.[52] And, as elsewhere, the struggle to police a dense web of regulations, collect new taxes and conscript labour for conservation work aroused resentment and opposition among peasant cultivators who had hitherto regarded government with indifference as at least remote if not benign. Moreover, as chiefs and chief-dominated native authorities were used to enforce the new rules, they became increasingly unpopular with, and alienated from, their local communities.[53] The effect was to encourage political activity and organisation in rural areas where previously chiefly rule had been unchallenged, and to open the door to the small group of urban politicians whose Tanganyika African Association (TAA) had only rarely made any impression on government since its foundation in 1929. But it was the threat of multiracialism that made Tanganyikan nationalism a living force.

The pressure to extend Tanganyika's representative institutions was almost entirely external in origin; there was little sign of strong new political and social forces within the country.[54] On the one hand, London was anxious to impress the United Nations Trusteeship Council with the progressiveness of its rule.[55] On the other, the policy makers were determined that Tanganyika's constitutional development should be carefully meshed with that of Kenya. Thus when the programme of reform was launched after 1949, it prescribed parity for African and non-African interests in the legislature in a territory where for every European there were 4 Asians and 430 Africans.[56]

The effect of this would be, as larger doses of self-government were administered, to convey more and more power not to African leaders but chiefly to Europeans and Asians, together with whatever African allies they were able to attract: so that in fact Tanganyika's political and social future would conform far more closely to the model of Kenya and the Rhodesias than to that of Uganda or West Africa. To strengthen the growth of what became the official policy of multi-racialism, the Tanganyika government set out after 1952 to reform local government along the same lines. The creation of new elected bodies to replace the old 'native authorities' was to bring a striking innovation. Henceforth the new local authorities, hitherto purely African in membership, under the eye of a British district officer, were to contain European or Asian representatives: a novelty which could only be regarded in the countryside as a deadly new threat to the influence of the chiefs and to the interests of the African community at large.[57]

More than anything else, it was multiracialism at a local level which drove rural chiefs and notables to support the anti-government campaign of the TAA which was renamed the Tanganyika African National Union (TANU) in 1954 under the presidency of Julius Nyerere.[58] TANU denounced multiracialism and demanded that the primacy of purely African interests be recognised. The reaction of the government revealed the importance it attached to the success of its bold experiment. TANU was harassed by coercive legislation, by the banning of speakers and by the prohibition of its branches in certain localities.[59] The government actively encouraged the formation of a multiracial party, the United Tanganyika Party (UTP) and tried to revive the prestige of the chiefs whose unpopularity often assisted TANU's cause.[60] Multiracialism in local government was pushed forward; and perhaps to strengthen its appeal to Africans it was proposed in March 1955 to institute direct election to the legislature on a highly qualified franchise,[61] designed so as to compel each voter to choose a candidate from each racial group. Those African politicians who wished for a larger share of self-government would have to share power with Europeans and Asians. But all these plans foundered: the UTP could make little headway against the fierceness of rural opposition to the infiltration of Europeans and Asians into local government.[62] At the elections of 1958 TANU-supported candidates swept the board and the new legislative council contained an elected majority bitterly opposed to the centrepiece of government policy.

A new governor announced the end of multiracialism as a political system.[63] But not until some fourteen months later, amid circumstances to be discussed in the next chapter, was a further step taken in the direction of self-rule. Multiracial rule had been abandoned; colonial rule remained.

In Uganda the British approach to the problems of representation, self-rule and African nationalism was at its most convoluted and Machiavellian. On the face of it, the political situation was simpler: there was no settler community to block African advancement by local opposition or pressure in London. But Uganda had to be fitted for a likely future in a federal East Africa – a prospect which held little appeal for African notables fearful of domination by the Kenya whites. Above all, there was the problem of Buganda.

Like many of Britain's African dependencies, the Uganda Protectorate in the early 1950s had little internal cohesion except for what was provided by a skeletal British administration. It was not a nation-state in embryo but a congeries of tribes and petty kingdoms loosely administered before 1939 in a decentralised system. Of the Bantu kingdoms, the best organised and largest was Buganda on the shores of Lake Victoria. Buganda had long enjoyed considerable autonomy and British favour in a partnership which looked back to the years before 1900 when the Christian Ganda had helped the British to establish their protectorate.[64] It had a monarch, the *Kabaka*, who enjoyed wide popularity and prestige, and a parliament, the *Lukiko*, as well as a notable class who were determined to preserve their social and political authority. Thus, when the British began after 1945 to plan the economic development of Uganda, candidly admitting that some degree of compulsion might be necessary,[65] the kingdom of Buganda lay like a great roadblock across the path of progress. For their part, the Bugandan leaders were intensely suspicious that economic development would mean more European and Asian interlopers, and that the immigrant communities would be given an equal political voice to theirs. Above all, they dreaded amalgamation in a Greater East Africa.[66]

Matters came to a head in 1953 when the Colonial Secretary in London imprudently let slip his desire for the dreaded federation. British denials and reassurances were unconvincing and the *Kabaka* demanded what amounted to complete autonomy and a timetable for Buganda's separate independence;[67] demands which, if conceded, would have ruined not only all hope of eventual federation but the viability of Uganda as well. So the British response to *Bugandan* nationalism was trenchant: the *Kabaka* was deported to London forthwith. But the crisis in Buganda, and the resentment against the coercion of the *Kabaka* also pushed the British into other more subtle countermeasures. The *Kabaka* was allowed to return in 1955 and Buganda was given almost complete internal self-government. But at the same time the British set out to demolish Bugandan separatism, not by main force, but by the encouragement of an all-Uganda nationalism. The character of Uganda, promised London grandly, was to be 'primarily African' and its government was to be 'mainly' in the hands of Africans.[68] More important, London deliberately set out to magnify the status and prestige of the Uganda Legislative Council, creating first an African majority among the unofficial members[69] and then a ministerial system with five African ministers. Outside Buganda, government set out to build a sense of Ugandan nationhood and a heightened political awareness. Then in October 1957 the principle of direct election to the Uganda legislature was laid down.

The aim of British policy was clear enough. Buganda was to be held in check by the growth of political activity among other tribes and peoples whose leaders strongly supported London's desire for a unitary constitution and a strong central government.[70] And the people of Buganda were to be encouraged to look to the Uganda legislature, rather than to their own *Lukiko*, as the real representative of African interests, and the real fount of power, patronage and money. Whether or not the British still hoped that the new Ugandan nation they were struggling to manufacture could be cajoled into an East African grouping is unclear. But certainly in the early months of 1959, as they girded themselves for the final struggle with Buganda, there is little sign that they regarded the infant nationalism into which they had breathed life as a serious threat to their continuing influence. On the contrary. Promoting the development of national politics, devolving power to African politicians, promising further constitutional progress were all intended to propagate a new breed of Ugandan politician: one eager to carry forward administrative centralisation and economic development; and a zealous ally in the deflation of Buganda. Nationalism might be no friend of imperialism: but, so the British reasoned, on separatism it would have no mercy.

In the three main East African territories, British policy in the 1950s stood in striking contrast to the pattern displayed in West Africa, and far from relapsing into passivity or pessimism in the face of the surge of nationalism, colonial rule in its last decade and a half showed remarkable vigour and an almost reckless confidence in its constitutional innovations. All over East Africa, African cultivators were badgered to improve, while sweeping changes in land tenure were introduced. The British plotted unavailingly to bundle the territories into federation. In Kenya and Tanganyika they embarked on a bold experiment to frustrate African nationalism through an elaborate mechanism of power-sharing labelled multiracialism. And in Uganda, in a blunt reversal of 50 years of policy, they planned the absorption of Buganda within a new unitary state. By the late 1950s, one after another, these ambitious policies were breaking down, as local opposition rose. But for all the emergence of new groups of African politicians, and the electoral triumph of TANU in Tanganyika, there was as yet little sign that the era of colonial rule, let alone of British influence, would shortly be terminated. At a conference of governors in January 1959 at Chequers a tentative schedule was laid out. Tanganyika, it was thought, might be given independence in 1970 with Uganda following on. But Kenya, the 'fortress colony', where strategic needs and settler interests were much greater, would remain a colony until after 1975.[71] In a matter of months this leisurely timetable had been cast aside.

CENTRAL AFRICA

In West and East Africa after 1945 colonial rule was forced to adjust sometimes rapidly, more often gradually, to the mobilisation of African opinion and the emergence of political movements for whom independence and black majority rule were two sides of the same coin. But in Central Africa circumstances were very different. For here the authority of the imperial government and the survival of colonial rule were threatened by a force whose organisation, solidarity and effectiveness were greater than those of any indigenous political movement and whose only weakness lay in sheer weight of numbers. Of all the African nationalisms the British encountered, none was to cause them more trouble than the white settler nationalism of Central Africa.

Settler nationalism in Africa has usually been characterised as unbending reaction blindly resisting its inevitable destruction. But until 1959–60 it was a force which still bid fair to dominate the future of Central as well as Southern Africa, and which had once aspired to reshape the politics of East Africa as well. As it turned out, settler nationalism in Kenya was unable to overcome the entrenched authority of the colonial administration before its fate was sealed by the outbreak of Mau Mau and reliance upon British troops and imperial cash to end the insurrection. When the crisis of European rule arrived, the settlers' response was crippled by weakness and division. But in Central Africa historical circumstances and the pattern of settlement gave white nationalism a much stronger base and far more bargaining power when dealing with London. Nyasaland (now Malawi) was a 'black man's country' with only a handful of settlers and officials amid a black population of over three million. But in the Rhodesias there were some 300,000 whites, increasing steadily with the inflow of new settlers after 1945 and forming a society five times the size of the settler community in Kenya.[72] Moreover, white nationalism in the Rhodesias was far better organised politically and far stronger economically than its counterpart further north.

Of crucial importance was the fact that Southern Rhodesia had enjoyed almost complete internal self-government since 1923. In theory, legislation affecting the African population and changes in the constitution required British approval, but in practice London had not intervened in Southern Rhodesia's affairs, even in the field of 'native policy', and the governor was purely a constitutional figure-head. Defence and internal security were controlled by local settler politicians. White Rhodesians north of the Zambezi, living under Colonial Office rule, regarded this enviable autonomy as a birthright wrongfully withheld, and white opinion in the south encouraged them to do so. In effect, Southern Rhodesia's curious semi-independence served to stimulate demands for equal status north of the Zambezi, and for full independence in the south. Nor could London easily dismiss the white Northern Rhodesians' case, rooted as it was in the analogy of longstanding British policy south of the Zambezi. Above all, white Rhodesians, north and south of the river, looked towards South Africa where since 1910 white rule had been untrammelled by any external authority. South Africa's very proximity inevitably encouraged white Rhodesian nationalism while making it harder for London (eager for Pretoria's financial and strategic cooperation) to resist its claims.

But to a large degree the vigour of white Rhodesian nationalism derived from the character of white society. White nationalism was not an affair of a few wealthy farmers eager to preserve a semi-feudal dominance, conservative in outlook and ill-suited to sustained political agitation. In both Rhodesias the great majority of whites earned their living in the towns and in industry, commerce and transport. In both there was a large class of skilled or semi-skilled whites strongly trade-unionised and as determined as their British counterparts to protect and enhance their living standards. What the Depression was to the folk memory of British trade unionism, fear of cheap black labour was to the white Rhodesian. Thus the central object of white nationalism in both the Rhodesias was the final destruction of British control over the legal and constitutional apparatus on which the industrial colour bar ultimately depended. No white politician could ignore this insistent demand while in both territories all adult whites (but scarcely any blacks) had the vote and while official policy in London remained formally opposed to the colour bar. In Northern Rhodesia the Colonial Office confronted this feeling directly. Here the power of the white unions in the copper mines – the largest employer of labour and the principal source of government revenue – and on the railways to disrupt the economy forced London to proceed with great caution.[73] This was particularly true at a time when Northern Rhodesian copper was vital to the war effort and to sterling's struggle to survive after 1947. 'As long as we must have copper we are in the hands of the Mine Workers' Union',[74] Harold Macmillan had remarked with characteristic pragmatism in 1942.

Settler nationalism was at heart a knife and fork question. But white anxiety to gain full control over all aspects of government stemmed also from the perpetual physical insecurity of a small and privileged minority and the fear, especially in the later 1940s, that without rapid progress towards full settler control in the North and complete independence in the South, London might encourage the growth of black African nationalism– as it appeared to be doing in West Africa. Indeed, the closer that Africans elsewhere moved towards self-rule, the louder grew white demands for immediate self-government – before black nationalism could rouse a mass following. But for all its apparent selfishness and the powerful unifying influence of job protection and the industrial colour bar, white settler nationalism was not simply the programme of a brutal vested interest. White leaders in Central Africa believed that they represented a superior civilisation whose destiny was to rescue the African from barbarism. To them the primitiveness of the black majority was self-evident and the notion of majority rule absurd and outrageous. They assumed (as did most economic writers and official opinion) that the presence of settlers was beneficial to the whole community and that white privileges were necessary to economic progress and justified by a general rise in living standards. They persuaded themselves that black nationalism elsewhere in Africa was a fraud worked by self-seeking agitators on backward and credulous tribesmen and rejected outright the claims of black politicians in Central Africa to represent the African masses. By the 1960s and 1970s all or most of these beliefs were regarded in the West as at best ludicrous and at worst the sinister expression of racial bigotry. But in the 1950s they were far less out of tune with the outlook of politicians and officials in Britain. That fact was to be critical in the making of the Central African Federation in 1951–53.

Until the late 1950s the forcefulness of white settler nationalism was unmatched by any comparable movement among black Africans in Central Africa. In both Nyasaland and Northern Rhodesia grinding rural poverty was the lot of most of the population: political organisation outside the traditional hierarchy of chiefs was difficult if not impossible and until the 1950s nationalist politics held little meaning for a countryside where white settlers and officials were extremely few and far between.[75] On the Copperbelt, the loyalties of the African workforce were largely channelled into the trade unions whose leaders resisted direct political involvement.[76] In Southern Rhodesia it was not until the war accelerated the flow of Africans to the towns that political and trade union organisation began to take root: the haphazard 'general strike' in Salisbury and Bulawayo in 1948 was an early sign of what the Southern Rhodesian premier called 'the emergence of a proletariat'.[77] And in Southern Rhodesia at least white nationalism had both the will and the means to deal firmly with black political activity. Over the whole of Central Africa, then, the 1940s and early 1950s presented white nationalism with what its leaders sensed was a golden opportunity to reshape the politics of the region after their own hearts. The Depression with all its constraints had given way to prosperity bringing a surge of immigration and investment to both Rhodesias. The value of Rhodesian copper and tobacco was greater than ever to a dollar-starved Britain. And London was eager to improve the efficiency and representativeness of its colonial governments.

The long-term objective of settler nationalism may have been complete independence from Downing Street and the Colonial Office and equal status with Canada, South Africa, Australia and New Zealand. But the immediate target in 1945 was the *amalgamation* of the two Rhodesias into a single self-governing colony. This was a long-cherished ambition among whites on both sides of the Zambezi which had gained new fervour when the inter-war Depression had threatened living standards in both colonies.[78] So strong had been the pressure that London had reluctantly appointed a commission to inquire into the question in 1938. Its report had recognised the desirability of amalgamation from an imperial and local point of view but insisted that the political development of the two Rhodesias and Nyasaland was as yet too uneven for either amalgamation or federation to work.[79] After the war, however, settler leaders revived the issue and by 1948 their case had grown much stronger. The economic viability of the Rhodesias was no longer in doubt. The Southern Rhodesian government was committed to amalgamation. Constitutional changes in Northern Rhodesia had given settler opinion there a much larger voice in government. Above all, after the electoral triumph of the National Party in South Africa in 1948, there was growing anxiety in London that Afrikaner nationalism, with its open hostility to British imperial influence, would infect settler opinion in Central Africa – especially since there was an increasing number of Afrikaners among the white immigrants flowing into Northern Rhodesia. There was a real danger, wrote one of the leading settler politicians there, that without federation even the existing measure of self-government 'may easily mean Afrikaner domination in a very few years – an awful thing . . . to contemplate'.[80]

Thus when the new round of agitation began in 1949, London abandoned its opposition. It permitted a conference of officials from all three Central African territories to meet in London in 1951 to draft a federal scheme – a task in which the Colonial Office's principal African expert, coincidentally the architect of phased decolonisation in tropical Africa, played a leading role.[81] The arrival of a Conservative government accelerated the proceedings and a series of conferences in 1952 and 1953 hammered out a federal constitution. But it was federation not amalgamation on which London insisted: for amalgamation would have meant the simple absorption of Northern Rhodesia into a self-governing settler-ruled Rhodesia and the eradication of almost all British control. London also insisted that the federation should include the poor and debt-ridden Nyasaland protectorate. Lastly, London imposed a series of safeguards designed to reassure

Africans in the northern territories and concerned opinion at home. The existing colonial administrations in Northern Rhodesia and Nyasaland were to remain under the supervision of the Colonial Office. They and not the new federal government would be responsible for internal security and the political advancement of the African population: both reservations of critical importance. They would continue to be staffed not, as the settlers wanted, by locally recruited whites, but by members of the British Colonial Service appointed in London and loyal to London. And as a watchdog on the federal legislature an African Affairs Board was set up with the power to refer discriminatory legislation to London. For there could be no doubt that in the foreseeable future white electors and white politicians would predominate in federal politics.[82]

Thus the federation set up in 1953 fell far short of white aspirations for full independence, and perpetuated the authority of the Colonial Office in its northern territories. On the other hand, much depended on how willing the British government would be, once the initial excitement had died down, to advance a white-ruled federation steadily towards dominion status. London had dismissed African opposition to federation in Northern Rhodesia and Nyasaland as confused, wrong-headed and misconceived, and assserted that federation would be good for Africans especially through the expected benefits of accelerated economic development.[83] The refusal to grant full independence and the insistence on safeguards owed little to any warmth of feeling towards African nationalism. It arose largely out of an eagerness to avoid serious controversy at home, out of a desire to postpone independence until the constitutions of the three territories were more compatible, and out of a fear that without some control from London white brashness and impatience might upset the apple-cart and discredit the federal plan. It seems likely, however, that London hoped and expected that the settlers would succeed in obtaining sufficient African political participation, through an elaborate franchise system, to justify complete internal self-government and then independence within a decade or so. This was thought to be the significance of the British promise in 1957 to bring forward the constitutional review laid down in the 1953 act to the earliest possible moment.[84] Moreover, in 1957 the British government overrode the objections of the African Affairs Board and approved the federal government's constitutional amendment which, while preserving the same proportion of African representatives, substantially enlarged the Federal Assembly – making it easier to find a two-thirds majority (for constitutional change).[85] And, as if to vindicate London's judgement and settler claims, African political activity fell away sharply once the battle against federation was lost.[86]

There was, therefore, some reason for settler buoyancy. But the crucial question had still to be faced: the reconciliation of constitutional advancement in the two northern territories with the survival of a white-led federation. The federal government and the Northern Rhodesian whites were determined to gain a large measure of self-government for Northern Rhodesia and reduce the power of the Colonial Office.[87] At their insistence, London began in 1957 to recast the Northern Rhodesian constitution but endowed it with a complicated franchise system designed to encourage voting along non-racial lines.[88] At the same time, constitutional reform was promised to Nyasaland for 1959. Among whites and blacks alike there was keen awareness that, with the federal constitutional review on the horizon, these constitutional changes were likely to determine whether London conceded full internal self-government and dominion status to the federation. Among Africans in the northern territories the spectre of white independence encouraged a new and far more determined surge of political organisation. But by the latter part of 1958 African nationalism in Northern Rhodesia had split between those prepared to work the new multiracial constitution and those under Kenneth Kaunda pledged to boycott it as part of the struggle against federation. Meanwhile in Nyasaland the return of Hastings Banda signalled the onset of a fierce campaign for majority rule and secession. The scene was set for four years of political crisis which ended with the collapse of the federation and the rolling back of settler nationalism to the historic frontier of the Zambezi – where it was to stand for nearly twenty years.

It is an interesting question why African nationalism in Northern Rhodesia and Nyasaland was to prove so much more effective after 1958 than it had done in the abortive struggle against federation in 1950–53. Economic development in Northern Rhodesia had brought a large increase in the black population of the towns, especially on the Copperbelt where, for example, the African population of Ndola grew sevenfold between 1944 and 1963.[89] Here too the aggressive tactics of white trade unionism encouraged a steady growth in black labour militancy through the 1950s,[90] creating an important pool of mass support for a nationalist movement.[91] Perhaps, too, economic expansion and the growth of government created greater awareness of how an independent federation would affect African job opportunities – if white immigration continued and if the administration came to be recruited locally on the Southern Rhodesian model with even the lower echelons reserved largely to whites. African politicians could also take heart from the increasing volume of criticism directed at the federation by the Labour Party in Britain which was widely expected in 1958 to win the next general election. Again, in both Northern Rhodesia and Nyasaland, the opportunities for political organisation were much better by 1958–59. Africans were elected, indirectly, to the Nyasaland legislature for the first time in 1956, while in Northern Rhodesia the government itself, in the effort to breathe life into the new constitution, made efforts to awaken potential African voters to their rights. But above all, perhaps, it was the experience of federation itself, and the fear aroused by the white drive for control of Northern Rhodesia which made African opinion not only more receptive but also more inflammable than it had been a few years earlier. 'The fact is,' claimed Hastings Banda in 1952, 'that federation has given birth to a strong feeling of nationalism in Nyasaland if not in Northern Rhodesia.'[92] By 1958 that claim could no longer be so easily dismissed. The struggle of rival nationalisms was about to begin.

But in 1958 the British were still deeply committed to the success of federation and to the conception of 'partnership' between the races that it was supposed to embody. 'Partnership' was widely spoken of, but rarely defined, for in its ambiguity lay its acceptability. To London it meant the steady evolution of blacks towards social and political equality, a definite rejection on the one hand of African nationalism and on the other of white supremacy and segregation. To white settler leaders it meant European leadership for the indefinite future, although in a constitution without a formal colour bar. To the British, federation still seemed to serve several vital purposes: it deferred a decision on the political and economic future of the northern territories; it put off a direct clash between colonial rule and white settler interests in Northern Rhodesia; and, so long as the credibility of 'partnership' lasted, it resolved the dilemma of choosing between a white minority and a black majority. The policy makers were still reasonably confident that by skilful statecraft they could hold enough black and white support for federation to work. If the constitutional machinery was carefully designed, they argued, the moderates of both races would triumph. But as the next year was to show, the stakes had grown too high for moderation.

SOUTH EAST ASIA

In South East Asia British imperial interests were far more vulnerable to external pressures and disruption than they were in any part of sub-Saharan Africa in the 1950s. The struggle against communist insurgency in Malaya and the defusing of racial tensions between Malays and Chinese in the colony had to be pursued against a background of communist China's growing influence, of Indonesia's newfound independence and of a colonial war in Indo-China. In Singapore, the British ruled over a city-state colony whose strategic and economic value to them depended upon their success in containing the volatile urban politics of an overwhelmingly Chinese community. On the island of Borneo, two thirds of which was Indonesian territory, were two British possessions whose constitutional development had scarcely begun and whose political future was as yet obscure.

In Malaya, as we have seen, the British had been anxious to push ahead with constitutional changes that would draw Malayan leaders, Malay, Chinese and Indian, into active participation in government. As elsewhere in the colonial empire, British policy was framed on the assumption that only the promise of eventual self-government would draw diverse regions and communities into voluntary political co-operation and allow the creation of a modern, unified and economically progressive state. But before 1955 Malaya had had no experience of electoral politics, except at a local level, and the British were reluctant to press on with self-government until there was more evidence of political cooperation between the three main communities.[93] With the Emergency still in force, there was some reason to fear that electoral competition could easily decline into a bloody communal struggle. Ideally, therefore, London would have liked to see the emergence of multiracial parties appealing to all communities as a preliminary to self-government.[94]

In the course of 1954–55, however, this cautious approach was cast aside. Despite the growing popularity of the two main communal parties (the United Malays' National Organisation and the Malayan Chinese Association) joined since 1952 in an alliance, and their local successes against the non-communal party (Party Negara), the British accepted the report of the Malayan government's Elections Committee which called for an elected majority in the Legislative Council of the Federation. Faced in June 1954 with a boycott of the state and federal governments by the Malay and Chinese Alliance Parties (UMNO and the MCA) the high commissioner agreed that the nominated members of the council (32 out of a total of 99 members) would be selected in consultation with the leaders of the elected majority.[95] Then, after the elections of 1955 which gave the Alliance Parties (now joined by the Malayan Indian Congress) all but one of the elected seats, Lennox-Boyd, the Colonial Secretary, promptly agreed to negotiations about self-government and *merdeka* – independence. The Alliance leaders had called in 1955 for independence in *four* years. But following a constitutional conference in London in January and February 1956 the date for *merdeka* was fixed for August 1957.[96]

Why was there such a sharp acceleration in the programme for Malayan independence, and why did London drop its previous requirement that a multiracial political movement was needed before real constitutional progress could be made? There are a number of possible explanations. The British may have reasoned that the Alliance was the best multiracial movement they were likely to get. They may have been intimidated by the Alliance boycott of 1954. They may have hoped that the three party alliance would do less well in the 1955 elections but accepted with good grace that self-rule was irresistible after its landslide victory. And they may have felt that after eight years of the Emergency, it was essential to devolve power into local hands as quickly as possible. But it is likely that other calculations were crucial if not decisive. At the very time in 1954–55 that London was weighing its policy in Malaya, seismic changes were under way in the politics of South East Asia. The end of French colonial rule in Indo-China left Britain as the only significant colonial power in the region (discounting Portuguese Timor and Dutch New Guinea) – a distinction London scarcely relished. American policy insisted that the containment of communist influence in Vietnam required the abolition of colonialism and partnership with popular nationalist movements.[97] Meanwhile, in Indonesia, with whom the Malayans shared both a culture and the archipelago, the Bandung conference of 1955 signalled the attraction of many new Asian states to non-alignment and their sympathy and respect for communist China. There were, therefore, powerful, even overwhelming, international reasons for taking a much more flexible attitude to Malaya's constitutional development and installing a suitable independence regime as quickly as possible.

This decision was made much easier by the fundamental conservatism of the Alliance parties with whom the British now had to deal. For all their tough talk, the Alliance leaders had no desire to break Malaya's connections with Britain: they were still dependent on British aid to end the Emergency. Nor could they embark upon a programme of full-scale civil disobedience without risking the stability of their fragile coalition or coming into open conflict with the traditional rulers of the states whose influence was still considerable. Malayan independence was the product not of conflict but of genial complicity. In the constitutional negotiations in 1956 the British promised to assist independent Malaya with both internal and external security. In their turn, the Malayan leaders undertook to remain within the Sterling Area, banking their valuable dollars in London.[98] For both sides the arrangements were highly satisfactory. For the British, certainly, this was independence as it ought to be: Malaya, far from slipping her imperial moorings and turning instead to regional friendships, remained firmly within a trading, financial and strategic system that made Britain, Australia and New Zealand her closest partners.[99] Moreover, for those politicians in Kuala Lumpur who looked forward to Malaysia – a Greater Malaya embracing Singapore and the Borneo colonies – there was every motive to preserve the closest harmony with Britain while she was still a territorial power in South East Asia.

In Singapore, too, throughout the 1950s, the British were able to retain the benefits of colonial rule while enlarging the participation of local politicians in the government. In the aftermath of the war which had left Singapore's economy in ruins, there had been considerable labour unrest and the British had also watched nervously for signs that China's post-war status would excite nationalist feeling among overseas Chinese communities. In 1948 a new constitution gave Singapore a legislative council with six elected members, increased in 1951 to nine. But a narrow franchise, insistence on English as the official language and the suppression of left-wing organisations under the Emergency that was extended to Singapore, ensured that active political life was largely confined to a wealthy conservative minority represented by the Progressive Party.[100] The British were eager to transfer a larger share of local power to the Progressives whom they saw as a bulwark against more radical movements, and the Rendel constitution of 1955 was intended to reward them with a mainly elected assembly. But the emergence in 1954 of more popular parties, the Labour Front and the People's Action Party, together with the widening of the electorate in 1955, wrecked this genteel arrangement. The Labour Front won the election and Marshall, the new chief minister, was soon threatening resignation if self-government was not conceded immediately. With the Labour Front and its rival the People's Action Party, competing in militancy and radicalism, the prospects for a satisfactory compromise looked slim.

For the British the sticking point was their determination to continue to make full use of Singapore as a military and naval base and to have ultimate control over the external defence and internal security of the island. Constitutional talks in 1956 broke down over this and Marshall resigned. But in 1957 a new round of negotiations produced agreement. Under its terms, Singapore was to enjoy full internal self-government, with a prime minister, a cabinet and a Malayan-born head of state appointed by the Queen. Defence and foreign affairs were reserved to the British government. The most sensitive question was internal security, since the British were well aware that their 'full right to the occupation, control and use of the bases and installations in Singapore'[101] would be of little value if they could not prevent internal subversion. Singapore susceptibilities were overcome by agreeing that the proposed Internal Security Council, whose decisions would be binding on the Singapore government, should have three British representatives, three from Singapore and one, with an effective casting vote, to be nominated by the independent Malayan government. The British Commissioner on the island was still to have the power to suspend the constitution if internal security required. London obtained one other significant provision. The Singapore government, while free from responsibility for defence and foreign policy, was not to be allowed to disclaim all association with them. An inter-governmental committee was to meet frequently to allow consultation and discussion.[102]

These terms were accepted by the Singapore assembly and embodied in the 1958 constitution setting up the State of Singapore. They permitted the British to bind Singapore into their regional design of a Malaya that would play a key economic and strategic role in the Commonwealth. British influence in South East Asia would remain strong and effective, with the prospect of a Greater Malaya being formed under British auspices. For their part, the leaders of the Labour Front and the People's Action Party, sensitive as they may have been to the appeal of communism to the large proletariat of the city, had two reasons for backing away from any confrontation with Britain. They were fiercely anti-communist and feared the effects of a violent anti-colonial struggle on their own position. And they were in favour of joining the mainland in a Malaysian federation, as the best guarantee of Singapore's economic and political survival. With the Malayan leaders in harmony with Britain and the clear evidence of London's unbending determination to retain the base, here, as in Kuala Lumpur, the benefits of collaboration outweighed the rewards of revolt.

THE MIDDLE EAST

In sub-Saharan Africa in the 1950s, the British were largely able to manage colonial politics as if external pressures were of little direct significance. In South East Asia, as we have seen they were favoured by local circumstances, especially the fundamental conservatism of the political leaders of Malaya and Singapore. In the semi-colonial region of the Middle East, however, the British were not so lucky. Here, as it turned out, circumstances were less propitious, their interests more vulnerable and the character of local nationalism radically different. At the outset of the 1950s, the British were determined to retain their great base at Suez as well as the air bases in Iraq. They were also anxious to strengthen the barriers to Soviet influence in the Middle East as well as guarding Britain's large investment in oil installations chiefly located in Iran and Iraq. They wanted to exclude any hostile influence from the Persian Gulf and maintain their position there as the premier external power. The defence of all these interests depended partly upon military strength but even more on a working partnership with Egypt and the Hashemite kingdom of Iraq with each of whom Britain still had in 1950 a treaty of alliance. As long as both these states were closely aligned with her, Britain could overawe the lesser Arab states; while the bases at Suez and near Baghdad provided not only the vital connecting links in a strategic chain stretching to Singapore and the Far East, but could also serve as launching platforms for military intervention throughout the Middle East.

Of the two it was Britain's relationship with Egypt which had been, since the 1880s, the foundation of her Middle Eastern power. As we have seen, in the early post-war years London had failed to renegotiate the Anglo-Egyptian treaty of 1936 in a way that would preserve

British use of the Suez base in case of need while conciliating Egyptian nationalism through the withdrawal of Britain's obtrusive military presence. Instead the British stood firm along the Canal, relying on their treaty rights and the sheer weight of their manpower at the base – some 80,000 men in the early 1950s.[103] But this wait and see policy became increasingly difficult chiefly because of the turbulence of Egyptian politics, the growing social unrest in the country[104] and the spread of fiercely anti-British feeling among the masses. In the past, the British had been able to rely on the fact that although the ruling class in Egypt had frequently expressed violent nationalist sentiments it had almost always drawn back from fomenting a mass movement against the British presence in fear of the social consequences. Moreover, Egyptian politics had been dominated not by the common struggle of all patriotic Egyptians against the occupying power but by an internal struggle between the king on the one hand and an alliance of landowners and middle-class interests on the other: a struggle in which the British had often been able to act as umpire and arbitrator. But by 1950 the political scene was changing drastically. Post-war economic instability, inflation and unemployment intensified discontent with a social and political system controlled by a small elite of wealthy landowners and their allies. Unrest was reflected in the growth of extremist politics: the communists and the Muslim Brotherhood – an Islamic fundamentalist movement which by the later 1940s had become the most powerful mass organisation anywhere in the Middle East.[105] In 1948–49 a further deadly ingredient was added to the political cauldron: the triumph of Israel in the Palestine war and the humiliating defeat of the Egyptian and other Arab armies. Nothing could have been better calculated to lash popular Muslim feeling to new fury, to erode the prestige of the old regime, to generate resentment in an army which ascribed its failure to political corruption and treachery,[106] and to redouble Egyptian hostility to Britain on whose 'betrayal' of the Palestine Arabs the catastrophe could conveniently be blamed. Amid fresh waves of popular unrest and Muslim agitation, and with the loyalty of the army in doubt, it was little wonder that the king and the politicians vied with each other in striking violently anti-British attitudes; that any proposal which would leave British troops on Egyptian soil was vehemently rejected. Ultimately, with no sign of a voluntary British withdrawal, the Egyptian government unilaterally abrogated the treaty in October 1951.

The British stayed put, but the price of confrontation steadily mounted. The hostile political atmosphere led to the almost complete withdrawal of local labour from the base – a considerable inconvenience. British camps, installations, transport and personnel were attacked by terrorists whose activities the Egyptian police refused to curb. As the spiral of violence increased, the British reacted with growing severity, until in January 1952, determined to disarm the troublesome auxiliary police, they attacked a police barracks with tanks, killing 41 Egyptians. The next day anti-foreign riots swept Cairo: eleven British were killed and much property destroyed.[107] For the Egyptian monarchy the collapse of order and the sequence of humiliations at home and abroad was the beginning of the end. In July 1952 a conspiracy of junior officers under Neguib and Nasser swept away the old regime. The army was in power and the Arab revolution had begun.

For the British the new regime presented both a danger and an opportunity. There could be no doubting the ardently nationalist outlook of the 'free officers'. Nevertheless they seemed at last to be a government with whom it was possible to deal and who had the power to fulfil their promises. In 1953 and 1954 the British strove for a rapprochement that would meet their most important requirements and restore some harmony to Anglo-Egyptian relations. In 1953 they agreed to end British rule in the Sudan, Egypt's former colony but a British dominated condominium since 1899, within three years in return for the abandonment of Cairo's longstanding demand for the 'unity of the Nile Valley'.[108] Then, in the autumn of 1954, the great question of the Canal Zone was settled between Eden and Nasser: British troops were to be withdrawn over a period of twenty months, but the facilities of the base were to be available in the event of an external threat to any Arab state in the Middle East or to Britain's NATO partner, Turkey. The 'temporary occupation' of Egypt, begun in 1882, was to end after 74 years.

There were strong British misgivings. Churchill, in his last year as premier, tried to block the agreement.[109] Its terms meant entrusting the Suez Canal to Nasser and the loss of a base that had served as the 'Clapham Junction' of imperial communications since before 1914. There was also the risk that the pro-Egyptian parties in the Sudan would be tools of Cairo and carry a disruptive Egyptian influence deep into colonial Africa. But standing pat would mean ever-worsening relations with Egypt and the embarrassment of Britain's other partners in the Islamic world. It would lock up a garrison of 80,000 men in unpleasant and perhaps dangerous conditions. The government's most senior military advisers, for long so adamant against withdrawal, were eager for a treaty. The acquisition of the hydrogen bomb as a strategic weapon made the Suez base less vital anyway in the deterrence of Russia – or so Churchill claimed in the House of Commons. And London was under steady pressure from the United States to end the quarrel with Egypt over Suez and the Sudan.[110] Nor is it likely that Eden and his colleagues regarded giving up the base in peacetime as a signal for Britain's general withdrawal from the Middle East. There remained other British bases, not least at Aden, a British possession. Jordan and Iraq were Britain's allies. With the Suez question settled, there was some hope that Egypt would eventually join a new Middle East defence organisation under Anglo-American auspices. With luck, Nasser might turn out to be another Kemal Ataturk, content, once full independence was won, to concentrate upon the internal modernisation of his country in friendship with the West. Perhaps, too, the British calculated that if he got out of hand joint Anglo-American political and economic pressure, coupled with Egypt's economic fragility, would bring him quickly to heel.

But if these were the calculations which justified the policy of 1953–1954, they were to be savagely demolished over the next three years. Nasser was not to be mollified by the concessions he had gained and may have regarded them as evidence of weakening British resolve. More to the point, powerful domestic and external pressures drove him forward into confrontation with the British. The loss of Egypt's claim to the Sudan and the prospect of nearly two more years of British occupation of the Canal Zone could not be presented as an outright national triumph: the day after the signature of the Suez agreement, Nasser escaped assassination by a hair's breadth. The Muslim Brotherhood was banned and its leaders hanged, but the emotions it voiced could hardly be ignored, especially in a climate of severe economic austerity. The fierce mutual antagonism of Egypt and Israel, punctuated by raids and counter-raids, militated against the calmer atmosphere the British needed and served as a perpetual reminder to Nasser of the insecurity of his position and his dependence on the loyalty of the army. Above all, Nasser came to believe that neither his regime nor Egypt's independence would be safe until Egypt had established her claim to be the premier Arab power in the Middle East and Cairo became the acknowledged centre of the Arab world. Egyptian nationalism was not enough. Power, independence and prosperity dictated a pan-Arab policy: the alternative was weakness, isolation and poverty – and the eventual collapse of his regime.

So, in the course of 1955 Nasser's intention of challenging British influence all over the Middle East became painfully clear. In particular, he was determined to check the ambitions of the two Hashemite kings of Iraq and Jordan, close partners of the British and the strongest rivals to Egyptian influence among the Arabs. For the Hashemites were eager to enlarge their power, to bring Syria into their camp and to impose on Egypt precisely the isolation that Nasser dreaded.[111] For as long as the British preserved their special relationship with the Hashemites, therefore, they could count on Nasser's hostility and Egyptian propaganda would denounce Anglo-Arab collaboration as the conspiracy of devils with traitors. The internal divisions of the Arab world, exacerbated by the consequences of the Egyptian revolution and the ulcerating sore of Palestine, ruled out the general Anglo-Arab rapprochement that the British sought so anxiously. Yet the British could not give up their special friendship with Iraq and Jordan. Indeed, they hoped to use it to force Egypt into a more compliant attitude. Thus, in 1955, to Nasser's fury, they promoted a defence pact between Iraq and Turkey which Britain herself joined in April. The aim was plainly to draw the eastern Arab world into a bloc centred on Iraq and sympathetic to Britain. The Baghdad Pact, so-called, offered further advantages too tempting to resist. It would help guard the northern limits of the Middle East against Soviet influence; it would check the growth of American influence, especially in Iraq;[112] it might help the security of Britain's extensive oil investments in Iraq and the Persian Gulf which were of growing value and importance; and it would solve the delicate problem of how to provide for necessary British air bases in Iraq when the Anglo-Iraqi treaty expired.[113] Egyptian resentment counted for little against such apparently solid gains; and the enforced withdrawal from Suez had to be balanced by the strengthening of British influence elsewhere.

But the conclusion of the Baghdad Pact was the starting signal for an intensified Anglo-Egyptian rivalry which culminated spectacularly in the Suez crisis eighteen months later. Against the British Nasser could deploy two powerful weapons. He played on the widespread suspicion that any Western defence pact was merely veiled colonialism and that Arab disunity and weakness – especially in the struggle with Israel – was a consequence of British machinations. Secondly, he obtained the help of Saudi Arabia whose rulers were hereditary enemies of the Hashemites (and in close touch with Washington) to frustrate Anglo-Iraqi efforts to pull Syria, Jordan and the Lebanon into the orbit of the Baghdad Pact. In the autumn of 1955 a series of striking diplomatic successes showed how easily Nasser could stand up to British influence. Syria was joined to Egypt in a defence agreement. British efforts to draw Jordan directly into the Baghdad Pact were humiliatingly sabotaged by a violent internal agitation orchestrated from Cairo. And in September Nasser broke dramatically free from the Western monopoly of arms supply by reaching an agreement with the Czechs (but really with Moscow) to provide him with modern weapons. By January 1956 it was clear to an anxious conference of British officials in London that pan-Arab nationalism under Nasser's leadership was threatening to roll up British influence all over the Middle East.[114]

The stage was now set for crisis. The British were eager to win American support (and hence Saudi acquiescence) for the taming of Nasser.[115] Washington was unresponsive: after all, America's principal Middle East client was as opposed to Iraqi aggrandisement as Nasser. But then in July 1956, chiefly for financial reasons, Washington abruptly withdrew support for the Aswan dam project in Egypt – the main economic carrot the Western powers had held out to Nasser. Nasser's response was swift and devastating. On 26 July 1956 he nationalised the Suez Canal: the vital strategic waterway whose security had preoccupied British strategists since the 1870s passed under the direct physical control of a local power fiercely hostile to British influence. Now the full measure of Britain's Middle Eastern weakness became painfully apparent. The full withdrawal from the Suez base, for which Nasser had discreetly waited, meant that no swift military counterstroke was possible. Eden pinned his faith on winning American and wider international support that would force Nasser to give way, hoping perhaps that diplomatic humiliation would be his downfall.[115] But the American government, mistrustful of British motives and increasingly mindful of the approaching presidential election, fought shy of any open confrontation with Egypt and made public their opposition to the use of force. Eden was boxed in. Direct British intervention alongside France[117] seemed to be ruled out: not only would it offend Washington but it seemed likely to damage relations with Britain's main Commonwealth partners and arouse a fiercer anti-British feeling than ever in the Arab world. Moreover, it would be strenuously opposed at home by the Labour Party and by some influential Conservatives. On the other hand, to do nothing would risk the complete collapse of British prestige in the Middle East and the despair and defection of Britain's friends and allies in the region. Nor could Eden ignore a strong Conservative feeling that his 1953–54 settlement with Nasser had been a disastrous miscalculation: the parallel with Munich and its aftermath was too close for comfort. It was these relentless pressures that drove Eden to the desperate remedy of secret collusion with France and Israel, whereby a 'spontaneous' attack by Israel on Egypt was to justify Anglo-French military intervention to 'separate the combatants', and, coincidentally, demolish Nasser.[118] On 29 October 1956 the Israeli attack was launched. A week later British and French troops landed at Port Said and began to take control of the Canal. But within 24 hours an ultimatum from Washington stopped Eden in his tracks with the threat of intolerable pressures on sterling and the restriction of American oil supplies to Britain and France (at a moment when Middle East oil was already running short). On 3 December the British and French agreed unconditionally to withdraw their troops. By 23 December that withdrawal, and their humiliation, were both complete. In the eighteen months that followed the last traces of Britain's erstwhile supremacy in the region melted rapidly away. Jordan denounced her treaty with Britain. In July 1958 the Hashemite regime in Iraq, Britain's staunchest ally, was overthrown and its leaders murdered. The Hashemite monarchy in Jordan just survived by dint of British military assistance, an operation of which Washington approved. But by the end of the 1950s, British influence had been driven to the maritime periphery of the Middle East at Aden and along the Persian Gulf where sea power and the conservative instincts of the local rulers preserved a temporary foothold.

The dizzying speed with which British power and influence was washed away by the floodtide of Nasser's Arab nationalism highlighted the conditions on which the survival of British interests now depended in regions where supremacy had once been easy. For much of the interwar period the British had enjoyed an authority based ultimately on their military power and the absence of any serious great power rivals in the Middle East. They were able to manage the politics of the region in a way that avoided as far as possible the provocation of pan-Arab sentiment. Even the thorny problem of Palestine had been contained though not resolved. But to an extent that only gradually became clear the impact and aftermath of the Second World War destroyed the political foundations of Britain's position. The social and economic consequences of a struggle of which she was a reluctant epicentre plunged Egypt into a gathering crisis that ended in revolution. The question of a Jewish home in Palestine ceased to be a regional issue and became a world problem. The prospect of Soviet expansion into the Middle East, and the region's hugely enhanced significance for their home defence, reinforced the determination of the British to retain their bases and military installations, already greatly enlarged by the war and a standing provocation to Arab feeling. Far more than elsewhere in their imperial system, the British allowed strategic priorities dictated by global rivalry to run sharply against the grain of local Anglo-Arab cooperation. Above all, perhaps, the outcome of the Palestine conflict pursued British efforts at an Anglo-Arab rapprochement like an avenging fury: creating just that common object of pan-Arab feeling which pre-war policy makers had striven to prevent. The Palestine conflict also revealed how deadly to British influence was the intrusion of another, greater power. It was the irresistible force of American pressure which destroyed the last faint hope of a solution in Palestine acceptable to Arab opinion. American sympathy strengthened Nasser's hand in the negotiations over withdrawal from the Suez base in 1954, while their open distaste for confrontation undermined the diplomatic coercion of Egypt in the earlier phase of the Suez crisis. And at the moment of Anglo-French military intervention, it was American opposition that shattered all hope of recovering the Canal and toppling Nasser.

In fact, of course, as Attlee had seen as far back as 1945, the Middle East was a highly vulnerable frontier region in which the task of maintaining British influence was bound to be particularly difficult and dangerous. British authority outside Egypt had never been firmly entrenched and over most of the Arab world had barely existed until after the First World War. The impress of British social and cultural influences had never been very deep, partly because of the resilience of Islam. No other 'colonial' region shrugged off Britain's embrace so easily or retained afterwards fewer marks of the imperial presence. The post-war economic transformation brought by the oil industry came too late to strengthen British influence or raise up a class of Arab middlemen closely bound by self-interest in Britain. Coupled with the seismic effects of the war and the Palestine conflict, this background would have made British efforts to create an informal partnership with the Arab states acutely difficult in any circumstances. But to make matters worse, the British, for their part, lacked by the 1950s the financial and military power to sustain a forceful or seductive diplomacy. In so disordered a region and with the Americans infringing their diplomatic monopoly more and more, the old British penchant for great power privileges on the cheap could no longer be indulged: informal empire could not work in such rough conditions. In the end, like the Habsburgs in 1914, they were driven to upholding their interests by a desperate military gamble. And, like the Habsburgs, it might be thought that an imperial power driven to such desperate remedies, and with so little success, was near the end of its tether.

CYPRUS

If the British had had to endure humiliation in Egypt in 1956, in Cyprus they suffered the frustration of a terrorist struggle which for long appeared insoluble: politically London could neither advance nor retreat. In Cyprus, however, the situation was very different from that in Egypt. Cyprus had been leased from Turkey in 1878 and was annexed to the British empire when war with Turkey broke out in 1914. Four fifths of its population were Greek in language, culture, religion and politics; one fifth was Turkish. The Church, an autonomous branch of the Greek Orthodox communion, was the most powerful social force and had agitated since the earliest years of British rule for *enosis*, union with Greece.[119] An insurrection in 1931 led the British to exile the turbulent bishops and ban Greek flags.[120] Despite occasional public hints that *enosis* might ultimately be considered, after the Second World War the British set out to defuse the issue by offering larger doses of self-government that would give Cyprus a stronger separate identity. But these efforts broke down against the monolithic solidarity of the Greek community and Church.[121] By the early 1950s a stalemate had been reached. The mobilisation of Greek Cypriot opinion by the ethnarch Makarios was matched by the insistence of successive British governments, Labour and Conservative alike, that the question of Cyprus's future was closed.[122]

What transformed this grumbling colonial difficulty into an insurrection with major international implications was not so much the strength of Greek Cypriot feeling as the intervention of Greece in

1954. A new Greek government, anxious to demonstrate its nationalist credentials and less deferential to Britain than its predecessors, pressed London hard for bilateral negotiations over Cyprus. Eden's response was firm, and eventually vehement, ruling out any discussion of sovereignty.[123] Then in the middle of 1954, amid a new attempt to break the local impasse with proposals for enhanced local autonomy, came the notorious declaration of Henry Hopkinson, Minister of State at the Colonial Office, that Cyprus would 'never' attain full self-government.[124] The constitutional proposals offering limited elective membership in a new legislative council, were rejected by Greek Cypriots in this unpromising atmosphere as 'something for Zulus'.[125] The Greek government, perhaps with some reluctance abandoned the hope of bilateral discussion with Britain and appealed instead to the General Assembly of the United Nations, while in Britain, the restrictive terms of the government's policy for Cyprus were fiercely attacked by elements of the Labour Party, and especially by Aneurin Bevan. In this climate of rising tension, and with generous signs that British policy would come under heavy international and domestic pressure, Makarios as the *de facto* leader of the Greek Cypriot community authorised recourse to armed struggle by the forces of EOKA under Grivas in January 1955.[126] On 1 April 1955 the terrorist campaign began.

For the next three years the British were confronted by a terrorist enemy which, while incapable of driving them out of Cyprus, threatened progressively to erode public acceptance in Britain of the human and material costs of maintaining the imperial presence – as had happened eight years earlier in Palestine. At the same time it appeared that no concession that fell short of *enosis* would bring the conflict to an end. Makarios's skill especially in rousing international sympathy, the highly effective organisation of the EOKA terrorists that made them difficult to track down or penetrate, and the open support of Athens, made this a colonial problem more intractable than any other in the later 1950s. For their part, the British ruled out either *enosis* or British military withdrawal, and even any major concession in this direction. In that sense, their policy showed a determination and a severity which, given the 'advanced' character of Cyprus as a European colony, appears as a striking anomaly alongside the rapid preparation for Ghanaian independence and Nigerian self-government.

The inflexibility of British policy was a consequence of three different pressures to which London was exposed. The first was strategic. The Suez Agreement of 1954 had laid down a timetable for the withdrawal of all British troops from the Canal Base, hitherto the centrepiece of British military power in the Middle East. The only alternative location from which military operations could be mounted in the region, and from which the Canal Base could be speedily reoccupied in the event of an 'external' threat (as provided for in the Agreement) was Cyprus; and it was to there that Middle East G.H.Q. was moved in 1955. It followed from this, in the view of the British Chiefs of Staff, that *enosis* was ruled out as a practical policy. Britain must retain full sovereignty over the whole of Cyprus, they argued, if the bases were to remain viable and escape the fate of the Canal Base. Moreover, were Greece to acquire Cyprus, they reasoned, British use of the bases, however guaranteed in an international agreement, might become impossible if Greece were to come under heavy diplomatic pressure from the Arab states.[127] The second argument was, in 1954–55, no less telling. To shore up their position in the Middle East and to guard against the growth of Russian influence in the region, the British had promoted the Baghdad Pact, the source, as we have seen, of much friction with Egypt. To have shown any sign of weakness over *enosis* in 1954 would have dealt this ambitious plan a double blow. It would have undermined the confidence of Britain's intended partners in an effective British contribution to regional defence, and, above all, it would have alienated Turkey whose strategic cooperation in the eastern Mediterranean had become, partly as a result of Anglo-Egyptian disharmony, a cardinal factor in British policy. Finally, even if all these objections had been overcome, there remained a major, perhaps decisive obstacle to concession. Eden's Suez Agreement had exposed him to accusations of weakness and appeasement from the right of the Conservative Party to which he was very sensitive.[128] Neither he nor Churchill, while still prime minister, were likely to court the risks of a second and much less urgent retreat in the eastern Mediterranean.[129]

Thus, despite the military strain and periodic atrocities of the EOKA campaign, which tied down some 25,000 British troops,[130] at no point did the British consider yielding to the demands for *enosis*. In 1956 the constitutional concessions offered in the Radcliffe plan envisaged a local legislature enjoying wide internal autonomy, but with foreign affairs and defence reserved to British control. Despite Makarios's release from detention to encourage discussion, a move that prompted Lord Salisbury's resignation from the British cabinet,[131] there was little chance at this stage that Greek Cypriot leaders would accept this renunciation of their goal. Nor could EOKA terrorism, for all its ruthlessness, apply sufficient pressure, whether internationally or through the disillusionment of British opinion. Instead Makarios and EOKA were outflanked by Macmillan who recognised that the key to defeating *enosis* lay in associating Greece and Turkey with the negotiation of Cyprus's future. Indeed, by 1958, as the *enosis* struggle widened into a communal conflict between Greek and Turkish Cypriots, the Cyprus question threatened to rupture NATO's precarious solidarity in the eastern Mediterranean. Under the Macmillan plan of 1958 each community was to have its own legislature, while representatives of Greek and Turkish governments were to 'assist' the British governor. The status of Cyprus as a British possession was to remain unchanged for seven years: thereafter sovereignty might be shared with Greece and Turkey.[132]

As we shall see, although this plan was unsuccessful, Macmillan's internationalising strategy, substantially modified, forced Makarios to abandon *enosis* in September 1958, and secured a treaty that preserved British sovereignty over the military base areas in perpetuity. But by the time of the Cyprus treaty in 1960, the strategic and diplomatic imperatives so pressing in 1954–55, had undergone a striking change.

THE CARIBBEAN

By comparison with their possessions in Asia, Africa and the Middle East, the British seemed to regard their Caribbean territories with an indifference all the more striking in view of the legendary value of the 'sugar islands' in the eighteenth century. There were, however, good reasons for this neglect. The Asian colonies had offered wealth, power and a certain glamour: there still seemed in the 1950s much to be gained from close association with the successor states of South and South East Asia. In colonial Africa, the challenge of building new states, societies and economies in lands (as it was thought) without a history exercised a powerful hold on the British imagination. In the 1950s, much of tropical Africa still seemed a 'new frontier' with vast resources to exploit. But the British West Indies were a monument to colonial failure: poverty-stricken, politically backward, economically as well as politically fragmented, with a golden past and a leaden future. West Indian societies may have lacked the long and sophisticated cultural history of, say, India: but equally, they could not be briskly modernised through the kind of constitutional reforms the Colonial Office had in mind for its African territories. They had old constitutional traditions and a long history of obstructiveness to the imperial government.[133] Poor, uncooperative, without evident strategic or economic value,[134] yet loyal to Crown and empire, there seemed little chance amid all the pressing imperial problems with which London had to contend, that the British Caribbean would receive much attention in the mother-country. And so, generally, it proved.

Nevertheless the Caribbean territories could not be left where they stood in the 1930s: politically stagnant and sliding deeper into economic depression with its grim accompaniment of malnutrition, illiteracy and agricultural deterioration.[135] Riots and disturbances in the later 1930s had shown that depression provided fertile soil for labour unrest and political agitation. The Royal Commission under Lord Moyne (1937–38) reached a conclusion that had become almost a commonplace in other parts of the empire, that under the existing system of limited popular representation in the island assemblies, with executives answerable only to the governors, the tendency towards political obstruction and non-cooperation was accentuated. The Commission recommended *progress* towards universal suffrage, but shied away from self-government, arguing that so long as the islands depended upon British financial assistance, London must have real control over their affairs. But the fillip that the disturbances had given to political activity was now powerfully reinforced. With the outbreak of war, the Caribbean ceased to be a quiet colonial backwater. American interest in the region, long matured,[136] now became a potent factor in British policy. Under the destroyers-for-bases pact, an American military presence was established. In March 1942 the joint Anglo-American Caribbean Commission to foster cooperation between British and American territories[137] was set up, at the height of the diplomatic offensive in Washington against the unreconstructed imperialism held responsible for Britain's humiliation in Malaya.

In these circumstances, the British found it inexpedient to stand firm against the demand of the Jamaica assembly for universal suffrage and for an executive answerable to the assembly.[138] Under the new constitution of 1944, universal suffrage was introduced and five members of the executive council (out of ten) were to be elected from the Lower House, in a form of 'quasi-ministerial' government.[139] Jamaican politics had undergone a transformation. Henceforth the growth of party organisations and popular politics, together with the glittering prospect of full internal self-government, set the pace of constitutional change.

What the British had conceded in Jamaica in the special conditions of wartime they could scarcely hope to deny to their other Caribbean colonies,[140] least of all in Trinidad, less populous but wealthier than Jamaica. But, as we have seen elsewhere, London combined a pragmatic acceptance of widening local participation with a resolve that constitutional change should also create viable colonial states capable of carrying through ambitious programmes of economic development, capable, that is, of acting as useful partners to Britain in the post-war world. The innumerable islands and islets which, with the two small mainland colonies (British Honduras and British Guiana), made up the British Caribbean were thus a peculiarly baffling problem. What gave the policy makers hope was the enthusiasm shown by Caribbean political leaders themselves for a West Indian federation. A conference of Caribbean politicians at Montego Bay in Jamaica in 1947 endorsed closer association.[141] The Jamaica assembly voted unanimously for federation in August 1951:[142] and where Jamaica led, surely others would follow.

This favourable attitude derived from several influential assumptions among West Indian leaders. To some it was self-evident that only the forging of a common British West Indian nationality would provide the basis for the independent nationhood which the war had brought into (distant) prospect. To others, it seemed obvious that Britain would never concede full self-government and equality of status with Canada, Australia and the other dominions in the Commonwealth unless the islanders agreed to federate.[143] To yet others, the urgent need for economic development could only realistically be tackled by a government capable of planning and mobilising resources over the whole of the British Caribbean.[144] But enthusiasm for federation still had to compete with the strong local patriotism of the island populations and the reluctance of local politicians to give up to a new federal centre the powers that were just beginning to be devolved by the imperial government. As a result, even though by 1957 the omens for federation seemed very favourable, with the passage of the British Caribbean Federation Act through Parliament in 1956, the price of agreement was a federal government of very limited scope that was forced to share its powers especially in finance. Worse still, in the first federal general election in 1958, the supporters of federation did badly in the two major islands of Jamaica and Trinidad where growing prosperity weakened the appeal of economic cooperation with the poverty-stricken lesser isles.[145] The mainland colonies of British Honduras (now Belize) and British Guiana (now Guyana) had rejected federation. In British Guiana where, uniquely, Indians from South Asia formed a majority of the population, a political movement of avowedly communist sympathy under the charismatic dentist Cheddi Jagan, together with growing communal tensions in the colony, strengthened British reluctance to permit rapid progress to full self-government.[146]

The ill-fated West Indian Federation lasted only four years and never achieved independence. Its doom was sealed by the defection of Jamaica which had earlier extracted from London the promise of full self-government in return for continued membership of the federation. Despite British efforts, including a visit by Harold Macmillan in March 1961, the tide of opinion in Jamaica was too strong and the federation's largest and strongest unit withdrew to receive separate independence in August 1962. Trinidad elected to take separate independence in the same month. The remaining islands followed slowly and sometimes painfully in their wake. For some, separate independence seemed viable; for others, associated status with Britain being responsible for their defence and foreign relations appeared better suited to their limited means. But even for the very smallest and weakest the tug of local loyalties and the desire for local autonomy was strong.[147]

Thus a *West Indian* nationalism never rose to challenge British imperialism: only Jamaican, Trinidadian, Barbadian or Grenadan. Nor were these island nationalisms quite like the colonial nationalisms the British encountered elsewhere. As colonists themselves, however involuntary, the West Indians had no indigenous pre-colonial past to evoke, although images of Africa exercised a powerful fascination in the home of Garveyism. Language, tradition, sport and new patterns of post-war migration drew them towards Britain. Here the Crown was not a symbol of alien domination but a popular institution: the Queen remained head of state in the independent islands. Perhaps, too, fear of absorption by the larger islands, or even by American influence, moderated anti-colonial feeling. The British, for their part, had little to lose from the advance of self-government in the region:

their prime requirement was that its beneficiaries should be 'reliable' and 'moderate' and that the island colonies should, by hook or by crook, be lashed together into a federation, however gimcrack, rather than becoming petty, insolvent dominions, a burden and an embarrassment to the mother-country. This ambition governed their whole approach to the question of constitutional advance after 1945. Their efforts failed. But for the most part, despite economic frailty and with some notorious exceptions, the island governments proved far less prone to financial or political disorder in the aftermath of independence than had often been feared.[148] But by a curious paradox, at the very time when the last traces of British rule in the Caribbean were disappearing after 350 years, the West Indian connection was becoming a major political issue in Britain herself.

6   Winds of Change

Two short periods since the Second World War stand out as phases of rapid change in Britain's relations with her empire and in her general international position. Between 1945 and 1948, the bulk of her Asian dependencies were granted independence, Britain abandoned the Palestine mandate and the goal of self-government was loudly proclaimed in the West African colonies. The primacy of American power in the West was recognised and the overriding importance of close Anglo-American cooperation became the leading principle of British foreign policy. Britain's place in the world was broadly redefined in official thinking to accord with these new conditions. Then, between 1959 and 1964, further and more drastic changes took place which marked the onset of Britain's final transformation from a global power with an overseas empire and considerable capacity for independent action, into a regional power whose remaining overseas possessions were more of an embarrassment than a source of strength, trade or influence; and a power whose economic performance placed her at best somewhere below the top of the second division. In this second and decisive period of readjustment, almost all the remaining colonial territories passed rapidly into independence; the connections with the Commonwealth states were steadily attenuated by Britain's declared intention to seek membership of the European Economic Community; growing economic weakness undermined British influence and imposed new constraints on Britain's military capability; and the consolidation of Western Europe under French leadership eroded Britain's old status within the Western Alliance and inflicted a punishing series of diplomatic defeats on London. With the decay of the long-cherished connections in the extra-European world and the sharp reduction of British influence in Europe, the real decline of British power by the later 1960s had proceeded further and faster than could have seemed remotely possible at the end of the 1940s. The mordant observation of Dean Acheson in 1962 that Britain had lost an empire and not yet found a role appeared a cruel but accurate epitaph on two decades of post-war decline.

In retrospect the Suez crisis serves as a convenient watershed to separate the years in which Britain's survival as an independent world power seemed possible (and desirable) from the subsequent era which saw the rapid liquidation of the colonial empire and the scaling down of Britain's global commitments. It has sometimes been argued that the humiliating outcome of the expedition played an important part in the reshaping of British world policy on more modest lines: by revealing to the world at large the hollowness of Britain's great power pretensions; by forcibly educating official and public opinion at home in the reality of Britain's reduced circumstances and the dangers of 'gunboat diplomacy'; and by stimulating the political appetite of colonial nationalists. Suez, on this view, was both symptomatic of Britain's declining international position and instrumental in promoting a more flexible response to it, especially on the key issue of how long the framework of imperial commitments could be maintained.

There could be no doubting the shock that Suez dealt British diplomacy, strategy and politics. It was a stunning blow to those who supposed that the post-war redistribution of global power and influence had been completed by the early 1950s. It brought about the severest rupture of Anglo-American relations since the Second World War and cast doubt over the future of the 'special relationship'. It precipitated a crisis within the Commonwealth which was fiercely divided over the propriety of British action. It revealed the vulnerability of sterling to American financial pressure and the danger that independent action might jeopardise Britain's revival as a premier trading and financial power – a prime object of government policy. It generated acute political division at home, enforced a change of prime minister and threatened to bring down the government altogether. And it exposed the weaknesses of British military power and the unreliability of foreign bases in time of crisis.[1] But the precise effects on British attitudes towards the timing of the transfer of power in the colonial territories are much more difficult to gauge. It is too facile to see the accelerated colonial withdrawal after 1960 as a direct consequence of the humiliation of 1956. Nor is it clear that Suez extinguished the great power aspirations of British leaders or their readiness to defend far-flung interests by military action.[2] But equally plainly, no British government thereafter was likely to risk the domestic and international consequences of foreign intervention (let alone full-scale colonial repression) except under the most favourable political circumstances and with the widest measure of international support.

The immediate consequence of the crisis was to elevate Harold Macmillan to the premiership. Macmillan's earlier political career had been devoted to social and economic questions: he had been an ardent advocate of government action to alleviate mass unemployment and a fierce critic of Chamberlain and the National Government. During the war, however, he acquired a new range of experience as the coordinator of British policy in North Africa and the Mediterranean and developed close contacts with senior American policy makers, especially with Eisenhower. Macmillan had been one of the most bellicose proponents of military intervention in 1956. But the real key to his attainment of the premiership and to the style and substance of his diplomacy was his status as Churchill's leading protégé. From Churchill, certainly, he inherited the most far-reaching conception of British power and influence in the post-war world. Britain must remain a global power by virtue of her Commonwealth connections and colonial interests. She was to be the leading power among the West European states – a status that was hers by default after 1945. And she was to enjoy a special understanding, both European and global, with the United States. Indeed, each of these roles leaned heavily on the others: the tripod needed all three legs if it was to remain in place.

Macmillan recognised that the recovery of British influence required first and foremost the healing of the open schism with the United States and lost no time in establishing friendly contact with Eisenhower and Dulles. In October 1957 he secured 'the great prize':[3] the restoration of full Anglo-American cooperation in the development of atomic weapons, suspended since 1946 and essential if Britain's independent nuclear armoury was not to be prohibitively expensive.[4] Here the revival of the 'special relationship' was given concrete and valuable form, marking, so it seemed, a return to the hey-day of Anglo-American friendship during the Second World War. In 1959–1960, Macmillan's influence as a leader of the Western Alliance reached its peak with the death of Dulles and the vacillation and uncertainty of Eisenhower's last year and a half of the presidency. Macmillan's journey to Moscow in 1959, his efforts to promote a summit conference and his highly successful performance at the United Nations in

September 1960 seemed to suggest that Britain's unique position as an Atlantic, European and Commonwealth power would continue to secure an influence far greater than that justified by her military or economic resources alone. Macmillan himself had no doubt about the foundation of his success. 'From Bermuda [in March 1957]', he told Selwyn Lloyd at the end of 1959, 'I set myself to rebuild the Anglo-American alliance to its former strength. This has been achieved and must never be abandoned'.[5]

But Macmillan's panache could not conceal a decisive shift in the relative positions of Britain and the United States which proceeded inexorably between 1957 and 1964. Before 1957, while close Anglo-American understanding was the keystone of British foreign policy, independent British action without American approval still seemed possible – as the cabinet's policy towards Suez indicates. Large parts of the non-communist world still lay more obviously under British influence than American – including the Middle East. The scope for British world power still seemed relatively wide in a world whose partition between the superpowers was far from complete. But after 1957, the forward movement of American influence steadily demolished any such assumption. Britain's dependence on American defence technology became greater and greater until by the time of the Skybolt crisis in December 1962 it was clear that the core of Britain's claim to great power status, her independent nuclear deterrent, existed only by American grace and favour. Implicit in the revived special relationship after 1957 was the understanding that Britain would never again embark upon such a major operation as Suez without American knowledge and tacit approval. Thirdly, the years after 1957 saw the steady expansion of America's global commitments and her entry into regions previously reserved to British or European influence. The Eisenhower doctrine of 1957 asserted American concern for the security of the Middle East in the wake of Britain's disaster at Suez. Henceforth, in Middle Eastern affairs, the leading voice among the Western Powers, once conceded by the United States to Britain, was to remain firmly in Washington. In South Asia, too, after 1956, American influence largely replaced British, partly, perhaps, for financial and economic reasons.[6] From the late 1950s onwards Washington was drawn more and more directly into the politics of South East Asia, first in Laos and then in Vietnam. And while American policy makers were cautious about upsetting their NATO partners by strident declarations about African nationalism, there was, from the time of Vice-President Nixon's African tour in 1957 a steady growth of American diplomatic activity in the continent marked by a quintupling of economic aid between 1958 and 1963.[7]

These developments, coupled with Britain's financial weakness after 1960 and her reliance upon American help to preserve sterling's role as a reserve currency,[8] changed the character of Anglo-American partnership, especially with the extension of cold war rivalry into new spheres of the world after 1960. America's delayed emergence as a power with interests in every important region swept away the old assumption that Britain would retain a privileged position as the leading Western power in Africa, the Middle East and South Asia, co-planner with the United States of the West's global strategy.

One factor in the growing readiness of the United States to supplement or supplant British influence may have been the fear that Britain with her still extensive colonial commitments would be an unsatisfactory champion of Western interests among new states whose leaders were pathologically sensitive on colonial issues. Indeed, Britain's claim to be a vital bridge between the West and the new Afro-Asian nations looked distinctly implausible after the diplomatic debacle of Suez. Before Suez, Indian cooperation had helped the British to moderate American policy in East and South East Asia.[9] But over Suez India supported Nasser's nationalisation of the Canal and denounced British intervention with unequivocal severity.[10] Indo-American relations improved and India's membership of the Commonwealth was the subject of vigorous debate in New Delhi.[11] Ceylon and Pakistan were at pains to dissociate themselves from British actions. The Suez affair highlighted the deep divisions of interest and outlook throughout the Commonwealth. Australia and New Zealand gave London strong support and incurred American displeasure as a result. South Africa preserved a tactful silence. But the Canadian government, with its special empathy for American opinion, opposed military intervention forthrightly because of its dangerous effects on the United Nations, Anglo-American relations and the unity of the Commonwealth.[12]

Hence the second of Macmillan's priorities in his effort to revive British influence and prestige was to rebuild good relations especially with the countries of the Asian Commonwealth and to insist that Britain still intended to play a great power role in the Far East. This was the purpose behind the prime minister's Commonwealth tour in early 1958.[13] By his own account Macmillan was exhilarated by the discovery that British influence was still so great in Australia and New Zealand.[14] For all the changes of the post-war world and the stresses of Suez the Commonwealth still seemed a workmanlike instrument for maximising British influence and promoting British interests in regions where Britain's physical power had sharply declined. But Macmillan was also greatly concerned with a larger issue, potentially of historic significance: whether the new states of Asia and Africa would lean towards the West or be won over by Marxism. His eastern tour impressed him with the vigour and independence with which the new Commonwealth states viewed international affairs, but also with the fragility of the new ruling elites, with their Western sympathies, in the face of enormous social and economic difficulties. 'The danger here', he noted of Ceylon

(as elsewhere throughout the East) is the collapse of the agreeable, educated, Liberal, North Oxford society to whom we have transferred power, in the face of the dynamism of Communism with all the strength of Russian imperialism behind it.[15]

The lesson he drew was that not only must the West assist the economic progress of the underdeveloped countries,[16] but that if the Commonwealth was to provide an effective counter to the growth of a worldwide Marxism, friction between Britain and the new member-states – above all over the issue of colonial self-government – must be reduced to the minimum. British interests and Western influence alike required the smoothest transition from colonial rule to independence.

That was not to say, of course, that colonial rule was to be terminated with all possible speed. As we have seen, even in the spring of 1959 the schedule for the transfer of power in East Africa was leisurely and British attitudes to anti-federation nationalism in Central Africa profoundly unsympathetic. What it did mean was that London's approach was to be increasingly influenced by what appeared the wider British interest in preserving the Commonwealth as a system of influence and by calculations about the place of colonial policy in the global rivalry of East and West. These preoccupations led to a further inflation of the windy rhetoric about the Commonwealth's uniqueness as a multiracial association which served, perhaps unconsciously, to veil its defects as a vehicle of British influence and its lack of more than the most rudimentary community of outlook in international affairs – a shortcoming starkly revealed in the Suez crisis and progressively accentuated as new members entered through the 1960s. Macmillan himself had pondered what unifying principle could hold together an association of disparate cultures and constitutions.[17] How so loosely articulated a political community as the Commonwealth was to resist the centrifugal pressures – economic, political, strategic, ideological – whose force had already broken the back of the empire itself was indeed a question. But not perhaps until the complacent presumptions about the continuity of Britain's influence in the post-colonial states began to collapse in the mid-1960s could it be answered realistically.

If Suez drove a wedge into Anglo-American relations and revealed the divergences of outlook in the Commonwealth, it was also a great political crisis at home with major implications for the future conduct of foreign policy and the maintenance of imperial commitments. After a short bipartisan honeymoon Eden's efforts to protect Britain's interests in the Canal had come under increasingly heavy attack from the opposition as well as from elements in his own party. The resort to force, however disguised as 'separating the combatants', brought forth a storm of criticism denouncing such 'gunboat diplomacy' as incompatible with the internationalist ideas embodied in the UN Charter and as counterproductive in its alienation of international opinion. The total failure of the military operation as a result of American pressure drew on Eden the resentment and contempt of those who had favoured firm action against Nasser, vindicated those who had opposed it on principle and ensured his political downfall. Assailed by vituperation at home and abroad, condemned to a painful diplomatic acquiescence in Nasser's victory and with its own supporters divided and demoralised, the government tottered on the brink of collapse. The price of defending what had seemed so vital a national interest had proved high indeed. Moreover two questions were immediately raised. If it had proved impossible to rally full public support for the use of force on an occasion when, by general agreement, Britain's national interest in the outcome was very great, how easy would it be to win public sympathy for the defence of less prominent imperial interests against internal or external attack? And having failed by its own yardstick to protect British interests in what it had claimed was a crucial encounter with an irresponsible nationalist dictatorship, had not the government itself destroyed the credibility of military action to protect imperial interests in the eyes of opinion at home?

It might be argued, then, that the political response in Britain to the course of the Suez crisis indicated a growing popular indifference to the symbols and substance of imperial power and an impatience with the great power pretensions of British leaders. But this is almost certainly too bold a conclusion. In the hey-day of Victorian and Edwardian imperialism, empire-minded politicians had railed against the ignorance and indifference of opinion at home and its parochial preoccupations. 'One must unfortunately explain to these d – d fools why we want an Empire', complained Lord Milner in 1906, 'and it pinches one in dealing with the methods of maintaining it'.[18] Those who had conducted Britain's worldwide diplomacy at the height of her power or who had added to her imperial commitments in the age of imperial expansion had never felt able to rely on public enthusiasm at home and had generally preferred to dampen rather than fire public interest. Consequently the 'education' of public opinion in times of emergency was a slow and uncertain operation that required skilled management and considerable luck. Public confusion and division at the time of Suez reflected the absence of both in the government's handling of its case[19] far more than any deep-seated change in popular attitudes – or so the apparent course of public feeling during the Falklands crisis would suggest. Nor was there much sign of the development of new and more liberal attitudes on more strictly colonial issues. Even in the Labour Party with its long tradition of sympathy for colonial nationalism grass roots response to imperial questions was minimal in the 1950s.[20] On the other hand, the deeply-felt humiliation of Suez bred on the Right of the Conservative Party a fierce resistance to the conciliation of Afro-Asian nationalism which acted as a brake on the pragmatism of ministers.[21]

But did Suez prompt a radical rethink among ministers and policy makers about the utility of Britain's colonial possessions? It has often been suggested that the rapid colonial withdrawal after 1960, especially from Africa, stemmed from just such an agonising reappraisal undertaken, so it is said, with cool, ruthlessly unsentimental pragmatism, by Harold Macmillan. As will be suggested later in the chapter it is not necessary, and probably misleading, to see the actual course of Britain's colonial retreat after 1960 as a consequence chiefly of a sharp change of policy in London. To that extent, the search for the causes of a new outlook on colonial matters in British politics may be redundant. Secondly, the evidence for such a rethink is at best indecisive. The notorious colonial cost-benefit analysis carried out in 1957 at Macmillan's instigation is sometimes cited in evidence of the new mood. But its conclusions were scarcely drastic:

> Any premature withdrawal of authority by the United Kingdom would seem bound to add to the areas of stress and discontent in the world. There are territories over which jurisdiction might be surrendered without prejudice to the essentials of strategy or foreign relations, and at some modest savings to the Exchequer. But would we stand to gain by thus rewarding loyalty to the Crown which is an enduring characteristic of so many colonial peoples? The United Kingdom has been too long connected with its Colonial possessions to sever ties abruptly without creating a bewilderment which would be discreditable and dangerous.[22]

On these criteria there was little scope for rapid colonial disengagement.

Nevertheless, the political trauma of the Suez crisis undoubtedly had an effect upon the calculations which British leaders were bound to make about the domestic repercussions of their external policies. Suez highlighted the dangers of allowing the defence of Britain's overseas interests to become a battleground of party warfare – not least for the sake of the credibility of British policy abroad. It emphasised the value of restoring some measure of bipartisanship in external policy and avoiding the open hostility of influential religious and secular figures.[23] For Conservative leaders particularly the drama of Eden's fall was a grim lesson in the unpredictable consequences of a prolonged international confrontation both for the authority of the government and the loyalty and confidence of its supporters – especially under a barrage of international criticism. No subsequent Conservative prime minister was likely to take the same risks as Eden or carry his colleagues with him in the attempt: certainly not in the decade over which Suez cast its shadow. There were other lessons too less narrowly relevant to party advantage.

Politically, the most dangerous and demoralising aspect of the crisis had been Britain's international isolation alongside France, and her public condemnation in the forum of the United Nations – an institution of which Britain had been a founding member and whose authority British governments had, prior to Suez, been at pains to uphold. In international affairs (as perhaps in private life) isolation and general condemnation can erode self-confidence at terrifying speed, especially in an open society where the press and public comment are unrestricted. For the makers of British policy the experience was novel and intimidating. What made it the more painful and bitter was the long and powerful tradition in British foreign policy of preserving the maximum international support and sympathy for its actions and of supporting (largely in Britain's own interest) broadly internationalist principles in world affairs – the renunciation of force, the freedom of trade and communications, the promotion of international cooperation. Indeed, of all the major powers, Britain's political tradition was the most international and the least isolationist.[24] Consequently, no lesson of Suez was more telling or perhaps more widely influential on the whole conduct of Britain's external policies than the fear that by incautious commitment or inflexible conservatism Britain might again find herself isolated and friendless, jeopardising in the process valuable friendships and reserves of goodwill around the world.

The effects of the Suez crisis upon Britain's imperial role were, therefore, certainly not obvious, simple, clear-cut or immediate. It did not create a revulsion against empire at home: indeed, as if by common consent, the whole affair dropped out of political debate with remarkable speed.[25] It did not destroy the will or ability of British governments to intervene militarily to protect other British interests. Nor did the loss of Britain's premier position in the Middle East produce any rapid change in her readiness to shoulder military commitments east of Suez – as the Anglo-Malayan Defence Agreement of 1957 reveals. Nasser's success may have whetted the appetites of colonial nationalists in the empire, but the special circumstances which permitted his triumph had little relevance to those dependencies where self-government had yet to be introduced. Moreover, as we have seen, the main lines of British colonial policy had already been laid down before the confrontation with Egypt became acute. The impact of the crisis was more subtle and diffuse. Inevitably, it helped to reinforce the constraints on British policy, to emphasise the domestic and external difficulties posed by actions which might isolate Britain and to point up the dangers of armed intervention except under highly favourable circumstances. Suez did not make a rapid colonial withdrawal inescapable, but it signalled the strength of the new pressures on Britain deriving, especially, from the Commonwealth. As political change rolled through the system with ever-increasing speed after 1958, the British were bound, out of concern for their wider interests, to take full account of what Suez had taught them. The alternative – proud defiance – was possible, but it might drive Britain into the precarious and insular position occupied for so long by that most resolute of colonial powers – Portugal.

There was one further influence, only indirectly linked with Suez, that came to bear on British policy after 1957: the shift in Britain's relationship with the Western European states. In the late 1940s and early 1950s, Britain had been, in terms of economic strength, military power and political cohesion, indisputably the premier European member of the Western Alliance. Her dual character as both an Atlantic power enjoying special intimacy with the United States and as a European state with a vital interest in continental defence conferred a special influence in Western European affairs greater than Britain had possessed at any time since 1918–19. British leadership in Europe seemed a fact of life to the architects of economic and political reconstruction on the continent. In 1954 Eden's whirlwind tour of European capitals and his pledge of a permanent British military contribution to the land defence of Europe broke the deadlock over Germany's rearmament. At the time of the earliest plans for the creation of a European economic community at the Messina conference of 1955, it was taken for granted that Britain would accept membership in some form.[26] But, notoriously, British attitudes towards Europe were deeply ambivalent. Churchill had spoken of European unity and Bevin had dreamt of a 'third force' of the Commonwealth and Western Europe under British leadership.[27] However, European cohesion under British leadership was one thing: the notion of supranational European institutions or of a political community quite another. Throughout the 1950s, it remained an absolute orthodoxy of British policy that membership of such a community, or even of a European customs union, was fundamentally incompatible with Britain's Commonwealth links, her global commitments and even with her special relationship with the United States.

British coolness towards the idea of an economic community and the refusal to contribute positively to its planning reflected London's confidence that without British participation such schemes would make little progress.[28] As the extent of this miscalculation became clear, the British, while maintaining their opposition to membership of a customs union or a political confederation, strove to preserve their European links by negotiating a free trade area which would allow the free movement of manufactures, but not of foodstuffs, between Britain and the members of the projected economic community. The virtue of such an arrangement in British eyes was that it would keep open European markets to British industrial products while allowing Britain to maintain the system of Commonwealth preferences which gave privileged access to Commonwealth foodstuffs in Britain and to British manufactures in the Commonwealth. It would also check any tendency by the new European combination to shut out British influence.[29] But this bold attempt to gain the best of both worlds came to nothing. French resistance and the anxiety of the pro-Europeans in other countries lest the dilution of the community and the alienation of agrarian interests destroy its fragile new unity were too strong.[30] By the end of 1959, with the European Economic Community in successful operation, with the advent of De Gaulle to power in France, with a newly sovereign West Germany[31] suspicious and resentful of British enthusiasm for detente with Russia and inclined towards an 'unholy alliance'[32] with France, British influence in Europe, so powerful five years earlier, seemed to have reached a nadir.[33]

The effect was to prompt a far-reaching reappraisal in London. By the summer of 1960, the cabinet had endorsed the view that some move towards closer association with the EEC must be made. Macmillan himself brooded gloomily over the prospects facing Britain:

Shall we be caught between a hostile (or at least less and less friendly) America and a boastful, powerful 'Empire of Charlemagne' now under French but later bound to come under German control. Is this the real reason for joining the Common Market (if we are acceptable) and for abandoning (a) the Seven (b) British agriculture (c) the Commonwealth? It's a grim choice.[34]

Perhaps a majority of the cabinet still favoured some form of association rather than full membership, even if on less attractive terms than had been sought in 1957–58. But by the spring of 1961, French insistence had made it clear that no such halfway house would be tolerated: if Britain wished to revive her European links she must apply for full membership. On 9 August 1961, after an abortive attempt to gain Commonwealth approval, and with little sign of public interest or sympathy at home for the 'European idea', formal application was made. Some sixteen months later, after arduous negotiations, a French veto abruptly terminated the proceedings.

Coinciding as it did with the decision to accelerate Britain's colonial withdrawal from Africa, with the onset of aggravated economic difficulties at home, with the failure of Blue Streak and Britain's real independence in nuclear weaponry, and following so closely on the heels of the Suez debacle, the application to the EEC appears irresistibly as an historic watershed in British world policy, marking the moment of decisive choice between the global ambitions and imperial commitments of the past and a future as a member nation of a united Europe with its supranational ideals and dynamic economy.[35] But that it appeared so to Macmillan or his colleagues in 1960–61 is much more doubtful.

Undoubtedly, what weighed most with the cabinet in London was the political danger of British isolation in Europe, the fear that in such crucial matters as the management of NATO and the defence of Western Europe British views and interests would count for little between the United States and a United Europe. Deprived of her pretensions to an influence in Europe, moreover, British leverage on the United States could only decline. By some means the European leg of the Churchillian tripod had to be restored, and the dramatic decline of British authority in European affairs since 1955 made good: for to be forced on to the periphery of European affairs seemed as fatal to British power and independence as the most far-reaching concession to European supranationalism. From this point of view, British insistence that membership of the EEC was compatible with Commonwealth links was more than just an empty platitude. It reflected the conviction, implicit in the Churchillian tripod, that Britain could no more depend on her Commonwealth connection *alone* than she could upon the 'special relationship' or her European links. Macmillan's own determination to enhance Anglo-American friendship, and his unyielding insistence on preserving Britain's nuclear deterrent at the Nassau conference in 1962 indicated indeed how far he was committed to maintaining Britain's special status as an Atlantic power, even while negotiating for membership of the EEC. The whole aim of British policy was thus to keep a careful balance between the three spheres and to avoid an overriding commitment to any. In this there was no novelty. The British had never accepted in the past that their imperial interests should dictate their whole external policy. Their long attachment to free trade, their recognition that vital interests were at stake in 1914 and 1939, their participation in NATO, reflected the historic diversity of British interests and the inescapable geographical fact that Britain's own security was bound up with the security of Europe. What British ministers were saying in 1961 was not only that Europe and the Commonwealth were compatible interests, but that, in London's view, they *must* be. That the application for EEC membership has come in retrospect to *seem* a decisive turning away from the empire-commonwealth may be ascribed chiefly to the fact that whereas in the past Britain's links with the empire countries had been strong enough to counteract her commitments in Europe, after 1961 those links were more attenuated, and the price of a British role in Europe much higher, than ever before in peacetime.

Here then was a fourth and powerful factor to set beside the other constraints on policy whose impact was greatly enhanced after the Suez crisis. From the summer of 1960 until the veto of January 1963 Britain's approach to her colonial commitments was necessarily influenced by the assumption that sooner rather than later she would be a member of the EEC, and that, as De Gaulle recognised for France, British influence in a revived and vigorous Europe would be jeopardised by ugly colonial confrontations for which her European partners would have no sympathy. Neither sensitivity to American, Commonwealth and domestic opinion, nor their new European policy required an *abandonment* of global influence or the erasure of all post-colonial relations. But they imposed great circumspection in their management.

THE ECONOMICS OF DECLINE

In the late 1940s the British had constructed a closely integrated trading and currency bloc – the Sterling Area – embracing almost all the empire-Commonwealth. A coordinated policy of discrimination against dollar goods, close cooperation in the regulation of exports and imports, the preferential supply of development capital from Britain, and the management in London of the gold and foreign currency reserves of the whole Area were the essential features of the system. With about a quarter of the world's population and a quarter of its trade in 1950 this was an economic empire that was not to be sniffed at. Its perpetuation under British management was a central object of British policy, and secured for Britain not merely a considerable influence in the affairs of the member states but a powerful position in international economic diplomacy as the leader of an economic bloc which, in population and geographical scope if not in wealth, far outstripped its principal rival the dollar area. Indeed, leadership of the empire-commonwealth, and of the Sterling Area, together with her status as a nuclear power, helped to make Britain, if not a superpower, certainly a world power of much more than the second rank at the start of the 1950s.

British confidence in the post-war Sterling Area as a vehicle for what London saw as Britain's beneficent influence in international affairs rested upon a series of crucial assumptions about the future of the world economy and of the relations between Britain and her Sterling Area partners. In the first place the shortage of dollars and the difficulties of trading with the dollar area (which justified the apparatus of regulation and exchange control) was expected to be of indefinite duration. So long as this was true the sterling countries would have to cling together for mutual protection.[36] Secondly, it seemed likely that the strong demand for the primary products which the Overseas Sterling Area economies supplied would continue and grow, so that the relative value of primary goods would increase against manufactured. Keynes had argued in the 1920s and 1930s that gradual industrialisation in less-developed countries would make primary products scarcer and dearer.[37] This would tend to make Commonwealth-Sterling Area markets richer and more valuable than those of industrial countries, especially since Britain would enjoy favoured access to them. Thirdly, Britain's own position as an industrial producer and exporter, although not free from considerable strains and difficulties, still looked secure: by 1949–50 most European countries had climbed back to pre-war levels of output,[38] but Britain enjoyed a share of world trade unmatched since before the First World War.[39] British industrial power, bolstered by war-induced technological innovation, would complement the agricultural and mineral wealth of the sterling-Commonwealth. Fourthly, while American aid and investment flowed, partly for political reasons, into Europe, Britain would continue to supply the great bulk of the sterling-Commonwealth's requirements of capital, an arrangement which would give London enormous leverage in adjusting the external policies of other member states to Britain's economic and currency needs. Hence there were good grounds for thinking that the bonds of trading complementarity and financial partnership would be proof against the effects of political and constitutional change, so that the transfer of power would leave intact the basic elements of Britain's relationship with her erstwhile colonial possessions. 'Commonwealth trade,' Edward Heath told an audience of EEC ministers in October 1961, 'is one of the strongest elements in maintaining the Commonwealth association.'[40]

In fact of course none of these assumptions survived much beyond the end of the 1950s. The dollar shortage steadily declined and with it the incentive for the close alignment of trade policies. Secondly, the assumption that the agricultural and mineral-based economies of the Commonwealth-Sterling Area would experience the most rapid growth on the strength of rising commodity prices turned out to be wrong. The terms of trade of developing countries deteriorated by some 16 per cent between 1955 and 1965:[41] in consequence they became less valuable as markets. The most buoyant sector of world trade in the 1950s and 1960s was the exchange of manufactured goods between industrialised countries:[42] it was the United States and the rapidly growing economies of Western Europe which offered the best long-term prospects for British industry.[43] By neglecting European markets for the softer outlets of the Commonwealth where preferences reinforced the advantages of exchange control, Britain's exports grew less rapidly than those of her main competitors. Thus, as the other great industrial economies revived, Britain's share of world exports declined from 29 per cent (1948) to 20 per cent (1954) to 13.7 per cent (1964).[44] Indeed, it was the *relative* failure of British exports to earn more abroad that increasingly threw doubt upon Britain's capacity to sustain her banker's function in the Sterling Area and the heavy burdens of overseas aid, investment and military expenditure – those indispensable instruments, so it was thought, of world power.

The heart of the problem lay in the fact that Britain's ability to act the part of the world's banker and investor was much less assured than before the war, and the pressure on her resources much greater. Before 1930 the sterling balances held in London by Britain's Sterling Area partners had been amply covered by Britain's own reserves of gold and foreign currency. After 1945 the disproportion was acute.[45] The danger of this was that if other members of the Sterling Area ran up deficits in their foreign trade and then drew upon their large sterling balances in London to meet them, Britain's own balance of payments would rapidly be threatened, with grave consequences either for the value of sterling or for the management of the British economy. In the later 1950s and 1960s this is precisely what happened, and the adverse consequences were reinforced by the growing tendency of the Sterling Area countries to turn for development capital to other countries besides Britain, entailing a further burden of dividends and interest payments.[46] The relaxation of controls with the end of the dollar shortage, Britain's inability to supply all the capital required in the Commonwealth-Sterling Area and the appearance of other suppliers and a reluctance to court the political risks of disciplining her sterling partners, reduced the leverage over the policies of the overseas members which had seemed London's birthright only shortly before.[47] More and more the British found themselves in the position of a bank forced into risky or unprofitable business by cavalier clients whom it feared to offend. By the later 1950s it was questionable whether the Overseas Sterling Area as an economic empire over which the British had hoped to preside was really more of a liability than an asset.[48]

Official attitudes, however, remained entrenched in the orthodoxy that economic and financial leadership of the Sterling Area and Commonwealth was indispensable to Britain's international position, on grounds of trade and diplomacy alike; and that the burdens and obligations of leadership simply had to be borne. In 1957 the British government rejected any suggestion of joining the European Economic Community, urging instead the formation of a free trade area confined to industrial goods – a provision which would have destroyed the Community's appeal to the huge and powerful lobby of European food producers. London's reasoning revealed its devotion to the Commonwealth connection:

> There are . . . substantial reasons why the United Kingdom could not become a member of such a Union [as the projected EEC]. They arise in particular from the United Kingdom's interests and responsibilities in the Commonwealth. Her Majesty's Government could not contemplate entering arrangements which would . . . make it impossible for the United Kingdom to treat imports from the Commonwealth at least as favourably as those from Europe . . . . It is essential that the United Kingdom should be able to continue the preferential arrangements which have been built up over the last twenty-five years.[49]

Any thought of sharing control of Britain's currency with the European states (whose political and economic stability was still regarded in

1957 with a suspicion bordering on contempt) was unhesitatingly rejected by the Treasury.[50] By contrast, at the Commonwealth Trade Conference at Montreal in 1958, London affirmed its faith in the Commonwealth as a trading bloc and promised a substantial increase in the provision of development capital from government funds – both to enlarge the market for British manufactures and to safeguard the political stability of the least developed countries.[51] This decision increased the burden of overseas aid by 100 per cent between 1957 and 1960.[52]

Solicitude for the Commonwealth was matched by an unchanging commitment to preserve for Britain her historical importance as a prime financial centre and a principal source of overseas investment. The Radcliffe Report in 1959 insisted that it was still in Britain's interest to maintain the Sterling Area system:

> We do not think it possible to dissociate these arrangements either from the longstanding trading relationships that lie behind them or from the political and other links by which most members of the area are joined in the Commonwealth. What is decisive . . . is the general harmony of interest between the United Kingdom economy and that of the rest of the Sterling Area . . . .[53]

The Committee accepted without demur the official view that Britain must strive to invest more abroad. Britain's large overseas investments in the past had reduced transport costs and enlarged the world market. 'They are also an integral part of the system that binds together in mutual dependence the economies of the United Kingdom and the great primary producing countries of the world'.[54] Britain, it concluded, had no choice but to continue along the same path since the government was committed (partly for political reasons) to the more rapid development of Commonwealth countries and because any sharp reductions in the supply of capital would react unfavourably on British exports.[55] What was needed was a substantial increase in Britain's export earnings to strengthen Britain's reserves as a banker of the Sterling Area and to provide the funds for heavier investment overseas.

Here then on the eve of the final and decisive wave of decolonisation was a remarkable reaffirmation of the old doctrine that British prosperity and influence was embodied in her role as the supplier of capital and manufactures to a worldwide network of primary producers, many of them linked to her through the commercial and political ties of the Commonwealth. Closely connected with this was the longstanding desire, shared by all the more powerful centres of British economic policy-making, to restore London's pride of place as a centre of international finance, and the widest use of sterling as a currency for international trade – attributes which, it was assumed, had conferred on Britain before 1939 substantial benefits in profit and influence. This drive culminated in the return of sterling to full convertibility 'in a blaze of confidence'[56] in 1958. As is sometimes the case, confidence preceded calamity.

The urge to maintain Britain's economic orientation towards the Commonwealth and her leadership of the Sterling Area did not mean that governments in London were blind to the limitations on Britain's economic strength. Since 1951 successive Conservative cabinets had been anxious to speed economic growth by the reduction of regulation, expenditure and taxation – the hallmarks of the austerity era under Labour. Indeed the defeat of the Labour Party and the revival of Conservatism seemed clear evidence that the electorate had grown impatient with the burdens loaded on to it after 1945. One of the earliest acts of Churchill's government had been to cut back considerably on the colossal rearmament plans adopted by the Labour cabinet at the time of the Korean war, and impose a far more modest programme.[57] In the summer of 1956 Eden set up a cabinet committee to push through further defence economies by cutting commitments and reducing the manpower of the armed forces – with the objective of improving the balance of payments by the large figure of £400 million a year.[58] Disillusionment with the services and heightened sensitivity to Britain's international financial weakness intensified the pressure for reduction in the aftermath of Suez.[59] Macmillan, now in Eden's place, was determined to drive this home against the wishes of the service chiefs. The result was the notorious defence white paper of April 1957 which stressed the excessive burden of defence expenditure in previous years, proclaimed a new and supposedly more economical reliance on nuclear deterrents as the centrepiece of defence policy and promised the end of conscription as soon as possible.[60] Macmillan's economising zeal was no doubt partly inspired by the need to recapture the middle ground of politics for a party and government punch-drunk after the Suez debacle: ending national service was clearly a popular move, a sign that austerity and emergency were over. But it was also intended to release manpower resources (especially in engineering) and technological expertise for a renewed export drive while simultaneously relieving the balance of payments of overseas expenditure. Manpower was to be brought down to some 375,000 for all three services by 1962[61] – less than half the figure for 1956.

But if the policy makers hoped that this streamlining of commitments and a new buoyancy in exports would lead to an improvement in Britain's economic position, to the reinforcement of sterling's role as a reserve currency and to the strengthening of economic and political ties with the new and emerging states of the Commonwealth through a larger volume of investment, they were to be disappointed on a grand scale. Between 1959 and 1965 everything went wrong. The promised export boom of 1960[62] produced a colossal deficit.[63] A great sterling crisis followed in 1961, inaugurating the series of restrictive measures since characterised as 'Stop-Go'. Britain's share of the world's manufactured exports steadily declined.[64] Meanwhile the cost in foreign exchange of overseas defence and aid rose sharply and painfully, more than doubling in net terms between 1958 and 1965.[65] An even larger deficit in 1964 led to a further series of crises for sterling, a continual resort to foreign creditors and eventually devaluation in 1967. The result, from 1960 onwards, was a steady shift in the prevailing assumptions that were still being echoed so confidently at the end of the 1950s.

The early signs of this reappraisal were to be found in the growing preoccupation with what were regarded as 'structural' defects in the British economy: the search for an incomes policy, for a regional policy and for better control over public expenditure.[66] A more dramatic indication of the new outlook was the new interest in the 'remarkable success'[67] of the EEC and the application for membership in the autumn of 1961 in the aftermath of the sterling crisis. The failure of the application, anxiety about Britain's economic performance, continued difficulty with the balance of payments and then the succession of sterling crises in the mid-1960s hammered home the lesson that Britain's economic power and influence were in steep decline and that the economy could no longer bear the external burdens which the policy makers of the late 1950s had enthusiastically heaped upon it. By the time that the Labour government's 'National Plan' was drawn up in the autumn of 1965 a sense of growing economic weakness and decline, amounting almost to a crisis, dictated the tone of official pronouncements.[68] Government must stop the increase in defence expenditure, especially net expenditure overseas; aid would have to be 'restrained'; the net outflow of long-term private capital would have to be reduced.[69] Something must be done to stimulate exports and check the incessant increase in manufactured imports. After 1965, indeed, overseas investment inside and outside the Sterling Area was restricted by 'voluntary agreement' and exchange control,[70] while the level of government overseas expenditure was first stabilised and then slightly reduced.[71] Even so, by the time that devaluation was eventually resorted to in November 1967, the British government had proportionately the largest foreign debts of any country in the world[72] – and had become 'the ward of the other developed countries of the non-Communist world' who exercised 'the same watchful concern over the British economy that the Aid Consortia exercised over those of India, Indonesia or Turkey'.[73] The contrast with the position of strength from which the policy makers of the late 1950s had proposed to play their hand could scarcely have been more vivid or more humiliating.

Thus it was that just as the full transformation of Britain's colonial role got underway, a series of changes, cumulatively of decisive importance, swept away the economic landmarks which had guided and encouraged political calculation. The long-term decline of Britain's export competitiveness, masked as it was by the artificially favourable conditions which prevailed until the end of the 1950s, was part of the explanation. But there were new factors at work as well. After 1945 Britain's overseas earnings from 'invisibles' – foreign investments, shipping, banking and insurance services – covered a much smaller proportion of the cost of her imports than before the war. Wartime sales and post-war inflation had reduced the *real* value of Britain's huge overseas investment to 20 per cent of its pre-war value by 1950.[74] At the same time, Britain's share of the world's shipping declined steeply from some 30 per cent in 1929 to 16 per cent in 1960,[75] so that after 1960 it ceased to yield any income at all.[76] Yet Britain had acquired, as a result of the war, vast new liabilities to her Sterling Area partners whose economic policies from the mid-1950s frequently embarrassed the limited reserves of foreign exchange held in London. Foreign investment was rebuilt after the war, reaching the figure of £10,000 million by 1962. But arguably this diversion of capital abroad, whatever its beneficial effects in terms of foreign income and the stimulation of British exports, reduced vital investment at home with damaging long-term effects on productivity and competitiveness. Lastly, the economic burdens of empire and world power proved remarkably inflexible: the costs of aid and defence spiralled at the very time that direct colonial rule was being phased out. All these adverse circumstances came together with devastating suddenness around 1960, just as the accelerating power of foreign industrial competition, the end of dollar discrimination and import controls in the sterling countries[77] and the long-heralded return to full convertibility exposed the hidden weaknesses of the British industrial economy. Nemesis had been delayed, but not for long.

It remains to ask the larger questions: what was the effect of Britain's economic decline upon her ability to remain a world power and on her approach to the key issue of when and how to concede independence to her colonial territories? The answer is paradoxical. Plainly the relatively smaller scale of Britain's economy imposed greater restraints on her ability to service, hold and defend zones of exclusive influence and control in an age dominated by two super-powers. Even so, for some fifteen years after 1945 there still seemed room in a world, whose partition between the superpowers was very far from complete, for a third bloc pivoted on a British economy that remained highly geared to the exchange of manufactures and capital against primary products. There had never been a time, even at the height of British imperial power, when the management of the empire had been free from economic and financial considerations. What is striking about the years after 1945 is the readiness of British govern-ments to sustain external burdens of aid and defence far greater proportionately than had been tolerated in the salad days of imperial-ism after 1918. Moreover, as we have seen, post-war economic vulnerability had driven the British towards a 'forward policy' of colonial development and had sharply raised the value of some of their dependencies: forging new and closer economic links which London was anxious to preserve intact after the formal transfer of power. What impelled the British towards the promise of self-government was not anticipation of imminent economic decline, but the pragmatic discovery that a steady devolution of power was the price of stability and cooperation in a developing colonial economy.

More to the point, it seems clear that the key decisions to schedule the gradual transfer of power in most colonial territories were taken while the old pre-1960 assumptions about Britain's general economic position still held good. The complementarity of economic needs between Britain and especially the less industrialised members of the empire-commonwealth was still taken for granted. Britain's capacity to remain the single most important source of development capital and economic aid remained an article of faith. The prospects for sterling as a reserve currency were deemed to be bright.[78] The workability of arrangements whereby new independent members of the Commonwealth banked their foreign earnings in London, and subjected the management of their local currencies to London's supervision was not yet in doubt.[79] In short, the survival of Britain's historic commercial and financial dominance was the invisible counterpoint to constitutional change, the guarantee that political and constitutional independence would be kept within bounds. It seems likely, too, that the dramatic decisions to accelerate political advance in colonial Africa taken in the course of 1960 were made before the new economic pessimism at home had taken root and derived chiefly from political and strategic, not economic, calculations.[80]

The real effect of economic weakness was not, therefore, (directly at least) to accelerate the end of colonial rule. But what it did was to destroy both the exercise of a predominant economic *influence* and, (partly through financial stringency) the apparatus of strategic protection by which the British intended to uphold their great power status in Africa, the Persian Gulf and the Far East after the concession of independence. The conversion to 'informal empire' turned out to have been made on the fallacious assumption that Britain would have the economic strength and resources to provide enough capital and military muscle to hold together a highly decentralised Commonwealth as a far-flung sphere of influence. To some extent, of course, this notion was founded anyway on strong elements of wishful thinking. The new states were, perhaps, always likely to turn away from their over-close economic relations with Britain, to seek to diversify their commercial and financial contacts and to yield to the protectionism of local vested interests.[81] Moreover, the perpetuation of British military bases as a permanent feature of the international scene could not confidently be assumed after the experience of the Suez base and Cyprus. But there can be no doubt that Britain's steep decline after 1960 as an industrial, commercial and financial power set the seal of failure on this dream-like vision of Britain's post-imperial future.

BRITAIN'S WITHDRAWAL FROM AFRICA 1959–64

Between the later 1950s and the middle 1960s the direction of British policy in Africa ceased to be the secluded preserve of colonial experts and specialists and became a central preoccupation in British policy-making. At times it threatened to become a major issue in British politics as well. The future of the 'dark continent' whose affairs had rarely attracted wider interest became, all of a sudden, the focus of attention in international diplomacy, the object of intense moral and ideological scrutiny and, for some, a key to the relations between the West, the Communist bloc and the nations of the Third World. The intensity of feeling generated by African issues, which would have astonished its inhabitants, rulers and ruled, a few decades earlier, was of course partly a reflection of other contemporary conflicts elsewhere which their protagonists sought to portray not as parochial disputes but as part of a decisive worldwide struggle between nationalism and imperialism, or between white supremacy and black freedom. But the main reason for Africa's sudden prominence in world politics was simple enough: between 1959 and 1965 the *political face* of the continent was transformed. British, French and Belgian colonial rule disappeared from tropical Africa. The white-dominated Central African Federation was dissolved. Algeria achieved independence. With the exception of Portugal's African colonies, white rule had been obliterated north of the Zambezi. With staggering rapidity nearly 30 African states had been born.

But at the end of the 1950s, this transformation had scarcely begun and its radical scope could not easily be foreseen. The Gold Coast had received full sovereignty in 1957 and Nigeria was set for independence in 1960. Over the rest of their African empire the British had accepted for some time that an increasingly elaborate apparatus of representation was inevitable and necessary, to keep pace with the effects of an ever-growing administrative machine. The desirability of promoting self-government was not in doubt. But British policy in the two main groups of British territories in East and Central Africa was as yet very far from being committed to the swift installation of African majority rule and full independence. In Kenya a further constitutional conference had been scheduled for 1960 but the Emergency remained in force until November 1959, and Jomo Kenyatta, still the most authoritative African politician, remained in gaol. In Uganda, where the struggle against Buganda separatism was London's chief concern, the struggle to integrate the refractory kingdom was approaching its climax and no date for internal self-rule, let alone independence, was yet in sight, despite further progress towards representative government. In Tanganyika, where separatism was absent and the settlers weak, a directly elected legislature and internal self-government were in prospect but not certain. Further south the chances of a constitutional breakthrough to majority rule and independence seemed much more remote. Emergency rule was in force throughout the Federation. In Nyasaland and Northern Rhodesia, those African politicians who had agitated most fiercely against a white-led federation were in gaol and their organisations proscribed. The constitutional future of both territories, for which London was directly responsible, was obscure.

Even by the latter months of 1959, therefore, large issues were still unresolved. Was Kenya to move towards majority rule and become a 'Black Man's Country' or would Britain continue to underwrite a system of power-sharing which would protect the social and economic position of the immigrant communities, European and Asian? Would the Buganda problem obstruct progress towards Ugandan self-government indefinitely or enforce a gimcrack federal solution? How could Tanganyika be permitted internal self-government or promised independence without making necessary similar concessions to African politicians in Kenya? And what was to become of the Federation in the light of the irreconcilable opposition to it that the Devlin Inquiry had found in Nyasaland? If Nyasaland were granted majority rule and allowed to secede, how could Northern Rhodesia's African majority be persuaded to settle for less? What would be the effect in white-ruled self-governing Southern Rhodesia of any British concessions to African nationalism north of the Zambezi? Would the collapse of federation polarise Central Africa driving the whites towards the South African laager and the blacks into an immoderate anti-Western nationalism? – perhaps with devastating consequences for British influence and interests. Could the Federation be saved in any form? In short, in the middle of 1959 most of the important questions about the shape of decolonisation in Africa remained open, and their resolution a matter of bitter controversy among the local antagonists.

Less than four years later almost everything had been resolved. In rapid stages from January 1960 power-sharing in Kenya was abandoned and the way opened for African majority rule under the leadership of Kenyatta whose permanent exclusion from political life had so recently been a cardinal precept of British policy. Tanganyika went rapidly forward to self-government in 1960 and independence the following year. A rickety compromise was patched up in Uganda to allow independence there in 1962. In mid-1960, Nyasaland was granted a new constitution with majority rule. Two years later a similar constitution in Northern Rhodesia brought the electoral triumph of a fiercely anti-federation party under Kenneth Kaunda. In March 1963 the British government reluctantly decided that the ten-year-old Federation must be dissolved. The problem of Southern Rhodesia remained: for no compromise could be found between the constitutional concessions London demanded as the price of independence and the determination of the white electorate to resist the acceleration of black majority rule. The unilateral declaration of independence of November 1965 which signalled the political and economic rupture of Central Africa graphically illustrated the wreck of British hopes for the region, the speed and completeness of the revolution whereby white minority rule had become an unacceptable anachronism in the eyes of British policy makers and the emptiness of Britain's claim to influence the affairs of what was still, constitutionally, a colonial territory. But to most whites in East Africa, the Rhodesias and South Africa, the course of British government policy after 1960 reeked of treachery and moral collapse.

The causes of this decisive shift in the approach of the British towards the political development of their African possessions will remain obscure until the archives for the 1960s are opened up. It is most unlikely however that the policies pursued in the different territories of East and Central Africa stemmed from any general cabinet decision to withdraw quickly from Africa: indeed Iain Macleod who, as Colonial Secretary from October 1959 until October 1961, presided over the crucial decisions to accelerate majority rule, explicitly denied that any such formal cabinet resolution was made.[82] Nevertheless the speed of change and the consistency of its direction indicate that something more than a haphazard series of pragmatic local adjustments was at work. One influential explanation has been that such an evolution was the deliberate intention behind British policy all along, but that the transfer of power was merely speeded up to take account of the growth of African nationalism. Another, espoused by Macleod himself, was that by the early 1960s any course other than a rapid devolution of power would have produced insurrection and bloodshed on a large scale. Both these explanations, while containing perhaps some grain of truth, were designed more to fend off contemporary criticism than to offer a candid statement of political motive. Both gloss over the impact of other important considerations, as well as the real gulf between the main drive of British policy in both East and Central Africa before 1959 and the rapid acceptance of majority rule thereafter. It is, moreover, far from clear that even the political decisions taken after the end of 1959 were intended to have the consequences which actually followed from them. We may suspect that accurate prophecy and farseeing calculation were no more commonplace in colonial affairs than in other realms of governmental activity.

Nevertheless, it is clear that after October 1959 British policy in Africa displayed greater flexibility than before, and greater ruthlessness in disposing of unwelcome commitments and redundant allies. Macmillan, whose authority over British external policy, foreign, Commonwealth and colonial was at its height, had been deeply impressed by the need to adjust to the new pressures set up by the cultivation of an intimate Anglo-American partnership, the danger of a serious rift within the Commonwealth, and the growing competition for influence in the Third World between the West and the Communist bloc. He was, for global reasons, acutely anxious that Britain should not find herself embroiled in costly and embarrassing colonial conflicts, of which the Algerian war was an awful example. This meant that the arguments for the appeasement of colonial nationalism were getting stronger and sharper. But there were in Africa from the late 1950s onwards other more immediate reasons for the course which Macmillan and Macleod were to plot.

The first of these was the growing evidence that the colonial territories in Africa would soon be disturbed by the kind of large-scale unrest which had swept across Asia at the end of the war. The most striking example of this was to be found not in tropical Africa but in Algeria in the Muslim Mediterranean north, but the fierceness of the struggle there which had already, by 1958, brought down the Fourth Republic in France, seemed likely to encourage anti-colonial resistance elsewhere. In 1959 the contagion seemed to have spread rapidly south. In January there were violent disturbances in Léopoldville, in the hitherto placid Belgian Congo. In March, British officials in Nyasaland detected a 'murder plot' and in the ensuing violence 51 people were killed and 79 injured. In May there was a well-organised popular campaign of violent intimidation directed against Asian traders in Buganda: the dangerous implications for the authority of the colonial administration were clear enough. And in the later part of the year there were serious riots in two urban areas in South Africa. Whether any common causes lay behind these upheavals was doubtful. But it was clear that they could not be dismissed as tribal and atavistic – the official view of the Mau Mau troubles in Kenya.[83] Indeed it seemed most likely that they reflected a mixture of social grievances – especially among town-dwellers faced by unemployment and constricting administrative controls – and resentment at the lack of greater African representation in government. In 1960 the spiral of violence and confrontation appeared to intensify – significantly in those regions of Africa where white rule was most deeply entrenched and least compromising. In January, nine policemen were killed in riots in Durban in South Africa. Then violent demonstrations at Sharpeville and near Cape Town in March led to the shooting of over 70 Africans by the police, and a wave of strikes and unrest in the following weeks. In July and again in October there were widespread riots in Salisbury and other towns in Southern Rhodesia. To some outside observers, and to whites in South and Central Africa, the prospect of a general insurrection against white rule or, at least, of widespread, prolonged and violent disturbances, with devastating economic and social consequences, seemed frighteningly close.

These developments were bound to make policy makers in London rather thoughtful. It was not that British colonial policy shrank on principle from the use of force to quell disturbance or violent opposition. Indeed the Nyasaland disturbances had been suppressed with abundant vigour to London's approval. But the evidence of general upheaval in different parts of colonial Africa suggested that something more than minor and localised unrest was to be expected. In that event the political difficulty of preserving control was bound to be much greater, and the strain on Britain's military manpower, scheduled for rapid contraction with the ending of national service in 1960, potentially intolerable. There was, moreover, the question of how any systematic repression of unrest would be viewed at home and internationally. The British government had already been embarrassed by revelations about the maltreatment of Mau Mau detainees at the Hola Camp in Kenya, worse was to come. The Devlin Report on the Nyasaland disturbances, published in the middle of 1959, roundly condemned, with the authority of a distinguished British judge, both the aims and the methods of the colonial administration there.

The Report made three damaging charges against British rule in Nyasaland. It discovered a widespread and ineradicable popular antipathy to the Federation which the Nyasaland government, committed as it was to membership, resolutely ignored.[84] Secondly, it rejected the whole approach of the Nyasaland administration towards the Nyasaland African Congress. The assertion that nationalism was confined to a small troublesome minority was dismissed.[85] The claim that the leaders of the Congress relied on intimidation to mobilise support was rejected.[86] The characterisation of Banda as an extremist on the evidence of extracts from his speeches was condemned as misleading and unfair.[87] And the justification advanced by the Nyasaland government for the proscription of the Congress and the arrest of its leaders – that a violent insurrection or 'murder plot' had been planned – was treated with polite but unconcealed disbelief. No evidence for such a plot had been found, the Commission concluded.[88] Indeed far from upholding the actions of the government, the Commissioners turned their fire on its proceedings. They accused it of intolerance of all opposition and of having resorted to a repression whose purpose was not the preservation of order but the coercion of African opinion.[89] In the process, they said, it had employed 'unnecessary and . . . illegal force'.[90] In a calculated phrase, which rang like a pistol shot, the Commission declared that Nyasaland had become 'no doubt only temporarily, a police state'.[91] Less than fifteen years after the defeat of Hitler, the implicit parallel with fascism had a peculiar and brutal force. No colonial government in living memory had been so savagely criticised by an official enquiry.

The Devlin Report appeared at what was perhaps a crucial time. It threw the Colonial Office on the defensive, not least over its commitment to the Federation.[92] It raised the prospect that forceful action to deal with nationalists elsewhere in colonial Africa would be castigated by future inquiries as Devlin had castigated the Nyasaland government and its superiors in London. It was bound to cause unease among the government's own supporters in and out of Parliament, both by its implicit claim that to ignore the wishes of the population was to violate the trusteeship tradition in colonial policy, and by its explicit statement that the colonial government had acted illegally as well as tyrannically. Its remarks about the strength and popularity of nationalism and its blunt denial that the disturbances could be attributed merely to troublemakers and agitators plainly had a wider application in Africa. Above all, the Report decisively rejected what had long been the classic but unspoken defence of colonial administrators and white settlers alike – that the difficulties of keeping order among primitive and volatile indigenous peoples justified the use of brusque and arbitrary methods of government.[93] After 1959 London may have feared further disturbances in its African territories; but perhaps it feared the spotlight of inquiry even more.

The second large fact of which policy had to take account after 1959 was the actions of the other colonial powers in Africa. For there was no tradition of friendship or cooperation between these powers in the colonial sphere. No imperialist solidarity front was formed to co-ordinate resistance to Afro-Asian nationalism. On the contrary. Empire was a competitive business and the age of decolonisation after 1945 saw a scramble for influence as fierce as that which had precipitated the partition of Africa in the 1880s. After the Second World War Italy was stripped of her colonies as Germany had been in 1919. The British had pressed the Dutch to hand over power in Indonesia – in the interests of their own position in South East Asia. With British encouragement French rule had been ended in Syria and the Lebanon in 1946, and there was little British sympathy for France's plight in Indo-China or, after 1954, in North Africa. But ironically in the later 1950s the difficulties of Britain's colonial rivals in Africa came to have embarrassing consequences for British policy as well. In 1956 the French Fourth Republic, grappling with insur-rection in Algeria, tried to rally the loyalty of its other African territories by an extension of representative government. Two years later the Republic itself was overthrown as a direct consequence of the Algerian rebellion. The new constitution framed by De Gaulle offered French Africa self-government within a French Community and then, as the struggle in Algeria intensified, full independence inside or outside the Community.[94] 'L'indépendance', De Gaulle had declared in Brazzaville in August 1958, 'Quiconque la voudra pourra la prendre aussitôt'.[95] This siren-song had its effects on the other side of the Congo and almost certainly contributed to the abrupt decision of the Belgians in January 1960 to offer the Congolese independence by mid-summer. With characteristic impetuosity De Gaulle had trans-formed, within the space of two years, the political geography of colonial Africa. In 1960 no less than sixteen new African states entered the United Nations, almost all of them francophone or sympathetic to France.[96]

The British had no Algeria to jerk them into the concession that De Gaulle had made. But they could not afford to treat his African policy with lordly indifference. The hectic speed with which the French colonies had reached independence made nonsense of the measured timetable laid down by the Colonial Office. More dangerously, it undercut the claim, on which the British had plumed themselves, that the constitutional progress of the British colonial empire had been more liberal than that of any other colonial system and gave Britain a special empathy with the new Afro-Asian states. How important this was to Macmillan we have seen in the previous section. Henceforth it would be difficult to justify the denial of independence to British colonies whose economic and political development already out-stripped that of France's former colonial territories or the notoriously backward Belgian Congo. Moreover, the prospect of a large new contingent of African states at the United Nations as an advertise-ment for the generosity of France (and an implicit condemnation of British intransigence) was all the more uninviting as the competition for influence in the Third World seemed to be accelerating. British interests now required a Gallic suppleness. Then, in the course of 1960, these international pressures on colonial policy acquired a new and dramatic urgency as the Congo exploded into anarchy.

As had been agreed in Brussels in January, the Congo became independent on 30 June 1960. Its troubles began immediately. On 5 July the army, the *Force Publique*, mutinied against its Belgian officers and in the ensuing chaos perhaps 300 European women were raped. A number of Europeans were killed in Katanga, the remote south-eastern province whose copper wealth was the mainstay of the Congo's economy. Belgian troops were sent to Léopoldville (now Kinshasa) in substantial numbers (some 10,000 by 13 July).[97] Then on 11 July Katanga declared itself an independent state, and success-fully appealed for Belgian technical and military aid. For their part, the Congolese government in Léopoldville denounced Belgian inter-vention and Katanga's secession and appealed to the United Nations for help. A UN resolution was passed demanding Belgian withdrawal and by the end of July a mixed force of some 10,000 troops had arrived under the banner of the UN to help the Congo put its house in order. But although the Belgians were persuaded to withdraw their troops both from Katanga and the rest of the Congo, the political situation deteriorated rapidly. Confusion reigned in the Congolese capital as president and prime minister dismissed and counter-dismissed each other. The purpose of the UN presence became a matter of acute controversy in the Congo, at the UN headquarters in New York and in great power diplomacy. And all the time the collapse of any semblance of orderly, unified administration in the Congo proceeded apace. By the latter part of 1960 perhaps two-thirds of the country had thrown off the authority of the central government: not only Katanga, but the central province of Kasai and the large eastern province centred on Stanleyville were practically independent.

The British could scarcely view the anarchy in the Congo other than with extreme anxiety. Uganda and Tanganyika shared a frontier with the eastern Congo; Northern Rhodesia, a component of the Federation, bordered Katanga whose share of the Copperbelt projected almost like a wedge into Rhodesian territory. The political evolution of all three territories was at a delicate stage. The greatest danger, in London's eyes, was that the collapse of central government would turn the Congo into an international cockpit with open rivalry between the Eastern bloc and the West. To Macmillan, still depressed by the failure of the Paris Summit, it seemed in August 1960 as if the Congo might even play the incendiary role of Serbia in 1914 and ignite a vast international conflict.[98] For this reason the British supported UN intervention to hold the Congo together and successive resolutions which denounced Katanga's secession. The emphatically pro-Western stance of the Katanga government, its close cooperation with European mining interests, the large European element in its administration and its friendly relations with the Federal government in Salisbury incited much British sympathy. But the danger that open support for Katanga's independence would turn the central government towards Russia, or invite communist aid to a separatist pro-communist regime in the eastern Congo was too great to be risked.[99] The Congo could not be allowed to become a second Korea. Nor could the good relations that Macmillan was eager to build with the Afro-Asian states (most of whom regarded Katanga as a colonialist stooge) be jeopardised.

Unfortunately, however, UN intervention brought no quick solution to the problems of the Congo. For much of 1961 anarchy, separatism and secession predominated.[100] The full effects on British policy can only be guessed at. In East Africa it is likely that the grim example of the Congo accelerated London's desire to construct regimes to whom power could be transferred safely before the turbulence spilt across the frontiers or the intense international excitement generated by the Congo's misfortunes spread to neighbouring territories. In Central Africa the problem was more complicated. Here London was engaged after 1960 in a threefold task of the greatest difficulty. Nyasaland and

Northern Rhodesia were to receive a larger measure of self-government and in Northern Rhodesia a new balance had to be struck between the influence of whites and blacks on the government. At the same time, great efforts were being made to save the Federation and to find a new formula of cooperation which could at least hold together the two Rhodesias. Thirdly, to ease this task, and to pave the way for the future independence of the Federation, the British were extremely anxious to liberalise the constitution of settler-ruled Southern Rhodesia, to increase African representation and to ensure that a moderate and liberal-minded government remained in power there. The course of events in the Congo could hardly have been less opportune. Inevitably the fate of Katanga was a matter of keen interest to whites in the Federation. Here was a regime which had apparently rejected the extremes of African nationalism for a workmanlike collaboration with European enterprise and white expertise. Its orderliness was in sharp contrast to the chaos that ruled the rest of the Congo. It symbolised the kind of partnership between whites and blacks which seemed possible in Central Africa.[101] To the Federal government the case for sympathy and support seemed overwhelming. By the same token, the Tshombe regime was anathema to the anti-Federation nationalists in Northern Rhodesia.[102]

British policy had to weigh the dangers of the Congo's disintegration, and the resentment of Afro-Asian opinion, against the risk that support for the destruction of Katanga's independence would bring the influence of a radical and perhaps communist inspired central government into the heart of Central Africa. It had also to take account of the fierce reaction of whites in both Northern and Southern Rhodesia against UN efforts to knock down the Tshombe government. For by the end of 1961 the tale of atrocities and the impact of the panic-stricken exodus of Belgian refugees, many of whom passed through the Rhodesias on their way home, had made the Congo a byword among whites for the awful consequences of black rule when unrestrained by white advice or control.[103] To white opinion, the efforts of the UN to force Katanga under the anarchic rule of Léopoldville and drive out the white advisers and mercenaries seemed evidence of a ruthless conspiracy against all European influence in Central Africa. Moreover, at a time when Northern Rhodesia itself was the scene of violent disturbances in the latter months of 1961, the prospect of Katanga's outright military defeat by UN forces seemed likely to encourage anti-Federation feeling in the territory and to foment further unrest.[104] Calculations of this sort pushed the British towards a middle course: to try to check the operations intended to unseat Tshombe, but to propel him towards a political settlement in which Katanga would form one element in a federal Congo. Between September and December 1961 London strove to restrain the UN force and cajole Tshombe into compromise.[105] But, as it turned out, this halfway house was untenable. Weakened by the forcible removal of its European officials and mercenaries, the Katanga regime proved no match for the UN troops when, after abortive negotiations through much of 1962, a further military onslaught was launched against it. By the end of that year all traces of independent Katanga had been erased.

But the effects of the 'Congo Disaster' remained to haunt British policy in Central Africa. The failure of Katanga's bid for real independence – a failure that was apparent by the end of 1961 – was a fillip for anti-Federation sentiment among Africans in Northern Rhodesia. The presence of a UN army just across the frontier in Elizabethville – an army whose masters seemed dedicated to the cause of 'anti-colonialism' – could only have weakened the prestige and authority of British rule and of the federal government in Salisbury and excited hopes of 'liberation'. Conversely, the horrific images conjured up by the stories (multiplied and exaggerated) of barbarity in the Congo, and of atrocities committed by UN troops in Katanga, bred among whites a greatly heightened fear of African nationalism and an intense resentment at what seemed the weakness and prevarication of British policy. The fate of the Federation was decided against the ghastly backcloth of the Congo. How far it contributed to the victory of anti-Federation sentiment in Northern Rhodesia cannot be measured; but that it helped to produce the white reaction in Southern Rhodesia which led first to the electoral victory of the Rhodesian Front in December 1962 and ultimately to the Unilateral Declaration of Independence in 1965 seems highly probable. But above all, perhaps, the lesson of the Congo for British policy makers was the appalling risks entailed, both locally and internationally, by retaining any direct responsibility for the government of Central Africa.

Had they occurred separately, or at a slow tempo over a long period, the surge of unrest in Southern and Central Africa in 1959–60, the impetuosity of France's colonial retreat in West Africa and the Congo anarchy of 1960–62 might have appeared as local difficulties for British policy in Africa; serious enough but insufficient to create a new climate of policy. But combining as they did in a sudden multiple series of detonations, they thrust Africa to the forefront of international diplomacy and challenged the assumptions of the 1950s about the inevitability of gradualism in colonial affairs. Now some stability had to be found and British interests and influence protected in a new climate where the gentle zephyr of political change had turned inexplicably into a hurricane.[106] New policies and new techniques had to be found; old interests reappraised; old allies jettisoned; discontent forestalled; rebellion anticipated. None of this meant however, a common policy indiscriminately applied across the face of British colonial Africa. The policy makers had to take account of political conditions that varied greatly from colony to colony. The course of decolonisation and the shape of the successor states it threw up closely reflected the local balance of social and political forces and the influence of the different social patterns laid down in the colonial era. To this more detailed examination we must now turn.

(i) East Africa

In East Africa the British had to deal with territories whose social and political character displayed important differences but whose proximity meant that their fates had to be settled together and along broadly similar lines. Thus the political development of each colony (unlike the progress of naval convoys or wagon trains) had to proceed at the pace set by the fastest, regardless of local conditions. They had also, as it turned out, to march to the drums beaten in far-off West Africa where British and French territories alike mostly received independence in 1960 (Sierra Leone in 1961). This fact in itself reveals the reluctance or inability of the British to impose their own timetable according to what they thought were the individual requirements of the colony – just as had been the case in India, Burma and Ceylon in 1947–48.

By the spring of 1959 it was clear that the electoral machine that Nyerere had forged under the banner of the Tanganyikan African National Union (TANU) enjoyed overwhelming support among Africans in Tanganyika. Its demand for full self-government in the near future, backed up by the threat of demonstrations, strikes and boycotts, could not easily be resisted without recourse to repression and emergency rule which would impose enormous strains on the administration and which, in the absence of any alternative set of political allies, could achieve little. The British responded by offering a further round of constitutional change which greatly increased the African electorate and reduced the seats reserved for Europeans and Asians in the Assembly to a rump. Macleod, the new Colonial Secretary after October 1959, agreed that cabinet or responsible government would follow elections under the new constitution which were to be held in September 1960. With this the Tanganyika politicians seemed satisfied; they expected to wait a further five or ten years before internal self-government was converted into independence.[107] But when Nyerere went to London in March 1960 he was encouraged to shorten his sights and ask for swift independence. In October, after the elections, Nyerere as the new prime minister sought and received the promise of full independence by December 1961.[108] With almost miraculous ease, Tanganyika had become the first East African territory to emerge completely from colonial rule.

What was remarkable about Tanganyika's progress was the rapidity with which the British had moved forward from the creation of a more representative legislature and the offer of internal self-government to the ultimate step of granting independence and full *external* autonomy. Internal self-government was perhaps the inevitable consequence of the growth of governmental activity since 1945 and the circumstances which had enabled Nyerere to construct a movement with wide popular support in town and countryside. But in the past the British had usually hesitated before agreeing to the final transfer of sovereignty. Ultimate British responsibility, it was argued, was a guarantee of stability and good government, a salutary check on the abuse of power by colonial politicians. The over-hasty concession of independence would encourage unreasonable aspirations and demands in other colonies where the appropriate conditions for self-government were lacking: a careful and measured pace had to be maintained. Thirdly, independence had always seemed to carry the risk of international complications, either as a result of foreign interference in a fledgling post-colonial state or because that new state misbehaved or struck up undesirable international friendships. All these reasons argued for the delay of independence for as long as was practicable. What then lay behind the drastic acceleration of constitutional progress in Tanganyika?

The answer is, perhaps, unlikely to be found in the new liberalism of British colonial policy after Macmillan's electoral victory in October 1959 or in a sudden loss of British nerve or in the intensification of

Tanganyikan nationalist pressure. Tanganyikan independence was not the fruit of nationalism's overthrow of imperialism, but the outcome of tacit conspiracy between policy makers in London and politicians in Dar es Salaam. At bottom, the reason for British haste was that precisely those considerations which had once argued against the early concession of independence now made it appear the safest course. Tanganyika was not a British possession in the strict sense but a trust territory under the supervision of the United Nations. For much of the period since 1945 this fact had made little real difference: until the very end of the 1950s Tanganyika had lagged behind Kenya and the West African colonies in political development. But with the approach of 1960, it was clear that Tanganyika's special status would attract far more international attention: the United Nations had become (or so it appeared) the great forum in which East and West competed for the favour of the Third World; and the Organisation itself, with the addition of sixteen new African members in 1960, was changing the balance of its membership and perhaps its character as well. Two powerful new factors had now to be weighed in British calculation. The denial of Tanganyikan independence was certain to become an issue at the United Nations where direct pressure on Britain could be brought to bear through the Trusteeship Council. In the task of cultivating Afro-Asian opinion this would be a serious embarrassment and would probably stimulate intensified political activity in the territory. Secondly, it was plainly advantageous that African voices sympathetic to Britain should be added to the francophone chorus in the General Assembly. Prompt independence was thus the best guarantee that unwelcome international interest in Tanganyika would be kept to the minimum and the loyalty to Britain of the territory's leaders subjected to the least strain.

The countervailing arguments for hesitation were, by contrast, weak. Nyerere's demeanour was friendly and amenable; he was not tainted, like Kenyatta, with the suspicion of terrorism; he aroused no comparable antagonism either in the territory or in the British parliament. There was no rival to TANU and a marked absence of the tribal divisions and animosities to be found in Kenya and Uganda – perhaps because most tribes were small and weak. The European community was much less entrenched and influential than in Kenya. Nor in Tanganyika was there any vital strategic interest (in the form of a base) or major economic stake which independence might jeopardise. On the other hand, the proximity of the Congo to the west served after July 1960 to strengthen rather than weaken the argument for a prompt and complete transfer of power. Circumstances, therefore, conspired not just to advance the case for the swift constitutional progress of the African colonies in general, but to place Tanganyika at the top of the list in East Africa. But special circumstances or no, Tanganyika's favourable treatment was bound to set a precedent for the rest of British East Africa.

In Uganda the pace of constitutional advancement, given the seriousness of the political obstacles to be overcome, was scarcely less hectic. At the end of 1959 the British set their face against the early introduction of universal suffrage, or of responsible government, fearing perhaps that this would lead to a direct confrontation with the recalcitrant kingdom of Buganda whose leaders regarded the creation of more representative government for Uganda as a whole as the deliberate subversion of Bugandan autonomy.[109] In August 1960, after London had refused to delay the next round of elections to the Ugandan legislature, the Buganda government boycotted the registration of voters and, after further attempts at delay, the Buganda parliament, the *Lukiko*, voted to secede from the Protectorate on 31 December 1960. The portents for any early independence for Uganda could hardly have seemed less favourable nor the risks entailed by a rapid British withdrawal more obvious. Yet, by September 1961 a compromise had been patched up by which Buganda was to enjoy federal status within Uganda; and a constitutional conference in London agreed upon a timetable of internal self-government by March and full independence in October 1962. And so it came to pass.

Even less than in Tanganyika was rapid independence in Uganda the consequence of an abject surrender or retreat by the British in the face of an irresistible Ugandan nationalism. Indeed, in Uganda, the main political conflicts and antagonisms were not between the colonial rulers and the disparate peoples and tribes of the Protectorate but between the kingdom of Buganda and the non-Ganda peoples to the north and west. These peoples feared and resented Buganda's claim to a special privileged status,[110] seeing it as a tactic to extract concessions from the British and as a cover for the eventual domination of Uganda as a whole by its wealthiest and most cohesive unit. The British too were determined to check Buganda's separatist ambitions, believing that if they did not Uganda would fragment into an anarchy of warring tribes. With this in mind, they had pressed steadily forward through the 1950s building up the prestige and authority of the central government and the all-Uganda legislature to unite the non-Ganda peoples and to put pressure on the leaders of Buganda: an elected central assembly of growing importance would, it was thought, stimulate demand for political democracy in Buganda and force the Ganda leaders to recognise the impracticality of separate Buganda independence. But Buganda had proved a tough nut to crack.

The key to Uganda's forced march to independence in 1961–62 lay in the sudden abandonment by the British of their long-cherished objective of creating a unitary state on the one hand, and on the other the effectiveness of the financial sanctions they used to checkmate Bugandan secession.[111] The Munster Report of June 1961 offered Buganda federal status and the right to control the selection of her representatives to the Uganda parliament – a concession greatly to the advantage of the kingdom's traditional aristocracy.[112] By this carefully calculated concession the British created the opening for a bargain between the Bugandan leaders and the Uganda People's Congress (UPC) which had been formed by Milton Obote in March 1960 – originally to unite the non-Ganda peoples against Buganda's pretensions. For Obote and the Buganda aristocrats had a common enemy in the Democratic Party which appealed especially to Catholic Christians outside Buganda and which enjoyed considerable support amongst commoners inside the kingdom as well.[113] The Democratic Party had actually won the elections of March 1961 and threatened to carry off the spoils if and when Uganda obtained self-government. The terms of the bargain were simple. Obote and the UPC accepted the terms of the Munster Report and federal status for Buganda. In return the Buganda government would participate in the national elections to ensure the defeat of the Democratic Party. Representatives loyal to the *Kabaka* would support Obote and the UPC in forming a new central government. For both sides, the prospect of independence held out by the British if the constitutional problem could be solved (or at least shelved) was a keen inducement. The alliance held, and in May 1962 Obote took office with support from the *Kabaka's* followers. Both parties to this alliance of strange bedfellows reckoned, no doubt, that once the British had gone the way would be open to pursue their real objectives. Both counted, no doubt, on eventual success.

One last but significant obstacle remained before the final transfer of power could be completed. A further constitutional conference was necessary in June 1962 to consider the demands of the smaller Bantu kingdoms to the west of Buganda for federal status as well. Perhaps with an eye to the turbulence across the frontier, this was conceded. The road to independence was now open, but the unitary state had been reduced to a patchwork quilt of local autonomies. Indeed it can scarcely be supposed that the plunge into federalism which was so drastic a reversal of the centralising drive of British policy since 1945 was undertaken except with the earliest termination of British rule in mind. The British had long realised that the forging of a unitary state was difficult; but throughout the 1950s they had been ready to harass and coerce Buganda in that direction. But the events of 1959–60 in Buganda – the attack on Asian traders, the boycott of registration, the secession of December 1960 – showed how difficult it would be to combine continued pressure on Buganda with further doses of self-government. Uganda, like other parts of Africa in 1959–60, seemed on the verge of becoming ungovernable – or governable only by repression. Fear of local anarchy, not the threats of nationalist politicians, pushed the British towards a compromise that would allow further instal-ments of self-government. By the early months of 1961 such a course seemed only prudent. To refuse Uganda what Tanganyika was about to receive would be sure to cause trouble. It might revive Buganda separatism; it was certain to make the task of persuading Bugandan leaders to cooperate with other Uganda politicians infinitely harder. On the other hand, the promise of independence might prove the effective catalyst of unity, the crucial incentive for accommodation.

By 1961, therefore, local events had probably persuaded the British that if they did not seize the opportunity to nudge Uganda into independence they might find themselves condemned to hold the ring in rapidly deteriorating circumstances and with disagreeable conse-quences. It was the wider international factors of which, as we have seen, London had to take such major account that made such a course unthinkable. By hook or by crook, some settlement must be found to allow formal British rule a graceful exit. Local difficulties and wider fears had converged to make independence the safest option. But the legacy of this judicious withdrawal was the slide towards the horrors and excesses of the 1970s, followed by invasion, civil war, famine and anarchy.

At the end of the 1950s Kenya remained the most valuable of Britain's East African possessions. It had the wealthiest and most diversified economy and its strategic value as a military base had been considerably enhanced by the final liquidation of Britain's military facilities at Suez.[114] In 1959 its political development still seemed firmly set in the mould of multiracial power-sharing under a constitution which gave Europeans and the African majority an equal number of elected representatives (the Arab and Asian communities were represented more modestly). In the early part of 1959 the Colonial Secretary in London bluntly rejected the request of the African elected members in the legislature for a further constitutional conference. Altogether the obstacles to majority rule in Kenya seemed infinitely greater than in Tanganyika or the Uganda Protectorate. The legacy of Mau Mau had left British policy makers with a deep suspicion of any African political organisation except at a local level while anything that smacked of concession to Kikuyu politicians still faithful to Kenyatta was likely to encounter fierce criticism from Conservative parliamentary opinion at home. Added to that, the opposition of the white settlers, who were vociferous, resourceful and well-connected politically in London, could be expected to make any move that could be represented as a 'sell-out' to African nationalism. Nevertheless, despite these apparently formidable roadblocks, progress towards majority rule, self-government and independence came rapidly. At the Lancaster House Conference in January 1960 the principle of self-government under majority rule was laid down. In 1961 African ministers formed a government enjoying substantial local autonomy. Further constitutional changes cleared the way for full internal self-government under the premiership of Kenyatta himself in June 1963, and then for independence at the year's end. In three years the unthinkable had become a fact.

At the outset several factors hastened progress towards self-government and prodded the British into constitutional changes which they had so recently regarded as dangerous and unworkable. The first of these was undoubtedly the awareness among British officials in Kenya and in London that constitutional advances conceded in Tanganyika and Uganda would have to find their counterpart in the wealthiest and most advanced part of British East Africa. To refuse to do so would alienate even friendly and cooperative Africans in Kenya; it would draw unwelcome attention from abroad to the privileges of the whites in the colony; and it would (as was the danger elsewhere) invite invidious comparison with French and Belgian policy the trend of which was clear enough by the end of 1959. But desirable as it was to give British rule in Kenya a progressive face, it would hardly have been possible to do so without the influence of two other local factors whose significance for Kenya's politics was not, perhaps, fully appreciated until the end of the 1950s.

As we have seen, the British had responded to the shock of Mau Mau in two different ways. The first was to impose a vigorous emergency regime in Kikuyuland with an elaborate programme for the detention and rehabilitation of Mau Mau suspects. This had been coupled with the ban on all political movements above local level. But it was the second response whose results were to prove more durable. This was the Swynnerton plan of agrarian reform, the aim of which was to transform African agriculture, especially in the Kikuyu heartland, into a commercial, market-oriented enterprise with the consolidation of land into individual property. This was backed up by an extensive campaign to improve techniques of cultivation and to provide better marketing and credit facilities. The motive was clear enough: to raise up a large class of property owners with a vested interest in order and stability and to relieve the rural poverty that was thought to lie behind the explosion of Mau Mau.[115] The effect, however, was actually to create a large new body of rural notables who had every reason to want to influence the policies of the colonial government and whose local prestige was being enhanced by the government's own actions. Moreover, the government itself, having once embarked on the Swynnerton plan, had a vested interest in the contentment of its progeny and could scarcely resist the demand of the notables for a larger representation in the legislature – unless it was ready to risk all the political benefits which rural development was supposed to bring. Indeed, the inevitable social tensions and grievances which the consolidation programme generated in the countryside made it all the more important to demonstrate that local cooperation with the government would be rewarded by a greater influence over its operations.[116]

Thus the attempt to cure the disease of which Mau Mau was thought to be a symptom ended by forcing the colonial administration to be far more attentive than ever before to the interests of African notables rather than white settlers. Crucially, the settlers proved to be unable to check Kenya's rapid change from a 'white man's country' to a black man's. The power they had enjoyed in the 1940s declined in the 1950s and all but vanished between 1959 and 1961. The way was left clear for London to come to terms with African leaders (in striking contrast to the position in Southern Rhodesia) to the surprise perhaps of both the settlers and the British officials who had treated them for so long with wary respect.

The weakness of settler resistance arose partly from the character of European society in Kenya. The great majority of Europeans were not settler farmers in the White Highlands but town-dwellers, engaged in commerce, the professions or administration.[117] There was not that stratum of white manual workers, dependent on a code of job reservation, that stiffened settler nationalism in the Rhodesias. On the other hand, many of the new European residents who had arrived after 1945 (since when the white population had tripled) were employees of government, subject to its discipline and with the option of returning home on a pension at the end of their service. The public service was not recruited locally – another contrast with Southern Rhodesia. Thus the marked expansion of the white population had had the effect of diluting the permanent settler element and of creating new divisions of interest and outlook. Added to that was the fact that by the later 1950s the old settler community of the White Highlands had largely lost the social and economic value which, during the war and the violent phase of the Emergency, had made government so attentive to its views. By 1960, the large farms or plantations (not the smaller mixed farms of the White Highlands) accounted for some 80 per cent of Kenya's overseas exports.[118] These farms were commonly owned by companies based abroad and managed by expatriates who expected like the public servants to return home at their career's end. No longer could the settlers threaten the colony with economic ruin if it ignored their wishes. Indeed, once government became committed to the Swynnerton plan, the fate of the smaller mixed farmers of the White Highlands became at best a matter of indifference; at worst the officials hoped to reschedule white land to ease the land hunger of the Kikuyu.

The settler community, then, was poorly placed to fight for its survival. Their earlier failure to obtain internal self-government on the model of Southern Rhodesia turned out to be decisive. In the 1930s they had been too few. In the 1940s, during the war and its aftermath, London had been determined to retain control for strategic and then economic reasons. In the 1950s Mau Mau had exposed their vulnerability and their dependence on military and financial aid from Britain. With Mau Mau the settlers lost whatever chance they ever had of winning that vital control over internal security and defence which allowed the white Rhodesians to bargain on more than equal terms with London and to stage their bloodless rebellion in 1965. Instead, the growing pressures for political and social change created not the solidarity characteristic of whites south of the Zambezi but division, uncertainty and weakness. 'Our weakness is the split among Europeans in Kenya itself', wrote a settler leader mournfully.[119]

It was on this – the second great local factor – that the policy makers in London capitalised in 1959–60. The Colonial Office had first refused the Africans a constitutional conference. But then in April 1959 Michael Blundell, a leading settler with considerable commercial interests and in close touch with the Colonial Office,[120] had formed the New Kenya Group (NKG), the aim of which was to break the mould of settler politics, knock down racial barriers in political life and form a party that would appeal to Africans, Europeans and Asians equally. The Group was backed financially by commercial organisations in Kenya and politically by a majority of the European members of the legislature, most of whom were, however, either governor's nominees or the indirectly chosen special members.[121] London's decision to permit a conference after all in January 1960 may well have been an attempt to propagate this hopeful new growth and to modify the constitution in its favour. Certainly, Blundell's own connections and the fact that a leading figure in the NKG was the brother of Iain Macleod ensured a favourable hearing in London.

The Lancaster House Conference inaugurated a new era in Kenya's politics. A delegation of African politicians attended alongside representatives of the NKG and the more conservative settler group who opposed it. Iain Macleod's chief purpose as Colonial Secretary, it may well be thought, was to encourage the emergence of a moderate African party who would cooperate in government with the NKG or perhaps even fuse with it. The Emergency had been ended and now the ban on African political movements was lifted. A constitution was devised which gave elected Africans a majority in the legislature, the best guarantee, it was thought, of winning the cooperation of those who had emerged as the leaders of African opinion. A long stride had been taken towards self-government with African majority rule and it came like a bombshell to the settler community. But behind Macleod's insistence on an African legislative majority there lay a calculation and a hope. Since the conference had been planned, the rapid advance of French and Belgian Africa towards independence had become unmistakeable,[122] South and Central Africa had been rocked by major disturbances and constitutional progress in Tanganyika accelerated. If, as *The Economist* remarked, the Kenya conference ended in bitterness and recrimination, 'the impact could be disastrous'.[123] That was the calculation. The hope was that the African leaders would be cajoled into cooperation with the white moderates of the NKG to form a government that would safeguard private property and Kenya's close connection with Britain. For it was not intended at this stage that *independence* would come swiftly.[124] And to hammer home the point that only moderate Africans were acceptable, Macleod refused to release Kenyatta from detention, and the Kenya African National Union (KANU), one of the two African parties to emerge in the aftermath of the conference, was refused permission to register him as its titular president.[125] Macleod had, after all, to guard his flank against Conservative backbench feeling on the right of the party where Kenyatta's identification with Mau Mau still aroused strong emotions.

The first signs were hopeful. Two African parties had been formed in 1960: KANU was dominated by Kikuyu and Luo politicians and regarded Kenyatta as its real head; KADU, the Kenya African Democratic Union, was a loose alliance of tribes who feared and resented Kikuyu power and influence. Unlike KANU, KADU's leaders were ready to form a multiracial government with the NKG and did not insist on Kenyatta's release beforehand. Nor were they as concerned, as KANU were, with appeasing Kikuyu land hunger in the White Highlands.[126] The 1961 elections gave KANU a majority of seats in African constituencies but KADU won enough to hold power with NKG support and the aid of the governor's nominees. But if London hoped that this alliance of moderates would prove stable, or that it would succeed in attracting leading figures from KANU, they were to be disappointed.

There were several reasons for this. The KADU leaders might have appeared more cooperative than KANU; and they were not tainted by association with Kenyatta and Mau Mau. But with self-government in the offing, they could not afford to appear mere tools of the British, particularly if they hoped to break down the uncertain solidarity of KANU's alliance of the Kikuyu, Luo and some lesser tribes. So the KADU government demanded the release of Kenyatta (he was released in August 1961), land for land-hungry peasants[127] and a new constitutional conference to advance Kenya towards independence. Inter-party rivalry was setting the pace of constitutional change. The

British were unwilling to deny their protégés' request, being anxious to improve their political credit. A further round of constitution-making in 1962 introduced universal suffrage and gave Kenya almost complete internal self-government. To meet KADU fears of a unitary state under Kikuyu domination considerable powers were to be devolved on regional assemblies.[128] But try as they might, the KADU leaders were unable to split the Kikuyu-Luo entente that was the heart of KANU or exploit effectively the rivalry of Kenyatta's two lieutenants, Mboya and Odinga. Kenyatta's status as the pre-eminent champion of African nationalism in Kenya and his skill as a politician were too great. And KADU itself suffered from tribal divisions and from its evident dependence as a government on nominated or European members who were to disappear under the new constitution. In May 1963, in the first universal suffrage election, KANU won by a landslide.

In fact, whatever their reservations about Kenyatta and KANU, the British had been eager since the spring of 1962 to speed up the progress towards independence. As in Uganda they were fearful that delay would harden the tribal conflicts implicit in the KANU-KADU split and wreck the prospects of stable self-government. The devastat-ing economic effects of political uncertainty and the growing financial burden on the British Treasury were an added spur.[124] Nor could the threat of a new wave of Kikuyu insurgency be ruled out. Thereafter, at every stage, London strove to promote cooperation and agreement among Kenya politicians and to adjudicate their continuing consti-tutional differences over federalism. The two parties were cajoled into a reluctant coalition government in April 1962. With London's encouragement the elections under the new universal suffrage con-stitution were hurried on. With most of the rest of Africa north of the Zambezi already independent by early 1963, the British had little taste for remaining as an unpopular policeman in Kenya. Moreover, for all their earlier mistrust of KANU and Kenyatta, the British now began to see the social conservatism of most Kikuyu politicians and their devotion to private property and a strong central government as the best defence against the anarchic pressures of land hunger and tribal separatism. Swift independence would give them a vested interest in promoting tribal unity as well as close political and commercial links with Britain.[130] Consequently, once Kenyatta had come to power, the British made haste to ratify the final arrangements which brought Kenya independence in December 1963.

In Kenya, as elsewhere in Africa, it seems likely that the British, far from willing the outcome of their constitutional changes, repeatedly found themselves overtaken by events. It made sense to rally moderate African opinion, especially in view of the new international scene in Africa after 1959, the surge of black unrest in Central and Southern Africa and the social changes wrought in Kenya itself by the Swynnerton plan. But as the British had found in West Africa, and years before in India, the sudden introduction of electoral politics produced very unpredictable consequences. Party competition, and the sheer difficulty of managing parties in colonial societies, made the new politicians acutely anxious to control all the sources of power and patronage lest they fall, or be slipped, into the hands of their rivals. Hence, the inevitable corollary of electoral politics was the demand for complete self-government – in the interests of party survival. But, at the same time, electoral politics and the approach of self-government were likely to accentuate mutual mistrust and hostility among the different tribes and communities that made up colonial society. It was an explosive mixture.

In these new and much more fluid circumstances, the price of exercising colonial authority went up sharply. To resist the pressures of the politicians, and to manage their rivalries in the interests of imperial power was now likely to require a considerable reserve of physical force and a readiness to use it, if necessary for a period of two or three years, to impose the kind of political settlement compatible with continued imperial over-rule. Twice between 1918 and 1939 the British had repressed Indian political non-cooperation in this way to enforce a constitutional system of their own choosing, and to preserve their control over the commanding heights of external affairs and defence. But neither in Kenya, nor anywhere else in Africa after 1960, was there any question of the British being prepared, or able, to counteract by main force the unwelcome effects of political change. Indeed, having embarked on a new course in Africa to protect their international influence, to have done so would have vitiated the whole object of their policy. Nor was there by 1961 the military capability, let alone the political will, to accept large *new* internal security burdens in colonial Africa. As a result, wherever they initiated party government in Africa, very quickly the British found themselves obliged to accelerate sharply the march to independence. Only thus could the divisions of colonial politics be kept within bounds, and the British themselves escape from the toils of communal, tribal or regional conflict into the sunny uplands – as they hoped – of diplomatic partnership, economic collaboration and informal influence.

(ii) Central Africa

In East Africa, once London had decided to accelerate majority rule, self-government and independence, it had not proved difficult to break the back of settler resistance and the main obstacle encountered by the policy makers was (in the case of Uganda and Kenya) how to cajole the main African interests to agree upon an independence constitution. In Central Africa the termination of colonial rule was infinitely more arduous and bitter. British control over the protectorates of Northern Rhodesia and Nyasaland was complicated by their membership of the white-ruled Central African Federation whose leaders had their own views on the political development of the two territories. The whole future of the Federation rapidly came to turn on the constitutional arrangements made for the protectorates. Britain was also ultimately responsible for the constitutional progress of the third member of the Federation, self-governing, but not independent, Southern Rhodesia where white settler control over all internal matters had been practically absolute since 1923. Inevitably political change, or the lack of it, in each territory of the Federation produced a reaction in the others, and upon the political structure of the federal system as a whole. This fact, together with the great differences of social and political character between the component territories, maximised the resentment and mistrust between all the parties concerned with the Federation's future: the British government, the African nationalist movements and the white settlers. But perhaps the greatest contrast with East Africa was the strength and determination of settler nationalism in Central Africa, above all in Southern Rhodesia.

In the later 1950s the British government was still firmly committed to the federal system in Central Africa. White dominance of the federal government and parliament would, it was hoped, be gradually offset by greater African participation through a franchise based on property and literacy qualifications. There is no sign that London believed that the policies pursued in West Africa – universal suffrage and majority rule – were necessary or appropriate in a region where white settlement (although small in total numbers) had created an entirely different political and social structure. Despite criticism of its failure to extend African political representation, the Federation had received London's seal of approval in November 1957 and the promise that its constitution would be reviewed in 1960 to consider whether Commonwealth status – i.e. independence – should be granted.[131] Had this occurred (as was generally expected) a white-ruled federation in Central Africa would have joined the Commonwealth alongside Nigeria.

But before the Federal Review Conference could take place, politics in Central Africa which had been relatively placid since federation in 1953, were transformed by a series of violent explosions. In Nyasaland, Dr Hastings Banda returned in the middle of 1958 to lead the campaign of the Nyasaland African Congress for an African majority on the Legislative Council in the constitutional discussions London had promised for 1959. The excitement generated by Banda's speeches, the eagerness of some of his followers in the NAC to challenge the Nyasaland government openly, and, perhaps, their desire to shake the loyalty of chiefs and other government employers, created growing unrest and disorder.[132] At the beginning of March 1959, acting on a report that the NAC planned to murder the government officials as part of an insurrection, a state of emergency was declared and the government decided upon 'a vigorous policy of harassing and breaking up Congress organisers, supporters and hoodlums at a lower level . . .' as well as arresting the Congress leadership.[133] In the police and military operation that followed some 51 Africans were killed and 79 injured before order was restored. In Northern Rhodesia, meanwhile, where elections under the new constitution were due, the African National Congress had split between those prepared to take part in the elections and those who formed the Zambia African National Congress (ZANC) under Kenneth Kaunda with the object of boycotting it and mobilising wider African opposition.[134] The success of the ZANC campaign and pressure from white settler members of the executive council led on 11 March 1959 to the banning of Kaunda's movement and the rustication of its leaders. A fortnight earlier, the Southern Rhodesian government had declared its own emergency and arrested some 500 African political activists. In neither of the two Rhodesias was there any parallel to the violence that broke out in Nyasaland.

There can be little doubt that the federal government in Salisbury was eager to check and if possible destroy the growth of anti-Federation movements in both Nyasaland and Northern Rhodesia and that action in all three territories was carefully coordinated.[135] The Devlin Report dismissed the Nyasaland government's claim that it was acting to prevent the 'murder plot' as little more than an excuse,[136] and declared that its main purpose was to suppress the anti-Federation agitation.[137] The object in Northern Rhodesia was the same.[138] Nor can it be seriously doubted that the London government approved of the policy, since the governors of Northern Rhodesia and Nyasaland, not the federal government, were directly responsible for internal security and could scarcely have acted against the nationalist movements without London's permission. Indeed a remarkable and angry letter from the Northern Rhodesian governor strongly implies that the suppression of the ZANC was undertaken on the explicit instructions of the Colonial Secretary.[139] All this serves to indicate how ardent was London's desire that the Federation should not be undermined by intransigent African politicians, and that African political leaders should accept the federal system and its very gradual extension of political rights to the African majority as a 'fact of life'. Cooperation was to be rewarded and anti-Federation 'extremists' given short shrift. But, to London's embarrassment and Salisbury's ruin, this bold stroke went badly wrong. The scale of disorder and loss of life in Nyasaland made an independent inquiry unavoidable. Its report, the Devlin Report, was a crushing public condemnation of the method and the aim and a clear endorsement of the anti-Federation movement's popularity. In Northern Rhodesia the government's action failed to knock out the ZANC organisation.[140] Instead of quietly burying dissident opinion, the Emergency led to a searchlight of British and international interest just at the moment when elsewhere on the African continent majority rule and independence were advancing rapidly, and when London itself began to fear the international consequences of seeming to pursue a reactionary colonial policy. Far from being a skilful prelude to the conferment of independence on the Federation, the 1959 Emergency turned out to be its death warrant.

The crucial difficulty which confronted the white politicians in Salisbury and the policy makers in London after 1959 was the sheer strength and scale of African nationalism in Northern Rhodesia and Nyasaland. As elsewhere in Africa, the growing appeal of nationalist movements may have owed a good deal to the desire of both urban and rural interests to protect themselves against the increasing intervention of the colonial state in their local affairs, especially through its efforts to regulate agriculture. It may also have reflected a clash between rival social leaders in the African communities as the spread of the money economy created new sources of wealth to challenge the position of chiefs and other established notables. On the Northern Rhodesian Copperbelt, the close proximity of 'poverty-stricken, underprivileged Africans and a rich white elite operating a blatant colour-bar'[141] and the four-way conflict between the African mineworkers, the white mineworkers, the mining companies and the government, taught both the necessity and the advantages of organisation and solidarity. In Nyasaland the pressures of land hunger gave the nationalist leaders a cause of obvious mass appeal. And, as we have seen, the constitutional changes of the later 1950s in both protectorates gave African politicians an immediate incentive to construct organisations which could gather votes in elections. But without doubt the factor which accelerated African political awareness most and gave it a far greater intensity of feeling was fear that a confident and aggressive settler nationalism would repeat in Northern Rhodesia and Nyasaland the triumph it had already achieved south of the Zambezi; above all the fear that superior political organisation by the whites would carry the Federation to independence in 1960 and that federation would then become the Trojan Horse of an irrevocable settler supremacy. More than anything else, resentment against the Federation united rural and urban Africans, old-style chiefs and new-style politicians all of whom saw in its triumph the loss of the status, influence and opportunities they enjoyed under British protection.[142] As the leaders of the Central Africa Party (a white liberal party) ruefully told the Monckton Commission, 'Federation has been a rocket booster to African nationalism'.[143]

Thus the very imminence of the promised conference on the Federation's progress towards full independence acted to goad African leaders into desperate efforts to mobilise last-ditch opposition. Despite the efforts to repress them, they enjoyed in the protectorates a number of crucial advantages which ultimately ensured their survival. After the embarrassment of the Devlin Report, London was reluctant to embark on a further round of coercion: indeed the scale of violence in Nyasaland may well have had a sobering effect on official thinking. Secondly, in Northern Rhodesia and Nyasaland British colonial rule relied heavily on the cooperation of chiefs and other notables, especially in the countryside. In Nyasaland, and over almost all of Northern Rhodesia, there was nothing like the spread of white rural settlement which allowed the Southern Rhodesia government to keep a firm grip on its African population.[144] Once the extent of anti-Federation feeling even amongst chiefs and native authorities in the countryside became clear, the colonial administrators faced the dilemma that the effort to destroy the nationalists and force the territories into an *independent* federation under white rule might produce a breakdown of authority on a grand scale, multiplying, not simplifying, Britain's colonial responsibilities. As they pondered these lessons, the policy makers in London turned for relief to the tested expedient of a baffled bureaucracy: the advisory commission to review the federal constitution.

The report of the commission (the Monckton Commission) in October 1960 wasted few words in demonstrating the 'almost pathological' dislike for the Federation in the protectorates.[145] But equally it argued that the experiment in multiracial partnership embodied in the federal system should not be allowed to fail, not only for local reasons but for the sake of the influence which its success might have on the political development of the rest of Africa.[146] How then was the pathological dislike of the Africans to be exorcised? The commission urged a series of sweeping and rapid changes in the structure of the Federation and in the politics of its component territories. The Federation itself should devolve much of its power to the territories, leaving mainly external affairs, defence and the broad control of the economy to the centre.[147] Parity of representation for whites and blacks should be introduced immediately into the Federal Assembly.[148] African majorities in the legislatures of Nyasaland and Northern Rhodesia were equally essential if African fears of settler supremacy were to be calmed.[149] And of the heartland of white power, the commission tersely commented: 'no new form of [federal] association is likely to succeed unless Southern Rhodesia is willing to make drastic changes in its racial policies'[150] – in its pass laws, in the allocation of land and in the industrial colour bar. Even the location of the capital, and the name of the federal association should be reconsidered. In short, almost every aspect of the Federation which secured white settler control or promoted settler interests in particular should be dismantled or recast.

It is likely that in its broad approach the commission reflected the new thinking in London. Doubtless ministers were anxious that the Federation should survive in some form[151] both for its supposed economic benefits and as a device for moderating both African nationalism and the danger that the Rhodesian whites would turn south towards South Africa and perhaps precipitate the worst of all worlds – a racial conflict in Central Africa that would destroy British influence for ever. To achieve this they were ready to throw over the uneasy alliance with the white federal politicians and propel them towards an accommodation that would satisfy the leaders of African nationalism. Even while the Monckton Commission deliberated this steady realignment went forward. Kaunda and Banda were released. Nyasaland was promised an African majority in its legislature. A constitutional conference for Northern Rhodesia was announced. Among white leaders in the Rhodesias this rapid volte-face since the emergency of early 1959 bred an increasingly bitter mistrust sharpened by the belief that anti-federal agitation was factitious and could easily be suppressed by resolute action; and by the insecurity brought on by events in the Congo and elsewhere. As London practised its smiles, settler intransigence hardened rapidly. Here then was one obstacle to the imperial design. The second was just as deadly. African majorities in the legislatures of Northern Rhodesia and Nyasaland were intended to disarm the objections to federation: but equally they armed the leaders of African nationalism with powerful new weapons to fight the battle for secession and independence. On the horns of this dilemma, federation and British policy were painfully impaled.

The conference to consider the federal constitution was opened in London in December 1960 and quickly adjourned until agreement could be reached on modified constitutions for Northern and Southern Rhodesia, as a basis for a new federal structure. Everything now turned on whether the African leaders in Northern Rhodesia would agree to terms acceptable to whites in both Northern and Southern Rhodesia, and to the federal government responsible to a predominantly white assembly and electorate; and equally on whether the Southern Rhodesian government would accept constitutional changes which African leaders north and south of the Zambezi would swallow. From the outset London pressed Welensky, the federal premier, and the white leaders to accept an African majority in Northern Rhodesia.[152] Their resistance rapidly led to deadlock. But in Southern Rhodesia, Sandys, the Commonwealth Secretary, persuaded the white ministers to accept a new constitution which gave Africans some 15 members in an assembly of 65, with the prospect of larger representation as more African voters qualified for the franchise. In return for this and for certain constitutional safeguards, London agreed to end its reserved powers over the administration of Africans, enabling Whitehead, the prime minister, to claim that Southern Rhodesia was independent in every respect except for the power to change its own constitution.[153] But if the British hoped that this agreement would allow a breakthrough in Northern Rhodesia, they were to be disappointed. African leaders north of the Zambezi bitterly attacked the maintenance of a white legislative majority in the south, fearing British pressure to settle for less than majority rule.[154] Under their heavy pressure, Nkomo the leading African politician in Southern Rhodesia, repudiated his acceptance of the Sandys constitution. Meanwhile the Colonial Office at last unveiled its plan for a three-part franchise in Northern Rhodesia, weighted to secure an African majority. Once more white resistance led to deadlock.

In London, the cabinet wavered. The arguments for conceding an African legislative majority were strong, as the Monckton Report had shown. But the unbending opposition of the whites raised other dangerous possibilities. In February 1961 there were strong rumours that the federal government was planning a *coup d'état* to throw off British rule in Northern Rhodesia and Nyasaland.[155] The prospect of armed struggle between British and Rhodesian troops at such a moment was nightmarish. Welensky also warned Macmillan that a triumph for the African nationalists in Northern Rhodesia would lead the Southern Rhodesia electorate to reject the Sandys constitution in the forthcoming referendum.[156] Within the British cabinet itself councils were divided on how best to preserve the Federation and whether to concede an African majority in Northern Rhodesia.[157] Eventually in June 1961, perhaps over Macleod's objections, a new constitutional scheme was proposed so weighted that it seemed likely to ensure a white majority in the legislature,[158] a compromise the white leaders gladly accepted. Satisfaction, however, was shortlived. The new Southern Rhodesia constitution was ratified in a referendum but north of the Zambezi violent disturbances inspired to some degree at least by the leaders of UNIP, convulsed the territory. In London, the policy makers gyrated once more. If the leaders of UNIP would halt the violence, further constitutional discussions would be permitted. In December 1961, Maudling, the new Colonial Secretary, bluntly declared that he was not bound by the proposals announced in June. Then in March 1962 he announced the final award: this time the constitution was weighted towards an African majority. UNIP accepted.[159] But the fate of the Federation was now all but sealed.

Why did London abandon the proposals of June 1961 and settle in the end for an African majority in Northern Rhodesia to the fury and consternation of most whites in the Federation? Part of the answer was undoubtedly fear of further disturbances in Northern Rhodesia at a time when a violent struggle just across the border in Katanga between the United Nations and Tshombe's forces[160] was imminent. Nor did London want to despatch British military forces to the area to help repress the disorders. In July 1961 it had its hands full with the defence of Kuwait. It was also doubtful whether the administration in Northern Rhodesia, with its heavy reliance on African cooperation in the countryside and with the large and combustible African town-ships on the Copperbelt, could stand the strain of a long campaign against UNIP to preserve a settler majority. But what may have weighed even more with ministers in London was the danger that by agreeing to destroy African opposition to federation, they would make themselves the captives of the federal government and be bound to follow its policy whatever the international or local conse-quences. The choice was stark, but London dared not give Salisbury a blank cheque. Moreover, the policy makers may well have judged that by the end of 1961 they no longer had to conciliate white opinion so fully. The disturbances had been an embarrassment but they had also revealed the weakness of the settlers' position in Northern Rhodesia, and the strain African opposition would have thrown on the federal armed forces and economy.[161] By the spring of 1962, London judged, the settlers could do less damage than the Africans. Majority rule must come, even if the Federation collapsed.

Nevertheless, at this late hour, there still remained in the British cabinet a considerable enthusiasm for some sort of federation in Central Africa. In March 1962, Macmillan appointed R. A. Butler, his principal lieutenant, to head a new Central Africa Office which would oversee British policy towards all three territories in the Federation, hitherto divided between the Commonwealth and Colonial Office. Butler was anxious to preserve at least the economic links of the federal system. He resisted any public declaration that either Northern Rhodesia or Nyasaland could secede from the Federation, hoping against hope that the Northern Rhodesia election might throw up a pro-federal majority, and fearing that Welensky might 'do a Samson' – instigate a coup.[162] Perhaps with its own backbenchers in mind, London shrank from being the Federation's public executioner. But the pressure grew relentlessly from Nyasaland,[163] and then as a result of the long-awaited Northern Rhodesia election in October 1962. There, the two African parties won a majority and after some hesitation coalesced to demand secession and independence. Then in December 1962 Welensky's pro-federal ally Sir Edgar Whitehead was swept away in the Southern Rhodesia elections by the new Rhodesian Front which campaigned on a platform of separate independence for Southern Rhodesia and whose triumph reflected partly the fear and antagonism whites there felt towards developments north of the Zambezi. By the end of the year, therefore, the Federation had been repudiated by the political majorities in each territory. Nothing now remained but to divide its assets and to draw up the schedule whereby each territory would go its own separate way. In Northern Rhodesia and Nyasaland there was no further reason to delay the concession of independence. In Southern Rhodesia the worst was yet to come.

What light does this tangled and bitter tale cast on Britain's approach to decolonisation in Central Africa? It suggests, in fact, a number of tentative conclusions. The first is that, as in East Africa, there was a sharp change of mood and outlook among British policy makers in the course of 1959–60 that was occasioned as much, if not more, by the new international considerations at work, both on the African continent and in the world at large, as by the constraints of the local situation. The judgement that African nationalism in Northern Rhodesia was irresistible was less an assessment of the local balance of power than a recognition that an open struggle between whites and blacks in which British power was deployed on behalf of white minority rule would be very damaging internationally and might jeopardise interests far more important than the Federation. Secondly, that as the struggle to reform the Federation reached its climax these international pressures on Britain also intensified, with the heightened East-West rivalry in the Third World, the new spirit in American policy, the crisis in the Congo and the danger of racial divisions in the Commonwealth, culminating in the withdrawal of South Africa in May 1961. There could scarcely have been a worse moment at which to contemplate the coercion of African nationalism. But, thirdly, what emerges forcibly is the continuing enthusiasm of the policy makers for some form of federation in Central Africa as a bulwark against instability and extremism and as a vehicle for economic and political influence. To preserve the Federation the

British had been ready to sanction a new constitution in Southern Rhodesia which fell far short of full political democracy and had tried briefly to extract or impose African consent for less than majority rule in Northern Rhodesia. Fourthly, that if *Realpolitik* rather than principle dictated British policy, this reflected the narrow limits of Britain's direct power in Central Africa, London's assessment of its resources, and the policy makers' resolute determination not to be dragged into open-ended commitments which would unbalance the defence of other vital interests around the world: in the Middle East[164] and in South East Asia as well as at home in Europe. The Northern Rhodesian disturbances of 1961 had made clear that an inflexible defence of the Federation might indeed have this effect. Lastly, the twists and turns of British policy between 1959 and 1963 reveal even more clearly than in East Africa that the British regarded their 'imperial' interests as quite distinct from the local interests of their kith and kin, the white settlers. As so often in the past history of the imperial system the allies of yesterday became the enemies of tomorrow. This was the bitter pill that white Rhodesians had to swallow.

STAYING ON: COLONIES AND STRATEGY

The termination of colonial rule and the rapid transfer of political control to local politicians was seen at its swiftest and most dramatic in East and Central Africa between 1959 and 1964. Elsewhere, too, this short five-year period saw striking changes in the pattern of British rule and influence. In the British West Indies, the absence of any complicating settler interest, the overpowering proximity of American influence, the social and economic problems (and their political legacy) and after 1959 the disturbing presence of a Marxist Cuba, provided good grounds, negative and positive, for a prompt transfer of power to a reliable class of local leaders. The only question was the economic viability of islands which suffered from overcrowding and unemployment. The remedy for this was intended to be a West Indies Federation to provide a common market and a higher credit rating for international borrowing. But when the federation failed, independence for the member islands could not be withheld. Here too the familiar pattern of decolonisation and withdrawal was in evidence. But the pattern was not universal, for the British did not display everywhere the extreme flexibility they showed after 1960 in

Africa. In particular they adopted a forceful, if not stubborn, attitude towards those dependencies to whose strategic usefulness they still attached great importance. Alongside London's insouciance about the political evolution of East and Central Africa should be set the old-fashioned austerity of their treatment of Malta, Cyprus, Aden and Singapore.

Up until the assertion of an American naval presence there in the early 1950s as a consequence of the Truman doctrine, Britain had been the premier naval power in the Mediterranean for over 200 years. This pre-eminence was founded upon the possession of a series of bases: Gibraltar; Malta, with its Grand Harbour; later Cyprus, Alexandria and Palestine. By the mid-1950s, Palestine and the naval facilities in Egypt had been lost. Gibraltar, whose mainland neighbour had enjoyed an uninviting reputation for civil strife, poverty and autocracy, was securely loyal to the British connection. But in Malta and Cyprus the British faced growing pressure for political change. Their response is instructive.

Of the two, Malta posed fewer problems. Since the 1930s when the British had deliberately encouraged a separate Maltese identity to exclude Italian influence,[165] the Maltese had favoured close cultural, sentimental and economic links with Britain, on whose naval expenditure the economy was overwhelmingly dependent. But in 1954, the clerical party, reacting to an increased American military presence, pressed for full self-government within the Commonwealth. The opposition Labour Party, more representative perhaps of the base and dockyard, won the next election on the platform of 'integration' with Britain. London's reaction was to hold a round table conference the outcome of which was the recommendation that Malta should be offered direct representation in the Westminster parliament. Remarkably, despite some reservations about the precedent set, this proposal was accepted by the British government in March 1956, and endorsed, despite the hostility of the Catholic Church in Malta, by a local referendum.[166] But London and the Malta Labour Party fell out over the scale of economic aid that was to accompany this change, and the call for integration turned into a demand for independence. In 1959, after fruitless negotiations, the constitution was suspended, and direct British rule imposed.[167]

This was an embarrassing impass and in 1960 a commission was despatched to find some new *modus* ι *ndi* with the Malta politicians. Its report, published in 1961, and pı nptly accepted by Macleod as

Colonial Secretary,[168] was strikingly different in tone from the reports and recommendations which poured into and out of London about British dependencies at the same period. Malta, it crisply declared, was too small and too important to proceed automatically down the primrose path of constitutional development. The Maltese should be given a wider local autonomy and should be encouraged to participate in matters of defence and external affairs (internal self-government had been permitted since 1947) but the powers of the Malta government in these respects should be 'concurrent' with those of London, whose wishes would prevail in any dispute, and the British parliament would retain its right to legislate for the island.[169] Both main Maltese parties rejected the proposed constitution: both, however, decided to contest the elections of February 1962. The clerical party, the 'Nationalists', won and took office, with the promise of certain constitutional amendments which nevertheless preserved Britain's control in defence and external relations. But the real nub of Maltese politics was economic aid. Failure to agree on this led the Nationalist premier to demand full independence in August 1962. At this point indifference became the mother of concession. The declining value of Malta had been clearly signalled in the defence white paper of 1962. Now London offered swift progress to complete self-government. In September 1964 Malta became independent. But Britain was to enjoy the right to station her forces there for 10 years in return for grants and loans of some £50 million over the same period: a redundant stronghold at a low rent.

The kaleidoscopic change in British attitudes to Malta between 1956 and 1964 closely reflected the changing estimate of Malta's strategic value and its rapid fall from grace in the defence review of 1962. As we have seen already, the situation in Cyprus was more complicated. There, by the middle of 1958, the Greek Cypriot struggle for *enosis*, originally waged against the British, had acquired an increasingly communal character as Turkish Cypriots and Greek Cypriots came to blows. It was at this point that the British had abandoned the attempt to find a purely local solution, and proposed through the 'Macmillan Plan', the direct involvement of Greece and Turkey in the government of Cyprus.[170] Despite the opposition of Greece and the Greek Cypriots, London publicly stuck to its plan.[171] But now a multiple series of pressures began to propel all the parties towards a negotiated political solution. The British watched with alarm the overthrow of the friendly regime of Nuri as-Said in Iraq in the middle of 1958, and with it the final demolition of the Baghdad Pact. Turkey's role in NATO and reconciliation between her and Greece became more important than ever. This view was shared in Ankara,[172] while in Greece, the support of the United States for the Macmillan Plan, the apparent solidity of British public opinion and reluctance to carry opposition to the point of leaving NATO predisposed Athens to search for agreement. It also seems likely that the urgency of a Greek-Turkish entente over Cyprus made London much more flexible than before over the question of British sovereignty. Finally, in Cyprus itself, Makarios himself had undergone a Pauline conversion to separate independence and had renounced *enosis* publicly on 22 September 1958.[173] Only Grivas remained briefly intransigent, and unleashed one last futile and bloody wave of terror in October and November.[174]

The crucial element in Makarios's calculations was that the alternative to independence was partition, either as a consequence of the implementation of the Macmillan plan or as a result of Turkish intervention in the escalating communal struggle on the island. Hence he, like the British government was prepared ultimately to accept the compromise hammered out in the arduous negotiations between Greece and Turkey at Zurich in February 1959. Under the new plan Cyprus was to be independent but its constitution would allow the two communities almost complete autonomy. London agreed, provided the bases at Dhekelia and Akrotiri remained sovereign British territory. 'We only need our Gibraltars', said Macmillan, 'this is vital to us militarily and politically'.[175] In the final agreement, Britain, Greece and Turkey were jointly to guarantee the independence and integrity of Cyprus (which was to be a member of the Commonwealth) and British sovereignty over the base areas was recognised in perpetuity.[176] Faced with this diplomatic *fait accompli* and the blunt warning that the alternative was partition, the Greek Cypriot leadership reluctantly acquiesced.[177]

As in Malta, the British had been determined to reserve their strategic rights, although in Cyprus the international complexities enforced, and local communal conflict made possible, an unusual solution to the problem. But ironically by the time that the Cyprus Treaty and the new Maltese constitution had been drawn up in 1961, Britain's main strategic concerns lay less and less in the Mediterranean, and were concentrated more and more in the wide maritime arc between Aden and Singapore.

The British had acquired the barren, treeless, waterless promontory of Aden in 1839 to guard the entrance from the Red Sea into the Indian Ocean. Subsequently they had established a loose protectorate over the southern fringe of the Arabian peninsula between Yemen in the west and Oman to the east. Aden was an important link in the chain of fortresses along the old imperial sea route through the Mediterranean, Suez Canal and Red Sea to India, the Far East and Australasia. It was the great bunker for coal and oil. In the 1950s, however, its value as a base appreciated rapidly. The loss of Suez, the fear that turbulence in the Persian Gulf would threaten Europe's oil supplies, and Aden's convenience for training and acclimatising British troops swiftly promoted it to Britain's principal military centre in the Middle East, while the number of British servicemen stationed there increased fourfold between 1957 and 1959.[178]

But every base has a hinterland, more or less predatory neighbours, and a local population on whose cooperation or acquiesence its usefulness depends. By a tiresome irony, the more the British grew to prize their possession of Aden, the greater became the difficulty of holding it with the necessary economy of effort. Two problems were pre-eminent. The rulers of Yemen were eager to absorb the petty Arab states of the Aden Protectorate by force or subversion. While in Aden proper (correctly the Aden Colony) the Arab population, swollen by migrants especially from the Yemen, became increasingly restive under British rule as the influence of Arab nationalism, greatly inflated by Nasser's triumph in 1956, played upon a volatile new urban society. By the end of the 1950s, strikes and election boycotts gave warning of what was to follow.

The British devised at first two political solutions. In the interior from 1954 onwards they set out to persuade the tribes and sultans to form themselves into a federation, the better to resist incursions from the Yemen or the siren-call of anti-British sentiment. Meanwhile in the Aden Colony the representative character of the local assembly was slightly increased with more elected members and a narrow franchise,[179] in the effort to draw in more local cooperation. By 1960, however, with continuing unrest in Aden, a radical new plan emerged. Aden would be given more self-government to defuse its discontents but only as part of the new federation set up in the interior in 1959. This scheme would have the extra merit of linking Aden's commercial wealth to the desperate poverty of the interior government. Security matters would remain under British control, and the radical element in Aden's politics would be checked by the conservative influence of the tribal interior. At almost the same moment as they were acquiescing in the break-up of the Rhodesian Federation, the British propelled the federal scheme through the Aden assembly on the votes of nominated or ex-officio members.[180] The Federation of South Arabia was set up in 1963.

But by 1963, even as the British were constructing, at heavy cost, new cantonments for the military base,[181] dangerous new pressures threatened their policy. In Aden itself, the radical nationalist movement based on the labour unions and immigrant workers from the Yemen mounted a terrorist campaign against federation and British rule which culminated in an attempt to assassinate the High Commissioner in 1963. The Yemen's revolution of September 1962 brought to power a regime that was closely aligned with the Aden radicals and which redoubled its efforts to drive British influence from the tribal interior, with active aid and support from Egypt. In the interior the appearance of a federal state, infringing tribal autonomy, inevitably bred new resentments and a violent insurrection in 1963–64. The British were driven to further measures to appease these various discontents and endow the fragile federation with greater prestige and authority. At a constitutional conference in 1964 it was decided that the Federation would become independent in 1968 but would be linked to Britain by defence and financial agreements which preserved British rights to the base and promised help to the federal government against its internal and external enemies. Here was a bold new commitment entered into just as the last vestiges of British rule were disappearing in tropical Africa. As we shall see, circumstances decreed that it would be short lived.

The South Arabian Federation was not the last exercise in constitutional fretwork in which the British indulged. In the Far East, they had long cherished the plan of building a great bloc of their colonial territories in Malaya, Singapore and Borneo into a federation that would be closely aligned to Britain and the West. In 1957, the Malayan states had attained independence in a peninsular federation bound to Britain by a defence agreement. The Borneo territories were politically dormant. But Singapore, with its large Chinese population, its vulnerability to communist influence, its enormous commercial importance and its vital strategic significance as the gateway between the Indian Ocean and the South China Sea, and as Britain's premier base east of Suez, posed an immediate political problem. How was

British control of the base and city to be protected against the social radicalism of this teeming metropolis? In 1956 and 1957 the British had successfully imposed a constitution in which, in return for full internal self-government, the local politicians had accepted British control over defence and external relations and the operation of the base; and joint British, Malayan and local control over internal security – still a matter of intense common concern to all three parties.[182] But with the new assertion of Chinese communist influence in South East Asia in 1960–61 and the stimulation of local Chinese-feeling the durability of British influence was placed in doubt, and with it the value of the base and the stability of Malaya.

The cue for British policy was the eagerness of the People's Action Party government in Singapore to achieve independence by a merger with the Malayan Federation as a means of checking communist influence and safeguarding Singapore's commercial future. In early 1961 a series of visits by the Commonwealth Secretary, the Secretary of State for War and Lord Mountbatten, Chief of Defence Staff, to Singapore and Malaya suggested how zealous London was to promote this idea.[183] The Malayan premier demurred, fearing the effects of what would be a majority Chinese population in the new state.[184] Fear and hope converted him: fear that growing communist influence in Singapore would jeopardise Malaya, especially if Singapore were granted separate independence; hope that the British would hand over the Borneo territories, with their critical non-Chinese population to the new federation.[185] In August 1961, Singapore and Malaya settled upon a merger subject to the inclusion of the Borneo states. The following November a conference in London brought Anglo-Malayan agreement: in return for Britain's freedom to use the Singapore base as she saw fit, a commission of inquiry would visit Sarawak and North Borneo to verify (with a strong positive presumption) the acceptability of a new 'Malaysian' federation.[186] That this Commission admitted that the 'Malaysian' proposal meant nothing to much of the interior population and enjoyed the firm support of at best one third of the population,[187] proved no bar to its report being regarded as the green light for federation.

One serious obstacle remained. Both the Philippines and Indonesia regarded the inclusion of the Borneo states in Malaysia with deep resentment. Despite an inquiry under the auspices of the United Nations, which supported the claim that the local populations favoured Malaysia, Indonesia in particular remained unreconciled, and celebrated the formation of the new Federation in September 1963 by severing relations with the Malayan government. But London refused to be deflected, despite the fact that it had undertaken in November 1961 to extend to the new Federation the defence agreement originally made with Malaya. Too much seemed at stake for compromise: the stability of Malaya and Singapore; a graceful release from colonial obligations in Borneo; above all the safety of the Singapore base and its hinterland. British devotion to these objectives was soon to be tested in a prolonged and expensive confrontation with Indonesia.

When we set British treatment of Cyprus, Aden and Singapore and the Borneo territories alongside London's policy elsewhere in the colonial empire, two features stand out strongly. The first is the determination with which the policy makers pursued their objects of control over defence and foreign relations, and, subsequently, the construction of what they regarded as the essential constitutional scaffolding for the support of Britain's strategic interests. In Cyprus they waged a fierce struggle against *enosis* and insisted upon a treaty settlement which preserved two colonial enclaves – hostages to fortune which London had carefully eschewed elsewhere in the retreat from empire. In Aden the British had repressed with rigour and showed minimal sympathy for any progress towards fully-fledged political democracy in the urban jungle of the Aden Colony. Moreover, they showed little hesitation in gerrymandering Aden itself into a gimcrack federation of sheikhs and sultans. In the Far East the same instinct was at work, for the Malaysian Federation, whose supreme usefulness was to solve the problem of Singapore's political future and create a stronger client state in South East Asia, was only possible because of London's readiness to push the Borneo territories into the new state with only the most token and impressionistic form of local consultation, and long before the mass of the population was capable of exercising a real choice through the ballot box. Precisely the kind of objection, it might be observed, that had been levelled against the Rhodesian Federation in the early 1950s and which was deemed to disqualify its claim to independence.

The second striking feature is the readiness that London displayed to assume substantial and potentially onerous commitments to insure these strategic benefits – the guarantee of Cyprus' integrity, the defence agreements with the two federations of South Arabia and Malaysia. What makes this readiness yet more striking is that they were undertaken between 1961 and 1964, at precisely that moment when, as has sometimes been argued, the swing towards Europe and the distaste for obsolete colonial responsibilities had become acute. Nor can this curious 'quirk' of policy be dismissed merely as an ill-considered attachment to a redundant imperial mentality.

In the mid-1950s the continuation of Britain's historic military presence in the Mediterranean, the Middle East (Cyprus and Aden rather than Suez) and the Indian Ocean was taken for granted. In 1954–55, at the same time as they contracted to maintain a permanent garrison of some 50,000 men in Germany as a contribution to Western defence, the British also entered the SEATO alliance for the defence of South East Asia, and the ill-fated Baghdad Pact to guard the Middle East, as well as renewing the Simonstown Agreement reaffirming their commitment to the naval security of the Indian Ocean and the South Atlantic. The Suez crisis and its aftermath led to the formulation of the Eisenhower doctrine and a more assertive American presence in the Mediterranean and Middle East; while the closing of the Suez route to the East as a strategic highway, reduced the naval importance of the Mediterranean in British eyes. But the Suez crisis did not lead them to lose interest in the Persian Gulf, the Indian Ocean and the Far East. Far from it. In fact the years after Suez saw a steady intensification of Britain's east of Suez commitments.

There were several reasons for this. By the later 1950s the defence of Western Europe and Britain herself came increasingly to be seen as a nuclear matter. This was the doctrine powerfully embedded in the Defence White Paper of 1957. Moreover, the threat of war, so keenly felt in the early 1950s appeared to have receded.[188] Britain's old naval hegemony in the Mediterranean had been taken over by the United States. Thirdly, the Suez crisis and its after-effects in the Arab world made London acutely conscious of the vulnerability of its oil interests in the Persian Gulf to local attack or Cairo-inspired subversion. British oil companies had fixed assets of nearly $700 million in the Gulf in 1959; Kuwait alone provided 50 per cent of Britain's oil requirements in 1957–61, the rest coming from the other Gulf states.[189] Fourthly, at the end of the 1950s the threat of communist expansion in Asia seemed to be growing steadily with the Indo-Chinese border war, the civil war in Laos, the threat to Thailand and the increasing Western anxiety over Vietnam. Here Britain had particular interests of her own and a shared interest in the containment of the communist world. Two further facts induced a reappraisal of British commitments east of Suez. The first was the after-effect of the Suez crisis in throwing up an 'air barrier' to the easy movement of men and equipment from Britain to the eastern theatres. The second was the eagerness of the Royal Navy to justify its existence in an era when, under the Sandys doctrine of 1957, the main burden of home defence would be met by nuclear weaponry. Together, these developments conspired to emphasise the necessity and feasibility of a new and stronger deployment of British forces east of Suez, and to create powerful advocates for such a commitment in the defence establishment. Old unspoken assumptions about Britain's world-power role, the desire to preserve the existing political order in the eastern world, and an 'ingrained sense of responsibility'[190] for the orderly transfer of power in Africa and Asia, were heavily reinforced.

The result was that between 1959 and 1964 Britain's strategic preoccupations swung more and more to the east even while the army's manpower was contracting sharply.[191] The navy was redeployed at the expense of the Mediterranean and Atlantic.[192] New cantonments were constructed at Aden and Singapore. Successive defence white papers stressed the importance of eastern defence. The Chiefs of Staff proclaimed in a paper prepared in January 1962 that the main dangers to Western security now lay in Africa and Asia and that here Britain would find her major role.[193] British forces, declared the Minister of Defence in May 1962, would henceforth be concentrated in Britain and at Aden and Singapore.[194] Even in 1965, as the economic storm clouds gathered, the new Labour government proclaimed its loyalty to this strategic orthodoxy,[195] despite the strains of the confrontation with Indonesia and the terrorist campaign in Aden. Two centuries of expansion into Asia had reached a bizarre finale.

What are we to make of this remarkable reorientation of defence policy carried through at the very moment when London was engineering a rapid withdrawal from the bulk of its direct colonial commitments? One answer may be that the inconsistency between Britain's enthusiasm for retreat in Africa and her more robust attitude, political and military, elsewhere was more apparent than real. The retention of Aden and Singapore and the ultimate conveyance of the bases to 'safe' local regimes securely tied to Britain was intended to ensure Britain's strategic grip in the Indian Ocean and to exclude the influence of any other major power – especially that of the Soviet bloc. It was, it may be suggested, precisely because it still seemed possible to retain strategic supremacy in the Indian Ocean that the policy makers could afford to view with such indulgence the independence of East and Central Africa. With a regional monopoly of military power, the sentimental and cultural links of the Commonwealth connection, and the continuation of close economic ties, there was reason to expect that independence, far from terminating British influence, would give its exercise a streamlined efficiency, shorn of the old causes of friction and conflict. In other words, if we look at British policy across the board in the period 1958–59 to 1963–64 there are strong grounds for supposing that its underlying theme was not the rapid liquidation of colonial or extra-European commitments preparatory to embracing a European destiny. It was instead an attempt, inevitably muddled and incoherent, to come to terms with a further contraction of British world power: an attempt, however, to *stabilise* Britain's world position, to retain its basic elements, not to abandon it altogether. To meet new international and local conditions, new allies had to be cultivated; new techniques of influence devised; new policies constructed; new commitments undertaken. Rationalisation and reappraisal were the order of the day. But if the transfer of power was, to some degree, the pursuit of empire by other, informal means, its success depended upon a range of favourable circumstances. The sentimental links would have to survive the strains of independence. The economic relationship would have to weather the rise of new pressures and vested interests. And Britain herself would have to be able to sustain the escalating burdens of economic, financial and military aid that were the price of influence and cooperation in the era of decolonisation.

7 Winding Up

The decline of Britain's ability to control or influence regions of the world far from her own shores was not just the outcome of changes at home or in the colonial territories. Between 1945 and 1965 or, on a longer view, between 1900 and the 1960s, the international conditions which had once allowed the British and (to a lesser extent) other European states to exert an astonishing preponderance over so large a part of the earth's surface gradually altered. The glacier-like inexorability of such changes, for so long of almost imperceptible slowness, came at last to be felt in its full strength not so much at the time when British leaders accepted the desirability of a full transfer of power in most of their possessions, but rather at the moment when the continuity of British influence, after the moment of independence, hung in the balance. It was when they tried to substitute influence for rule that the British really discovered how drastically their power had declined.

THE WITHDRAWAL FROM EAST OF SUEZ

At the time of the general election in October 1964, Britain still retained substantial commitments and obligations east of Suez. She was committed to setting up a South Arabian Federation which would receive, even after independence, substantial military aid and be bound in a military agreement allowing Britain to use the Aden base. In the Persian Gulf Britain was still responsible for the defence and external relations of the petty sheikhdoms that fringed the Arab shore of the Lower Gulf and held, in theory, a watching brief over the stability of the Gulf as a whole with its enormous oil trade. In the Far East lay the most extensive and demanding commitment of all: the defence of Malaysia and Singapore against the territorial claims and general hostility of Sukarno's Indonesia, whose apparent alignment with communist China had raised fears of a general communist onslaught on South East Asia through Vietnam and the Malay peninsula. At the height of the confrontation with Indonesia some 68,000 British servicemen were deployed in the Far East, together with a fleet of 80 ships including 2 aircraft carriers and a commando ship.[1] With the project to develop island bases for a new fleet of warplanes to provide 'air control' of the Indian Ocean into the 1970s,[2] Britain's determination to maintain her position as the mistress of the Indian Ocean appeared unshakeable. Here, as has been suggested, was the counterpoint to the ready transfer of power in East and Central Africa, and the enthusiasm for a Malaysian Federation. However much British power and influence had been straitened elsewhere in the world, in the Indian Ocean, fringed by the vital oilfields of the Gulf, bordered by former colonial territories in Africa, South and South East Asia, and traversed by vital air and sea routes to Australia and New Zealand, Britain was to remain a great power.[3]

The Labour government which came to power in October 1964 had been keenly critical of its predecessor's insistence on retaining an independent nuclear deterrent and scornful of the status which it was supposed to uphold. Significantly, once in office, the leaders of the new government rapidly abandoned the notion of scrapping Britain's nuclear weapons.[4] More striking, however, was the commitment of the prime minister, Harold Wilson, and the most powerful figures in the party leadership, to Britain's east of Suez role, which Wilson had championed long before Labour's accession to power.[5] At first sight, this appears at odds with the proverbial dislike of the party for overseas commitments and military expenditure, and its concern for domestic social priorities. But three powerful influences worked against any radical tendency in Labour's foreign policy. The first was the fear (which constantly tormented Labour leaders) that to be seen to favour the reduction of British world power and influence would expose them to Conservative attack and arouse patriotic resentment among Labour's own working-class supporters. The second was the power of the old Bevinite tradition which asserted Britain's claim to be the world's third power, independent alike of the United States and the Soviet bloc and looking outward to Britain's old imperial spheres of influence. This tradition had dominated the Labour government of 1945–51 to which Harold Wilson and his colleagues looked back for inspiration and from which they drew all their experience of government. The third influence was an amalgam of pride, habit and inertia: the almost invariable reluctance to abandon positions of status and influence (or their apparent benefits) until they became plainly untenable. For a government resting, as Labour did from October 1964 until March 1966, on a wafer-thin majority (of four) the electoral benefits of an assertive foreign policy were not easily forsworn. World power, after all, conferred domestic prestige. For all the emphasis upon Britain's commitment to international 'peacekeeping' as a member of the United Nations, and to the multiracial fraternity of the Commonwealth, there can be little doubt that the principal objective of deploying so much military power east of Suez was the retention of British influence there. In a phrase of which Lord Curzon might have been proud, Harold Wilson proclaimed in June 1965 in New Delhi that 'Britain's frontiers are on the Himalayas'.[6] That this self-assertion now seemed to enjoy American support and approval was an additional encouragement.[7]

But if the Labour leaders had come to power in the hope of preserving Britain's world-power status while overhauling and modernising the British economy, they were to be disappointed on both counts. Almost from the moment they took office a succession of crises in Britain's balance of payments removed almost all scope for economic initiative and battered ministerial morale. Between November 1964 and June 1966 there were three major sterling crises[8] enforcing deflation, cuts in government spending and heavy borrowing from central banks overseas. And the worst was yet to come. In the effort to reduce the outflow of sterling and to check public expenditure, overseas defence spending in particular and defence spending in general came under close scrutiny. In the first year of the Labour government this concern for economy had little effect on strategic policy. The Defence White Paper of 1965 indicated that both Aden and Singapore would be retained. To a fierce critic within the cabinet of the east of Suez policy, it seemed that the prime minister was determined to maintain 'our imperial position East of Suez' at considerable economic cost chiefly to meet American requests and cement Anglo-American friendship.[9] But a revolution was in the making, for in the course of 1965 the Treasury was able to insist that henceforth the defence budget should be restricted to £2,000 million and that Britain's strategic coat should in future be cut according to her financial cloth. The result in 1966–68 was the most far-reaching change in Britain's world position to occur since the withdrawal from India twenty years before.

The first and perhaps decisive round was fought over the 1966 Defence White Paper, the terms of which were hammered out in more than twenty meetings of the fourteen-strong cabinet defence com-mittee.[10] What gave the terms of the White Paper such far-reaching importance was the fact that in 1966 the intense pressure to hold down defence spending collided head on with the need to decide upon the shape of Britain's military presence east of Suez well into the future. In particular, if the ageing force of aircraft carriers which formed the backbone of that presence were to be replaced at the end of their life in the mid-1970s, new ships would have to be ordered and their design approved. This was the crunch. The cost of new aircraft carriers was unacceptable to a cabinet acutely conscious of economic weakness and of unfulfilled pledges in domestic policy. Despite the resignation of the navy minister and the Chief of Defence Staff, no new carriers were ordered. When the existing force became obsolete it was to be replaced by land-based aircraft. In the meantime, the White Paper laid down three new strategic principles. Henceforth no oper-ations of a large-scale kind were to be contemplated without an ally; no assistance was to be offered unless the country concerned could offer appropriate facilities – presumably air bases; and no attempt was to be made to preserve defence facilities in an independent country unless it wanted them.[11] The Singapore base was to be retained. But Aden was to be abandoned when the South Arabian Federation became independent in 1967 or 1968. Nor was the new Federation to be offered the defence agreement that had been promised at the time when its progress to independence was laid down in 1964.

The 1966 White Paper was intended to be a compromise: to preserve a British presence but to escape the massive cost of aircraft carriers and the unrewarding drain of defending Aden and South Arabia. To a restive parliamentary Labour Party, Wilson insisted that 'though he was prepared to withdraw and reduce the number of troops East of Suez he would never deny Britain the role of a world power'.[12] But the pressure for further economies continued. At a meeting of the cabinet defence committee in December 1966 it was proposed to cut the British forces in the Far East by half and those in the Middle East by one third. But any notion of a full-scale with-drawal was firmly rejected.[13] In the early part of 1967 a further defence white paper promised complete withdrawal from South Arabia on independence and further reductions in South East Asia.[14] But if the prime minister hoped that this would satisfy critics within the party and the cabinet,[15] he misjudged their mood. After a major revolt in the party, a supplementary defence statement in July 1967 promised withdrawal from Malaya and Singapore by the mid-1970s while the effort to negotiate South Arabia into independence was accelerated. By September, the British had abandoned all hope of preserving the compliant federal government in South Arabia which was now defunct and were negotiating for early withdrawal with the rival groups of nationalists who dominated Aden itself. But at the same time as the decision to leave Aden in November 1967 was made public, the Foreign Office hastened to reassure the sheikhdoms of the Gulf that Britain intended to maintain her presence there and would continue to honour her commitments to them.[16]

This latest formula had a short life. Aided by the Middle East war and the closure of the Suez Canal, Britain plunged in the autumn of 1967 into the fourth and worst sterling crisis since Labour came to power. In mid-November, devaluation, so long resisted, became inevitable. The result for British defence policy was twofold. In the first place the recovery measures to take advantage of devaluation and to meet the requirements of the International Monetary Fund dictated a further round of expenditure cuts, of which defence would have to take its share. No less important was the fact that devaluation had broken the old solidarity of the 'Bevinites' in the cabinet – George Brown, James Callaghan, Denis Healey and Michael Stewart – who had resisted any early or general withdrawal from east of Suez; and, with the promotion of Roy Jenkins to the Treasury, altered the balance of authority within the government. Jenkins was determined to secure withdrawal from east of Suez by 1970 or 1971. At three fierce meetings, of the inner cabinet on 4 January 1968, and of the full cabinet on 12 and 15 January, the resistance of the Bevinites was broken.[17] The die was cast. Britain was to leave Malaysia, Singapore and the Persian Gulf by the end of 1971. The fleet of F-111 aircraft, originally intended to provide an air power replacement for the obsolete carriers, was cancelled. Britain was to retain no special capability to intervene militarily east of Suez. The Indian Ocean, the last sphere in which Britain had retained a world-power status, was to be given up.

In retrospect it may seem less remarkable that the British should have decided to withdraw from the Indian Ocean by 1971 than that the decision took so long to reach. Even after the confrontation with Indonesia had been ended by the Bangkok Agreement of August 1966, the strategists in London still planned to keep a military presence in the Far East based, if necessary, in Australia. And even after it had been decided that Aden's value as a base was outweighed by the likely costs of its defence, the retention of Britain's Gulf role had been reaffirmed – as late as October 1967. The eventual decision to withdraw from the Far and Middle East by the end of 1971 was hotly contested in cabinet and for a brief moment seemed likely to be reversed.[18] As we have suggested, part of the reason – perhaps the most important part – for the reluctance to contemplate *complete and final* withdrawal was a view of Britain's interests and place in the world that was emotional and romantic rather than coldly rational and cost-effective. Richard Crossman railed against the 'Great Britain' mentality of the senior ministers which virtually excluded, until 1967, discussion of either withdrawal or the devaluation of sterling – which was seen in the same way as a gesture of retreat and despair that would signal the renunciation of world-power status.[19] It is also clear that the British government was under strong pressure from Washington to maintain its Eastern commitments at a time when the American involvement in Vietnam was growing steadily, and that American sympathy in Britain's economic difficulties was partly dependent on this.[20] There was, in addition, an anxiety in London to strengthen relations with the United States as a counterpoise to Britain's continued exclusion from the EEC and the steady weakening of her influence in Europe. Finally, there was no doubt a genuine, if exaggerated belief that, even with the end of confrontation in the Far East, a British presence was necessary to prevent potentially dangerous local crises and to help contain the growing influence of both Soviet and Chinese communism.

It is usual to attribute the dramatic abandonment of these convictions in January 1968 to the pressure of economic circumstances, in particular to the need for major economies in the aftermath of devaluation. Clearly the steady decline in Britain's international competitiveness, in her relative prosperity and in the stability of sterling as an international currency undermined confidence among the policy makers about the viability or wisdom of maintaining commitments which might become unmanageable and end in humiliation. The effort to remain a great power east of Suez seemed certain to become *more* burdensome, if only because of the frightening escalation of defence costs and the sluggishness of the British economy. Nevertheless, ultimately the decision to withdraw was a *political* choice not a financial imperative. Twenty years before a Labour government facing an even grimmer economic future gritted its teeth and retained peacetime conscription to maintain Britain's overseas garrisons. It has also been argued that withdrawal was not so much the product of either strategic or economic calculation as a sop to the vociferous Left of the party which was dismayed by further deflation and expenditure cuts.[21] Undoubtedly the cabinet faced a restive and rebellious parliamentary party, but the decision to give up the east of Suez policy almost certainly derived from a wider range of pressures and calculations. Indeed, it might almost be argued that devaluation and the cabinet reorganisation which followed it were as much the occasion as the cause of a fundamental change of perspective on Britain's overseas interests.

An important factor here was growing support within the cabinet and the parliamentary party for a second approach to the Common Market. It was the alliance of Europeanist MPs with the Left in the party which made opposition to east of Suez commitments so formidable. Moreover the decisive lead in the cabinet decision on withdrawal was taken not by the Left but by Jenkins.[22] In October 1966, a meeting of ministers had heard the argument that Britain must join Europe 'as the only way to make sure that Britain retained a place at the top table'.[23] In May 1967 the application was made. And even though this second application foundered like the first on De Gaulle's veto, it marked the emergence of entry into the EEC, and the revival of British influence in Europe, as the first priority of foreign policy. By contrast, the east of Suez commitment was a diversion of resources, and might even be regarded by European countries as a 'negative dowry' – a British liability which her future partners in the EEC might have to share. Certainly, Healey as Defence Secretary could argue in the foreign affairs debate in January 1968 that the concentration of Britain's military power in Europe would strengthen her voice in European affairs.[24] In short, an alternative strategy for maintaining Britain's world status now commanded wide support.

Perhaps a second factor was the increasing difficulty which even the most ardent champions of the Eastern commitment found in demonstrating that the retention of a military presence yielded any special advantage to Britain. It was tacitly admitted that Britain's continued presence was, to a considerable extent, at American behest and for American convenience. Moreover, the Defence White Paper of 1966 had openly declared that Britain could undertake no major operations without an ally – so that the protection of peculiarly *British* interests could not be guaranteed. Perhaps a sense of impatience at an expensive proxy role combined with another powerful feeling increasingly at work since 1949 and particularly since the late 1950s. This was the recognition that the defence of Britain's most vital interests was no longer in the hands of British leaders, but rested with the policy makers in Washington. The habit of dependence inevitably lessened the impact of such decisions as those of January 1968.

The last factor to be considered is the local situation in the Middle and Far East. Aden was the first casualty of strategic revision in 1966. It was also the most exposed of Britain's remaining outposts, especially to a campaign of nationalist terrorism, financed from Cairo and supplied through neighbouring Yemen – an Egyptian satrapy. The creation of the Federation had done nothing to reconcile the politicians of Aden to a British presence. For the British Aden was a growing embarrassment and a considerable drain on manpower. Moreover, with the decision to phase out the use of aircraft carriers and to rely on airpower in the Indian Ocean, Aden's value as a long-term commitment plummeted. Nevertheless, it is likely that the impact of withdrawing the promise of a defence agreement upon the unstable politics of the Federation was not appreciated in London, and the speed with which the federal government collapsed after 1966 took the policy makers by surprise.

Elsewhere, in the Far East and the Persian Gulf, the British were under no direct pressure to withdraw. Indeed, notoriously, the rulers of the Gulf States and of Malaysia and Singapore begged for a postponement of British departure. Nevertheless changes had occurred in local politics since the early 1960s which weakened the case for a British military presence. The rapprochement of Malaysia and Indonesia in 1966 ended the danger of Malaysia and Singapore being overrun and absorbed into a Greater Indonesia. There was also a growing feeling in Britain, influenced perhaps by the pattern of conflict in Vietnam, that if resistance to communist expansion was to be successful, much greater involvement in their own defence by the local powers was essential. This idea – that the *local* power balance would prove decisive – had been voiced by Enoch Powell as Conservative defence spokesman at the somewhat unlikely venue of the Conservative Party Conference in 1965. Significantly, though Conservative leaders denounced the withdrawal announcement in January 1968 for its abruptness and haste, when a Conservative government returned to power in 1970 it confined its efforts to negotiating a contribution to a five-power force (Australia, New Zealand, Malaysia,

Singapore and Britain) rather than resuming the defensive obligations of the Anglo-Malay defence agreement.[25]

In the Persian Gulf there were even stronger arguments for doubting the value of Britain's existing military commitments. The 1960s had seen a rapid growth in the wealth and power of the two main Gulf States, Iran and Saudi Arabia. In the face of their increasing self-assertion, Britain's treaty obligation to defend the tiny sheikhdoms of Bahrain, Qatar, Abu Dabi or Shahjah, once effortlessly maintained by sea power, came to appear burdensome out of all proportion to its benefits. Apart from the discharge of treaty obligations, the main arguments for retaining a British presence in the Gulf were that it would ensure stability (and the exclusion of unwelcome influences) as well as providing a guarantee of the West's oil interests in general and Britain's large stake in particular.[26] But by 1968 these arguments could be stood on their head. Both Saudi Arabia and Iran appeared stable, and possessed considerable military power. To become embroiled with either would be embarrassing and counterproductive. Secondly, the great bulk of Britain's oil interests was to be found in Iran and Kuwait[27] – both states that pressed for British withdrawal – and would hardly benefit from a clash with either. To be the watchdog of Europe's oil supply at the risk of losing their own investment with its vital foreign exchange, was scarcely a role for the British to relish. Thirdly, the rapid economic development of Saudi Arabia and particularly of Iran with its large population and industrialisation programme suggested that Britain's interest in particular was better served by cultivating close economic and political ties with the most powerful states in the region than by clinging to an obsolete and potentially embarrassing commitment in the Gulf itself.[28]

Whatever the force of the various arguments for scaling down or abandoning completely military commitments in the Middle and Far East, it was not to be expected that such a major policy change woud be easy or uncontroversial. Old established policies usually have well-entrenched defenders; long-standing commitments generate an impetus of their own. Moreover, so drastic and sudden a withdrawal inevitably called Britain's identity as a world power into question. The 'status barrier,' remarked Richard Crossman ironically, 'is as difficult to break through as the sound barrier: it splits your ears and is terribly painful when it happens'.[29] Whatever the inner logic of withdrawal from the point of view of Britain's interests and economic capability, it required perhaps the disruptive shock of devaluation and the associated political changes in the cabinet to allow the break to be made, and the realignment of external policies to occur. Far more than any weakness on the ground it was the almost accidental convergence of economic crisis, internal political pressure on an irresolute left-centre government, and anxiety about British relations with Europe which cleared the way for winding up the remnants of the world role. Together with other changes in world affairs, it helped to transform the *partial* withdrawal which the British intended to be the result of the colonial transfers of power into a conscious retreat from the old burdens and privileges of imperial power.

THE DECLINE OF INFLUENCE

There can be little doubt that when the British formally transferred power over their colonial possessions in Asia, Africa, the Caribbean and elsewhere, they both hoped and expected to wield a very great influence over the post-colonial states that they had helped to construct. As we have already seen, the later phases of British colonial policy were frequently geared chiefly to making sure that the emerging state would be a useful and stable partner for Britain after independence – an asset and not a liability or a loss. Wherever possible, indeed, London intended to construct a 'special relationship' with the ex-colony, on the assumption that the new rulers would turn to Britain for their external needs – capital, technical assistance, defence aid – and align themselves closely to her in their external policies. This was why such stress was laid upon the attractions of Commonwealth membership; why successive British governments were at such pains to inflate the Commonwealth's significance and prestige as a worldwide organisation; why London rejected any notion of a two-tier Commonwealth of old (mainly white) and new (mainly Asian or African) members;[30] why the British government undertook after 1958 to increase drastically the economic aid it made available to Commonwealth countries; and why educational links were carefully fostered. The flexibility and informality of Commonwealth relationships, the readiness to accommodate republican constitutions as long as the Queen's status as head of the Commonwealth was recognised, the absence of binding treaties between Britain and the ex-colonies did not betoken indifference or expectations of a rapid divergence of interests. They indicated the eagerness of the British to make

Commonwealth membership as easy and attractive as possible, in the fond hope that once in the club the old links with the ruling power would be strengthened and solidified in a new and acceptable form.

The objects of British influence were plain enough. The ex-colonial states were to be drawn towards the West, and kept from the contagion of communism. In political and strategic terms, they were to be oriented, however discreetly, towards the Anglo-American camp. Then economic development was to be encouraged along lines compatible with British interests and in cooperation with British overseas enterprises. London hoped no doubt that if the new states in Africa and Asia continued to look to Britain for markets and capital, and for financial expertise in banking and economic planning, they would have a strong incentive to maintain 'open' economies attractive to British business and investment.[31] This was not mere neo-colonialist greed. It was widely thought that only economic policies of this kind would attract sufficient development capital or stimulate internal economic change sufficiently. Finally, of course, it was hoped that the social and cultural identity of the new state would develop along lines that were especially sympathetic to the British model. Here the new university colleges set up after 1945, the prestigious high schools like Achimota in Ghana or Alliance in Kenya, the professions with their British style and training, and the magnetic power of English language and literature were all expected to play their part. With effort, tact, goodwill and wise spending, thought the optimists, the ties between Britain and the Afro-Asian Commonwealth might be almost as close as the more instinctual bonds that linked Britain and the old dominions.

These hopes were, of course, to be disappointed in large measure principally because they ran counter to what can be seen with hindsight as the economic, political and social realities of the era of decolonisation – realities which, as we shall see, affected Britain as well as her prospective partners in the post-colonial world. The ex-colonial states were more than willing to remain in the Commonwealth which provided a useful range of diplomatic contacts as well as an international stage on which to strut. But they were not prepared to give invariable priority to their Commonwealth links, and regarded them as merely one aspect of their external relationships. In the same way, their ties with Britain were balanced in many cases by the fostering of new connections with the United States or other major powers. Notoriously, the model constitutions with which Britain endowed her former colonies in Africa and elsewhere did not stand the test of time. Many post-colonial states found constitutional and political inspiration more readily in American, Russian or even Chinese experience. Because of her elaborate political and social system, and the enormous emphasis that was always placed upon slow, evolutionary development in her society and politics, Britain's attractiveness as a paradigm of national progress was perhaps less than that of rival types, more dynamic and rough-hewn. Economic connections languished. British enterprises were required to adapt to very different types of political economy, in which state control was very pronounced, and where, in some cases, private assets were confiscated or nationalised. In a number of former British colonies, indeed, the new rulers seemed eager to advertise their repudiation of Britain and the Western world and, far from demonstrating fraternal sympathy or filial respect, showered British governments with criticism and abuse. 'All over the world,' recorded Richard Crossman plaintively in July 1967, 'we're having trouble with people assaulting and insulting us, and it's natural enough because we're going rapidly downhill'.[32] Over British handling of the Rhodesian question in particular, Afro-Asian criticism swelled into a chorus of vituperation.[33] By the early 1970s, it was clear that in most cases Britain's past constitutional and political bond with her ex-colonies no longer conferred, *ipso facto*, any special claim on their loyalty or support in world affairs.[34]

How is the erosion of British influence to be explained? Perhaps a better question is why Britain failed to maintain her special status as the major external friend and partner of the former colonies, or to preserve those aspects of the former colonies' political and economic life to which the British had attached great importance at the time of independence. Clearly an important part of the answer is to be found in the fact that a power which desires to exert influence must have something to offer its would-be clients. Influence is a two-way bargain. A small power in search of a patron was likely to choose one who promised the best returns, whether in terms of protection, diplomatic support, military or economic aid. Britain's very visible economic difficulties in the later 1960s inevitably raised questions about the value of her patronage. Her supply of economic aid levelled off after 1964 and was in any event scarcely a tithe of what the United States could offer, and substantially less than that provided by France.[35] In military terms, the withdrawal from east of Suez and the self-denying

ordinance about military capability in this theatre laid down in
January 1968 indicated the very limited nature of any future British
diplomatic commitments outside Europe – even if delusions persisted
to the contrary. 'We had an utterly futile paper on non-military
methods of preserving our influence East of Suez' wrote Crossman
acidly in July 1968. 'I found it a kind of schoolboy essay on diplomatic
relations and [said] so.'[36] It turned out that the Foreign Secretary
himself had drafted it. Britain suffered as well from two further
disabilities in her relations with much of her new Afro-Asian Commonwealth. In South Asia most spectacularly, but also in Nigeria and
East and Central Africa, the transfer of power produced local conflict
and rivalry which made it extremely difficult for close relations to be
established with the successor states and where mistrust of British
intentions was mixed with accusations of her past responsibility for
current difficulties – the partition of India, the Nigerian civil war, the
tensions between Uganda and her neighbours, the Cold War along
the Zambezi. Secondly, British determination to adhere very closely
to the American alliance throughout the 1960s, whatever its merits as
a policy, inevitably tended to lessen Britain's value as an 'alternative'
Western partner for Third World countries critical of United States
involvement in Vietnam, but reluctant to desert the Western camp. It
was Gaullist, not British, diplomacy that aspired to be the third force
in world affairs.

But if the deterioration of Britain's military, economic and diplomatic circumstances provide part of the answer for her declining voice
in the ex-colonies, there were other factors at work as well. To an
extent that was difficult to predict at the moment when the transfer of
power was effected, independence led to an accelerating divergence of
interests and sympathies between Britain and her ex-colonies – with
few exceptions. Political, diplomatic, social, cultural and economic
pressures upon the governments of new states made a close relationship with Britain less and less viable or attractive so that in many
cases the transfer of power was followed to greater or lesser degree,
and over varying periods, by gradual disengagement.[37]

On the face of it, the atmosphere of goodwill and mutual esteem
which accompanied the formal transfer of power in most British
colonial territories after 1945 promised well for the future. The
British went to considerable trouble to cosset the dignity of the
colonial politicians who were to succeed them once the timetable to
independence was laid down. But tact and courtesy could not prevent

the growth of new political interests and demands in the emergent states. In the first place, for all the bonhomie of independence ceremonies, the transfers of power were usually preceded by hard bargaining in which the rulers-to-be had been obliged to make concessions on the constitutional structure to appease their local rivals and satisfy the British: for example, regionalism in Ghana and Kenya; the special position of Buganda in Uganda. Painful compromises of this kind, and the more general desire to build up the prestige and authority of the new government made a proud assertion of independence, and the rejection of any deference to the old colonial power, desirable if not essential if the jibes of local political rivals were to be answered convincingly. Moreover, there were new supporters to be rewarded and old enemies to be punished; powerful interests to be conciliated and won over; popular expectations to be fulfilled, or redirected to new objects. Almost everywhere, after an interval, these kinds of political pressure drove the ex-colonial states into actions which repudiated the legacies of colonial rule. The impartiality of the civil service was abandoned; the constitutional checks and balances dispensed with; economic privileges conferred on favoured groups and interests; and a vigorous anti-colonial rhetoric deployed to divert the inevitable disillusionment with the material fruits of independence. The mutual trust and esteem of the former colony and the erstwhile rulers underwent a decline since the pragmatic adjustments of post-independence politics constituted, in many cases, an attack upon the institutions and practices painstakingly built into the independence agreements, which had enabled London to claim that the end of colonial rule would not endanger democratic government along Western lines.

If post-colonial politics often made close relations between Britain and the ex-colonies a source of *mutual* embarrassment, the new diplomatic alignments of many emergent states also accelerated the drift away from reliance upon British help and advice on defence and external relations. The assumption, all too easily made, that the new states would have the same external concerns and interests as in colonial times was belied by events. Thus the British had hoped, in the prelude to Indian independence, that the foreign policy of the new state would lead to close cooperation with Britain; that India would seek British assistance to guard against Russian aggression; and that India would help safeguard South East Asia as a sphere of Western influence. But as it turned out, the government of independent India was unwilling to play such a subordinate role, or pay for new military burdens, and aspired to an independent and more prestigious role in world politics as a non-aligned power and the leader of the independent states of Africa and Asia. Such a course enhanced the dignity and status of India and improved its bargaining power in extracting aid from the West. Thus in the 1950s, while remaining generally friendly to Britain, India resisted any close diplomatic alignment and was a violent critic of the Suez expedition in 1956. In the 1960s, however, the Anglo-Indian relationship became progressively more remote. War with China in 1962 led the Indian government to abandon its old aspirations to leadership of the non-aligned nations and to turn instead towards the Soviet Union as the best and most effective ally against China.[38] Then in 1965 war with Pakistan, the suspension of British military aid to both sides and fear of American support for Pakistan, reinforced this new tendency in Indian foreign policy and led eventually to the Indo-Soviet treaty of 1971. Less than two decades after independence, the regional pattern of rivalry and conflict had completely reversed the expectations of the policy makers of 1945–47.

A similar pattern of disengagement may be seen in the case of Nigeria. Here independence in 1960 seemed to make little difference to the substance of Anglo-Nigerian relations. Britain provided nearly half Nigeria's imports and took nearly half her exports.[39] Some 75 per cent of the foreign capital at work was from Britain or the Sterling Area. The new Nigerian government emphasised their loyalty to Britain and their hostility to communism. Nigeria's interests in Africa seemed perfectly complementary to her links with Britain. In 1960–61 the Lagos government obliged London by recognising the Federation of Rhodesia and Nyasaland with its controversial constitution and by accepting an Anglo-Nigerian defence agreement which gave Britain overfly and staging port rights. But the honeymoon was short-lived. Within Nigeria, the dissatisfaction of the Action Group – one of the three main parties and based in the Yoruba south-west – with the federal constitution pushed it towards a more radical position. The parties in power were attacked as the clients and lackeys of British influence. Closer contacts with the Eastern bloc were demanded.[40] Moreover, after 1961 the Nigerian government itself aspired to play a leading role in the Pan-African movement and to exercise the degree of influence in Black Africa to which Nigeria's wealth and size entitled her. But the price of this new orientation was to dispense with the

Anglo-Nigerian 'entente', and, in particular, to dispose of the embarrassing defence agreement of 1961. Then, by degrees, Nigeria's external relations were diversified: the sterling reserves in London were run down; a republican constitution drawn up; and defence assistance sought elsewhere.[41] Once again, in the pursuit of its regional objectives, an ex-colony found its British connections either redundant or counterproductive.

Diversification and disengagement were, to an even greater extent, the keynotes of economic relations. As we have seen, at the end of the 1950s, when the transfer of power in Africa was sharply accelerated, it was expected that the trading and financial links between Britain and the Commonwealth and colonial territories would remain broadly unchanged: an assumption which helped take some of the sting out of constitutional change. But, as it turned out, the 1960s were a decade of rapid and accelerating change in the economic interests and orientation of Britain and the Commonwealth countries alike.

In the mid-1950s nearly 43 per cent of British exports were being sent to the Overseas Sterling Area – broadly coextensive with the empire and Commonwealth countries.[42] In the same period some 58 per cent of British overseas investment was to be found in the Sterling Area as well.[43] Complementarity between industrial Britain and the commodity-producing Commonwealth seemed assured, reinforced as it was by the habits built up in the long period of dollar shortage, inconvertibility, exchange control and import licensing. In fact, however, this economic nexus was already in decay by 1960 and was to undergo an increasingly rapid decline in the decade thereafter. Thus in 1950, 47.7 per cent of British exports were directed to Commonwealth countries. By 1960, the proportion was still high at 40.2 per cent. By 1970, however, only 24.4 per cent of British exports went to the Commonwealth and South Africa – scarcely half the level 20 years before.[44] The same tendency held true of imports. In 1950 Britain drew 41.9 per cent of her imports from the Commonwealth; in 1960, the figure was 34.6 per cent. But in 1970 the proportion had declined to 25.9 per cent.[45] Instead a greater and greater proportion of British trade was being conducted with the industrial countries of the West. The United States and the six countries of the EEC took 16.3 per cent of British exports in 1950, but 33.3 per cent in 1970.[46] In 1950 they provided 20.8 per cent of British imports, but 33 per cent by 1970.[47] Investment followed trade. In 1960 some 60 per cent of British foreign investment was flowing into Sterling Area countries, and

and 40 per cent elsewhere. Ten years later the pattern had been more than reversed: 38 per cent going to the Sterling Area and 62 per cent elsewhere.[48]

This was an historic shift in the whole direction of Britain's economic interests. Ever since the early years of the century British trade and investment had tended to drift more and more into the sheltered and attractive opportunities of the empire and Commonwealth. After 1960 it was abundantly clear that the opposite movement was occurring. The driving force behind this change was the realisation that the industrialised and developed countries of the West offered larger and richer markets as well as better investment opportunities, and that their economic growth, once recovery from war damage was complete, was more rapid than that of most countries in the Commonwealth. But economic disengagement was not one-sided. If British trade was changing direction, so too was that of Britain's old trading partners in the Commonwealth. By 1966–67, Japan had replaced Britain as Australia's single biggest customer,[49] while the United States, at the same time, overtook Britain to become the largest foreign investor in the country. In the case of India, the speed of economic disengagement in the 1960s was especially dramatic. The real value of British exports to India fell by two thirds during the decade;[50] and while India sent 26 per cent of her exports to Britain in 1960–61, the proportion had collapsed to 11.6 per cent by 1969–70.[51]

Undoubtedly, part of the explanation for these trade movements lay in purely economic factors: the appearance of more attractive markets elsewhere or, in the case of India and Britain, the growing incompatibility of two economies *both* suffering from slow growth and foreign exchange problems. But equally certainly, the political changes that followed on the transfer of power and the attainment of independence accelerated the process. The 'open economy' of the colonial era was supplanted by the 'closed economy' characterised by the much closer restriction on the activity of foreign enterprises and interests.[52] In the colonial period, British territories were required to keep their foreign earnings in London and to have their local currencies regulated so as to conform with British practice. The habit of keeping substantial sterling balances in London facilitated commercial and investment links with Britain.[53] But in the 1960s, many former colonies steadily reduced their London balances, partly as a gesture of independence; and, in response to local pressures, threw off the shackles of external control over their currency administration.[54]

The demands of local manufacturing interests, anxiety to promote employment and suspicion of the influence of large foreign enterprises, encouraged many new states to impose import controls and promote import substitution wherever possible. Where, as often happened, efforts at economic development ran into foreign exchange difficulties, governmental control over foreign trade came to appear all the more necesssary.[55] Moreover, most new states inherited from the colonial period an apparatus for state control of the economy.[56] Inevitably, once the full possibilities of political independence had been grasped, new vested interests moved in to exploit the possibilities of licensing, regulation and monopoly, while the political and financial benefits of extending state control over ever-wider sectors of the ex-colonial economy appeared unanswerable.[57] As the principal foreign economic influence in her erstwhile colonies, Britain was the prime loser from these new developments. In addition, the increasing tendency among the new states of the Commonwealth to look to multilateral agencies, such as the World Bank, for economic aid, weakened the cosy relationship of former times when British economic assistance generated demand for British exports. Thus the emergence of new industrial and commercial rivals in the world economy, Britain's own deteriorating performance as an industrial producer, and the loss of privileged access to so many colonial markets helped to dissolve or sharply reduce the economic elements of British influence in the extra-European world – and, as we have seen, it was the 1960s which really saw the disappearance of the old comfortable pattern.

Military withdrawal from east of Suez, the political and diplomatic side effects of colonial independence and the end of the old 'imperial economy' combined after 1960 to transform Britain's relations with those regions that had once seemed so securely under her influence. To some extent, the decline of British influence reflected the strength of new world powers, above all the United States. Decolonisation was partly a redivision of spheres of influence in the less-developed world, a redivision that reflected shifts in the relative wealth and power of the industrial states of Europe and the West. But it would be facile to conclude that American influence simply inherited the special position that Britain (or France) had so long enjoyed in their colonial empires and spheres of informal dominance. Changes in world politics in the 1950s and 1960s tended instead to create a more open and competitive environment which allowed the new states of Africa and Asia a greater bargaining power in their relations with the great powers and made the exertion of a monopoly influence by a great power very much harder (if not impossible) than it had been before 1939. Not even the United States with its vast military power and massive economic base, was able to exercise the extraordinary far-flung authority and influence that the British enjoyed at the peak of their imperial career. The risks and difficulties of overt military and political intervention became far greater. Thus, though the loss of influence suffered by Britain was real, it was not simply a consequence of British decline, but part of the post-war transformation of the international system.

LIMPET COLONIES

By the later 1960s Britain had largely completed the transfer of power. To all intents, it was impossible to deny independence to any colonial territory that asked for it. For their part, the British were anxious to terminate colonial rule in their remaining dependencies and, where necessary, were prepared to nudge reluctant colonial politicians into asserting the demand for a full and final transfer of power. There was little to be gained by retaining power. Colonial rule was at best an embarrassment in international affairs. And though the British had a strong preference for merging the smaller dependencies into larger and supposedly more viable units, the readiness of these smaller territories to remain within the Commonwealth seemed to be an adequate safeguard of their independence and integrity, and the best hope for orthodoxy and restraint in their economics and politics.

Even so, in the early 1980s a handful of territories had yet to achieve independence. Some of these territories were so small that like Pitcairn Island (population 54) or Tristan da Cunha (population 298) it was clear that independence would simply impose futile administrative burdens. St Helena (population 5,268) and Ascension (population 689) also fell into this category, although Ascension Island at least also had an importance as an air base and communications centre which made direct British rule convenient. But population and economic viability were not the only or most important yardsticks in deciding whether a colonial territory should proceed to independence or not. In the 1960s and 1970s independence was granted to a number of colonies whose poverty and low population were equally striking. Nauru, with an indigenous population of 4,174 became independent in 1967, the Seychelles (population 64,000) in 1976. There seemed little at first sight to differentiate those West Indian islands which took full independence – like Barbados or Grenada – from those that remained under colonial rule – like the British Virgin Islands – or which chose in the 1970s to remain as Associated States whose external relations were dealt with by London – the Cayman Islands, Montserrat, St Kitts, Nevis, Anguilla and the Turks and Caicos Islands.[58]

But in the three most notorious cases where British rule has survived and power seemed to be non-transferable, it is clear that the dominant consideration has not been the nature of the colony's internal policies so much as wider international considerations. The cases of Gibraltar, Hong Kong and the Falkland Islands illuminate not so much the internal difficulties that may arise in the demission of empire and the transfer of power, but rather (by contrast) the necessary external preconditions for the successful termination of colonial rule. Examination of their cases brings out more clearly the favourable circumstances which made the actual transfer of power in most of Britain's empire such an easy and painless process which opinion in Britain was brought to accept with remarkable non-chalance. More Gibraltars and Falklands might have made decolonisation an infinitely more painful and protracted operation.

Gibraltar[59] is a minute colony of 2½ square miles, with a population of 26,833. It was captured by Britain in 1704 and ceded in perpetuity by Spain under the Treaty of Utrecht in 1713. The Spanish population departed in the period of conquest and was replaced by a new community mainly of Genoese stock, but with other Mediterranean elements. Nevertheless, for many years connections with the neighbouring Spanish region, the 'Campo', were close with commercial contact and intermarriage. But although Britain's possession of the Rock was inevitably a sensitive point for patriotic Spaniards, it was not until after 1945 that it became a live issue, as Britain's decline as a Mediterranean power and the new approach to colonial policy encouraged Spanish hopes of recovering the territory.

Ironically, it was the application to Gibraltar of the principle of greater local representation and autonomy which provoked Spanish anger. The 1950 constitution which introduced elected members into the assembly and executive was followed by a campaign of harassment at the frontier post, when Madrid's request for negotiations over the colony's status was rejected. In 1963, on the eve of further constitutional changes that delegated internal affairs to an elected Council of Ministers,[60] the matter was taken up at the United Nations and further Anglo-Spanish exchanges began. The Spanish government denounced the proposals to give Gibraltar greater self-determination as a breach of the Utrecht Treaty, and referred contemptuously to the Gibraltarians as an 'artificially constituted human group'.[61] Plainly, at the heart of Madrid's objections was the fear that the greater the degree of local autonomy and representation, the harder it would become to effect a simple territorial transfer, a retrocession of the colony by Britain to Spain. When the Spanish pressed further at the United Nations, the British government responded by holding a referendum in the colony allowing the 12,762 voters to choose between association with Britain and association with Spain. 12,182 voted altogether, but only 44 for Spain. Madrid's response was to cut off altogether all direct links between Spain and Gibraltar.

In 1967, a British minister had declared in ringing tones that 'decolonisation cannot consist in the transfer of one population, however small, to the rule of another country, without regard to their own opinions and interests'.[62] While Franco remained ruler of Spain, such a handover remained, indeed, unthinkable. But the dilemma of British policy was that Gibraltar was by the 1970s of marginal importance as a naval base. Cut off from its normal sources of labour and food, and from its natural market, its survival required a considerable British subsidy. It was an undesirable complication in Anglo-Spanish relations. Gibraltar could not be sloughed off into independence since that would be tantamount to retrocession – of a particularly undignified kind. Public opinion, and, more particularly, parliamentary opinion, in Britain would not tolerate Gibraltar's involuntary transfer to Spanish sovereignty, even in a disguised form. And having conceded the principle of self-government and self-determination at a time when the colony's future was thought to be firmly in association with Britain, the views of the population could not now be disregarded. In these circumstances, London took refuge in a tactic of agreeable cynicism. To circumvent a United Nations' resolution calling for the end of Gibraltar's colonial status by October 1969, Gibraltar was declared in May of that year to be no longer a colony but 'the City of Gibraltar . . . part of Her Majesty's dominions'.[63] Even so, Gibraltar residents were not admitted as British citizens under the recent Nationality Law of 1982,[64] in a further effort to soothe Madrid's feelings.[65]

Gibraltar was thus a conundrum. It could not become independent. Spain's territorial claim was overt and aggressively vocal. Yet the local population had a sense of separate identity, and enjoyed too much self-government to be nudged into an accommodation with Spain. Above all, opinion in Britain, suffused still with memories of Gibraltar's importance, loyalty and symbolic value, was unlikely to countenance any bullying of the local population by Whitehall. Colonial status was unacceptable to the United Nations, but integration with Britain would merely outrage Spain still further. Between the irresistible and the immovable, Gibraltar remained in suspended animation, a colony in all but name.

The second case, Hong Kong, represented a curious variation on these themes. Like Gibraltar, Hong Kong was originally a colony of conquest, taken from China by the Treaty of Nanking (1842) and the Convention of Peking (1860). Its function was to serve as a naval base from which the China coast could be policed, and subsequently as a great entrepôt port under British control, gathering the coastal trade of south China.[66] But Hong Kong, unlike Gibraltar, developed first into a major commercial centre, and after 1950 into a great industrial city-state ranking, by the 1970s, sixteenth in world trade. More extraordinary still, it had become by the late 1970s the world's third most important financial centre after New York and London,[67] the pivot of the rapidly growing Far Eastern economy. Even more than that other economic Sparta, Singapore, this tiny city-state with a population of five million had become a major economic power in its own right. It had become, in short, a very bizarre kind of colony.

Yet there was not and never had been, any question of Hong Kong becoming independent – unlike Singapore which became so in 1965. With a population practically 100 per cent Chinese, and a geographical position that makes it indefensible (and certainly irrecoverable) by Britain against any assault by mainland China, it nevertheless remained a colony throughout the heyday of decolonisation. This political status had little to do with any decision taken in Britain, or indeed with the state of British world power. It arose essentially from three facts. The first was that a large proportion of Hong Kong's territory outside the original cessions of 1842 and 1860 consisted of the New Territories leased not ceded to Britain under the Anglo-Chinese agreement of 1898. That lease falls due in 1997. Hong Kong, therefore, did not enjoy territorial integrity in a real sense. Secondly, both the British and the Chinese politicians in Hong Kong recognised that China would not tolerate any enhancement of the colony's international status, let alone full independence, and that, even if granted, such independence would merely be the prelude to a traumatic intervention. The third fact was the attitude of the Peking government. Whatever its long-term objective, Peking appeared in no hurry to repossess Hong Kong. The extent to which China had invested in Hong Kong, and Hong Kong's economy had become profitably interlocked with that of neighbouring Chinese regions[68] gave Peking a strong vested interest in the colony's political and financial stability: some 40 per cent of China's export earnings were acquired through Hong Kong. Moreover, Hong Kong's enormous importance as a financial and industrial centre ruled out precipitate action which might have had far-reaching – and devastating – economic side effects. So, up until 1984, China was content to allow this colony-by-universal-consent to perch on her southern flank, confident that it had no independent future, and no future at all except in the closest cooperation with the Peking government.

These peculiarities of Hong Kong's colonial status were closely reflected in the terms of the Anglo-Chinese Agreement on the Future of Hong Kong concluded in September 1984.[69] In 1997, when the lease on the New Territories expired, the whole colony would revert to Chinese sovereignty. But the exercise of that sovereignty would be qualified by the promise, among others, that no change would be made in 'the current social and economic system . . . and . . . the lifestyle' for 50 years after the transfer. Hong Kong would enjoy a high degree of autonomy, especially in its international economic relations. It would be a free port and issue its own travel documents. Indeed, in many respects, the transfer of sovereignty appeared merely to hand-over the limited supervisory powers of the colonial power to a new office in Peking, with all sides agreeing that, so far as was possible, the colony itself should be insulated from the political effects of the exchange. Whether it can remain so will be seen in the long and delicate approach march to 1997.

The third case, that of the Falkland Islands, was the most spectacular. With a population of under 2,000, the Falkland community was less than one tenth the size of Gibraltar's. Its economy was precarious, depending on wool and philately, and barely viable.[70] It suffered from poor and costly communications, and a slowly declining population. Although, together with its outlying dependencies such as South Georgia, it had some value as the base for British activity in Antarctica, there was little likelihood of the colony itself acquiring commercial significance as a source of offshore oil or minerals in the foreseeable future. In short, the Falklands were as remote and indefensible as Hong Kong, but without any of the economic importance that made Hong Kong's stability a question of worldwide interest.

Although British sovereignty over the Falklands had been spasmodically disputed by Argentina, the issue became live during the 1960s as the progress of decolonisation worldwide accelerated sharply. In 1965 a United Nations resolution required Britain and Argentina to discuss this colonial problem. From the first, British attitudes were far more flexible than over Gibraltar. Sovereignty was negotiable the Argentines were told in 1967, a promise repeated again ten years later.[71] From London's point of view, flexibility made sense. Britain's title to the Islands, though it rested on long effective occupation, was less clear cut than in the case of Gibraltar. The Islands were extremely remote: a far-off colony of which British opinion knew nothing. There was no Franco to arouse the ire of the Left. And restraining Argentina by diplomatic means was certain to be less easy than restraining Spain.

In the late 1960s therefore, the Labour government moved discreetly towards transferring sovereignty to Argentina, while insisting that they would only do so if they judged it to be in the Islanders' interests. Under heavy pressure in Parliament, however, this ambiguous commitment had to be transformed into a promise that the Islanders' consent would first be sought.[72] Throughout the 1970s, ways and means were sought of persuading the Falklands population that closer association with the Argentine was desirable and economically advantageous. Then in 1979–80, to break the deadlock in Anglo-Argentine negotiations, the Foreign Office minister responsible proposed that sovereignty over the Islands should be transferred, but a lease agreed upon which would allow Britain to administer the Islands for the foreseeable future. This proposal was contemptuously rejected by the British House of Commons in December 1980.[73] The following March, the policy of 'seduction', persuading the Falklanders to consent to their transfer, was abandoned as futile. There was, in fact, nothing of substance left to negotiate about. A year later, with vehement parliamentary approval, a naval task force was despatched to recover the Islands from the Argentine invaders.

The contrast with British attitudes towards Hong Kong is instructive, and may be explained by three circumstances. The first was undoubtedly the mode and manner of the Argentine claim and occupation of the Islands. The second was the fact that, by an accident of geographical isolation, the Falklanders, unlike the population of British stock in Argentina, had retained a British identity and a strong sense of separateness from the mainland, to which political opinion in Britain responded sympathetically. The third was the disreputable nature of the Argentine military regime, and the success with which the opponents of concession played upon its misdemeanours. As it turned out, these were sufficient to mobilise opinion – the majority of parliamentarians at least – behind the military repossession of the Islands with the inevitable consequence that the colony would become that expensive luxury, a remote, redundant fortress. The same constraints which had always afflicted the settlement of Gibraltar applied here with the same paralysing force.

The limpet colonies provide a striking reminder of the potential difficulties and dangers of imperial withdrawal, and an illustration of the favourable conditions required if a transfer of power was to be carried out without political turbulence at home. What Gibraltar and the Falklands suggest, in different ways, is the importance of the sentimental factor, the reluctance of British opinion to 'abandon' populations that either were British, or claimed plausibly to be so (as in the case of Gibraltar). Secondly, it is clear that the consideration of great power dignity played an influential part in shaping the British response, official and non-official, to the issues involved. Nor was this uncalculated: other interests elsewhere might suffer from a colonial humiliation; diplomacy like high finance depends on confidence. Most important of all, perhaps, Hong Kong, the Falklands and Gibraltar revealed the extreme delicacy of a transfer of power where it meant not the creation of a new society or a 'daughter-state' but the physical transfer of land and people to another power. Where this could be viewed as handing over a 'British' population to a different, and less prestigious, culture, the delicacy of the matter became almost tangible.

Thus the general course of Britain's imperial retreat after 1945 profited by two uncovenanted benefits of great though unnoticed importance. It was possible in almost every case to transfer power to local political leaders, almost all of whom showed *some* enthusiasm for continued links with Britain. The illusion of 'nation-building', of creating new societies, was not punctured. Almost nowhere did

British policy makers have to reckon with a powerful neighbouring state with a belligerently articulated territorial claim on the colonial nation-to-be. Where such pressures did exist, they were mostly ineffectual, although London waited, in the case of Belize, for American support against Guatemala, before proceeding to full independence.[74] The second blessing was the absence of more small settlements of British stock scattered round the globe, with avaricious neighbours and no prospect of effective self-defence. Had there been more Gibraltars and more Falklands, had more British colonies been threatened by annexationist neighbours, the whole history of Britain's retreat from empire might have been very different – more painful, and much more controversial.

RHODESIA

Until the eruption of the Falklands war in 1982, no aspect of Britain's imperial withdrawal since the partition of India in 1947 threatened so much danger or embarrassment as the problem of Rhodesia. From 1964 until 1980 it remained a constant source of anxiety, and of periodic humiliation, to every British government. Abroad it exposed the weakness and, in the eyes of many states, the duplicity of Britain's decolonising policy in Africa. Its effect on British authority and prestige, as the leading member of the Commonwealth, was damaging. At home, it destroyed many of the comfortable illusions about the transfer of power in Africa and the perpetuation of British influence. The logic of denouncing kith and kin in Rhodesia as racialist tyrants, in deference to Afro-Asian states whose own record of internal administration left almost everything to be desired, was not always popular and seldom dignified. In particular, the sympathy of Conservative Party rank and file for the Rhodesian rebels, consistently expressed at party conferences from 1965–71[75] highlighted the antagonism now felt towards a predominantly Afro-Asian Commonwealth by those whose instinctive first preference had once been for the preservation of Britain's overseas connections. The identification of most Commonwealth leaders with the coercion of white Rhodesia may have played a considerable part in dulling by 1971 the old loyalties to Commonwealth which had divided Conservative opinion over earlier applications to join the European Common Market.

The Rhodesian problem arose directly out of the reluctant decision to dissolve the Central African Federation and advance Northern

Rhodesia (now Zambia) and Nyasaland (Malawi) to full independence. Rhodesia, (as Southern Rhodesia was usually called after
1964) remained, of course, a white-ruled self-governing colony, whose
leaders showed no signs of readily enlarging the very modest representation allocated to Africans in the legislature or of willingly abolishing
the laws which, for example, reserved large tracts of the best agricultural land for white ownership and cultivation. Nevertheless, the
white Rhodesian politicians, and almost all Rhodesian whites, were
determined that if Zambia and Malawi gained their independence,
their own colony, self-governing since 1923, should also do so. Their
reasons are not difficult to understand. White Rhodesian opinion had
already been deeply offended by what it regarded as London's absurd
and treacherous deference to African 'agitators' in refusing to concede
independence to a white-dominated federation and then breaking it
up. To be denied independence when Zambia and Malawi received
it, was to add humiliation to injury. But more important, perhaps,
were two other circumstances. The whole period from 1960–65 was
one of considerable, and sometimes acute, insecurity for white communities all over Central, Eastern and Southern Africa. The transfer
of power in Kenya, the agony of the Congo, the battle over Federation
in Central Africa, had bred a siege mentality among whites south of
the Zambezi, which was inimical to rational argument or external
persuasion. Secondly, Rhodesian whites and their leaders were convinced that so long as London retained any authority, however
shadowy, in their affairs, African leaders would refuse to accept the
constitution and, far from cooperating with white rule, would exploit
every opportunity to rally sympathy and support in Britain, if necessary by violent agitation. From Salisbury's point of view, therefore,
pride, security and stability all required the early termination of
Rhodesia's colonial status, and her recognition as an equal and
sovereign member of the Commonwealth.

In London, however, the politics of Rhodesian independence looked
very different. There could scarcely have been a worse time to
contemplate conceding independence to a state under white minority
rule. The 'crisis of Africa' was still at its height. The independence of
Zambia and Malawi as states with black majority rule was an
inconveniently immediate precedent. Worse still, how London would
handle the issue of minority rule and control its refractory white
subjects had become a matter of intense interest among the Afro-
Asian members of the Commonwealth. The same international

considerations which had made rapid decolonisation in Africa desirable, still argued against any policy which appeared to align Britain with a white settler regime against an African majority. On the other hand, the fear of a Unilateral Declaration of Independence (UDI) was very real, and for good reason. It would force on the British government of the day painful and embarrassing choices. It would probably turn the handling of the Rhodesia question into a party issue at home. It would tend to internationalise the problem and expose the region to the unpredictable consequences of this. It would signal a definite parting of ways in Central Africa. And, almost certainly, it would reveal Britain's impotence to restrain the Rhodesian whites and bring down on London's head the bitter reproaches of the other African states.

In these circumstances, the Conservative government under Sir Alec Douglas-Home refused Rhodesian calls for immediate independence, not on grounds of principle but out of diplomatic pragmatism. What was needed was some Rhodesian move to soothe the Afro-Asian Commonwealth. 'Sir Alec', concluded a Rhodesian cabinet paper in February 1964, 'made it very clear that he wanted a facade as it was a question of presentation to the world. He was quite cynical about this.'[76] How little flexibility there was likely to be on the Rhodesian side was signalled by the removal in April 1964 of Winston Field as prime minister after he had denied any plan for UDI and his replacement by Ian Smith whose outlook was much closer to that of the white Rhodesian electorate. Later in the year, in August 1964, the banning of the principal African parties and the detention of their leadership provided further indication of how little Salisbury was disposed to compromise. In November 1964 a referendum among the mainly white electorate produced an overwhelming majority for independence.

Faced with this attitude and no less fearful than its predecessor of UDI the new Labour government after October 1964 struggled to find a way out. UDI, Wilson told his cabinet colleagues in October 1965, might result in a conflict with the settlers which would be 'ruthlessly exploited' by the Conservative Party; it would risk the stoppage of Britain's copper supplies from Zambia; and it might provide opportunities to the Russians to take part in a United Nations operation and march into Rhodesia.[77] The object of this highly-charged language was of course to win his colleagues' support for a further round of negotiations with the indefatigable Smith. But every effort to find some compromise formula broke down against the reluctance of white political opinion in Rhodesia to tolerate any real constitutional concession to the black majority. Nor were the Rhodesian leaders prepared to risk the test of all Rhodesian opinion, black and white, required by the British government before independence under any constitution could be granted. A last minute visit by the British prime minister failed to avert the inevitable, and UDI was declared on 11 November 1965.

As it turned out, the Rhodesians had picked a remarkably favourable moment for their act of rebellion. The London government had a wafer-thin majority, and was beset by financial and economic troubles. Wilson, as prime minister, was extremely anxious to avoid any action which would allow the Conservative opposition to rally popular feeling at home against him. His notorious public renunciation of the use of force before UDI was declared weakened his hand against the Rhodesians. But it was probably designed chiefly to preserve a bipartisan approach at home and win the backing of Conservative leaders.[78] But even if the political damage of UDI at home could be limited, it rapidly came to dominate Britain's relations with the Afro-Asian Commonwealth. 'How can we ever rid ourselves of this appalling liability?' groaned Richard Crossman in August 1966.[79] Between 1966 and 1972, two British governments made three strenuous efforts to shift the hump on their back – each time without success.

The first round of negotiations, the talks held on HMS *Tiger* in December 1966, broke down over the arrangements for an interim government while a new legal independence constitution was drawn up. It seems likely that, on consideration, the Rhodesian leaders decided that the suspension of the legislature, the resumption by the governor of direct control of the armed forces, the broadening of the government to include independents and Africans, as well as the British government's right to send military reinforcements in case of need, would destroy their control over the government at a crucial and delicate stage, when African opinion was likely to be very volatile.[80] On the second occasion, the talks on HMS *Fearless* in October 1968, the interim arrangements were left much less explicit, but negotiations broke down in this case over the Rhodesian ministers' refusal to agree to an appeal to the Judicial Committee of the Privy Council being built in to the independence constitution as a guarantee against its discriminatory amendment. It is likely that on neither occasion were the Rhodesians really prepared to accept the concessions on which London insisted, and that their object was really to wear the

British down. But what is striking is how far the British were from demanding in either 1966 or 1968 anything approaching rapid majority rule. The constitutional package put forward on both occasions envisaged the extension of the vote to all Africans over 30, but on the 'B' roll, a second class franchise requiring a lower qualification and electing fewer seats than the 'A' roll. 'B' roll seats in the legislature were to be increased from 15 to 17 (out of 65). There was in addition to be a Senate of 12 Europeans, 8 elected Africans and 6 Chiefs which, voting with the Lower House, was intended as a check on constitutional amendments. In 1968, the British government added a promise to subsidise African education, in order to speed up the qualification of more Africans for an 'A' roll vote. Nevertheless, how quickly such a representative system would bring about African majority rule was anyone's guess. But one sophisticated analysis by the leading expert on Rhodesian constitutional law concluded that, even if there was no obstruction or delay in the interval, the earliest date at which African voters could command a majority in the legislature lay 30 to 35 years away.[81]

The final British effort to negotiate a settlement followed the installation of a Conservative government in 1970. This time the British offered terms modified still further, suggesting that African majority rule would be a good deal more than 30 years away, indeed a 'distant prospect'.[82] Vigorous criticism was directed by other African states in the Commonwealth at these proposals as well as by liberal opinion at home. But London staked everything on the 'test of acceptability' – the one unchanging element in every formula for Rhodesian independence since 1963. If an impartial test of opinion could show an African majority in favour of the proposals, their legitimacy could not be denied and, London reasoned, the clamour against the settlement would shortly die away. A commission of investigation was assembled under Lord Pearce, a High Court judge, and despatched to Rhodesia where, as agreed, African opinion was to be allowed to express itself freely. The outcome was to be a bitter disappointment to the architects of the agreement. The commission found that almost all sections of African opinion were opposed to independence on the terms put forward. In effect, the test of opinion had turned into a referendum on the popularity of the white government and into a golden opportunity for a new African political organisation, Bishop Muzorewa's African National Council (ANC), to mobilise the popular support previously enjoyed by the banned

parties. In an atmosphere of intense political excitement and expect-
ancy unmatched since 1964, tame acceptance by the African majority
of the *status quo*, or even of a modified version of it, soon proved an
unlikely result. The commission's negative conclusion, announced in
May 1972, was a humiliation to London and Salisbury alike. It was
the last British attempt to settle the Rhodesian question by bilateral
negotiation with the white government.

But four years later, on 24 September 1976, Mr Smith announced
Rhodesian acceptance of majority rule within two years. Before
another four years had passed, and after a series of unpredictable
twists in local politics, a black majority government, comprised of Mr
Smith's bitterest opponents, had gained internationally recognised
independence in a transfer of power presided over by a British governor. This was an astonishing climax to the years of impotence and
humiliation, but, as so often in Britain's colonial withdrawal from
Africa, the outcome was only indirectly a consequence of British
actions, and its substance largely inimical to British desires. The key
factor in breaking the resistance of the settler regime to majority rule
was the seismic change in the regional balance of power brought
about by the Portuguese coup of 1974 and Portugal's rapid withdrawal from Angola and Mozambique in 1975. Rhodesia's eastern
frontier now became a launching pad for guerrilla warfare. For
the whole of white-ruled Southern Africa the strategic problem had
been momentously transformed. It was this which bred a new enthusiasm in Pretoria for a Rhodesian compromise. By 1976, pressure from
South Africa (on whom the Rhodesians had become increasingly
dependent for economic and military assistance) and the United
States had become irresistible and Salisbury conceded the principle of
majority rule. But after further rounds of bargaining and manoeuvre
no solution emerged which could assure Rhodesia of international
recognition. Instead, in May 1978, Smith reached his own 'Internal .
Settlement' with the veteran African nationalist Nabadingi Sithole
and Bishop Muzorewa. The leaders of the 'Patriotic Front' parties,
Joshua Nkomo and Robert Mugabe, rejected the terms offered and
continued the guerrilla struggle. A year later, in April 1979, the
Internal Settlement was consummated by an election on a universal
franchise in which Muzorewa's United African National Council was
supported by more than 60 per cent of the electorate and he became
prime minister. 'Zimbabwe-Rhodesia' now had a black prime minister
and a constitution apparently approved by an absolute majority of its

black population. On the face of it, the Six Principles on which the British government had insisted as the condition of recognised independence had been met. But the war in eastern Rhodesia between the Rhodesian security forces and Mugabe's guerrilla army grew fiercer.

At this moment, in May 1979, a new Conservative government was returned to power in London. Almost immediately it set out to resolve the perennial Rhodesian problem once and for all. Boldness was prompted by necessity and opportunity. There was strong sympathy within parts of the Conservative Party for recognition of the new regime in Zimbabwe-Rhodesia. The government itself would have to show its hand before long over the annual renewal of the economic sanctions order: and renewal was known to be against Mrs Thatcher's inclinations.[83] At the same time, the prospects for achieving international acceptance of the Internal Settlement, however modified, seemed markedly favourable. That over 60 per cent of the estimated total voting population had taken part in the elections of April 1979 was widely recognised as a setback to the claims of the Patriotic Front, whatever allegations might be made about intimidation by the security forces.[84] There were signs that the 'Front-line states' most closely involved in the guerrilla struggle, Zambia and Mozambique, were growing weary and might pressurise their guerrilla guests into compromise.[85]

It has sometimes been suggested that what London would have preferred was international recognition of Bishop Muzorewa's regime, with only the mildest constitutional adjustments.[86] This is not implausible. The Internal Settlement gave white MPs a veto over further constitutional changes for ten years and, through the device of independent commissions, preserved white leadership in the civil service, judiciary, police and army. It also protected white property against expropriation. Nevertheless, its democratic credentials were at least defensible (admirable by African standards) and it appeared to offer the prospect of political and economic stability, the defeat of a guerrilla movement avowedly Marxist in sympathy and the wider advantage of encouraging a similar settlement in Namibia as well as promoting a climate of moderate reform throughout south-central Africa. But Britain was not strong enough to procure international recognition by her own efforts. And, as rapidly became clear, it would first be necessary to win the agreement of most Commonwealth countries to any settlement before there could be much hope of obtaining wider international acceptance.

The Lusaka meeting of Commonwealth heads of government in August 1979 thus became a crucial test of the Conservative government's intentions. The atmosphere was tense and suspicious. It was soon clear that a formidable bloc of Commonwealth states, including Australia, so often in the past Britain's closest ally in Commonwealth affairs, would oppose any outcome that left the substance of the Internal Settlement intact. To obtain Commonwealth support for the summoning of a new constitutional conference that would lead to an independent Zimbabwe, and to win the cooperation of Zambia and Mozambique on whose goodwill the guerrilla armies depended, Mrs Thatcher made two crucial concessions. As part of any constitutional settlement, there were to be fresh elections in which the 'external parties', i.e. of the Patriotic Front, would be allowed to participate freely. Secondly, there were to be Commonwealth observers to monitor the elections, on whose report international judgements about their fairness would be based. Implicitly, the role of these observers was to protect the followers of the external parties and their guerrilla armies from interference by the Rhodesian security forces. With these concessions, the heads of government communiqué approved the summoning of a new conference which the two Patriotic Front leaders, despite evident misgivings, found it politic to attend. On 10 September 1979, the Lancaster House Conference opened in London.

Three issues dominated the agenda: the constitution; the ceasefire; and the interim administration. The constitutional issues were the least troublesome. Various amendments to the Internal Settlement were made: the number of white seats was reduced and the white MPs' veto of constitutional change given up; the provisions protecting white influence in the security services and civil service were sharply modified; and the term of the entrenched clauses was reduced to seven years. As in the Internal Settlement, white property was effectively protected by the requirement for full compensation to be paid. It was over the ceasefire arrangements that the crucial negotiations took place, for on the relative positions of advantage of the guerrillas and the Rhodesian security forces was likely to depend not only the electoral influence of the internal and external parties but also, in the worst case, their strategic situation in the event of the war being resumed. The instinct of the British government seems to have been to fall in with the proposals of the Rhodesian commander-in-chief, General Walls, which required the guerrilla armies to assemble in some fourteen locations and to permit a ceasefire and elections to take place.[87] This, and the observance by the Rhodesian security forces themselves of the ceasefire, was to be monitored by a minimal number of British observers. Not surprisingly, perhaps, the Patriotic Front leaders were deeply apprehensive about the vulnerability of their guerrilla armies, especially since the deployment of the Rhodesian army and the Auxiliaries owing loyalty to Bishop Muzorewa seemed likely to continue. Not until late November did the Patriotic Front delegates, under pressure from their backers in Zambia and Mozambique, accept a series of ceasefire proposals. By then they had achieved certain significant amendments. There was to be a Commonwealth, not British, Monitoring Force of some 1,500 men to police the ceasefire and manage the Assembly points; and, formally at least, the guerrilla armies were to enjoy the same status as the Rhodesian army as 'forces of the Crown'. Final agreement on all these points was delayed until mid-December and only on 22 December did the Monitoring Force at last leave to take up its positions in readiness for a ceasefire. Two last questions remained to be decided. The first was settled by British agreement that a Commonwealth Observer Group would deliver the final verdict on the fairness of the election. The second by British insistence, reluctantly accepted, that in the interim period the Muzorewa government should make way not for an all-party administration but for a British governor who would exercise sole authority until independence was proclaimed. On 11 December 1979, following the ceasefire agreement, Lord Soames flew to Rhodesia as the last British governor.

The ceasefire was successfully put into effect. Some 20,000 guerrillas made their way to the Assembly Points. The election campaign followed, marked by sporadic violence and by claims and counter-claims about intimidation from both sides. As the campaign proceeded, it came to appear more and more likely that ZANU (PF), Mr Mugabe's party, would win most seats, especially among the Shona people of eastern Rhodesia, but fail, nevertheless, to win an absolute majority.[88] The result was a stunning surprise. ZANU (PF) won 57 of the 80 African seats and in coalition with its Patriotic Front partner dominated the new parliament. The election was declared to be 'fair'; and on 18 April 1980 Zimbabwe became an independent republic within the Commonwealth.

There can be little doubt that, despite London's brave smile, this was an unexpected, unintended and unwelcome consequence of British intervention, satisfactory only in so far as it removed a disabling hump from the back of British diplomacy. It had been easy to hope that, with the guerrilla war suspended on terms favourable to the Zimbabwe-Rhodesia regime, and following Bishop Muzorewa's remarkable electoral success in April 1979, a 'moderate' Muzorewa-Nkomo coalition would be the beneficiary of independence.[89] We can see in retrospect that this was one further instance of the extraordinary delusion so characteristic of British policy during the colonial withdrawal from Africa – that there existed a natural constituency for what London blithely defined as 'moderation', and that with a fair wind 'extremism' could be defeated. February 1980 demonstrated yet again the naive simplicity of this view of African politics. The triumph of ZANU (PF) may have reflected the fact that its grass roots organisation enabled it to intimidate more effectively than its rivals; Bishop Muzorewa may have been discredited by the very fact that he had voluntarily stepped down from power; but it is likely that two other factors played a much greater role in the victory of the Patriotic Front, and of ZANU in particular. The first was its success in persuading African voters that only by voting it into power would the guerrilla war be ended: the greatest failure of the Muzorewa regime had been its inability to end the war. The second was of much longer standing and, if anything, of greater force. As the remarkable study by Terence Ranger has shown, grievances over the loss of tribal lands were overwhelmingly the most important issue for most rural Africans.[90] They were likely to support whichever party offered the best hope of recovering farmlands alienated to whites: Bishop Muzorewa's United African National Council in 1979, Robert Mugabe's ZANU (PF) in 1980. In the rural politics of land, political labels invented in London had not the smallest significance.

Ironically, and to British relief, victorious 'extremism' rapidly assumed the character of wise 'moderation'. The constraints on the new government in Harare were extensive. The clauses in the Lancaster House Agreement barring constitutional change for seven years or the alienation of white property without full remittable compensation could not be breached without putting at risk British and American economic aid. Fears about the loyalty of the old Rhodesian army (which was to be the core of the new Zimbabwe army), the economic importance of the white community and the intimacy of Zimbabwe's commercial relations with South Africa enforced a cautious pragmatism. But perhaps the ultimate judgement on the last of Britain's African withdrawals will depend on the unpredictable consequences of its first – from South Africa in 1910.

BRITAIN AFTER EMPIRE

How has the disappearance of empire affected Britain herself? For the United Kingdom, along with all the once-dependent territories, was a successor-state of the old imperial system, even if the marked decentralisation long applied to the government of the empire reduced the visible impact of its dissolution on the mother-country to an almost imperceptible minimum. The end of colonial rule overseas brought no constitutional crisis, nor any such political upheaval as led, in the case of French Algeria, to a dramatic change in the government and politics of metropolitan France. Nor was Britain reduced, like Austria after 1918, to the mere rump of a previously integrated economic zone. The effects on Britain were altogether less dramatic and more subtle.

Certainly the 1970s, the first real post-imperial decade, appeared to be marked by a deliberate turning away from old imperial links and towards the European Community. The Conservative government's view on this was very explicit. The Commonwealth, remarked its white paper *The United Kingdom and the European Communities* (1971), did not 'offer us, or indeed wish to offer us alternative and comparable opportunities to membership of the European Community. The member countries of the Commonwealth are widely scattered in different regions of the world and differ widely in their political ideas and economic development. With the attainment of independence, their political and economic relations with the United Kingdom in particular have greatly changed and are still changing'. In 1975, the referendum on membership of the European Community resulted in a large majority for staying in. In a variety of ways, Britain's interests appeared to be becoming markedly more regional and less global, more continental and less maritime. The direction of British exports in the 1970s reflected the economic significance of new European links. The money value of all British exports rose between 1971 and 1980 from £9,071 million to £47,338 million, or approximately fivefold. In the same period, exports to European Community countries rose from £2,591 million to £20,540 million: this is approximately eightfold.[91] By contrast, the value of exports to Australia, usually Britain's best Commonwealth market, rose by less than three times from £365 million to £814 million. Another historic index of

Britain's oversea connections also suggested the waning of old patterns – in this case of emigration. In the 1960s, when an average of about 250,000 non-alien emigrants left Britain each year, normally about two-thirds went to settle within the Commonwealth – following a pattern of migration which had lasted since the early years of the twentieth century. In the 1970s the average number of emigrants dropped to below 200,000 a year, of which the proportion heading for Commonwealth countries declined from two-thirds towards one half. In 1978, indeed, more non-aliens emigrated to countries outside the Commonwealth than to countries in it.[92]

A similar disengagement seemed to be at work in defence policy carrying the great strategic revolution of 1968 through to its logical conclusion. Spending on defence declined slightly in real terms through the 1970s, while service personnel were reduced by about 10 per cent.[93] In 1975 the Labour government's defence review crisply condemned the somewhat equivocal attempt by the 1970–74 Conservative government to retain a skeletal military presence outside Europe. Henceforth, it declared, Britain's economic circumstances would require the almost total concentration of her defence effort in the eastern Atlantic and central regions of NATO.[94] Britain's naval presence in the Mediterranean was finally to be wound up. Forces still committed to the defence of Malaysia would be withdrawn, including the small garrison in Brunei. Bases at Gan and Mauritius would be given up. The two frigates normally based in the West Indies would be withdrawn and the Simonstown Agreement terminated. Small contingents would remain to assist the Sultan of Oman and to garrison Britain's dependencies: Hong Kong, Gibraltar, Belize and the Falkland Islands were the most important of these. But the distribution of British forces throughout the world, which still reflected in 1975 (if in a shadowy way) the old pattern of imperial defence, would be finally, definitely and drastically simplified.

There is, therefore, some excuse for arguing that between 1973, the year in which Britain entered the Common Market, and 1975, the year of the referendum and the defence review, Britain's imperial career, already on its last legs, was formally brought to an end and a new era, regionalist and continentalist, inaugurated in her international policy and outlook. But a number of factors caution against the overhasty dismissal of residual imperial influences. Even after 1975, of course, Britain retained her limpet colonies and remained embroiled in the affairs of Rhodesia-Zimbabwe. And although the

final achievement of black majority rule, independence and full
international recognition in 1980 removed the prime causes of British
involvement, the existence of a substantial white community, largely
of British birth or stock, preserves a direct British interest in the
stability of the new state. As we have seen, the British possessions of
Hong Kong and Gibraltar and their future continue to be a key factor
in Britain's relations with Spain and China. In 1983, the Crown's
constitutional link with the independent West Indian island of
Grenada threatened, at the time of the American intervention there, a
considerable upset in Anglo-American relations.

But the most dramatic example of how apparently obsolete colonial
responsibilities and commitments can still deflect the course of British
politics and foreign policy was provided by the Falklands war of 1982.
Whatever view is taken of the causes of the conflict, what is clear is
that the abandonment of even so remote a colony as these 'ice-cool
rocks' was unacceptable to almost the entire spectrum of *parliamentary*
opinion. The extraordinary emotions of the parliamentary debate
which followed the Argentine invasion made it inevitable that some
form of military intervention would be undertaken, despite the enormous political and military risks of the venture. In turn, military
success conferred enormous prestige and popularity upon the government of the day, whose electoral prospects improved dramatically
with the capture of Port Stanley. All the sage utterances and proph-
ecies of the strategic planners in 1966, 1968 and 1975 had been swept
aside. And not surprisingly, perhaps, the experience of the Falklands
war prompted some subsequent debate about the wisdom of concentrating Britain's defensive resources in north-west Europe. The
authoritative voice of *The Times* was raised to urge a reduction in
Britain's land commitment on the Rhine, the recognition that many
threats to Western security would occur outside the NATO area, and
the preservation by Britain of a 'global perspective' alongside the
United States as the other member of NATO with a major maritime
capacity.[95]

In other respects as well, Britain retains a distinctly uncontinental
outlook despite her decade or more of membership of the European
Community. France, like Britain, has a handful of overseas dependencies with a French settler population. But Britain is unique in
possessing a head of state who serves not only as head of the
Commonwealth – a constitutionally nebulous position, though one
invested with great dignity and prestige – but also as the sovereign of

Canada, Australia, New Zealand, Jamaica, Barbados, Papua New Guinea as well as a number of others. A total of sixteen independent Commonwealth States besides Britain recognises the Queen as head of state. There can be little doubt that the effect (and intended effect) of the frequent royal tours of the Commonwealth is to preserve close relations between Britain and the British Crown on the one hand and these 'core' states of the Commonwealth on the other. Indeed, as trade, migration and investment drop away, the common monarchy, by virtue of its mass popularity becomes ever more important in the perpetuation of old sentimental links. How strong the fellow-feeling between Britons, Canadians, Australians, New Zealanders and others who share both the monarchy and British origins actually is can only be guessed at. Yet, although we are unlikely ever to be able to measure how British opinion would react, for example, to the invasion of Australia, the existence of these far-flung connections, constitutional and sentimental, means that Britain's outlook on world affairs is likely to remain less emphatically 'European' than that of most of her Community partners.

This, however, is a much more modest legacy than was intended by those in the 1950s and 1960s who favoured Britain's early withdrawal from her colonial possessions. They expected that Britain would retain a much more prominent place in world affairs and enjoy the close cooperation and friendship of most if not all of the successor states. But the same international forces, both economic and political, that have demoted Britain in terms of wealth and power have sundered to a very large extent the special relationships which the wise men of two decades ago looked forward to. The proverbial visitor from Mars, arriving today, might have some difficulty in deducing that Britain once ruled or dominated so much of Africa and Asia, though he might quickly guess the connection between Britain and the old settlement colonies. But he would find in Britain numerous reminders of an imperial past: the obsolete nomenclature of official honours; the survival of pageantry and military ceremonial; and the very scale and style of so many public buildings.

It was once almost commonplace among more radical commentators that the end of imperial responsibilities would have a healthy and invigorating effect upon British society. An old tradition of thought looking back to Richard Cobden and J. A. Hobson believed that the possession of an empire propped up a reactionary social structure at home and diverted popular attention away from the necessary reform of domestic society. (In more explicitly Marxist circles it was held that the empire was the last crutch of a failing capitalism.) Thus sloughing off the outdated authoritarian attitudes characteristic of colonial rule, displacing the supposedly stuffy class which had presided over imperial government, shedding the financial burdens of defending the indefensible, and concentrating instead on the internal changes needed to make Britain more equal and more dynamic – ironing out what one influential writer called the 'imperial kink' – were expected to have the same liberating and energising impact on Britain as independence would have on the colonies.[96]

Even the most buoyantly optimistic observer might have some doubts as to how far these expectations have been fulfilled in post-imperial Britain. A sense of economic weakness as Britain's industrial base declines, of insecurity in the face of inflation, of declining opportunities as unemployment rose, of the strain of attempting to maintain the semblance of great power status, have all been more characteristic. Perhaps the most obvious reaction to the disappearance of empire was, in fact, indifference. This is not surprising. The end of empire for Britain did not mean emergence from a long, agonising series of colonial wars, as it did for France, nor escape from stifling authoritarianism as it did for Portugal. Nor did it lead to the return of large numbers of expatriate refugees to complicate domestic politics, as happened in both France and Portugal. Instead the end of colonial rule presented itself as an apparently inevitable sequence of constitutional transformations, enthusiastically welcomed by almost all shades of political opinion (except the Conservative right wing) as desirable, appropriate, unavoidable and compatible with continued British influence. The absence of public controversy suggests how little in fact colonial affairs impinged upon society at home.[97] But it is also a reminder that the real struggle to maintain British world power was not being waged on colonial soil, but against the slow, inexorable, glacier-like forces of economic and technological decline. It was failure on these unglamorous battlefields – a slow, cumulative, unspectacular defeat – which ensured that however shrewdly the British stage-managed the installation of successor-regimes, or fabricated the meccano-like constitutions which festooned Africa and Asia in their wake, they would lack the wealth and power to dominate their creations. The British did not acquire their empire 'in a fit of absence of mind'; but perhaps they lost it while looking the other way.

Conclusion

'Britain has lost an empire and not yet found a role'. This celebrated remark by a former American foreign minister has been widely adopted as an epitaph on Britain's decline from world power since 1945. Like many aphorisms, however, it carries an implication that is misleading. Whatever foreign observers may have thought, the possession of a colonial empire was not the sole preoccupation of the British in world affairs. Much as they may have valued their colonial property, British leaders had always recognised that Britain's world interests extended far beyond the bounds of her dependencies; this was true not only in Europe, but in the Middle East and the rest of Asia as well. Though they were bound to them by special ties, as well as by the force of public sentiment, the policy makers in London regarded the colonial territories, as well as Britain's Commonwealth partners, as merely pieces (however important) in the large and complicated jigsaw puzzle of British interests and commitments. Historically, too, British policy had declined to treat this 'formal' empire with special consideration, or to regard it as of intrinsically greater value than regions that were dominated 'informally' and enjoyed technical independence. It would be mistaken, then, to deduce, simply from the rapid advance of so many colonial territories to independence, that a fundamental change had necessarily occurred in Britain's world position. Yet, undoubtedly, British world power and the extent of Britain's colonial possessions did contract at the same time.

The suggestion advanced in this book is that there was no simple and straightforward relationship between these two developments. British power did not decline simply because the colonial territories became independent. Nor did these territories become independent merely as a consequence of a decline in British world power. A more complicated process was at work, pushing the British towards indirect forms of influence and control in possessions they ruled directly, but denying them, once direct rule had been given up, the influence they had expected to wield. For decolonisation in Britain's experience was a much more far-reaching change in their external relationships than the facile business of drafting independence constitutions and inventing flags. Nor is it, any more than the accompanying decline of British world power, to be explained by examining the changing relations between colony and mother-country in isolation from other world events. The most striking feature of British decolonisation was the failure to construct the expected close post-colonial relationships with the new states. To explain this, the decline of British power of which it was symptomatic, as well as the spasmodic but irreversible trend towards colonial self-government after 1945, we need to treat decolonisation not as a mere constitutional event but as a general change in the whole web of connections between Europe and Afro-Asia – perhaps between Europe and the rest of the world. This change affected Britain more than most countries because, of all the European colonial powers, she had built up the most extensive interests overseas.

If we look at decolonisation in this way, it is clear that explanations of it that depend upon one great cause, or upon particular developments in British or colonial society, are fundamentally unsatisfactory. Indeed, even if we focus simply upon the most dramatic element in decolonisation – the abandonment of colonial rule – isolating a single decisive reason appears a forlorn endeavour. It was, for instance, once fashionable to attribute the end of colonial rule mainly to the effects of Western education and the spread of Western ideas of democracy – until the workings of colonial politics came to be examined more closely. In Britain, it was for some time a political commonplace that the concession of colonial independence was an act of altruism, the climax of a careful programme of political apprenticeship. This account now appears merely ludicrous or at best self-deluding. A third explanation saw the abandonment of the 'colonial mission' as reflecting a decisive shift of opinion in the mother-country. A fourth that it was the result of irresistible political pressure from rebellious colonial peoples. Another, that it was a response to growing economic weakness. And yet another theory held that in the age of superpowers colonial dissolution was simply inevitable. But each of these explanations presents difficulties or raises further questions.

Thus, as we have seen, it would be a gross oversimplification to argue that domestic attitudes towards colonial affairs were transformed by a post-war revulsion against colonialism. Plainly British opinion was shaped by a variety of expectations, but one of the most important was the belief, constantly reiterated by British leaders, that, come what may, Britain would remain a great world power. There is a similar paradox in colonial politics, since, to a considerable extent, the growth of political organisation in the colonies was not purely spontaneous but was triggered by the behaviour of colonial governments. But why should they have been the authors of their own destruction? Economic weakness clearly affected Britain's ability to play a great power role and is an important part of the explanation of why her post-colonial relationships languished. But it is not a satisfactory explanation for the transfers of power which brought colonial independence, since independence was expected to add to Britain's economic burdens in the short term and was, in many cases, already scheduled before the full extent of Britain's relative economic decline was felt or appreciated in London. As for superpower dominance and its effects, superpower division of the globe was much slower in coming than is sometimes imagined and was never complete. In some ways, as we have seen, it worked to Britain's advantage. Many empires, any way, have survived the appearance of more powerful states and found, like the Habsburgs or Ottomans, a *modus vivendi* that permitted extraordinary longevity.

Rather than advancing various causes in isolation from each other, or even in parallel, it may be better to see the dual aspect of British decolonisation – the transfers of power and the decline of British influence in Afro-Asia – as the consequence of a broader change in world affairs: the breakdown of the old conditions which had favoured the existence of the European colonial empires. Thus the division of the Third World into colonial empires ruled over by Europeans, and the extensive influence, even control, enjoyed by the European states in countries that were technically independent depended upon a set of circumstances whose disappearance after 1945 constituted a revolution in international relations. Before 1939 the major powers in Africa, Asia and the Middle East were colonial powers in fact, if not in name. Those powers like Germany, Italy or Japan who lacked or had lost a colonial domain aspired to imperial grandeur. The Soviet Union and the United States, ideologically if not practically anti-colonial in outlook, played a self-effacing role in world affairs. As a result few colonial politicians could be in any doubt that, even were they to cast off the rule of their existing oppressors, new imperialists would hasten to fill the gap. Moreover, in few colonies before 1939 were the European rulers under serious pressure to accelerate the economic and constitutional progress of their possessions. The price that colonial leaders could command for their cooperation was thus relatively low and opportunities to mobilise an effective mass movement against colonial rule scant, or at best periodic. While colonial rulers took care to treat their colonies with 'salutary neglect', to avoid upsetting local feeling by administrative interference, and as long as economic conditions remained tolerable, the task of the colonial agitator remained almost impossibly difficult. And what was the use of being a nationalist if no national institutions existed, if the colony remained, as so many did, a rough amalgam of districts, tribes and zones?

Arguably, some of these conditions had begun to change in the aftermath of the First World War and amid the international tensions and economic dislocation of the 1930s. But the impact of the Second World War in generating a series of fundamental changes in world politics appears decisive. In its colonial aspect, it was a war of self-destruction by the imperial powers (including Japan) whose ferocious rivalries, so we can now see, hid from them the fragility of all colonial empires. The war wrecked the European economies, and hence the international influence of the European states, for a crucial interval. Its astonishing course between 1939 and 1941, by offering an irresistible opportunity for Japanese expansion, helped to smash the colonial system in Asia and set off further waves of turbulence across that continent. It forced the British to mobilise their colonial resources as best they could and drove them, most strikingly in India, into short-term policies that ran athwart their long-term interests. The demands and disruptions of a war economy strained the relations of colonial rulers with their subjects and provided welcome new opportunities for colonial politicians. The persistence of shortage and currency crisis into the post-war years prolonged and accentuated these disturbed conditions and the dependence of colonial governments upon local politicians. In some cases, to meet the new burdens placed upon them, colonial governments constructed new institutions whose effect was to enlarge considerably the role and scope of these same colonial politicians. Meanwhile, the eclipse of the European colonial powers by the new superpowers ended the era in which the possession of colonial territories was regarded as a normal attribute of great power status and, together with the reaction against Nazism and fascism, encouraged an ideological climate in which 'self-determination' and the unnaturalness of foreign rule became the most widely accepted of political dogmas, requiring almost universal deference. The establishment of the United Nations – significantly on American not European soil – gave an institutional focus to these beliefs.

These profound changes in international affairs created remarkably favourable conditions for the natural tendency of colonial politicians to seek the largest possible freedom from imperial supervision and control. Their demand for more power was ratified by the prevailing belief in self-determination. With the pressing demand for commodities and raw materials, tropical colonies in particular, acquired an economic value unimagined in the 1930s – provided that their peoples could be persuaded to accept sometimes uncomfortable development policies. Colonial notables could now extract fresh concessions from governors harassed by London's demands for economic progress, while, time and again, government's efforts at economic and social improvement merely played into the hands of local politicians eager to build up a mass following against colonial rule – because of the sheer unpopularity of reforms such as terracing or cattle dipping. And while the task of governing colonial possessions became generally more difficult, the gradual evolution of superpower rivalry in the two decades after 1945 brought the international competition for influence more and more into the Third World of colonies and 'semi-colonies', imposing an additional external constraint upon the policies of the imperial powers. In the British case, the effects of cold war were exacerbated by the financial strain, in an age when defence technology and its costs were advancing by leaps and bounds, of maintaining armed forces trained and equipped both for the primordial task of defending Europe against the Soviet Union and for general service as a colonial police force around the world.

The history of British imperial policy after 1945 was marked by a series of efforts to come to terms with these changes as their implications were gradually (and often indistinctly) perceived. As this book has tried to emphasise, British leaders after 1945 recognised that Britain's power base was weaker and her resources well short of those required for a superpower role. But they were uncertain how far this weakening had gone, how long it would continue, and what its effects would be. And they were determined to prevent the erosion of British world power except where the pressures were irresistible. They had remarkable confidence in the durability of British influence and the effectiveness of their diplomacy, a legacy, perhaps, of victory in 1945. Nevertheless, they sensed the need to shift the basis of their world power away from too much reliance upon formal colonial rule or visible coercion (as by their garrisons in Egypt). Pragmatically they saw the virtue of combining the economic development of the colonial territories with the widening of political participation and the promise of (eventual) self-government. But they were extremely reluctant to accept that even formal independence would end a relationship of special economic, political and strategic intimacy.

In fact, of course, the termination of British colonial rule and the advancement of the dependencies to sovereign status did not proceed as a carefully planned rolling programme. The break-up of the British empire was largely achieved in two great convulsive movements, one centred in Asia in 1945–48, the other in Africa between 1960 and 1964. In both cases, the actual outcome was largely unexpected and thoroughly unwelcome from a British point of view. In both, too, the rapidity of British withdrawal arose from the conjunction of colonial and international pressures. Uncertainties about their ability to check disruptive elements and restore political discipline without losing the cooperation of moderate politicians on whom they depended, were compounded by the fear that confrontation might occur in a number of colonies simultaneously as well as inflicting serious damage on other non-colonial interests. As a power with, even in 1960, such wide-ranging global concerns, the British were acutely sensitive to the risk of being over-committed in a particular region – for all that this imbalance often occurred. They were also, especially in 1960, extremely anxious to avoid the stigma of being 'old-fashioned' imperialists when their rivals for influence in the Afro-Asian world, and even fellow colonial powers like France, were competing to show their sympathy for Afro-Asian aspirations. There were, in London's view, too many important irons in the fire for an inflexible colonial policy to make sense. Colonial rule must die that influence might live: empire must be sacrificed to world power. The contrast with backward poverty-stricken Portugal is illuminating. Paradoxically the weakest and poorest of European colonial powers retained its colonies longest and fought hardest to keep them. But in Lisbon colonial policy was not so complicated by the pursuit of other conflicting interests, nor by the belief that the dissolution of colonial rule was the price of remaining a great power – quite the reverse.

But whatever the hopes they entertained of their more liberal policies after 1945, the British found almost everywhere that their assumptions about retaining a premier influence in regions where they had previously exercised colonial or semi-colonial domination were belied by events. In South Asia, the Middle East and then in Africa Britain lost her special position with startling speed. It is this, far more than the formal transfer of sovereignty, which indicates the true nature of the changes implicit in the term 'decolonisation'. In each region, the British found that the effort to move to a less formal kind of superiority proved unworkable in practice. Local politics, international competition, their own economic and military weakness were against it, except in certain favoured locations – such as Malaysia. Independence turned out to have many unintended consequences not least the eagerness of new states to conduct their own foreign policy and multiply their sources of economic assistance. So for the British decolonisation came to mean not a painless transition from empire to Commonwealth but a complex shift in the distribution of global power that gradually destroyed the favourable circumstances in which their imperial power had been constructed and defended. The climate had changed too drastically for any further evolution to be possible: extinction awaited. Yet it should be noted that no immutable law decreed the obsolescence of colonial empires; and the circumstances which made *European* colonial domination unviable after 1945 did not apply universally. In the vast realm of the Soviet empire perhaps a hundred nations wait to be born.

Notes and References

1. DECOLONISATION

1. For the nineteenth century, see the seminal article by J. Gallagher and R. Robinson, 'The imperialism of free trade', *Economic History Review* 2nd Series, vol. VI, 1 (1953); for the inter-war and post-war years, J. G. Darwin, 'Imperialism in decline?', *Historical Journal* 23, 3 (1980) and J. G. Darwin, 'British decolonisation since 1945: a pattern or a puzzle?', *Journal of Imperial and Commonwealth History* XII, 2 (1984).

2. Charles Wentworth Dilke, *Greater Britain* (London, 1869) p. 397.

3. See Darwin, 'Imperialism in decline?' p. 667.

4. The main point of Gallagher and Robinson, 'The imperialism of free trade'.

5. J. P. Halstead, *Rebirth of a nation: origins and rise of Moroccan nationalism, 1912–44* (Cambridge, Mass., 1967).

6. J. Duffy, *Portuguese Africa* (Cambridge, Mass., 1961).

7. Jomo Kenyatta, *Facing Mount Kenya* (London, 1938).

8. J. Nehru, *An autobiography* (London, 1936, new edn, 1942) p. 574.

9. This was the implied conclusion of the Kenya Land Commission's report, 1934. See C. G. Rosberg and J. Nottingham, *The myth of 'Mau Mau': nationalism in Kenya* (New York, 1966) pp. 155–160.

10. J. K. Fairbank (ed.), *The Cambridge History of China*, vol. XII, Part 2 (Cambridge, 1983) ch. 3; J. Ch'en, *China and the West* (London, 1979). In 1921 there were some 240,000 foreign residents in China: 144,000 were Japanese, the rest from the principal European states and the U.S.

11. C. Dewey, 'The end of the imperialism of free trade' in C. Dewey and A. G. Hopkins (eds), *The imperial impact* (London, 1978).

12. See B. R. Tomlinson, 'Britain and the Indian currency crisis 1930–32' *Economic History Review* 2nd Series, vol. XXXII, 1 (1979) pp. 88–99.

13. A fascinating study of the development of the concept of civilisation in international law is G. W. Gong, *The standard of 'civilisation' in international society* (Oxford, 1984).

14. See J. W. Burrow, *Evolution and society* (Cambridge, 1966).

15. R. Cruise O'Brien, *White society in black Africa: the French of Senegal* (London, 1972); D. Rothchild, *Racial bargaining in independent Kenya* (London, 1973).

16. See A. G. Hopkins, *An economic history of West Africa* (London, 1973) chs 5–7; D. Seers, *The political economy of nationalism* (Oxford, 1983).

17. For example, by restricting the commercialisation of land ownership and protecting tenant cultivators against eviction.

18. For the changing conditions in which foreign enterprise operated, see an excellent recent study by Charles Lipson, *Standing Guard* (Berkeley and London, 1985).

19. For this view, see especially R. F. Holland, *European decolonisation 1918–1981* (London, 1985).

20. H. Macmillan, *Pointing the way* (London, 1972) pp. 116–117.

21. H. D. Hall, *Mandates, dependencies and trusteeship* (London, 1948).

22. W. D. McIntyre, *Commonwealth of nations: origins and impact* (Minneapolis and London, 1977) p. 341.

23. Examples of this approach are: C. Leys, *Underdevelopment in Kenya: the political economy of neo-colonialism* (London, 1974); P. Gutkind and I. Wallerstein, *The political economy of contemporary Africa* (Beverley Hills and London, 1976). There is a vast literature along these lines.

24. As in the Anglo-American trade agreement, 1938.

25. See M. Howard, *The continental commitment* (London, 1972).

26. Following the Statute of Westminster, 1931.

27. A. H. M. Kirk-Greene, 'The thin white line: the size of the Colonial Service in Africa' *African Affairs* 79, 314 (1980) pp. 25–44.

28. S. Constantine, *The making of British colonial development policy 1914–1940* (London, 1984) is the most authoritative study.

2. WAR AND EMPIRE, 1939–45

1. See G. Monger, *The end of isolation* (London, 1963).

2. For naval deployment especially, see S. Williamson, *The politics of grand strategy* (Cambridge, Mass., 1969) and Paul Kennedy, *The rise and fall of British naval mastery* (London, 1976) ch. 8.

3. M. Gilbert, *W. S. Churchill* vol. V (London, 1976) p. 291.

4. A. J. Marder, *From the Dardanelles to Oran* (London, 1974) ch. 3.

5. For Britain's strategic dilemmas in the 1930s, M. Howard, *The continental commitment* (London, 1972) chs 4, 5, 6.

6. For this episode, P. Lowe, *Great Britain and the origins of the Pacific War 1937–1941* (Oxford, 1977).

7. For Churchill's optimistic judgement in March 1939 see his memo on seapower, 27 Mar 1939 in M. Gilbert (ed.), *Churchill Companion Volume V* Part 3, pp. 1414 ff. For Admiralty views, A. J. Marder, *Old friends, new enemies* (Oxford, 1981) pp. 40, 49, 57, 64–5; P. Haggie, *Britannia at bay* (Oxford, 1981).

8. On this theme, see the magisterial study C. Thorne, *Allies of a kind* (pbk edn, Oxford, 1979) esp. ch. 3.

9. Thorne, *Allies*, p. 102.

10. W. R. Louis, *Imperialism at bay* (Oxford, 1977) p. 158.

11. Louis, *Imperialism*, passim.

12. See the warning of the Permanent Under-Secretary at the Foreign Office, July 1944. Louis, *Imperialism*, p. 383.

13. Thorne, *Allies*, p. 274.

14. Louis, *Imperialism*, p. 187.

15. Thorne, *Allies*, p. 590.

16. For a perceptive introduction to Churchill's ideas, P. Addison, 'The political beliefs of Winston Churchill', *Transactions of the Royal Historical Society*, 5th Series (1980) pp. 23–47.

17. Addison, 'Churchill', p. 37.

18. W. K. Hancock and M. M. Gowing, *British war economy* (London, 1949) pp. 515–16.

19. Ibid., p. 438.

20. Ibid., p. 367.

21. Thorne, *Allies*, pp. 596, 598; Louis, *Imperialism*, p. 567; B. Rubin, *The great powers in the Middle East 1941–47* (London, 1980).

22. Louis, *Imperialism*, pp. 19, 366.

23. For the situation on the eve of Alamein, see the account in N. Hamilton, *Monty: the making of a general 1887–1942* (London, 1981) Part V.

24. See M. Hauner, *India in Axis strategy* (Stuttgart, 1981) for the best account.

25. Churchill's speech, 10 Nov. 1942, quoted in Louis, *Imperialism*, p. 200.

26. Thorne, *Allies*, p. 412.

27. Louis, *Imperialism*, pp. 525, 528, 530.

28. For a discussion of Anglo-dominion relations before 1939, J. Darwin, 'Imperialism in decline?', *Historical Journal* 23, 3 (1980) pp. 657–79.

29. See R. H. Davies, *Capital, state and white labour in South Africa 1900–60* (Brighton, 1979) ch. 7.

30. In a newspaper article, 28 Dec. 1941. N. Mansergh, *Survey of British Commonwealth affairs: problems of wartime cooperation and post-war change 1939–52* (London, 1958) p. 132.

31. Attlee to Curtin, 20 Feb. 1942, *Documents on Australian Foreign Policy 1937–1949* [*D.A.F.P.*] vol. 5, p. 547.

32. Evatt to McMillan, 22 Feb. 1942 (for Frankfurter); Evatt to Stirling, 22 Feb. 1942 (for Cripps), *D.A.F.P.* vol. 5, pp. 554–57.

33. Eggleston to Evatt, 30 June 1942, ibid., vol. 5, pp. 863–70.

34. Mansergh, *Survey*, pp. 68–9.

35. Its membership rose to 300,000 during the war. E. G. Malherbe, *Never a dull moment* (Cape Town, 1981) p. 243.

36. M. Chanock, *Unconsummated Union: Britain, Rhodesia and South Africa 1900–1945* (Manchester, 1977) p. 239.

37. B. R. Tomlinson, *The political economy of the Raj 1914–47* (London, 1979) p. 102; A. G. Hopkins, *An economic history of West Africa* (London, 1973) pp. 266–67; V. Harlow and E. Chilver (eds), *History of East Africa* vol. 2 (Oxford, 1965) p. 469; W. R. Crocker, *Nigeria: a political officer's diary* (London, 1936) p. 238.

38. D. A. Low and A. Smith (eds), *History of East Africa* vol. 3 (Oxford, 1976) p. 300.

39. Famine Inquiry Commission, *Final Report* (Madras, 1945) ch. 3; Tomlinson, *Political economy*, p. 99.

40. *Final Report*, p. 409.

41. For examples, Hopkins, *West Africa*, p. 257; J. Iliffe, *A modern history of Tanganyika* (Cambridge, 1979) p. 354; East Africa vol. 2, p. 536.

42. See Tomlinson, *Political economy*, p. 97.

43. Iliffe, *Tanganyika* p. 370; A. Clayton and D. C. Savage, *Government and labour in Kenya 1895–1963* (London, 1974) p. 239.

44. 100,000 Nigerians and over 86,000 from Tanganyika, as well as perhaps 2,000,000 Indians.

45. M. Wight, *The Gold Coast legislative council* (London, 1947) p. 190.

46. Colonial Office, *The Colonial Empire 1939–1947* para. 392.

47. Ibid., paras 394, 397–98.

48. Ibid., para. 388.

49. Clayton and Savage, *Government and labour*, p. 246.

50. R. D. Pearce, 'Morale in the Colonial Service in Nigeria during the Second World War' *Journal of Imperial and Commonwealth History* XI, 2 (1983) pp. 175–96.

51. Iliffe, *Tanganyika*, p. 356; Harlow and Chilver (eds), *East Africa* vol. 2, p. 535; J. Smith, *Colonial cadet in Nigeria* (Durham, N.C., 1968) p. 20.

52. Governor to Colonial Service, confid. minute, 17 Aug. 1942. Arthur Creech-Jones Papers, box 18, Rhodes House Library, Oxford.

53. S. Epstein, 'District officers in decline' *Modern Asian Studies* 16, 3 (1982) pp. 493–518, esp. p. 514.

54. A. H. M. Kirk-Greene, 'The thin white line', *African Affairs* 79, 314 (1980) pp. 25–44.

55. J. D. Hargreaves, *The end of colonial rule in West Africa* (London, 1979) pp. 30–1.

56. P. Woodward, *Condominium and Sudanese nationalism* (London, 1979) pp. 28–34; K. D. D. Henderson, *The making of the modern Sudan: life and letters of Douglas Newbold* (London, 1953 and 1974) pp. 556–7.

57. R. Robinson, 'Andrew Cohen and the transfer of power in tropical Africa 1940–51' in W. H. Morris-Jones and G. Fischer (eds), *Decolonisation and after* (London, 1980) pp. 55–56; for a study of British wartime thinking on East Africa, N. J. Westcott, 'Closer Union and the future of East Africa 1939–48', *Journal of Imperial and Commonwealth History* X, 1 (1981) pp. 67–88.

58. For the evolution of Colonial Office thinking during the war, J. M. Lee, ' "Forward thinking" and the war: the Colonial Office during the 1940s', *Journal of Imperial and Commonwealth History* VI, 1 (1977).

59. For an example of how far this new enthusiasm could go,

L. Barnes, *Soviet light on the colonies* (Harmondsworth, 1944).

60. *Native administration and political development in British Tropical Africa: a report by Lord Hailey 1940–42* (London, 1979 rep.) p. 11.

61. Ibid., pp. 3–4.

62. Ibid., p. 7.

63. Ibid., p. 5.

64. Ibid., p. 10.

65. Ibid., pp. 44–6.

66. For a general discussion, R. D. Pearce, *The turning point in Africa* (London, 1982).

67. See M. J. Cohen, *Retreat from the mandate: the making of British policy 1936–1945* (London, 1978).

68. Cohen, *Retreat*, p. 142; G. Kirk, *Survey of international affairs 1939–46: the Middle East in the War* (London, 1952) p. 23.

69. M. W. Wilmington, *The Middle East Supply Centre* (London, 1971) p. 148.

70. Ibid., pp. 122, 127–35.

71. Kirk, *Survey*, p. 267.

72. Cohen, *Retreat*, pp. 148–49; T. Evans (ed.), *The Killearn diaries 1934–46* (London, 1972) p. 282.

73. B. Rubin, *The great powers in the Middle East 1941–47* (London, 1980) pp. 193, 214; V. Rothwell, *Britain and the Cold War 1941–47* (London, 1982) p. 240.

74. Rubin, *Great powers*, pp. 47, 64.

75. P. T. Moon, *Imperialism and world politics* (New York, 1926) p. 359. Even in 1935 British empire countries took the largest share of China's trade. See S. L. Endicott, *Diplomacy and enterprise: British China policy 1933–1937* (Manchester, 1975) table 2.

76. Foreign Office memo, 8 Jan. 1930, *Documents on British Foreign Policy* 2nd Series, vol. VIII, p. 19.

77. For the official view of China as a potential trade 'eldorado', Endicott, *Diplomacy*, p. 22.

78. Lowe, *Pacific war*, ch. 3.

79. For wartime Indonesia, M. Ricklefs, *A history of modern Indonesia* (London, 1981) ch. 16.

80. Foreign Office memo, Sept. 1945 Thorne, *Allies*, p. 681.

81. Thorne, *Allies*, pp. 555 ff.; P. Lowe, *Britain in the Far East: a survey from 1819 to the present* (London, 1981) p. 202.

82. Ibid., p. 199.

83. Quoted in J. A. Gallagher, *The decline, revival and fall of the British Empire* (Cambridge, 1982) pp. 142–3.

84. For some discussion of these themes, J. Darwin, *Britain, Egypt and the Middle East* (London, 1981) chs 1, 2, 10.

85. See memo by Sir O. Sargent, 11 July 1945, *Documents on British Policy Overseas* 1st Series, vol. 1 (London, 1984) pp. 181 ff.

86. R. W. Ferrier, *The history of the British Petroleum company vol. 1: the developing years* (Cambridge, 1982) ch. 13.

87. B. Chatterji, 'Business and politics in the 1930s: Lancashire and the making of the Indo-British trade agreement 1939', *Modern Asian Studies* 15, 3 (1981) p. 540; J. Osterhammel, 'Imperialism in transition: British business and the Chinese authorities 1931–37', *China Quarterly*, June 1984, pp. 260–86.

88. J. Strachey, *The coming struggle for power* (London, 1932).

89. L. Barnes, *Empire or democracy?* (London, 1939) p. 261.

90. See e.g. its 1935 election manifesto.

91. P. S. Gupta, *Imperialism and the British labour movement 1914–1964* (London, 1975) p. 234.

92. Ibid., p. 229. This was not of course true of India.

93. Ibid., p. 227.

94. P. Addison, *The road to 1945* (London, 1975).

95. J. M. Lee and M. Petter, *The Colonial Office, war and development policy* (London, 1982) p. 159.

96. Ibid.

97. Compare, for instance, Labour Party election manifestoes 1918–35.

98. W. H. Beveridge, *Full employment in a free society* (London, 1944) p. 234 ff.

99. Hancock and Gowing, *War economy*, p. 551.

100. J. M. Keynes, 'Overseas financial policy in Stage III', printed in D. Moggridge (ed.), *Collected works of J. M. Keynes*, XXIV: *Activities 1944–46* (Cambridge, 1979) p. 280. At this time Keynes was the dominant figure in British financial policy.

101. 'Our overseas financial prospects', 13 Aug. 1945 in Moggridge, *Collected Works* XXIV, pp. 398–414.

102. Keynes had spelled out the implications of going it alone in his paper 'Overseas financial policy in Stage III'.

103. 'Our overseas financial prospects', p. 410 ff.

104. Ibid.

105. Sir Richard Clarke, *Anglo-American economic collaboration in war and peace 1942–49*, ed. Sir A. Cairncross (Oxford, 1982) p. 55.

3. THE CRISIS OF EMPIRE, 1945–48

1. See his remarkable letter to Attlee, 1 Jan. 1947, PREM 8/564, Public Record Office.

2. P. S. Gupta, *Imperialism and the British Labour Movement 1914–1964* (London 1975) pp. 250, 260, 265.

3. J. R. Seeley, *The expansion of England* first published in 1883.

4. Described by Cripps as 'socialist democracy'. E. Estorick, *Stafford Cripps* (London, 1949) p. 360.

5. Cabinet 16 (1946) 18 Feb. 1946, CAB 128/5.

6. Cabinet 54 (1946) 3 June 1946, CAB 128/5.

7. R. Clarke, *Anglo-American economic collaboration in war and peace 1942–1949*, ed. A. Cairncross (Oxford, 1982), p. 72–4.

8. H. Dalton, *High tide and after: memoirs 1945–1960* (London, 1962) pp. 170–1.

9. Note by Lord President of the Council, C.P. (47) 20, 7 Jan. 1947, CAB 129/16.

10. Memo by Chancellor of Exchequer 13 Jan. 1947, Cabinet Defence Committee D. O. (47) 9.

11. Dalton, *High tide*, pp. 193–8.

12. Dalton's Cabinet memos 21 Mar. and 28 May 1947 are printed in Clarke, *Economic collaboration*.

13. Ibid., p. 180. Memo by RWB Clarke, 23 July 1947.

14. Dalton, *High tide*, p. 259.

15. Ibid., pp. 241–4.

16. Cabinet 78 (47) 2 Oct. 1947, CAB 128/10.

17. Memo by Chancellor of Exchequer, C.P. (48) 35, 5 Feb. 1948, CAB 129/24.

18. Memo by prime minister, C.P. (45) 44, 1 Sept 1945, CAB 129/1.

19. Dalton, *High tide*, p. 101.

20. Ibid., p. 105.

21. Ibid.

22. *The memoirs of F. M. The Viscount Montgomery of Alamein* (Companion book club edn, London, 1958) p. 400.

23. Memo by Chiefs of Staff, 'the defence of the Commonwealth', 7 Mar. 1947, D.O. (47) 23, CAB 131/4.

24. Defence Committee 9 (48), 30 April 1948, CAB 131/5.

25. Montgomery, *Memoirs*, p. 444.

26. Memo by Minister of Defence, C.P. (48) 2, 24 Dec. 1947, CAB 129/23.

27. M. Gowing, *Independence and deterrence: Britain and atomic energy 1945–52* (London, 1974) vol. I, pp. 184–5.

28. C.P. (47) 11, 3 Jan. 1947, CAB 129/16.

29. The development of British policy in this period can be followed in: A. Seal, 'Imperialism and nationalism in India', *Modern Asian Studies* VII, 3 (1973) pp. 321–47; D. A. Washbrook, *The emergence of provincial politics* (Cambridge 1976); C. A. Bayly, *The local roots of Indian politics* (Oxford, 1975); B. R. Tomlinson, *The political economy of the raj 1914–47* (London, 1979).

30. For British policy and Indian nationalism in the inter-war years: J. Gallagher and A. Seal, 'Britain and India between the wars', *Modern Asian Studies*, 15, 3 (1981) pp. 387–414; B. R. Tomlinson, *The Indian National Congress and the Raj: the penultimate phase* (London, 1976); R. J. Moore, *The crisis of Indian unity* (Oxford, 1974); R. Coupland, *The constitutional problem in India* (Madras, 1945).

31. See J. O. Rawson, 'The role of India in imperial defence beyond Indian frontiers and home waters', D.Phil. thesis, Oxford, 1976.

32. The hope of Lord Irwin, Viceroy 1926–31. See C. Bridge 'Conservatism and Indian reform 1929–1939', *Journal of Imperial and Commonwealth History* IV, 2 (1976), p. 183.

33. Gallagher and Seal, 'Britain and India', p. 408.

34. See C. J. Baker, *Politics in South India 1920–1937* (Cambridge, 1976), pp. 53–4.

35. For Irwin's views, G. Peele, 'A note on the Irwin declaration', *Journal of Imperial and Commonwealth History* I, 3 (1973), pp. 331–7; for that of the Chiefs of Staff in March 1946, N. Mansergh (ed.), *The transfer of power 1942–7 (T.P.)* V, (London, 1976) pp. 1166–73.

36. For the view that the Cripps offer was undermined by Churchill and the viceroy, R. J. Moore, *Escape from empire* (Oxford, 1983), p. 12.

37. G. Rizvi, *Linlithgow and India* (London, 1978), pp. 206–7.

38. Ibid., pp. 237–9. For Attlee's view, in October 1942, Moore, *Escape from empire*, p. 4.

39. Thus the governor of one province told the Viceroy in November 1945 that he had 17 European (i.e. white) civil servants and 19 police officers for 18,000,000 people and 100,000 square miles. Twynam to Wavell, 26 Nov. 1945, *T.P.* VI, p. 543.

40. See C.P. (45) 137, 30 Aug. 1945, *T.P.* VI, p. 181.

41. P. Moon, *Wavell: the Viceroy's Journal* (London, 1973) pp. 165–9.

42. Cabinet 24 (45) 20 Aug. 1945, CAB 128/1; Cabinet India and Burma Committee (I.B.C.) 4 Sept. 1945, *T.P.* VI, pp. 211–12.

43. Ibid.; Wavell to Pethick-Lawrence, 5 Aug. 1945, *T.P.* VI, pp. 28–30; memo by Cripps, 3 Sept. 1945, *T.P.* VI, pp. 203–4.

44. See note by Cabinet Far East Civil Planning Unit, 14 Jan. 1946, *T.P.* VI, pp. 780–2; note by Pethick-Lawrence on draft Anglo-Indian treaty, 23 Feb, 1946, *T.P.* VI, p. 1051 ff.

45. Chequers discussion, 24 Feb. 1946: Cripps' draft directions for cabinet delegation to India. *T.P.* VI, pp. 1058, 1062.

46. Note by Far East Civil Planning Unit, 14 Jan. 1946; draft statement of Indian economic policy, n.d., *T.P.* VI, pp. 1035–7.

47. Hollis to Monteath, 13 Mar. 1946, giving views of Chiefs of Staff. *T.P.* VI, pp. 1167–73.

48. Wavell to Pethick-Lawrence, 27 Dec. 1945, *T.P.* VI, pp. 686–7.

49. See Nehru's angry letter to Cripps, 27 Jan. 1946, *T.P.* VI, pp. 852–8.

50. See remarks on political opinion in the Punjab in Jenkins to Wavell, 9 May 1946, *T.P.* VII, p. 484.

51. Nehru to Cripps, 27 Jan. 1946.

52. S. Gopal, *Jawaharlal Nehru* vol. 1 *1889–1947* (London, 1975) p. 327.

53. Nehru's phrase, letter to Cripps, 27 Jan. 1946.

54. Wavell to Pethick-Lawrence, 6 Nov. 1945, *T.P.* VI, p. 453.

55. I.B.C. 7 (45) 19 Nov. 1945, *T.P.* VI, p. 502.

56. Wavell to Pethick-Lawrence, 27 Dec. 1945, *T.P.* VI, p. 688.

57. Thorne (Home Member, Govt of India) to Abell, 5 April 1946, *T.P.* VII, p. 151.

58. Wavell to King George VI, 22 Mar. 1946, *T.P.* VI, 1233.

59. Thorne to Abell, 5 April 1946.

60. Cabinet 55 (46) 5 June 1946, Confidential annex, CAB 128/7.

61. I.B.C. 1 (46) 14 Jan. 1946, *T.P.* VI, p. 787.

62. See e.g. his memo of 18 April 1946, *T.P.* VII, pp. 303–5.

63. Ibid.

64. See Cabinet Delegation to Attlee, 8 May 1946, *T.P.* VII, p. 455; Moore, *Escape from empire*, pp. 106–7.

65. Moon, *Wavell*, pp. 370–4. 'I cannot carry Bengal for more than another twelve months', its governor told Wavell. Ibid. p. 370.

66. I.B.C. 8 (46) 11 Dec. 1946, *T.P.* IX, p. 332 ff.

67. For Wavell's plan as presented to ministers in a note dated 3 Nov. 1946, Moon, *Wavell*, p. 386 ff.

68. I.B.C. 13 (46) 20 Dec. 1946, *T.P.* IX, pp. 391–4.

69. Cabinet 108 (46) 31 Dec. 1946, Confidential annex, *T.P.* IX, pp. 427–31.

70. See notes by Attlee, n.d. but c. 14 Nov. 1946; Wavell's comment, Moon, *Wavell*, p. 398.

71. See note 69.

72. Ibid.

73. Bevin to Attlee, 1 Jan. 1947, PREM 8/564.

74. Moore, *Escape from empire*, p. 220; Cabinet 21 (47) 13 Feb. 1947, Confidential annex, CAB 128/10.

75. Attlee to Mountbatten, 18 Feb. 1947, *T.P.* IX, pp. 972–4.

76. Viceroy's personal report no. 1, 2 April 1947, CAB 127/111 (Sir Stafford Cripps papers).

77. The provincial assemblies were to decide between partition and unity. Mountbatten thought there was an 'outside chance' that Bengal would vote for unity and independence. Viceroy's personal report 5, 1 May 1947.

78. But see the discussion in Moore, *Escape from empire*, pp. 234–280, which suggests that Mountbatten himself was confused and uncertain about the implications of this first plan.

79. Gopal, *Nehru* vol. 1, p. 349; Moore, *Escape from empire*, pp. 276–7.

80. A deliberate decision by the viceroy. See personal report 17, 16 Aug. 1947, CAB 127/111.

81. Gopal, *Nehru* vol. 1, pp. 342–3; Moore, *Escape from empire*, pp. 239–42.

82. Ibid. Congress leaders tended to think that 'Pakistan' would be so truncated and feeble that its reincorporation into an Indian union would follow sooner or later.

83. Reinforcing Britain's military presence in India, the cabinet had concluded gloomily in June 1946 would put security at risk in Palestine and Greece. Cabinet 55 (46) 5 June 1946, Confidential annex, CAB 128/7.

84. See the account in M. Adas, *The Burma delta* (Madison, 1974).

85. See O. H. K. Spate, 'The Burmese village', *Geographical Review* XXXV, 4 (1945), pp. 523–43.

86. N. Mansergh, *Documents and speeches on British Commonwealth affairs 1931–52* II, (London, 1953) p. 762.

87. Ibid. II, pp. 762–5. These areas formed about 30 per cent of the whole area of Burma and had been excluded from the sphere of Burma's ministerial government 1937–42.

88. See F. S. V. Donnison, *British military administration in the Far East 1943–46* (London, 1956) pp. 332–4, 356, 365.

89. Governor of Burma (GoB) to Secretary of State for Burma (SSB), 17 Dec. 1946, CAB 27/128 (Sir Norman Brook papers).

90. I.B.C. 7 (46), 26 Nov. 1946, PREM 8/412.

91. GoB to SSB, 23 Jan. 1947; SSB to GoB, 25 Jan. 1947, PREM 8/412.

92. Cabinet 104 (46), 10 Dec. 1946, CAB 27/128.

93. GoB to SSB, 7 Dec. 1946; memo by SSB, 9 Dec. 1946; report by Chiefs of Staff, 18 Dec. 1946, all in PREM 8/412. GoB to SSB, 17 Dec. 1946, CAB 27/128.

94. Cabinet 9 (47) 17 Jan. 1947, PREM 8/412.

95. Conclusions of H.M.G. and delegation of Burma Executive Council, Cmd 7029 (1947), printed in Mansergh, *Documents* II, pp. 766–70.

96. See GoB to SSB, 9 June 1947; Governor-General Malaya to Secretary of State for Colonies, 27 June 1947, PREM 8/412.

97. GoB to SSB, 29 May 1947, PREM 8/412.

98. Adas, *Burma*, p. 208; M. Collis, *Trials in Burma* (London, 1938). Between ⅓ and ¼ of the cultivated land of Lower Burma was mortgaged to Indian bankers. See W. G. East and O. H. K. Spate, *The changing map of Asia* (4th edn, London, 1961) p. 175.

99. Controversy over the default on debts continued to bedevil Burma's relations with India long after independence. H. Tinker, *Ballot box or bayonet?* (London, 1964).

100. GoB to SSB, 8 June 1947, PREM 8/412.

101. *Report of the Special Commission on the constitution of Ceylon* (Donoughmore Commission) Cmd 3131 (1928) p. 31.

102. *Ceylon: report of the commission on constitutional reform* (Soulbury commission) Cmd 6677 (1945) pp. 20–3.

103. S. W. Kirby, *The war against Japan* II (London, 1958) pp. 107–8.

104. Ibid. II, p. 109.

105. *Soulbury report*, p. 27.

106. See the British government declaration, 26 May 1943, printed

in Mansergh, *Documents* II, pp. 714–16.

107. See *Soulbury report*, 25, pp. 60–4.

108. *Soulbury report*, p. 110.

109. Ibid., p. 60.

110. Ibid., p. 64.

111. *Ceylon: statement of policy on constitutional reform* Cmd 6690 (1945) p. 7.

112. *Round Table* 149 (1947) p. 455.

113. Ibid., pp. 455–7.

114. Cabinet 44 (47), 6 May 1947, CAB 128/9.

115. Texts in Mansergh, *Documents* II, pp. 749–51.

116. Memo by P. C. Gordon-Walker, C.P. (48) 91, Mar. 1948, CAB 129/26.

117. Ibid.

118. Ibid.

119. Ibid.

120. Figures quoted in Donnison, *British military administration*, p. 375.

121. See T. E. Smith, 'The immigration and permanent settlement of Chinese and Indians' in C. D. Cowan (ed.) *The economic development of South East Asia* (London, 1964), p. 180.

122. A. J. Stockwell, 'Colonial planning during World War II: the case of Malaya', *Jnl of Imperial and Commonwealth History* 2, 3 (1974), 337.

123. See memo by Colonial Secretary, C.P. (45) 133, 20 Aug. 1945, CAB 129/1.

124. See Sir Frank Swettenham, *British Malaya* (revised edn, London, 1948) p. vi.

125. Donnison, *British military administration*, p. 140.

126. See B. Simandjuntak, *Malayan federalism 1945–63* (London, 1969) pp. 39–41.

127. For the fear of communism, Donnison, *British military administration*, pp. 381–3.

128. Simandjuntak, *Malayan federalism*, pp. 45–9.

129. Cabinet 48 (47), 20 May 1947, CAB 128/9.

130. Memo by Chiefs of Staff, 7 Mar. 1947, D.O. (47) 23, CAB 131/4.

131. Ibid.

132. The British to show their good faith granted Trans-Jordan independence in 1946, but with a treaty of alliance. The Arab Legion retained its British officers.

133. In June 1946 there were some 38,000 British troops in the Cairo district alone. Cabinet 58 (46), 7 June 1946, CAB 128/5. This number alone represented a breach of the Anglo-Egyptian treaty of 1936.

134. Cabinet 7 (46), 22 Jan. 1946, CAB 128/5.

135. Cabinet 23 (46), 11 Mar. 1946; Cabinet 45 (46), 13 May 1946; both in CAB 128/5.

136. For the genesis of this offer see E. Lerman, 'British diplomacy and the crisis of power in Egypt: the antecedents of the British offer to evacuate 7 May 1946', in K. M. Wilson (ed.) *Imperialism and nationalism in the Middle East: the Anglo-Egyptian experience 1882–1982* (London, 1983) pp. 96–122.

137. Cabinet 42 (46), 6 May 1946, CAB 128/5.

138. Cabinet 57 (46), 6 June 1946, CAB 128/5.

139. Ibid.

140. I.e. Chief of the Imperial General Staff.

141. Cabinet 58 (46), 7 June 1946, CAB 128/5.

142. *Memoirs*, pp. 386–7.

143. Defence Committee 1 Jan. 1947, CAB 131/4.

144. See the authoritative study M. J. Cohen, *Palestine: retreat from the mandate 1936–1945* (London, 1978).

145. The best study of these efforts is now M. J. Cohen, *Palestine and the great powers 1945–1948* (Princeton, 1982).

146. The Haganah, the official Jewish underground, opposed the terrorist tactics of the Irgun and the Stern Gang. But official Jewish organisations like the Jewish agency were implicated in a number of violent attacks.

147. See Cohen, *Palestine 1945–48*, pp. 126–34.

148. Cabinet 22 (47), 14 Feb. 1947, CAB 128/9.

149. See B. Rubin, *The Arab states and the Palestine question* (Syracuse, 1981) ch. 10 for a recent discussion.

150. Cabinet 72 (46), 23 July 1946; Cabinet 73 (46), 25 July 1946; CAB 128/6.

151. Cohen, *Palestine 1945–48*, pp. 77, 240, 241, 247–8.

152. Ibid., ch. 10; N. Bethell, *The Palestine triangle* (London, 1979).

153. Cohen, *Palestine 1945–48*, p. 247.

154. Bevin's memo for Cabinet, C. P. (47) 259, 18 Sept. 1947, CAB 129/21.

155. See the gloomy forebodings of the chiefs of staff in the memo for Minister of Defence, C.P. (47) 262, 18 Sept. 1947, CAB 129/21.

156. Defence Committee 9 (48), 30 April 1948, CAB 131/5.

157. Memo by Foreign Secretary, D.O. (47) 65, 10 Sept. 1947, CAB 131/4.

158. See Cohen, *Palestine 1945–48*, p. 326 ff. But the British were anxious that Trans-Jordan should not affront the other Arab states. Rubin, *Arab states*, p. 181.

159. Cabinet 38 (47), 22 April 1947, CAB 128/9.

4.   WORLD POWER OR IMPERIAL DECLINE?

1. For the determination of the British to influence the post-war status of Japan, R. Buckley, *Occupation diplomacy* (Cambridge, 1982).

2. Minutes of discussion, 5 Jan. 1949. Sir R. Clarke, *Anglo-American economic collaboration in war and peace 1942–1949*, ed. A. Cairncross (Oxford,1982) p. 209.

3. The definition of a great power advanced in M. Wight, *Power politics* (London, 1946).

4. For this managerial characteristic of a great power, Hedley Bull, *The anarchical society* (London, 1977) p. 202.

5. Bevin to Attlee, 9 Jan. 1947. A. Bullock, *Ernest Bevin Foreign Secretary 1945–51* (London, 1983) p. 353. See also the judgement of Douglas, the American ambassador, 31 Aug. 1948, ibid., p. 602–4.

6. See the memo by R. W. B. Clarke, one of the most senior and influential Treasury officials, 27 Feb. 1948. Clarke, *Anglo-American economic collaboration*, p. 206.

7. Exports formed some 30 per cent of output in 1907, 16 per cent in 1935. A. E. Kahn, *Britain in the world economy* (London, 1946) p. 259.

8. This was the view, for example, of Indian businessmen. See B. Chatterji, 'Business and politics in the 1930s: the Indo-British trade agreement 1939', *Modern Asian Studies* 15, 3 (1981) p. 561.

9. See P. W. Bell, *The Sterling Area in the post-war world* (Oxford, 1956) pp. 335–7.

10. Thus British exports to Latin America fell by three quarters between 1937 and 1944. R. A. Humphreys, *Latin America and the Second World War 1942–45* (London, 1982) p. 223.

11. By agreements with India, Pakistan, Iraq and Ceylon; informally with the rest. Bell, *Sterling Area*, pp. 23–4.

12. G. N. D. Worswick and P. Ady (eds), *The British economy 1945–50* (Oxford, 1952) p. 536.

13. Bell, *Sterling Area*, pp. 314–16, 317 ff., 335–7.

14. Ibid., p. 28.

15. Ibid., pp. 389, 395.

16. Ibid., p. 62. See also remarks of Indian finance minister, Sept. 1949. N. Mansergh (ed.) *Documents and speeches on British Commonwealth affairs 1931–52* (London, 1953) vol. 2, p. 1036.

17. N. Mansergh, *Survey of British Commonwealth affairs: problems of wartime cooperation and post-war change 1939–52* (London, 1958) p. 344.

18. By 1950, 75 per cent above the pre-war figure.

19. S. Constantine, *The making of British colonial development policy 1914–1940* (London, 1984).

20. D. J. Morgan, *The official history of colonial development: the origins of British aid policy 1924–45* (London, 1980) ch. 15.

21. Memo by Minister of Food, C.P. (47) 10, 4 Jan. 1947, CAB 129/16.

22. Memo by Parliamentary Under-Secretary for Colonies, C.P. (47) 242, CAB 129/20.

23. Memo by Colonial Secretary, 1 July 1948, C.P. (48) 171, CAB 129/25.

24. See the table in Bell, *Sterling Area*, pp. 56–7.

25. Thus Tanganyika sisal producers were paid about 50 per cent of what producers in neighbouring Mozambique obtained. D. A. Low and A. Smith (eds), *A history of East Africa* (Oxford, 1976) vol. 3, p. 300. See also A. G. Hopkins, *An economic history of West Africa* (London, 1973) p. 268; Worswick and Ady (eds), *British economy*, p. 555.

26. Confidential note by W. A. Lewis, 2 July 1954, Creech Jones Papers, Box 44, Rhodes House Library, Oxford. Also W. A. Lewis, 'A policy for colonial agriculture' in W. A. Lewis, M. Scott, M. Wight and C. Legum, *Attitude to Africa* (Harmondsworth, 1951).

27. Especially in the writings of Professors Bauer and Yamey.

28. House of Commons, 5 May 1948. Mansergh, *Documents . . . 1931–52* vol. 2, p. 1131.

29. Ibid., vol. 2, p. 1137.

30. C. J. Bartlett, *The long retreat: a history of British defence policy 1945–70* (London, 1972) pp. 46, 51.

31. Ibid., p. 46.

32. Pointed out in B. H. Liddell Hart, *The defence of the West* (London, 1950) p. 210. In the Commons debate on the Brussels Pact and the North Atlantic Treaty neither set of front-bench spokesmen perceived new commitments.

33. See P. Darby, *British defence policy East of Suez 1947–68* (London, 1973) chs 1, 2.

34. Ibid., ch. 1.

35. Liddell Hart, *Defence*, p. 216.

36. Memo by Minister of Defence, C.P. (48) 276, 18 Nov. 1948 CAB 129/31.

37. Ibid.; Liddell Hart, *Defence*, p. 218.

38. In 1949, at approximately 400,000 men, the army was twice its pre-war size. Central Statistical Office, *Annual Abstracts of Statistics 1938–49* (London, 1951) p. 103.

39. Memo by Colonial Secretary, C.P. (48) 36, 30 Jan. 1948, CAB 129/24.

40. J. G. Darwin, 'Imperialism in decline?' *Historical Journal* 23, 3 (1980) pp. 657–79.

41. See, for example, speeches in 1944 by Lord Halifax, Foreign Secretary 1938–40, then British Ambassador in Washington. J. Eayrs, *In defence of Canada: peacemaking and deterrence* (Toronto, 1972) pp. 204–5.

42. See his memo C.P. (45) 144, 1 Sept. 1945, discussed in ch. 3.

43. Eayrs, *Canada*, p. 219.

44. Quoted in Canadian High Commissioner, London, to Secretary of State for External Affairs, 2 May 1946. *Documents on Canadian External Relations* vol. XII, p. 1309.

45. Minutes of prime ministers' Conference, 18th meeting, 22 May 1946. *Canadian Documents* vol. XII, p. 1267.

46. Dominions Secretary to Secretary of State for External Relations, 9 Nov. 1946. Ibid., vol. XII, p. 1342.

47. Same to same, 21 Sept. 1946, ibid., vol. XII, pp. 1330–1.

48. T. R. Reese, *Australia, New Zealand and the United States* (London, 1969) pp. 62, 108.

49. Ibid., pp. 122–33.

50. See J. Barber, *South Africa's foreign policy 1945–70* (London, 1973) pp. 62, 88; R. Ovendale, 'The South African policy of the British Labour government 1947–51', *International Affairs* 59, 1 (1982–83) pp. 41–58.

51. See memo by prime minister, C.P. (48) 244, 26 Oct. 1948, CAB 129/30: appendix 1 report by Cabinet Committee, 21 May 1948.

52. See the verdict of the Official Committee on Commonwealth Relations, 5th report, Jan. 1949, PREM 8/950.

53. Notably in P. Gordon Walker, *The Commonwealth* (London, 1962).

54. See memo by prime minister, C.P. (48) 244, 26 Oct. 1948 and appendices.

55. S. Gopal, *Jawaharlal Nehru* vol. 2 (London, 1979) p. 47.

56. Ibid.

57. Ibid., p. 50.

58. Ibid., p. 52.

59. Report by Lord Rugby, British Representative, 9 Aug. 1948 in C.P. (48) 205, CAB 129/29.

60. See Cabinet Committee on Commonwealth Relations, C.R. (49) 2nd Conclusions, 8 Feb. 1949, PREM 8/950.

61. Ibid.

62. Gopal, *Nehru* vol. 2, pp. 45–7.

63. See Official Committee on Commonwealth Relations, 1st meeting, 16 Mar. 1948, PREM 8/950.

64. Gordon Walker, *Commonwealth*, pp. 200–1.

65. Anthony Short, *The Communist insurrection in Malaya 1948–60* (London, 1975) p. 174.

66. Ibid., p. 32.

67. Ibid., pp. 294–5.

68. A. J. Stockwell, 'British imperial policy and decolonization in Malaya 1942–52', *Journal of Imperial and Commonwealth History* XIII, 1 (1984) p. 69.

69. A. J. Rotter, 'The triangular route to Vietnam: the United States, Great Britain and South East Asia 1945–50', *International History Review* VI, 3 (1984) p. 409.

70. Ibid., pp. 418–19.

71. Stockwell, 'Malaya', p. 72.

72. Ibid.

73. In a cabinet memo, 30 Aug. 1950. Stockwell, 'Malaya', p. 73.

74. Short, *Insurrection*, p. 334.

75. Stockwell, 'Malaya', p. 84.

76. 30 July 1951. W. R. Louis, *The British Empire in the Middle East 1945–51* (Oxford, 1984) p. 671.

77. For this episode, J. Darwin, *Britain, Egypt and the Middle East* (London, 1981) Part 3.

78. For an authoritative account based on the company's archive: R. W. Ferrier, *The history of the British Petroleum Company: vol. 1 The developing years 1901–32* (Cambridge, 1982). For an unsympathetic but well-informed view, L. P. Elwell-Sutton, *Persian Oil* (London, 1955).

79. G. W. Lenczowski, *Russia and the West in Iran 1914–48* (New York, 1949) pp. 310–14.

80. E. Abrahamian, *Iran between two revolutions* (Princeton, 1982) p. 189.

81. Ibid., p. 267.

82. Louis, *Middle East*, p. 668.

83. Ibid., p. 688.

84. Ibid., p. 664.

85. Holmes to Acheson, secret, 7 Jan. 1950; quoted in Louis, *Middle East*, p. 609.

86. P. M. Williams (ed.), *The Diary of Hugh Gaitskell 1945–56* (London, 1983) p. 226.

87. J. Mitchell, *Crisis in Britain, 1951* (London, 1963) pp. 50–4.

88. A. Seldon, *Churchill's Indian Summer* (London, 1981) pp. 21–22.

89. Churchill's cabinet memo 29 Nov. 1951. Bullock, *Bevin* (pbk. edn, Oxford, 1985) p. 787.

5.   NATIONALISM AND EMPIRE IN THE 1950s

1. D. J. Goldsworthy, *Colonial issues in British politics 1945–61* (Oxford, 1971) p. 359; P. S. Gupta, *Imperialism and the British Labour movement 1914–64* (London, 1975) pp. 372–3.

2. R. B. Smith, *The international history of the Vietnam War: vol. 1 Revolution versus containment 1955–61* (London, 1983) pp. 16 ff.

3. Ibid., vol. 1, pp. 38–9.

4. Colonial Office, *Report on the Gold Coast 1949* (HMSO, 1950) p. 72; F. M. Bourret, *Ghana: the road to independence 1919–1957* (London, 1960) p. 158. The Native Authorities Ordinance and its effect on chiefly authority are discussed in K. A. Busia, *The position of the chief in the modern political system of Ashanti* (London, 1951) pp. 158–64.

5. D. Austin, *Politics in Ghana 1946–1960* (pbk. edn, London, 1970) pp. 50–1.

6. Austin, *Ghana*, p. 27; Busia, *The chief*, p. 199.

7. The three largest towns doubled their populations 1931–48. D. Apter, *Ghana in transition* (rev. edn, New York, 1963) p. 163.

8. Ibid., p. 165.

9. Austin, *Ghana*, pp. 56–7; Apter, *Transition*, p. 69.

10. The Coussey Committee.

11. Heavily emphasised in K. Nkrumah, *An autobiography* (London, 1957).

12. See J. Dunn and A. F. Robertson, *Dependence and opportunity: political change in Ahafo* (Cambridge, 1973) ch. 8.

13. Nkrumah to James Griffiths, 14 Dec. 1956. A. Creech-Jones Papers 18/4, Rhodes House Library, Oxford.

14. For government expenditure, G. B. Kay (ed.) *The political economy of colonialism in Ghana* (Cambridge, 1973) p. 47.

15. Colonial Office, *Report on the Gold Coast 1953* (HMSO, 1954) pp. 6–7, 132.

16. Austin, *Ghana*, p. 158.

17. Dunn and Robertson, *Dependence* p. 324; T. P. Omari, *Kwame Nkrumah* (London, 1970) p. 41.

18. Cmnd. 71 (1957), *The proposed constitution of Ghana* pp. 3, 7.

19. J. S. Coleman, *Nigeria: background to nationalism* (Berkeley and Los Angeles, 1958) p. 320.

20. Ibid., pp. 80–1.

21. K.A.B. Jones-Quartey, *A Life of Azikiwe* (Harmondsworth, 1965) pp. 161–2.

22. In *The path to Nigerian freedom* (1947).

23. Coleman, *Nigeria*, pp. 291–5, 308.

24. J. D. Hargreaves, *The end of colonial rule in West Africa* (London, 1979) pp. 45–6.

25. For the weakness of traditional authorities in this respect, R. E. Wraith, *Local government* (Penguin West African series, Harmondsworth, 1953) pp. 20–8.

26. Memo by Colonial Secretary, C.P. (50) 94, 3 May 1950, CAB 129/39.

27. Ibid.

28. K. Post, *The Nigerian federal election of 1959* (London, 1963) pp. 46–9.

29. For the Eastern Region crisis of 1953, K. Ezera, *Constitutional developments in Nigeria* (2nd edn, Cambridge, 1964) pp. 159 ff.

30. Cmd. 8934 (1953), *Report by the Conference on the Nigerian Constitution* p. 3.

31. See J. Smith, *Colonial cadet in Nigeria* (Durham, N.C., 1968) p. 51.

32. Cmnd. 207 (1957), *Report by the Nigerian Constitutional Conference* p. 26.

33. Post, *Election*, pp. 19, 441.

34. By 1960 there were approximately 340,000 Asians in Kenya, Uganda, Tanganyika and Zanzibar.

35. These projects and their fate can be traced in P. Darby, *British defence policy East of Suez* (London, 1973).

36. 17,997 (1935–6); 55,759 (1962).

37. See M. P. K. Sorrenson, *The origins of European settlement in Kenya* (Nairobi, 1968).

38. The number of settler-farmers grew from 1,700 (1938–39) to 3,600 (1960). R. M. A. Van Zwanenberg, *An economic history of Kenya and Uganda 1800–1970* (London, 1975) p. 44.

39. Statement by Kenya government, 1952. Quoted in C. Rosberg and J. Nottingham, *The myth of 'Mau Mau': nationalism in Kenya* (Stanford, 1966) p. 225.

40. D. A. Low and A. Smith (eds), *History of East Africa* vol. 3 (Oxford, 1976) p. 110.

41. For a recent discussion, D. Throup, 'Origins of Mau Mau' *African Affairs* 84, 336 (1985).

42. Low and Smith (eds), *East Africa* vol. 3, p. 132.

43. Cmnd. 1030 (1960), *Historical survey of the origins and growth of Mau Mau* (Corfield Report) p. 284.

44. See Baring to Lyttelton (Colonial Secretary) 29 Oct. 1953. C. Douglas-Home, *The last proconsul* (London, 1978) pp. 271–2.

45. A point made strongly by the parliamentary delegation to Kenya in their *Report*, Cmd. 9081 (1954) p. 10.

46. Cmnd. 309 (1957), *Kenya: proposals for new constitutional arrangements* p. 3.

47. See the optimistic view in E. Huxley, *The new earth: an experiment in colonialism* (London, 1960) p. 265.

48. See Cmnd. 124 (1957), *Defence: outline of future policy* p. 4; Darby, *Defence policy* pp. 124, 125, 175, 203–6.

49. *H. C. Deb.* 5s, vol. 604, col. 563.

50. J. Iliffe, *A modern history of Tanganyika* (Cambridge, 1979) pp. 475, 477.

51. Ibid., citing Colonial Office correspondence.

52. Ibid., p. 473.

53. G. A. Maguire, *Towards 'uhuru' in Tanzania* (Cambridge, 1969) pp. 26, 112.

54. R. C. Pratt, *The critical phase in Tanzania 1945–1968* (Cambridge, 1976) pp. 21–2.

55. See Cohen to Twining, 1 Nov. 1949 in Iliffe, *Tanganyika*, p. 477.

56. Pratt, *Tanzania*, p. 29; Iliffe, *Tanganyika*, p. 477.

57. Maguire, *Towards 'uhuru'*, p. 203.

58. Ibid., p. 204; Pratt, *Tanzania*, p. 35.

59. Maguire, *Towards 'uhuru'*, p. 179.

60. Iliffe, *Tanganyika*, pp. 521–2, 535.

61. Ibid., p. 555; Low and Smith (eds), *East Africa* vol. 3, p. 183. This gave some 60,000 Africans the vote out of a total population of 10,000,000.

62. Maguire, *Towards 'uhuru'*, pp. 199–228.

63. Pratt, *Tanzania*, p. 42.

64. See V. Harlow and E. M. Chilver (eds), *History of East Africa* vol. 2 (Oxford, 1965) ch. 2.

65. See E. B. Worthington, *A development plan for Uganda, December 1946* (Entebbe, 1947) p. 100.

66. D. A. Low and R. C. Pratt, *Buganda and British overrule: two studies 1900–1955* (London, 1960) p. 285.

67. Ibid., pp. 324–9.

68. Ibid., p. 336.

69. Ibid., p. 339.

70. Low and Smith (eds), *East Africa* vol. 3, p. 91.

71. Darby, *British defence policy*, p. 206; Douglas-Home, *Proconsul*, p. 282.

72. S. Rhodesia: 220,000 (1961); N. Rhodesia: 74,000 (1961). The total population of the Rhodesias and Nyasaland in 1961 was 8.5 million.

73. See Elena J. Berger, *Labour, race and colonial rule: the Copperbelt from 1924 to independence* (Oxford, 1974).

74. H. Macmillan to A. Creech-Jones, 6 May 1942. Creech-Jones Papers, ACJ 22/3 Rhodes House Library.

75. For the limited impact of the Nyasaland African Congress, set up in 1945, R. I. Rotberg, *The rise of nationalism in Central Africa* (Cambridge, Mass., 1966) p. 199.

76. D. C. Mulford, *Zambia: the politics of independence 1957–64* (London, 1967) p. 26; Berger, *Labour*, pp. 132, 137, 138.

77. R. Blake, *A history of Rhodesia* (London, 1976) p. 240.

78. See Cmd. 5949 (1939), *Rhodesia-Nyasaland Royal Commission* (Bledisloe Report) pp. 107–16.

79. *Bledisloe Report*, general conclusions.

80. Sir S. Gore-Browne to A. Creech-Jones, 1 Oct. 1950. Creech-Jones Papers, ACJ 22.

81. This was Andrew Cohen. See Blake, *Rhodesia*, pp. 250–2.

82. The negotiations for federation can now be followed on the white Rhodesian side in J. T. Wood, *The Welensky Papers* (Durban, 1983).

83. See e.g. Cmd. 8411, *Closer association in Central Africa: H.M.G. Statement 21 November 1951*.

84. Mulford, *Zambia*, p. 51; R. Welensky, *Welensky's 4000 days* (London, 1964) pp. 76–7; *H. C. Deb.* 5s, vol. 578, col. 924.

85. C. Leys, *European politics in Southern Rhodesia* (Oxford, 1959) pp. 47–8.

86. Mulford, *Zambia*, pp. 36–8, 62; Rotberg, *Nationalism*, pp. 267–8.

87. Welensky, *4000 days*, pp. 72–3, 89 ff.; Mulford, *Zambia*, p. 50.

88. Mulford, *Zambia*, ch. 2.

89. Berger, *Labour*, p. 16.

90. Ibid., pp. 130 ff.

91. I. Henderson, 'The origins of nationalism in East and Central Africa: the Zambian case' *Journal of African History* XI, 4 (1970) pp. 591–603.

92. Hastings Banda to Creech-Jones, 3 April 1952. Creech-Jones Papers, ACJ 22/10/47.

93. A. J. Stockwell, 'British imperial policy and decolonization in Malaya 1942–1952', *Journal of Imperial and Commonwealth History* XIII, 1 (1984) pp. 68–87.

94. Ibid.

95. G. P. Means, *Malaysian politics* (London, 1970) p. 150.

96. Cmd. 9714 (1956), *Report by the Federation of Malaya Constitutional Conference* p. 18.

97. Smith, *Vietnam War* vol. 1, pp. 38–9.

98. *Malaya Constitutional Conference Report*, p. 9.

99. Australia and New Zealand formally associated themselves with the Anglo-Malayan defence agreement in 1959. Chin Kin Wah, *The defence of Malaysia and Singapore* (Cambridge, 1983) p. 3.

100. C. M. Turnbull, *A history of Singapore 1819–1975* (Kuala Lumpur, 1977) pp. 233–43.

101. Cmnd. 147 (1957), *Report of the Singapore Constitutional Conference* p. 8.

102. Ibid., p. 11.

103. Darby, *British defence policy*, p. 78.

104. See C. Issawi, *Egypt at mid-century: an economic survey* (London, 1954) ch. 13.

105. Patrick Seale, *The struggle for Syria* (London, 1964) p. 18.

106. See General Neguib, *Egypt's destiny* (London, 1955) chs 1, 2.

107. For these events, P. Calvocoressi, *Survey of international affairs 1951* (London, 1954) pp. 282–90.

108. I.e. the unification of Egypt and the Sudan. For the negotiations, P. Woodward, *Condominium and Sudanese nationalism* (London, 1979) p. 124.

109. D. Carlton, *Anthony Eden* (London, 1981) pp. 356–8.

110. Woodward, *Condominium*, pp. 124–5; Anthony Eden, *Full Circle* (London, 1960) pp. 253, 256–7, 260.

111. Seale, *Syria*, pp. 16–23, 194–211; M. H. Kerr, 'Egyptian foreign policy and the revolution' in P. J. Vatikiotis (ed.), *Egypt and the revolution* (London, 1968) pp. 121–2; P. J. Vatikiotis, *Nasser and his generation* (London, 1978) pp. 226–32.

112. See W. Gallman, *Iraq under General Nuri* (Baltimore, 1964) ch. 9.

113. E. Monroe, *Britain's moment in the Middle East* (London, 1963) p. 184; Selwyn Lloyd, *Suez 1956* (London, 1978) p. 35.

114. Lloyd, *Suez*, p. 34.

115. Carlton, *Eden*, p. 403.

116. Ibid., pp. 411, 416.

117. The French had a separate quarrel with Nasser over his support for the Arab insurrection in Algeria.

118. The best recent discussion of these events is to be found in Carlton, *Eden*.

119. Sir G. Hill, *A history of Cyprus* vol. 4 (Cambridge, 1952) ch. 13.

120. E. Monroe, *The Mediterranean in politics* (London, 1938) pp. 51–2.

121. S. Kyriakides, *Cyprus: constitutionalism and crisis government* (Philadelphia, 1968) pp. 28–31.

122. F. Crouzet, *Le conflit de Chypre* 2 vols (Brussels, 1973) vol. 1, pp. 311–14.

123. Crouzet, *Chypre* vol. 1, p. 382.

124. For this episode, Crouzet, *Chypre* vol. 1, p. 403.

125. Crouzet, ibid., vol. 1, p. 435.

126. Crouzet, ibid., vol. 2, p. 497.

127. Crouzet, ibid., vol. 1, p. 322, vol. 2 pp. 654–62 for diplomatic and strategic calculations in London.

128. *Full circle: the memoirs of Anthony Eden* (London, 1960) p. 414; Crouzet, *Chypre* vol. 1, p. 654.

129. R. Rhodes James, *Anthony Eden* (London, 1986) pp. 379–83.

130. F. Kitson, *Bunch of fives* (London, 1977) for this estimate.

131. Salisbury believed that Makarios's release was the first step on a path of concession. Crouzet, *Chypre* vol. 2, p. 919. For a different account of his resignation, Rhodes James, *Eden*, p. 608.

132. Crouzet, *Chypre* vol. 2, p. 1036.

133. For the constitutional history of the British West Indies, Hume Wrong, *The Government of the West Indies* (Oxford, 1922); A. Spackman (ed.), *Constitutional development of the West Indies 1922–1968* (Barbados, 1975).

134. Since c.1900, Britain had implicitly recognised United States strategic predominance in the Caribbean. See K. Bourne, *Britain and the balance of power in North America 1815–1908* (London, 1967).

135. For a graphic survey made in the mid-1930s, W. M. Macmillan, *Warning from the West Indies* (published as a Penguin special in 1938, first published in 1936).

136. See R. W. Van Alstyne, *The rising American empire* (Oxford, 1960).

137. *Report of the Anglo-American Caribbean Commission for 1942–3* (Washington, 1943) p. 3.

138. See minutes by Battershill and Lord Cranborne, Secretary of State for the Colonies, 12 November 1942, in H. Johnson, 'The Anglo-American Caribbean Commission and the extension of American influence in the Caribbean 1942–45', *Journal of Commonwealth and Comparative Politics* XXII, 2 (1984) pp. 190–1.

139. Spackman, *Constitutional development*, pp. 134 ff.

140. For the Windward Islands, A. W. Singham, *The hero and the crowd in a colonial polity* (New Haven, 1968) p. 117.

141. H. Mitchell, *Europe in the Caribbean* (Stanford, 1963) p. 48.

142. J. Mordecai, *The West Indies: the federal negotiations* (London, 1968) p. 41.

143. Ibid., p. 33.

144. For Eric Williams' 'Hamiltonian' views, S. D. Ryan, *Race and nationalism in Trinidad and Tobago* (Toronto, 1972) p. 112.

145. For these developments, Mordecai, *Federal negotiations*.

146. For Guyana, T. J. Spinner, *A political and social history of Guyana 1945–1983* (Boulder and London, 1984).

147. See D. Lowenthal and C. G. Clarke, 'Island orphans: Barbuda and the rest' *Journal of Commonwealth and Comparative Politics* XVIII, 3 (1980).

148. For some of these fears, see the interesting collection, D. Lowenthal and L. Comitas (eds) *The aftermath of sovereignty: West Indian perspectives* (Garden City, N.Y., 1973).

6. WINDS OF CHANGE

1. P. Darby, *British defence policy East of Suez 1947–68* (London, 1973) p. 99.

2. As for example in Malaya, Kuwait, Aden and, as late as 1982, the Falkland Islands.

3. H. Macmillan, *Riding the storm 1956–59* (London, 1971) p. 323.

4. On this J. Bayliss, *Anglo-American defence relations* (London, 1981).

5. Note to Foreign Secretary, 22 Dec. 1959. H. Macmillan, *Pointing the way 1959–61* (London, 1972) p. 112.

6. See M. Lipton, 'Neither partnership nor dependence . . . Indo-British relations since 1947' in W. H. Morris-Jones and G. Fischer (eds), *Decolonisation and after* (London, 1980).

7. See W. A. Nielsen, *The great powers and Africa* (London, 1969), chs 8, 9 and table 20.

8. See below, pp. 235 ff.

9. J. D. B. Miller, *Survey of British Commonwealth affairs: problems of expansion and attrition 1953–69* (London, 1974) p. 26.

10. M. S. Rajan, *India in world affairs 1954–56* (London, 1964) pp. 150–68.

11. Ibid., p. 334.

12. See Canadian prime minister to British prime minister, 1 Nov. 1956. L. Pearson, *Memoirs* vol. 2 (London, 1974) pp. 238–9.

13. See especially his remarks in Australia and New Zealand. Macmillan, *Riding the storm*, pp. 400–1, 404.

14. For his enthusiastic report to the Commons, *H. C. Deb.* 5th Series, vol. 582, col. 1215; and to the cabinet, *Riding the storm* p. 413.

15. Ibid., p. 395: note dated 19 Jan. 1958.

16. See Macmillan to Humphrey (U.S. Treasury Secretary) 28 Nov. 1958. Macmillan, *Pointing the way*, p. 47.

17. Macmillan, *Riding the storm*, p. 379.

18. Quoted in A. M. Gollin, *Proconsul in politics* (London, 1964) p. 106.

19. See the discussion in G. Parmentier, 'The British press in the Suez crisis', *Historical Journal* 23, 2 (1980) pp. 435–88.

20. D. J. Goldsworthy, *Colonial issues in British politics 1945–61* (Oxford, 1971) pp. 320, 334.

21. Ibid., ch. 9.

22. D. J. Morgan, *The official history of colonial development* vol. 5 (London, 1980) p. 102.

23. Goldsworthy, *Colonial issues*, p. 343; Lord Butler, *The art of the possible* (London, 1971) p. 209.

24. See Robert Skidelsky's penetrating account of Labour Party attitudes in 'Lessons of Suez' in V. Bogdanor and R. Skidelsky (eds), *The age of affluence* (London, 1970).

25. There was no grand inquisition into the causes of Britain's diplomatic humiliation.

26. M. Camps, *Britain and the European Community 1945–63* (London, 1964) pp. 30–1.

27. See Cabinet Defence Committee D.O. (48) 19th Meeting, 16 Sept. 1948, CAB 131/5.

28. Camps, *European Community*, pp. 45–8.

29. For this plan, Macmillan, *Riding the storm*, pp. 80–8.

30. Camps, *European Community*, pp. 147–72.

31. West Germany became a fully sovereign state in 1955.

32. Macmillan's words: memo to Selwyn Lloyd, 28 Nov. 1958. Macmillan, *Pointing the way*, p. 47.

33. U. W. Kitzinger, *The politics and economics of European integration* (rep., Westport, Conn., 1976) p. 191; Camps, *European Community*, p. 280.

34. Diary 9 July 1960, Macmillan, *Pointing the way*, p. 316.

35. For some traces of this, M. Beloff, *Imperial sunset* vol. 1 (London, 1969) ch. 1.

36. Susan Strange, *Sterling and British policy* (London, 1971) p. 181.

37. M. M. Postan, *An economic history of Western Europe 1945–1964* (London, 1967) p. 93.

38. D. H. Aldcroft, *The European economy 1914–1970* (London, 1978) p. 161.

39. M. W. Kirby, *The decline of British economic power since 1870* (London, 1981) p. 119.

40. Cmnd. 1565 (1961), *The United Kingdom and the European Economic Community* p. 8.

41. Postan, *Economic history*, p. 94.

42. Aldcroft, *European economy*, p. 180.

43. See J. Black, 'The volume and prices of British exports' in G. N. D. Worswick and P. Ady (eds), *The British economy in the 1950s* (Oxford, 1962) p. 129.

44. Postan, *Economic history*, p. 75. Britain's share was 22 per cent in 1937.

45. Cmnd. 827 (1959), *Report of Committee on the working of the monetary system (Radcliffe Report)* para. 653 ff.

46. See A. R. Conan, *The problem of sterling* (London, 1966) and the complaint voiced in *The Economist*, 13 September 1958, pp. 815–16.

47. See the case of India in 1956–57. A. Shonfield, *British economic policy since the war* (Harmondsworth, 1958) p. 130.

48. Shonfield, *Economic policy*, ch. 6 for a polemic.

49. Cmnd. 72 (1957), *A European free trade area: U.K. Memorandum to the O.E.E.C.* pp. 3, 6.

50. See the remarks to the Radcliffe Committee quoted in S. Brittan, *Steering the economy* (Harmondsworth, 1971) p. 223.

51. Cmnd. 539 (1958), *Commonwealth trade and economic conference 15–20 September 1958.*

52. Strange, *Sterling*, p. 193.

53. *Radcliffe Report* para. 657.

54. Ibid., para. 731.

55. Ibid., para. 739.

56. Brittan, *Steering*, p. 233.

57. C. J. Bartlett, *The long retreat* (London, 1972) pp. 64 ff.

58. Darby, *Defence policy*, pp. 101–2. Eden wanted to reduce manpower from 800,000 (1956) to 445,000 (1960).

59. Ibid., pp. 102–6.

60. Cmnd. 124 (1957), *Defence: outline of future policy.*

61. Ibid., p. 7.

62. See C. D. Cohen, *British economic policy 1960–69* (London, 1971) p. 18.

63. The worst balance of payments for a decade. See Brittan, *Steering*, p. 251.

64. See the table in Cohen, *Economic policy*, p. 183.

65. Ibid., p. 179.

66. Brittan, *Steering*, p. 227.

67. Edward Heath's phrase, Cmnd. 1565 (1961), p. 3.

68. See Cmnd. 2764 (1965), *The National Plan*.

69. Ibid., pp. 6, 70–1.

70. Brittan, *Steering*, p. 306.

71. Ibid., p. 307.

72. Strange, *Sterling*, p. 258.

73. Ibid.

74. See Worswick and Ady (eds), *The British economy 1945–50* (Oxford, 1952) p. 479.

75. S. G. Sturmey, *British shipping and world competition* (London, 1962) p. 403.

76. Conan, *Sterling*, p. 13, table.

77. For discussion of this, J. O. N. Perkins, *The sterling area and the Commonwealth: world economic growth* (Cambridge, 1967) pp. 33–5.

78. Cmnd. 539 (1958), p. 5.

79. See Strange, *Sterling*, pp. 97–105.

80. See next section.

81. See discussion of 'closed economies' in A. G. Hopkins, *An economic history of West Africa* (London, 1973) pp. 171–2; and of 'paraprotectionism' in Morris-Jones and Fischer (eds), *Decolonisation*, pp. 158–92.

82. See his article in the *Weekend Telegraph*, 12 Mar. 1965, quoted in R. Blake, *A History of Rhodesia* (London, 1976) p. 328.

83. Endorsed in the Corfield Report, Cmnd. 1030 (1960).

84. Cmnd. 814 (1959), *Report of the Nyasaland Commission of Enquiry* (Devlin Report) para. 45.

85. Ibid., para. 43.

86. Ibid., para. 40.

87. Ibid., para. 63.

88. Ibid., para. 149.

89. Ibid., para. 256.

90. Ibid., para. 254.

91. Ibid., para. 2.

92. For the Commons debate on the Devlin Report, *H. C. Deb.* 5th Series, vol. 610, cols 337–443.

93. Enoch Powell's much admired speech on the Hola Camp inquiry made the same point: *H. C. Deb.* 5th Series, vol. 610, col. 232 ff.

94. For these developments, W. J. Foltz, from *French West Africa to the Mali Federation* (New Haven, 1965); G. Barraclough, *Survey of international affairs 1959–60* (London, 1964) pp. 372–85.

95. Ibid., p. 398.

96. The Belgians were afraid that French influence might supplant theirs in an independent Congo. See C. Legum, *Congo disaster* (Harmondsworth, 1961) pp. 79–80, 85. For De Gaulle's explanation of French policy, see his *Memoirs of hope* (Eng. trans. London, 1971) pp. 37–67.

97. Barraclough, *Survey*, p. 412.

98. Diary, 4 Aug. 1960, *Pointing the way*, p. 264.

99. Ibid., pp. 263, 266.

100. For a survey, C. Hoskyns, *The Congo since independence* (London, 1965).

101. For white attitudes to Katanga, in Northern Rhodesia, D. C. Mulford, *The Northern Rhodesian general election 1962* (Nairobi, 1964) p.34.

102. Ibid., p.38.

103. For the effect on whites in Kenya, G. Wasserman, *The politics of decolonisation: Kenya Europeans and the land issue 1960–65* (Cambridge, 1976) p. 74.

104. Lord Alport, *The sudden assignment* (London, 1965) pp. 95, 106.

105. For a hostile view of these attempts, C. Cruise O'Brien, *To Katanga and Back* (London, 1962).

106. Macmillan's famous reference to a 'wind of change' was made in January 1960, well before its full strength had been felt.

107. J. Iliffe, *A modern history of Tanganyika* (Cambridge, 1979) p. 566.

108. Formalised at the Tanganyika constitutional conference, 27–29 Mar. 1961 at Dar-es Salaam. See *H.C. Deb.* 5th Series, vol. 638, cols 12–15 (11 April 1961).

109. D. A. Low, *Political parties in Uganda 1949–62* (London, 1962) p. 31.

110. 'African nationalism hates small states and will crush Buganda', remarked Milton Obote in Feb. 1960. *Keesing's Archives 1960*, 17259 (3 Feb. 1960).

111. See D. A. Low and A. Smith (eds), *History of East Africa* vol. 3 (Oxford, 1976) p. 96.

112. Direct election was applied elsewhere in Uganda.

113. Low, *Uganda parties*, p. 55.

114. Darby, *British defence policy*, pp. 125, 133, 185, 188, 203–5.

115. C. Rosberg and J. Nottingham, *The myth of 'Mau Mau': nationalism in Kenya* (Stanford, 1966) pp. 303–5.

116. Ibid., p. 307.

117. Wasserman, *Kenya Europeans*, ch. 2.

118. Low and Smith (eds), *East Africa* vol. 3, p. 257.

119. Wasserman, *Kenya Europeans*, p. 82.

120. Ibid., pp. 37–43.

121. Ibid., pp. 37–40. The chief appeal of the NKG was to whites in urban and commercial occupations, not to rural whites.

122. G. Bennett and C. Rosberg, *The Kenyatta election: Kenya 1960–61* (London, 1961) p. 18.

123. *The Economist*, 9 Jan. 1960.

124. Wasserman, *Kenya Europeans*, p. 46.

125. Bennett and Rosberg, *Kenyatta election*, p. 41.

126. Wasserman, *Kenya Europeans*, p. 63.

127. Ibid., p. 84; for KANU–KADU negotiations, August 1962, pp. 88–9.

128. Cmnd. 1706 (1962), *Report of the Kenya Constitutional Conference 1962*, appendix.

129. *The Economist*, 14 April 1962, claimed that Kenya was penniless.

130. An argument pressed on the Colonial Secretary by Blundell in Oct. 1962, Wasserman, *Kenya Europeans*, p. 95.

131. *H.C. Deb.* 5th Series, vol. 578, col. 924, 25 Nov. 1957.

132. *Devlin Report* paras. 104, 106–37.

133. Ibid., para. 258.

134. D. C. Mulford, *Zambia: the politics of independence 1957–1964* (London, 1967) pp. 73, 76.

135. Sir Roy Welensky, *Welensky's 4000 days* (London, 1964) p. 120.

136. *Devlin Report* para. 177.

137. Ibid., paras 43–5.

138. Mulford, *Zambia*, pp. 103–5.

139. Benson's letter to the Colonial Office, quoted in ibid. pp. 104–5.

140. Ibid., p. 107.

141. I. Henderson, 'The origins of nationalism in East and Central Africa: the Zambian case', *Journal of African History* XI, 4 (1970) pp. 598, 602.

142. See the memo of the Choma Tonga Native Authority, 18 Feb. 1960, Cmnd 1151 (1960), *Advisory Commission on the Review of the Constitution of the Federation of Rhodesia and Nyasaland, Report,*

Appendix VIII: Evidence vol. 1 (Northern Rhodesia) p. 3.

143. Memo by Central Africa Party, 15 Mar. 1960, ibid., vol. 1, p. 35.

144. In Northern Rhodesia the white population was concentrated on the Copperbelt and along the line-of-rail.

145. Cmnd. 1148 (1960), *Report of the Advisory Commission on the Review of the Constitution of the Federation of Rhodesia and Nyasaland* (Monckton Report) para. 27.

146. Ibid., para. 71.

147. Ibid., para. 123.

148. Ibid., para. 100.

149. Ibid., para. 114.

150. Ibid., para. 221.

151. See Lord Home, *The way the wind blows: an autobiography* (London, 1976) pp. 129–30.

152. Macmillan to Welensky, 9 Jan. 1961, *Pointing the way*, p. 307.

153. Cmnd. 1291 (1961), *Report of the Southern Rhodesia Constitutional Conference February 1961*.

154. Mulford, *Zambia*, p. 182.

155. Macmillan, *Pointing the way*, p. 311; Alport, *Assignment*, p. 32.

156. Welensky, *4000 days*, p. 306.

157. Macmillan's diary, 4 Feb. 1961, *Pointing the way*, p. 309.

158. Mulford, *Zambia*, pp. 194–6.

159. For details, ibid., p. 210.

160. See above p. 254–55.

161. See Mulford, *Zambia*, p. 207.

162. Butler to Alport, 23 Aug. 1962, *Art of the possible*, p. 218.

163. Ibid., p. 214.

164. Where Britain intervened to protect Kuwait in 1961.

165. E. Monroe, *The Mediterranean in politics* (London, 1938) pp. 46–7.

166. *Full Circle: the memoirs of Sir Anthony Eden* (London, 1960) pp. 385–9.

167. Cmnd 1261 (1961), *Report of the Malta Constitutional Commission* p. 6.

168. *H.C. Deb.* 5th Series, vol. 636, cols 471–7.

169. *Malta Commission report* pp. 3–4.

170. For this plan, F. Crouzet, *Le conflit de Chypre* 2 vols (Brussels, 1973) vol. 2, pp. 1036 ff.

171. Crouzet, *Chypre* vol. 2, p. 1111.

172. Ibid. vol. 2, p. 1109.

173. Ibid. vol. 2, p. 1073.

174. Ibid. vol. 2, pp. 1107, 1196.

175. Macmillan, *Riding the storm*, pp. 692, 695.

176. Cmnd. 1252 (1961), *Treaty concerning the establishment of the Republic of Cyprus*, Article 1 and annexes B–F.

177. P. G. Polyviou, *Cyprus: conflict and negotiation 1960–1980* (London, 1980) pp. 13–17.

178. Darby, *British defence policy*, pp. 125, 133, 209–10.

179. 21,000 voters in a population of 140,000.

180. F. Halliday, *Arabia without sultans* (Harmondsworth, 1974) pp. 186–7.

181. G. King, *Imperial outpost – Aden* (London, 1964) pp. 10 ff.

182. Cmd. 9777 (1956), *Singapore Constitutional Conference 1956*; Cmnd. 147 (1957), *Report of the Singapore Constitutional Conference, March–April 1957*.

183. D. C. Watt (ed.), *Survey of international affairs 1963* (London, 1977) p. 120.

184. B. Simandjuntak, *Malayan federalism 1945–63* (Kuala Lumpur and London, 1969) p.133.

185. Ibid., pp. 125, 128–9.

186. Cmnd. 1563 (1961), *Federation of Malaysia: joint statement by Governments of the United Kingdom and the Federation of Malaya*.

187. Cmnd. 1794 (1962), *Report of the Commission of Enquiry, North Borneo and Sarawak* (Cobbold Report) pp. 30, 42.

188. Cmnd. 124 (1957), *Defence: outline of future policy* p. 1.

189. Darby, *British defence policy*, p. 154.

190. Ibid., pp. 155–6.

191. Manpower was more than halved between 1956 and 1966. Ibid., p. 328

192. Ibid., p. 192.

193. Ibid., p. 218.

194. Ibid., p. 276.

195. Ibid., p. 283.

7. WINDING UP

1. Neville Brown, *Arms without empire* (Harmondsworth, 1967) pp. 66–8.

2. Ibid., pp. 51–7.

3. At this time approximately 25 per cent of British exports went to countries bordering the Indian Ocean and the western Pacific. See D. C. Watt, 'Britain and the Indian Ocean: diplomacy before defence', *Political Quarterly* 1971, p. 309.

4. Richard Crossman's judgement, 26 Nov. 1964. *Diaries of a Cabinet Minister* vol. 1 *Minister of Housing and Local Government 1964–66* (London, 1974) p. 58.

5. Brown, *Arms*, pp. 28–9, 39.

6. Ibid., p. 55.

7. See Crossman, *Diaries* vol. 1, p. 94 (11 Dec. 1964).

8. In Nov. 1964, June 1965 and June 1966.

9. Crossman, *Diaries* vol. 1, p. 156 (11 Feb. 1965).

10. Ibid. vol. 1, p. 455 (14 Feb. 1966). At this stage Crossman was not a member.

11. These principles were perhaps intended chiefly to justify the defence cuts in American eyes.

12. Crossman, *Diaries* vol. 1, p. 539 (15 June 1966).

13. Ibid. vol. 2 (London, 1976) pp. 155–56 (9 Dec. 1966).

14. P. Darby, *British defence policy east of Suez 1947–68* (London, 1973) p. 315; Cmnd. 3203, *Statement on the defence estimates February 1967* p. 7.

15. H. Wilson, *The Labour Government 1964–70: a personal record* (London, 1972) p. 376.

16. J. B. Kelly, *Arabia, the Gulf and the West* (London, 1980) p. 47.

17. See Crossman, *Diaries* vol. 2, pp. 634–5, 645–7, 649 ff.

18. Ibid. vol. 2, p. 649 (15 Jan. 1968).

19. See particularly ibid. vol. 2, p. 86 (22 Oct. 1966).

20. For instance, Crossman, *Diaries* vol. 1, p. 539, 456; vol. 2 p. 156.

21. E.g. D. C. Watt, 'The decision to withdraw from the Gulf', *Political Quarterly* 1968, p. 321; Kelly, *Arabia*, pp. 50–1.

22. Crossman, *Diaries* vol. 2, pp. 624, 645–7.

23. Ibid. vol. 2, p. 81.

24. *H.C. Deb*, 5th Series, vol. 757, col. 627.

25. See M. Leifer, 'Retreat and reappraisal in South-East Asia' in M. Leifer (ed.), *Constraints and adjustments in British foreign policy* (London, 1972).

26. See 'Aden's shadow over the Gulf' by Sir. W. Luce, Political

Resident in the Gulf 1961–66, *Daily Telegraph* April 1967.

27. British Petroleum took 40 per cent of Iranian production and 50 per cent of Kuwait's. Iran (168 million tonnes), Saudi Arabia (149 million) and Kuwait (129 million) were by far the largest Gulf producers in 1969.

28. Since 1800 British policy in the Persian Gulf had oscillated between defending Britain's interests in the Gulf itself and the pursuit of influence in Teheran.

29. Crossman, *Diaries* vol. 2, p. 639.

30. This had been Sir Robert Menzies' idea. J. D. B. Miller, *Survey of British Commonwealth affairs: problems of expansion and attrition 1953–69* (London, 1974) p. 412.

31. For the 'open economy' see A. G. Hopkins, *An economic history of West Africa* (London, 1973) pp. 168 ff.

32. Crossman, *Diaries* vol. 2, p. 450 (30 July 1967).

33. See Miller, *Survey*, ch. 10.

34. It is interesting to speculate how much support Britain would have received internationally over the Falklands question in 1982 had the Rhodesian issue not been settled to the satisfaction of the Afro-Asian Commonwealth countries.

35. For the statistics see OECD, *Development Assistance: efforts and policies 1966 Review* p. 147; *1970 Review* p. 170–1. This is not to argue that there is a simple equation between expenditure and influence.

36. Crossman, *Diaries* vol. 3 (London 1977) p. 159 (26 July 1968).

37. See M. Lipton and J. Firn, *The erosion of a relationship: Britain and India since 1960* (London, 1975).

38. Ibid., pp. 178–86.

39. O. Ojedokun, 'The Anglo-Nigerian entente and its demise 1960–62', *Journal of Commonwealth Political Studies* IX, 3 (1971) p. 223 ff.

40. Ibid., p. 222.

41. Thus West Germany was asked to train the air force. Ibid., p. 228.

42. Miller, *Survey*, p. 444.

43. Ibid., p. 447.

44. Lipton and Firn, *Erosion*, appendix 2, table 3.1. The percentages are by value.

45. Ibid., Table 4.1.

46. Ibid., Table 3.1.

47. Ibid., Table 4.1

48. Miller, *Survey*, p. 448.

49. Susan Strange, *Sterling and British policy* (London, 1971) p. 92.

50. Lipton and Firn, *Erosion*, p. 11.

51. Ibid., p. 45.

52. See M. Lipton, 'Paraprotectionism' in W. H. Morris-Jones and G. Fischer (eds), *Decolonisation and after* (London, 1980) pp. 162, 173.

53. The depletion of India's large sterling balances in 1958 marked the onset of her economic disengagement from Britain.

54. Strange, *Sterling*, pp. 100, 105.

55. For a general survey of these developments see the essay by Lipton in Morris-Jones and Fischer (eds), *Decolonisation*.

56. See P. Bauer, 'British Colonial Africa: economic retrospect and aftermath' in L. Gann and P. Duignan (eds), *The economics of colonialism* (Cambridge, 1975).

57. For the growth of 'parastatals' in Zambia, R. Sklar, *Corporate power in an African state* (Berkeley and Los Angeles, 1975) p. 194.

58. Under the West Indies Act, 1967.

59. The best recent history is G. Hills, *Rock of contention: a history of Gibraltar* (London, 1974).

60. See Cmnd. 2632 (1965), *Gibraltar: recent differences with Spain* p. 3.

61. Cmnd. 3131 (1966), *Gibraltar: talks with Spain May–October 1966*. Spanish statement, May 1966.

62. Statement by Miss J. Hart, 14 June 1967. Cmnd. 3325 (1967), *Further documents on Gibraltar October 1966–June 1967*.

63. Hills, *Rock of contention*, p. 466.

64. By contrast with residents of the Falkland Islands.

65. Spain's accession to NATO and the European Community has prompted further attempts to find a compromise.

66. G. B. Endacott, *An eastern entrepot* (London, 1964) pp. xi–xv.

67. At least according to the Hong Kong government. *Hong Kong 1982* an official publication.

68. See *The Times* 5 March 1981.

69. Cmnd. 9352 (1984), now embodied in the Hong Kong Act, 1985.

70. Cmnd. 8653 (1982), *Falkland Islands economic survey*.

71. Statement by Foreign Secretary, 26 April 1977, *H.C. Deb.* 5th

Series, vol. 930, cols 273–4; M. Hastings and S. Jenkins, *The battle for the Falklands* (pbk edn, London, 1983) p. 31.

72. Cmnd. 8787 (1983), *Falkland Islands Review* (The 'Franks Report') para. 25.

73. Ibid., para 82.

74. See *The Times* 21 Nov. 1980.

75. M. Hudson, *Rhodesia: triumph and tragedy* (London, 1981) p. 104.

76. R. Blake, *A history of Rhodesia* (London, 1977) pp. 356–7.

77. Crossman, *Diaries* vol. 1, p. 356.

78. Ibid., p. 351.

79. Crossman, *Diaries* vol. 2, p.18.

80. The interim arrangements were set out in Cmnd. 3171, *Rhodesia: documents relating to proposals for a settlement 1966* p. 9.

81. Claire Palley, 'No majority rule before 1999', *Guardian* 14 Nov. 1968. Reprinted in C. Legum and R. Drysdale (eds), *Africa Contemporary Record 1968–9* (London, 1969).

82. Hudson, *Rhodesia*, p. 99. Professor Palley's judgement this time was 80–100 years. See E. Windrich, *Britain and the politics of Rhodesian independence* (London, 1978) p. 179.

83. See P. Cosgrave, *Carrington: a life and a policy* (London, 1985) pp. 141, 143.

84. 64.45 per cent of the total estimated voting population took part.

85. For Mrs Thatcher's Commons statement of 25 July 1979 and ensuing discussion, *H. C. Deb*, 5th Series, vol. 971, col. 620 ff.

86. See the account by Anthony Verrier, *The road to Zimbabwe* (London, 1986). This is a generally persuasive version of events, marred in places by shrill partisanship.

87. Verrier, *Zimbabwe*, p. 265.

88. *The Times* 23 February 1980.

89. Cosgrave, *Carrington*, p. 118.

90. Terence Ranger, *Peasant consciousness and guerrilla war in Zimbabwe* (London), 1985) esp. ch. 4.

91. Central Statistical Office, *Annual Abstract of Statistics 1982*, p. 318.

92. Ibid., p. 26.

93. Ibid., p. 189–90.

94. Cmnd. 5976, *Statement on defence estimates 1975*.

95. *The Times* 21 June 1982.

96. See e.g. M. Nicholson, *The system* (London, 1964).

97. For two studies of the domestic politics of decolonisation, M. Kahler, *Decolonisation in Britain and France* (Princeton, 1984); J. G. Darwin, 'The fear of falling: British politics and imperial decline since 1900', *Transactions of the Royal Historical Society*, 5th series, vol. 36, 1986 pp. 27–43.

Select Bibliography

A full list of the sources used in this book may be found in the references for each chapter. The following selection indicates the published material likely to be of interest to a reader wishing to read further on the topics and issues discussed.

PUBLISHED SOURCES

The most useful are the following:

N. MANSERGH (ed.), *Documents and speeches on British Commonwealth Affairs 1931–1952*, 2 vols (London, 1953).

Foreign Relations of the United States (Washington): a large number of volumes dealing with the years after 1945 have appeared; those covering American diplomacy in the Middle East and South and South East Asia will be found most useful.

Documents on Australian Foreign policy (Canberra, 1975–   ) 6 vols so far.

Documents on British Policy Overseas (London, 1984–   ) 1st Series, 1945–1950; 2nd Series, 1950–1955. 3 vols so far.

Documents on Canadian External Relations (Ottawa), vols 9 (1942–43) and 12 (1946) were most useful for this study.

Constitutional Relations between Britain and India: the Transfer of Power 12 vols (London, 1970–83). Indispensable.

Constitutional Relations between Britain and Burma: the struggle for independence 1944–1948 2 vols (London, 1983–84).

GENERAL

J. A. GALLAGHER, *The Decline, revival and fall of the British Empire* (Cambridge, 1982).

R. F. HOLLAND, *European decolonisation 1918–1981* (London, 1985).

N. MANSERGH, *Survey of British Commonwealth affairs: problems of wartime cooperation and post-war change 1939–1952* (London, 1958).

J. D. B. MILLER, *Survey of British Commonwealth affairs: problems of expansion and attrition 1953–1969* (London, 1974).

W. J. MOMMSEN and J. OSTERHAMMEL (eds), *Imperialism and after* (London, 1986).

W. MORRIS-JONES and G. FISCHER (eds), *Decolonisation and after* (London, 1980).

B. PORTER, *The lion's share* (London, 1975).

TONY SMITH, *The pattern of imperialism* (Cambridge, 1981).

A. P. THORNTON, *The imperial idea and its enemies* (London, 1959).

THE HOME BASE: BRITISH POLITICS AND ECONOMICS AFTER 1945

S. BRITTAN, *Steering the economy* (Harmondsworth, 1971).

A. BULLOCK, *Ernest Bevin Foreign Secretary* (London, 1983).

A. CAIRNCROSS, *Years of recovery: British economic policy 1945–51* (London, 1985).

D. CARLTON, *Anthony Eden* (London, 1981).

RICHARD CROSSMAN, *The diaries of a Cabinet Minister* 3 vols (London, 1974–77).

H. MACMILLAN, *Riding the storm 1956–1959* (London, 1971).

————— , *Pointing the way 1959–1961* (London, 1972).

K. O. MORGAN, *Labour in power 1945–1951* (Oxford, 1984).

ANDREW SHONFIELD, *British economic policy since the war* (Harmondsworth, 1958).

SUSAN STRANGE, *Sterling and British policy* (London, 1971).

BRITAIN: EXTERNAL POLICIES

C. J. BARTLETT, *The long retreat* (London, 1972).

M. CAMPS, *Britain and the European Community 1945–1963* (London, 1964).

P. DARBY, *British defence policy east of Suez* (London, 1973).

ANTHONY EDEN, *Full Circle* (London, 1960).

D. J. GOLDSWORTHY, *Colonial issues in British politics 1945–1961* (Oxford, 1971).

P. S. GUPTA, *Imperialism and the British Labour movement 1914–1964* (London, 1975).

M. KAHLER, *Decolonisation in Britain and France* (Princeton, 1984).

SOUTH AND SOUTH-EAST ASIA

A. CAMPBELL-JOHNSON, *Mission with Mountbatten* (London, 1951).

R. COUPLAND, *The constitutional problem in India* (London, 1945).

J. A. GALLAGHER, G. JOHNSON and A. SEAL (eds), *Locality, province and nation* (Cambridge, 1973).

S. GOPAL, *Jawaharlal Nehru* vol.1 *1889–1947* (London, 1975).

M. LIPTON and J. FIRN, *The erosion of a relationship: Britain and India since 1960* (London, 1975).

D. A. LOW (ed.), *Congress and the Raj* (London, 1977).

R. J. MOORE, *The crisis of Indian unity 1917–1940* (Oxford, 1974).

————— , *Churchill, Cripps and India* (Oxford, 1979).

————— , *Escape from empire: the Attlee government and the Indian problem* (Oxford,1983).

G. RIZVI, *Linlithgow and India* (London, 1978).

B. R. TOMLINSON, *The Indian National Congress and the Raj: the penultimate phase* (London, 1976).

————— , *The political economy of the Raj 1914–1947* (London, 1979).

F. S. V. DONNISON, *British military administration in the Far East 1943–46* (London, 1956).

A. SHORT, *The Communist insurrection in Malaya 1948–1960* (London, 1975)

A. J. STOCKWELL, 'British imperial policy and decolonisation in Malaya 1942–52' *Journal of Imperial and Commonwealth History* XIII, 1 (1984).

C. M. TURNBULL, *A history of Singapore 1819–1975* (Kuala Lumpur, 1977).

WAH, CHIN KIN, *The defence of Malaysia and Singapore* (Cambridge, 1983).

THE MIDDLE EAST

M. J. COHEN, *Palestine: retreat from the mandate* (London, 1978).

————— , *Palestine and the great powers 1945–1948* (Princeton, 1982).

L. P. ELWELL-SUTTON, *Persian oil* (London, 1955).

R. W. FERRIER, *The history of the British Petroleum Company* vol. 1 (Cambridge, 1982).

Index